What You Will

What You Will

Gender, Contract, and Shakespearean Social Space

Kathryn Schwarz

PENN

UNIVERSITY OF PENNSYLVANIA PRESS

PHILADELPHIA

Published by
University of Pennsylvania Press
Philadelphia, Pennsylvania 19104-4112
www.upenn.edu/pennpress

Printed in the United States of America on acid-free paper
1 3 5 7 9 10 8 6 4 2

Library of Congress Cataloging-in-Publication Data
Schwarz, Kathryn, 1966–
    What you will : gender, contract, and Shakespearean social space / Kathryn
Schwarz.—1st ed.
        p.   cm.
    Includes bibliographical references and index.
    ISBN 978-0-8122-4327-7 (hardcover : alk. paper)
    1. Shakespeare, William, 1564–1616—Criticism and interpretation.
2. Shakespeare, William, 1564–1616—Characters—Women.   3. Women in
literature.   4. Femininity in literature.   5. Social role in literature.   6. Sex role
in literature.   I. Title.
PR2991.S37   2011
822.3'3—dc22   2011011190

For Katie

Contents

Illustrations

Note on Citation

In citing early modern texts, I have retained their spellings; however, I have modernized typography in several ways. Consonantal *u* and *i* have been revised to *v* and *j*, and vocalic *v* has been revised to *u*; long *s* has been revised to *s*; ligatures of æ and œ have been expanded; & and *yᵉ* have been altered to *and* and *the*; where a macron over a vowel indicates the suspension of *m* or *n*, I have supplied the letter.

Introduction

Virtue Trouble

Besides, if women be educated for dependence; that is, to act according to the will of another fallible being, and submit, right or wrong, to power, where are we to stop?

—Wollstonecraft, *A Vindication of the Rights of Woman*, 115

We give to necessity the praise of virtue.

—Quintilian, *De Institutione Oratoria*, 1.8.14

Livable Space

This book takes up sixteenth- and seventeenth-century representations of femininity, and traces a curious pattern: women pose a threat when they willingly conform to social conventions. Exemplary texts of the period tell stories of literal violence, describing chaste women who kill their rapists, constant wives who make marriage a space of enervating desire and debilitating commitment, and devoted mothers who destroy the fitness of children and the durability of patrilines. These mythologies of damage may titillate through their extravagance, but they also gesture toward the more common ways in which intentional virtue unsettles the tenets of heterosocial hierarchy. To explore this effect, I consider the problems posed not by women who challenge expectations of femininity, but by women who take those expectations as a mandate for purposeful acts. What happens when feminine subjects recognize and participate in the doctrines that govern them? Whose act of will is this?

For the early modern period, will is a dense and volatile theoretical concept. As the faculty that realizes abstract designs, will exemplifies the doubled and divided nature of agency: it functions both as a useful tool and as an independent, potentially renegade force. Personified in feminine terms and subordinated to masculine reason, will has the power to sustain or disrupt order, and bears final accountability for the relationship between cause and

Figure 1 (preceding page). William Austin, *Haec Homo* (London: Richard Olton for Ralph Mabb, 1637), 79. By permission of the Folger Shakespeare Library.

effect. If will does not enact the dictates of reason, the system suffers error, inversion, and chaos; in Robert Burton's formulation, "The actions of the *Will* are *Velle* and *Nolle*, to well and nill: which two words comprehend all."[1] The practice of gendering this faculty produces direct analogies to social roles, analogies which characterize will as the wife to reason and the mother to action, and underscore awareness that stable relations depend on a conformity grounded in consent.[2] Theorists of the faculties describe a vital but potentially wayward will that forms the hinge between idea and accomplishment; for social theorists, the complex, ambivalently valued intercessions of feminine volition serve a parallel purpose, translating disciplinary edicts into efficient procedures. Women who willfully do what they should further the projects of chastity, marriage, and patrilineal succession, but those projects appear as work, in which feminine subjects play intentional parts. Rather than liberate women from repressive dictates, this compromised mode of self-direction alters the meaning of compliance. The gap between decree and execution requires an acquiescence that is deliberate and transactional rather than innate; through the contradictory logic of prescribed choice, feminine will becomes the means of social contract.

In making this claim, I focus on the intra- and intersubjective systems of alliance that subtend formal bonds. Covenants of allegiance, affiliation, fidelity, and reciprocity have their basis in the capacity of persons to agree within and among themselves, to formulate priorities of intercourse that work against the drives of dominance and opposition, but respond to a more foundational imperative of coexistence. This is what I mean by "livable space": throughout this book, I take up the ordinary interactions which, however damaging to fantasies of self-sufficiency, weave networks of functional accord. Will is a crucial element in these processes, not least because its operations are at once internal and communal; it fuses the adversarial elements that circulate within persons, and, as it makes the integral subject both possible and conditional, it breaches the porous boundaries between other and self. Contractual agreements, in their more abstract and codified configurations, articulate a condition of interdependence that preexists and preconceives particular expressions of obligation and guarantee. That interdependence is a result not of organic unity or natural law, but of pragmatic and often laborious practices which turn unpredictable intentions and desires toward workable accommodations. These are the practices with which I am concerned. Their contingent intricacies are routinely masked by more absolute precepts and structures: imposition transmutes participation; hierarchy disguises mutuality; control overwrites consent.

And those second terms—which in a predicative sense must be first terms—tend to be figured by and immanent in volitional feminine acts. The correlation reflects a basic premise of patrilineal order: cultural self-perpetuation relies on feminine sexual choice.

This is obvious enough to go without saying, yet early modern texts cannot say it enough.[3] Normative femininity, that set of roles which organizes subjects toward the pursuit of proper ends, is a scheme that declares its agenda, as when Stephen Batman indexes his chapters on women: "of the maide; of the mother; of the daughter" (the chapters on men begin, "of a male; of a man").[4] Feminine virtue is neither a narrow subset nor a deceptive translation of social policy; the principles that inform chastity, maternity, and filial duty are to a substantial degree identical with heterosocial ideology on its broadest scale. The vital yet fragile link between self-restraint and social continuity stimulates a wide range of defensive tactics, and indeed we might understand the entire monumental apparatus of conduct literature, from exemplary catalogues to misogynist polemics, as a response to the crux of feminine choice. Joan Scott reminds us that when discursive systems constitute subjects, they also create agents: "They are not unified, autonomous individuals exercising free will, but rather subjects whose agency is created through situations and statuses conferred on them."[5] The agency conferred by social requirements mirrors those requirements, but it might reflect or distort; faithful replication derives from an informed sense of purpose. Good women have to know what they are doing, and, when the responsibilities incurred by embodiment are available as sets of data and accessible to acts of will, discipline is an effect of mutual affirmation. Barnabe Rich states the fact that controverts truisms of passivity, inertia, essential nature, and serviceable use: "And yet to speake truly women are commonly more abstinent from all manner of uncleanesse then men, neither are the most of them curbed in with any other bridle then what they willingly put uppon them selves."[6]

Accounts of sociality that isolate power at the top intersect this other story of formative assent. In "Governmentality," Michel Foucault associates early modern authority with a series of dilemmas that revolve around interrelation: "How to govern oneself, how to be governed, how to govern others, by whom the people will accept being governed, how to become the best possible governor—all these problems, in their multiplicity and intensity, seem to me to be characteristic of the sixteenth century."[7] Foucault distinguishes government from the sovereignty manifest in both divine and monarchical law: sovereignty encodes a tautological validation—"the end of sovereignty is the exercise of sovereignty"—while government constructs an elaborate complex of means and ends: "whereas the end of sovereignty is internal to itself and possesses its own intrinsic instruments in the shape of its laws, the finality of government resides in the things it manages and in the pursuit of the perfection and intensification of the processes which it directs; and the instruments of government, instead of being laws, now come to be a range of multiform tactics."[8] Government does not segregate a preeminent agent, but connects the levels at which authority operates; "multiform tactics" distribute regulation across a flexible, efficient, and interconnected scheme.[9] Such assiduous dispersal might produce a surfeit of effects, a potential Judith Butler highlights when she traces the genesis of resistance within Foucault's theories of discipline:

> In Foucault, the suppression of the body not only requires and produces the very body it seeks to suppress, it goes further by extending the bodily domain to be regulated, proliferating sites of control, discipline, and suppression. In other words, the body *presumed* by the Hegelian explanation is incessantly produced and proliferated in order to extend the domain of juridical power. In this sense, the restrictions placed *on* the body not only *require* and *produce* the body they seek to restrict, but *proliferate* the domain of the bodily beyond the domain targeted by the original restriction. In what many have come to see as a finally utopian gesture in Foucault, this proliferation of the body by juridical regimes beyond the terms of dialectical reversal is also the site of possible resistance.[10]

Even as power populates its domain with the bodies it needs, the process expands outward under its own weight, so that the bodily realm ceases to coextend with the initial, motivated constraint. This does not release surplus bodies into radical liberty; instead, as Butler notes, it creates a circumstance of doubt. "The possibility of this resistance is derived from what is *unforeseeable* in proliferation."[11]

For Butler, the texture of discipline might change with the incursion of a fraught reciprocity: "Does the regulatory regime not only produce desire, but become produced by the cultivation of a certain attachment *to* the rule of subjection?"[12] She hypothesizes a compliant desire that exceeds the purposes for which it is produced,[13] and her question, like the questions in which Foucault embeds government, focuses on how objects of control intersect the devices that define them. If, in Foucault's words, "the finality of government resides in the things it manages," those well-managed things delineate and certify the direction under which they take shape; if, to return to Butler's proposition, regulatory regimes produce an invested acquiescence only to be produced by it in turn, that acquiescence authorizes the methods to which it accedes. This sheds light on the issue of willful compliance with which I am concerned, and on the complicated mechanisms whereby instruments become integral to yet estranged within the systems that animate them as subjects. Regulation conveys the mandate of power through displacement, attenuation, and excess. Self-government is thus citational, both mimetic of and dislocated from the principles of subjugation; it performs an attachment in which the terms are only speculatively governed by the source. Transfer becomes translation not because the mandate changes, but because its locations multiply beyond the limits that determine its sense. Precise concurrence may have ambiguous effects: when subjects speak as they have been spoken for, the echo binds fixed requisites to a volatilized sense of place. For the regulatory regime of early modern heterosociality, this is the unforeseeable result of proliferation: feminine acts of will represent a dispersed repetition of directive strategies, which incorporates discipline in its constituent subjects and marks them as determined in both senses of the term.

As exemplary texts become increasingly methodical in their codification of roles, they reveal the arduous, awkward labor that sutures duress to self-control.[14] Confine your wives and dispose of your daughters, advice books insist, yet spend most of their ink on what women might choose to do. Chastity exemplifies corporeal passivity, unless and until virgins need to kill men. If "conception is the male having an idea in the female body," medical treatises nonetheless cite maternal imagination to explain why the child is a boy; is a girl; is a hermaphrodite; looks like the father; looks like a camel; looks like a Moor.[15] Besieged by this propensity for counter-examples, a defensively simplified account of gender draws on Aristotelian theory to argue that women are neither agents nor products of intention: "because nature doth always tend unto that which is best, therefore she dooth always intende to beget the male, and not the female, because that the female is only for the males sake, and a monster in nature."[16] Women are accidents and objects, who acquire value only through an enforced conformity that can be turned to good use.[17] As I will argue in the chapters that follow, however, willful acquiescence confounds the process of objectification as it answers the demand for compliance. Under the pressure of an enigmatic agency, philosophical questions become quotidian concerns: how can volition consummate its own surrender? what claims to self-possession does the self-forfeiting subject retain?

The fact that social order relies on an intentional paradox is largely transparent, and if this is not the whole story, it is far-reaching enough to inform the arguments of cultural survival. "The *Merchant* trusts his *credit* to the safety of his *Shippe*: And, the *husband* his *credit* to the *chastity* of his Wife," William Austin writes, framing dependence in proverbial terms.[18] Familiarity does not diminish the power of the image, and Rich infers an ominous corollary: "The *Harlot* is like to a ship too, but not like a marchantes ship, but in truth like a *Pyrat* a *Rover*, a *Frebuter* and like such a ship as lieth still in waite for rapine and for spoyle."[19] Caught in the mix of reliable and treacherous vessels, masculine subjects might escape the problem entirely, as in Roland du Jardin's parable: "Marchants being at Sea, and seeing their Shippe in danger to miscarry, resolved to cast forth some of their heaviest wares. Wherupon one cast forth his wife, saying, It was hard for the Ship to sustaine such a weight."[20] Or they might rely on virtuous feminine choice and hope to secure a plausible accord. Rich concludes, "she must be a stirringe ship quicke of stirrige, ready at a word of her husband, she must not be immoveable like some womenne that a man were as good to remove a house, as to remove them from their willes."[21] Obduracy sinks the boat, but a mobile acquiescence undermines any stable situation of command: assurances are itinerant and provisional, and heterosocial futurity abides in contracts that yoke feminine acts of will to masculine acts of faith. Rather than stand as a remote concern, this awareness comes close to home. Writing that "the household was routinely touted as the foremost disciplinary site in the period," Wendy Wall describes domestic space not as a model of effective regulation, but as a realm that mystifies familiar routines: "the question of *how* women worked and what their work meant—both to them and to a broader population—remained unresolved."[22] Such opacity undercuts hierarchical foundations as it withholds knowledge of fixed place or sure tenure: a vertical array of relations rests on the inscrutable, consequential work of feminine subjects whose methods and intentions resist subsumption.

Attempts to integrate feminine will into conventional arguments are inflected by caution, bracketed by risk, and seamed with counterfactual possibilities, as in Edmund Tilney's account of marriage:

> In this long and troublesome journey of matrimonye, the wise man
> maye not be contented onely with the Spouses virginitie, but by
> little and lyttle must gently procure that he maye also steale away
> hir privat will, and appetite, so that of two bodies there may be
> made one onelye heart, which shee will soone doe, if love raygne in
> hir, and without this agreeable concorde, matrimonie hath but small
> pleasure, or none at all, and the man, that is not lyked, and loved of
> his mate, holdeth his lyfe in continuall perill, his goodes in great
> jeoperdie, his good name in suspect, and his whole house in utter
> perdition.[23]

A transition from the dangers of "privat will" to the pleasures of "agreeable
concorde" presses toward reciprocity, but any false step exposes men to comprehensive loss. Assimilation and jurisdiction are contingent on feminine desire; that elective faculty enables viable arrangements as it reveals their
ceaseless vicissitude.[24] In her account of the threat posed by erotic attachments between women, Valerie Traub writes, "Woman's social role within a
system of procreation relies not only on her biological capacity to give birth,
but on her willingness to perform that labor and to enter into the lifelong
social bonds with men that legitimate maternity."[25] This seems clear common sense, but the fickleness of will galvanizes efforts to fix consent as a
synchronic fact and limit intention to an instrumental role. By confining
women to mediation, early modern texts assert that tools are baser and more
fallible than the aims that move them. All errors become errors of transmission, as Timothy Bright contends of the relationship between body and soul:
"I take generally the soule to be affected of the body and spirit, as the instrument hindreth the worke of the artificer, which is not by altering his skill, or
diminishing his cunning, but by depraving the action through untowardnes
of toole, and fault of instrument."[26] The phrase "depraving the action" registers the translative act through which bodies confute an implemental quies-
cence; for sexual hierarchies, this threat to adulterate is also and more
crucially a promise to augment. Feminine choice introduces a second site of
purpose into the production of social meanings, and defines an agent who
conceives on more than material terms.[27] Dolora Wojciehowski writes, "Ironically, to assert some form of freedom requires that one simultaneously admit
servitude or non-freedom, the condition from which one would ransom oneself by the payment of a certain argument. The expenditure of reason, will,

or words is a mode of procurement, but it is arguably never an entirely cost-effective procedure."[28] Mastery is bound by its supplement, and ransoms its arguments with a will it does not own.

Will is not simply the mechanism for a single choice between submission and rebellion, or for a sustained refusal to engage at all. The friction between "willing" and "willful" animates feminine social subjectivity, and if isolated masculine privilege risks stasis, this vitality offers a hazardous cure.[29] Disabling dependence can be recast as fruitful intersection, but the procedure conflates the founding and confounding premises of hierarchy, identifies foreign agents within the *heimlich*, and reinvests "the uncanny stranger on display" with constitutive power.[30] Feminine will is at once antithetical to and inherent in ideological reproduction. It generates artifacts that sustain heterosocial order as they alienate it from itself: the duality that defines women as both instrumental and autonomous; the reflexivity that makes authenticity and masquerade indivisible aspects of impersonation; the fractured temporality that sets teleology against reiteration. Intentional virtue yokes utility to volition. A durable patriline requires that women know what to perform and how to rehearse it. Consent is a recurrent decision that both affirms and vitiates the priorities of contract. Each of these statements might be reduced to flat contradiction, but early modern arguments instead expand them, in an attempt to articulate the forms of livable space.

Logical Extremes

My central questions—with what agency, and to what effect, do feminine subjects occupy the conventions of femininity?—are historically specific. They have particular forms and textures in early modern narratives, taking shape through the philosophical discourses of rhetoric and will, the didactic treatises that educate women into appropriate behavior, and the cultural place and material practices of the popular stage. At the same time, these questions engage recent theories of subjectivity that describe a disruptively compliant response to ideological constraints. Intentional femininity recalls Butler's concept of parody as transformative repetition and Luce Irigaray's model of mimesis as oppositional visibility; it evokes Slavoj Žižek's strategy of "simply taking the power discourse at its (public) word," and Leo Bersani's account of a drive that "combines and confuses impulses to appropriate and to identify with the object of desire."[31] These theories address the intimacies of knowledge, and investigate the ways in which a faithful reproduction of social codes can constitute betrayal. An active, informed, and willful conformity confounds distinctions between affective allegiance and appropriative defiance; the motives and capacities of the invested social subject are crucial but obscure. Questions of who acts on what prerogatives, with what meanings, and to what effects, multiply around agents who rearticulate dominant discourses from unexpected locations. In her analysis of "the inevitable effects of a fully articulated female masculinity on a seemingly fortified male masculinity," Judith Halberstam explores the diverse consequences of possessive identification. "Sometimes female masculinity coincides with the excesses of male supremacy, and sometimes it codifies a unique form of social rebellion; often female masculinity is the sign of sexual alterity, but occasionally it marks heterosexual variation; sometimes female masculinity marks the place of pathology, and every now and then it represents the healthful alternative to what are considered the histrionics of conventional femininities."[32] This outline resonates with the phenomenon I address: intersections of identity and alterity, of predicated modes and unassimilated iterations, reconfigure a category through the committed intentions of its inhabitants. But to imagine that female femininity might work in this way is surely somewhat odd.

This line of thought would not be possible without the previous interventions of feminist scholarship, which have resisted totalizing accounts of subordination and containment. Rather than take feminine subjectivity as fully conscripted to patriarchal ends, such scholarship reveals that women can transform, commandeer, or manipulate the terms of convention, and expands our understanding of what the enactment of social roles might mean.[33] As we question the scope of domination, we find alternative structures of choice: separatism; homoerotic desire; adultery and promiscuity; religious dissent; female ascendancy; transgendered identities and acts. We also recognize disruption from within, and consider forms of role-playing that revise the script. Karen Newman points out that overt regulation facilitates its own reversals: "Though there is no question that Renaissance discourses of femininity advanced social controls and the policing of female behavior, they also enabled opposing discourses, which though they often speak with the same vocabulary and from the same categories, were nevertheless tactically productive."[34] Disciplinary mechanisms are always double-edged: early modern discourses formulate rules only to produce culturally resistant subjects who are culturally literate as well.[35]

Through opportunistic agency, reclaimed autonomy, and strategic orthodoxy, such subjects challenge a monolithic patriarchal order, even when that construct delineates the space within which they contest their inscription.[36]

I build on these insights as I take up narratives in which women pursue conventional agendas without detachment or disidentification, alibis or escape routes. What does it mean for feminine subjects to speak what normally—normatively—speaks them? Constance Jordan argues that early modern feminism interrogates the idea of natural roles, and revises the symbolic status of woman: "In a sense, she becomes the symbol of the socially self-reflexive act, the image of a constructive form of doubt that qualifies the significance and usefulness of traditions, habits, and customs."[37] Two modern claims about customary habits might elucidate the stakes of that qualification. In "Toward a Butch-Femme Aesthetic," Sue-Ellen Case writes, "the female body, the male gaze, and the structures of realism are only sex toys for the butch-femme couple."[38] In *Doctrine for the Lady of the Renaissance*, Ruth Kelso writes, "Let a woman have chastity, she has all. Let her lack chastity and she has nothing."[39] Each statement establishes a relationship between tradition and self-possession. For Case, the break between social law and citational performance unlocks a space of enabling play, while for Kelso any discontinuity opens a gulf into which viable existence disappears. In both arguments a subject might own and use cultural knowledge, but the operations of that knowledge split, between unmooring and anchoring a referential frame. I am interested in sites where those operations instead cohere, and produce what I would call the identity effect of authentic impersonation: the performance of feminine roles answers the need for social stability, and privileges the issue of how virtue signifies over the question of whether it refers. Situational enactments of guarantee enable heterosociality to circulate as a "structure of realism," tethered to the meeting point of imposed doctrine and autonomous intent. Through that efficient and perverse coincidence, the reiteration of social norms presses toward a multiply vectored diffusion of control. Butler imagines something like this in *Excitable Speech:* "these terms we never really choose are the occasion for something we might still call agency, the repetition of an originary subordination for another purpose, one whose future is partially open."[40] The future is always the most urgent question: what might women, as the instrumental agents of a patrilineal order, make or do? By setting them in motion, does that order give too much away?

When Isabella reaches her chilling resolution in *Measure for Measure*—"Then, Isabel, live chaste, and, brother, die: / More than our brother is our chastity" (2.4.184–85)—or when Helena's constancy in *All's Well* emasculates her husband, or when Cordelia's defense of filial duty precipitates Lear's madness, such consequential self-assertions seem extreme. But these are the logical extremes of a structure that relies on feminine subjects to prove their own worth and extend that verification to the system they inhabit. The plays present women who restore equilibrium at the expense of men: Claudio and Bertram live to accept their obligations, while Lear's death exemplifies the price of refusal, but in each case the drive to recuperate social integrity damages masculine subjects as it hinges on feminine will. Feminine acts that answer ideological demands uncover the disparate priorities of structures and persons, and errant men fall into the gap. "It is a hard matter therefore in this age to distinguish betweene the good woman and the bad," Rich complains in *The Excellency of good women*, a tract somewhat incongruously subtitled "The infallible markes whereby to know them."[41] We might read this as a conventional condemnation of deceit, but I think we can hear as well the suggestion that knowing may not help, that distinctions between good and bad lose clarity when virtue works as a deliberate choice in the service of an abstract principle. Early modern theorists describe heterosocial proximities as both inescapable and unsafe; how, after all, does a single treatise move from "A woman of good lyfe feareth no man with an evill tong" to "Weomen by nature are borne malicious" without missing a beat?[42] Rather than segregate virtue from vice, such oscillations show that prescriptive categories neither discipline nor domesticate the force of feminine will. In this context, the suspicion that a virtuous woman might act for your own good is every bit as vibrant as the fear that a vicious woman might kill you in your bed.[43]

A powerful counter-strategy requires that women police only their own potential to contaminate, and limits proprietary volition to the efficient removal of bodies that have lost their use. When Edward Gosynhyll ranks the casualties of military conquest, he places virgins above infants because the virgins intend to die:

> Yet have these vyrgyns immaculate
> If any comparyson may be therto
> More mede of god, I suppose so
> These vyrgins for god dyed wyllyngly
> The infantes by force and knewe nat why.[44]

A self-sacrifice referred to another's agenda marks the high point of feminine choice. That idea informs Juan Luis Vives's chapter on exemplary virtue, with its numbing catalogue of victims who, having been raped or threatened with rape, retain just enough purpose to kill themselves.[45] But a less fettered will erupts into this pattern when Vives records a woman's revenge: "Greke writers tel of an other mayd of Thebes, that whan her ennemy a Macedon had deflowred her, a whyle she dissembled her angre, and after founde the corrupter of her virgynite slepyng, whom she slewe, and after that her selfe, for joye that she had avenged her selfe of that abhomynable vilanye."[46] The trajectory of sexual violence may recoil on itself to create a circuit that encompasses men, as when Richard Brathwait describes a virgin who confronts her would-be seducer: "shee tels him, how shee had vow'd never to consent to any man in that kind, till shee had first tri'd his mettall in the field. Draw he must, or she will disgrace him; in which combat, instead of a more amorous Conflict, shee disarm'd him, and with a kicke, wish'd him ever after to be more wary how he attempted a Maidens honour."[47]

If the first victory seems pyrrhic and the second merely comic, both chastise masculine degeneracy, and other texts stress the weight of that act. Thomas Heywood tells of a woman who, "being forcibly adulterated," tricks her assailant into looking into a well, whereupon, "she apprehending that advantage, thrust him headlong into the Well, and casting huge stones after him, revenged her selfe upon the Ravisher."[48] Violated women suffer social and often literal death, but they take men with them; as ravishment breaches bodies and contracts, it ties the destruction of feminine subjects to the voidance of heterosociality itself. In its analysis of ravishment, *The Lawes Resolutions of Womens Rights* first lists "when a woman is enforced violently to sustaine the furie of brutish concupiscence: but she is left where she is found, as in her owne house or bed, as *Lucrece* was," and concludes, "It seemeth the first kinde of rape deserved alwayes death by Gods Lawes, unlesse the woman ravished were unbetrothed, so that the ravisher might marrie her."[49] A horrific pragmatism conscripts rape to the cause of futurity; value can be recouped if the useful body is interned, however belatedly, in sanitized space. But willful virtue posits other solutions. Chaste women might take incontinent revenge, authorized by such exemplary precursors as Penthesilea and Diana, Boudica, Judith, and Philomel.[50] This distills an ideal to a deadly concentration: feminine subjects defend the standards by which they are defined, and contractual systems excise valueless men.

The premise of indispensable feminine virtue leads to a peculiar mode of licensed insurgence. Willful women operate within the space of institutional authority, and shore up the paradigms they seem to challenge. Yet the concept of challenge has relevance as well, for, if those paradigms accommodate volitional subjects, they do so by stretching their seams and even changing their shapes. In this sense feminine will cuts across categories of action, obscuring what Michel de Certeau describes as the difference between strategies and tactics. Strategies, de Certeau writes, "are actions which, thanks to the establishment of a place of power (the property of a proper), elaborate theoretical places (systems and totalizing discourses) capable of articulating an ensemble of physical places in which forces are distributed." A tactic, by contrast, "is a calculated action determined by the absence of a proper locus. . . . This nowhere gives a tactic mobility, to be sure, but a mobility that must accept the chance offerings of the moment."[51] These definitions call to mind a familiar split between patriarchal power and feminine resistance: masculine dominion forges a totalizing structure, which women disrupt only through local, ephemeral incursions. And yet, as I have argued, feminine will executes social imperatives, and plays a legitimate part in the operations of power. This is also and inevitably a questionable part, distrusted and disavowed, a contradiction which conjoins "the property of a proper" with something that cannot be properly situated or owned. If strategy, in de Certeau's terms, "is an effort to delimit one's own place in a world bewitched by the invisible powers of the Other," virtuous feminine will guards the borders, but also opens the doors to alien agents and unforeseen affiliations: "a tactic boldly juxtaposes diverse elements in order suddenly to produce a flash shedding a different light on the language of a place."[52]

Laurie Shannon illuminates one such juxtaposition when she links chastity to the privileged discourse of friendship. "Masculine friendship and female chastity both proffer self-sufficiency, autonomy, and constancy, as well as a freedom from servility, mutability, or contingency."[53] Shannon makes a critical distinction between the *consensio* that characterizes friendship and the hierarchical quality of other bonds: "Equality between agreeing parties suggests a balance of wills, and only that parity can ensure that a contract has been freely entered. It is this utopian parity that the other-self logics of friendship fundamentally concern themselves to address, rather than an avoidance of diversity or a hierarchizing of difference. Consent and hierarchy here exclude one another mutually."[54] Consensual homosocial parity draws chastity into a system that circumvents vertical differentiation. Shannon's compelling argument might enable us to approach heterosociality from an altered angle of view, and trace paths of interdependence—that "balance of wills"— through a system in which consent and hierarchy do not exclude one another at all, but engage in a fractious conflict between motivated segregation and

practical need. Masculine autonomy, with its warrant for top-down separatism, is the cover story of heterosocial order, but self-possession conveys only
a precarious entitlement to the good will of others. Where feminine subjects
act as agents of connection, the intricacy of social contracts redistributes the
claims that can be made by and on persons.[55] From this premise of reciprocal
commitment, consent speaks back to a factitious discipline. Althusser argues
that ideological articulation only flows one way: "As a first formulation I
shall say: *all ideology hails or interpellates concrete individuals as concrete
subjects*, by the functioning of the category of the subject."[56] But when that
category is itself a compressed space of call and response, the Althusserian
hail precipitates chiastic recognition, both of and by the subjected subject,
which constitutes feminine will through coincident yet discordant man-
dates. Acquiescence does not occur in silence. It is a discursive development, which crosses sites of investment and proliferates claims on intent.

In pursuit of that development, I explore the ways in which predomi-
nantly male-authored texts address the volition of women. Traub notes the
possibility that texts written by men about female desire might be deemed
irrelevant to "women's actual lives," but disagrees with that view: "I believe,
on the contrary, that male-authored discourses were an intrinsic, indeed,
constitutive part of women's lived experience. They provided the images and
idioms that women encountered, discussed among themselves, willfully appropriated, silently disavowed, and publicly contested."[57] Accounts of feminine practices tend to reach us through the distorting lens of masculine
unease, but distortion, as a sign of the torque that twists regulatory narratives
away from their declared ends, may be telling in itself. As Dympna Callaghan
reminds us, the absence of "actual" women does not limit the reach of representation:

> The paradox of representation is that it both produces and occludes
> subjectivities and while it may service the production and reproduc-
> tion of subjectivities, it cannot wholly determine them. Representa-
> tion exerts a pull on subjectivity, which can be variously, or even
> simultaneously, coercive and disciplinary, seductive and enthralling.
> That the categories of "woman," "African," etc., are always bound
> up with representation renders them profoundly cultural and com-
> plex rather than biological and essential—though no less real.[58]

In accounts of willing women, the "pull on subjectivity" pulls twice, on
the masculine subjects who make a case for social sovereignty, and on the

feminine subjects who appear in the gaps of that porous argument. The predicament of authority, in which domination is precisely a state of thrall, ruptures the framework of univocal claims. Whether we follow Callaghan's point about representation or Traub's about lived experience—or whether we simply imagine that the hectic proliferation of these texts must tell us *something*—we encounter the fact that male authors do not represent agency as the sole province of men. The patriarchal enterprise is far less than the sum of its parts, and stories about feminine volition divulge a great deal about the strains and the breaks.

Against the Grain

In the first section of this book, I concentrate on three influential discourses that interweave philosophical speculation and social practice: faculty theory, rhetorical theory, and misogyny. When they discuss will as an aspect of individual psychology, of language, or of gendered identity, the texts I consider participate in the project that sustains hierarchy through the disciplined use of subjected terms. Yet each discourse feminizes the faculty of action, and entangles the condition of mastery in an intimate association with the objects it would govern. Theoretical formulations are haunted by images of women, which they summon in the name of making social sense, and seem unable or unwilling to banish when that sense goes astray. In this way arcane, esoteric, or technical vocabularies—taxonomic, theological, psychic, and figural— enter secular, pragmatic conversations about everyday actions and roles. Faculty theory, which defines the tasks of psychic elements within the mind or soul, identifies will as analogous to and inherent in feminine subjects, populating intra- and intersubjective systems with agents that are both immanent and estranged. Rhetorical theory feminizes and sexualizes the effects of figuration, so that ambivalence about willful speech implicates broader concerns about utility, excess, desire, and control. Misogyny responds to the problem of feminine choice, and, because its methods are reactive and defensive, the impulse to define women in terms of essential nature is overshadowed by a wary regard for their conditional but formative agency. In chapters on each of these discourses, I trace connections between the quotidian work of feminine volition and the abstract tenets of social order.

Those connections shape the readings that comprise the book's second section. Each of the Shakespearean texts I discuss presents feminine subjects who directly engage conventions of gender, and thus alter the ways in which those conventions operate and signify. In *All's Well That Ends Well*, Helena poses a problem by pursuing what conservative values prescribe as her goal; her constant pursuits energize the trajectory of socialized desire, but deflect its meaning by determining its outcome. In the last section of the *Sonnets*, the intimacy of heterosocial exchange reflects a process of mutual constitution, an intersection of subjects that undercuts misogynist taxonomies. *Measure for Measure* begins with a ruler's abdication, and leaves Isabella to speak the law of marriage; the quality of her chaste will escalates friction between absolute ideals and compromised resolutions. *King Lear* realizes the possibility that feminine will might operate on its own terms, and, by playing out a fantasy of masculine isolation, sets even virtuous women at odds with patrilineal succession. These plays and poems present the deliberate, consensual participation of women as crucial to stability and continuity, and disclose the contingency of naturalized relationships, procedures, and aims.

In monitory texts, feminine will appears as a theatrical problem: "If she be faire, thy house shall then bee a Stage, the people Spectators, and thy wife the Actor of a Comedy."[59] Drama heightens the calculated artifice of social roles, connecting authenticity to performance by way of precedent need: if "women" provide a medium for the progress of traditional plots, they perform that function as a motivated exchange that takes the form of contract. What you see is what you hope to want, a subjective figment invented for a spectator who knows, yet resists knowing, that the spectacle does not guarantee truth but fulfills expectation and answers desire. Lorna Hutson acutely reminds us that the citation of cultural codes can intervene in their production: "If a form of representation involves narrative, as Renaissance drama does, there is no obvious reason why we should not ask how narrative itself, or the selection and sequence of represented actions, contributes to and reproduces, or transforms, the *doxa*, or the stereotypes of a particular culture."[60] Dramatic narratives give bodily form and motion to the effects of feminine will, and animate orthodoxies in ways that inseparably replicate and reshape their terms. Still, an obvious question remains: why, specifically, Shakespeare? Shakespeare highlights the intersection of established forms and volatile dynamics, through works that construct a belated relationship to generic conventions, and through the acute angles that link an idea of Shakespeare to Shakespearean texts. My primary interest lies in the issue of belatedness, and this rests in part on an entrenched fascination with Shakespeare as sign. Here as so often, "Shakespeare" is a *provocateur*: the author is not unique in his concerns, but his extravagant cultural presence begs the question of how will circulates and signifies through the coincidence of "Will."

By this I do not mean to say that Shakespeare's nominal "Will" is a coincidence, although for my purposes it largely is; rather, I want to focus briefly on the exposés of proprietary reference that surround a proper name. Across a range of approaches and agendas, scholars draw "Will" into nets of implication from which no self-possessed figure can emerge. In *Poetic Will,* David Willbern begins with the conventional notion of solitary genius, only to enmesh it in corollary terms: "Shakespeare's language, scenes, and characters emerge from his writer's quill, propelled by the genius of his poetic *will*—understood simultaneously as emotional erotic drive and intellectual artistic design (both conscious and unconscious) as well as literary legacy."[61] In *Will Power,* Richard Wilson describes legacy itself as a product of interlocked forces: "The local determination that prescribed the semantics of this author's name at a conflux of phallocentric violence and textual desire was also the field of force from which Shakespearean fiction drew a transcendent charge."[62] In *Reading Shakespeare's Will,* Lisa Freinkel shows that "Will" does not refer within a closed system, but facilitates the infinite regress of linguistic displacement: "It is, accordingly, precisely this figural notion of fulfillment that Shakespeare's *Will* challenges."[63] In "Shakespeare's *Will,*" Joel Fineman reads *The Rape of Lucrece* as a troubling collaboration—"Tarquin and Lucrece are inverse versions of each other, and for this reason *together* make the rape of Lucrece"—and traces the mark of Shakespeare's name in the poem to bind the author, too, to the genesis of story and act.[64] These studies employ various methods toward diverse ends, but each uses "Will" to explode autonomy and pursue entanglement. The indices of ownership evoked by will—body, legacy, language, name—become signs of connections forged at a cost, and consequential meanings emerge not from the enclosed space of intention, word, or person, but from the transactional force of bonds. In *Seizures of the Will,* Frank Whigham writes, "The acts of seizure examined below aim less, as the courtier did, to do something *before* others, striving to please an audience, than to do something *to* another, to write oneself man or woman upon the slate of another, to strive to become 'the deed's creature.'"[65] Only a violation of discrete subjects can conjure the experience of subjectivity itself: this sketches the logic of interrelation, at once coercive and fruitful, which will as a faculty works to impose.

"Will," as a proper name, leads to the vital, tricky, sometimes disabling, and often improper unions consummated by will as a transitive force. This recalls that most obvious of improprieties, the use of "will" as genital slang. I confess I had hoped to avoid the penis, but it has a certain utility, which we might extract from the entries in Gordon Williams's *A Glossary of Shakespeare's Sexual Language.* Under the heading "will," Williams gives "carnal desire" as his first definition; his second is "genitals, usually penis," with the added note, "Genital sense extends to include the woman's organ."[66] That extension of sense breaks open the possessive equivalence of "will" and "penis," which associates sexual capacity with the exclusivity of intent. If will names the sexed bodies of both men and women, it identifies neither in isolation, and engages a broader disquiet about the tenability of isolation itself. A raunchy joke carries a rueful comment on the contact points that define heterosocial relations. Despite its still-legible ancestry, this version of will has migrated some distance from Augustine's correlation of willful genitals with a post-lapsarian state. Amy Greenstadt draws out the masculine emphasis of Augustine's account: "Paradoxically, it seems, the Fall brought with it the uncontrollable rise of the male member as a visible sign or gesture that 'bore witness' or 'gave testimony' (*teste*) to the involuntary nature of carnal desire."[67] Augustine's corrupted will palpably distinguishes men from women, and emphatically separates intention from desire. In the early modern period, will cross-couples those bodies and faculties to enforce the intimacies of contract, and Shakespeare conveys that effect to us when we incessantly cite the *Sonnets* to illustrate will in its genital usage.[68] "Will" notoriously calls up a swarm of connotations in these poems, among which any specificities of body, person, desire, intent, or name are overwhelmed if not erased; to fix one meaning there is to embed it in a host of others.[69] For the *Sonnets* as for early modern texts more generally, will is a meeting point rather than a tool, a densely overwritten shorthand for the uncanniness of being bound.

Throughout this book, I am concerned with the interplay of familiarity and estrangement, and with culturally loaded figures that at once inhabit and exceed the forms for which they are taken as substantial signs. This quality describes will and women and Shakespeare, and it also characterizes the texts I have chosen: they fall into genres, but it is an awkward fit. *All's Well* and *Measure* are famously forthright about the hard work of comedy, bracketing happy endings with near-visible quotation marks. The *Sonnets*, whenever they were written, appear late in the tradition, and sustain a complicated theoretical engagement with their own conceits. *Lear* is not the last of Shakespeare's tragedies, but, as it begins with dislocated monarchy and ends with evacuated sociality, it meditates on the prospect of exhaustion.[70] Belatedness inheres less in radical change than in a sense of raised texture; gestures of generic compliance draw attention to structures which, even as they hold their shapes, are populated and organized in odd, unsettling ways.[71] Each text makes feminine subjects responsible for relational systems: chastity, desire, marriage, and patrilineality succeed or fail through the intercessions of women. Teleology is superseded by reiterative but conditional acts of will, which widen the gap between predestined results and manufactured effects, between the answer that must be right and a solution that can—perhaps—be made to seem true. Linda Charnes writes, "Shakespearean drama, perhaps more than that of any other playwright, demonstrates the ways in which absolutist ideologies can find themselves undermined in their deployment by the visual, spatial, and gestural choreography of their own performance."[72] If the texts I consider invoke the apparatus of mastery, they do so by regarding truisms from a crooked line of sight. For present-day audiences, the effect is heightened by canonicity: the formal and affective protocols of Shakespearean genres shape our frame of reference, even if we question the explanatory sufficiency of socialized desire, poetic power, or tragic flaws. When we encounter these texts, our knowledge precedes rather than discovers its reference points. If drama estranges the truth-claims of social performance, Shakespearean belatedness redoubles that effect, and creates an oblique refraction of reified norms.

In her remarkable study of Shakespeare, theology, and figure, Freinkel writes, "To read Shakespeare's *will* is to read the implosion of flesh into spirit, of spirit into flesh."[73] We might pursue this observation outside a theological frame, and consider its implications for the figures who both perform and refigure prescribed social roles. As drama animates ideas through artifactual bodies, it provides a testing ground for the infusion of social theory into social subjects. The illusion of personhood is shaped by questions of assigned and assumed purpose: what it means to act in context, to act on others, to act with consequence, to act as meant. Luke Wilson argues that a concern with intention shapes early modern theater: "this inclination to look carefully at the structure of intentional action and the reports made of that structure derives from the early modern theater itself, an institution and mode of representation profoundly invested in enacting the experience of intentional engagement with the world."[74] Such engagement exacts its costs, and scholarship has shown that Shakespeare's plays—perhaps most particularly his comedies—are far more troubled than they may appear. Here I look at plays and poems which, as they mobilize unmediated feminine will, strip away even the semblance of protected space or natural order, and leave only the counterpoised austerities of compromise and dissolution. Reading against the grain becomes reading for the plot. The fallen reciprocity of the *Sonnets*, the banished futurity of *Lear*, the forceful restitutions of *All's Well* and *Measure*: these intensely visible processes foreground the necessary but ambiguous interventions of feminine subjects. Through abdication in *Measure* and *Lear*, illness and flight in *All's Well*, and the poet-speaker's disavowal of self-sufficiency in the final *Sonnets*, each text carves out an absence in the space of masculine control. Feminine will circulates within heterosocial systems, but the veneer of extrinsic government no longer overlays its work.

Thus exposed, feminine will presents a fusion of compliance and purpose that puts the bones of the problem on display. Louis Althusser argues that ideology works in silence: "the 'obviousness' that you and I are subjects—and that that does not cause any problems—is an ideological effect, the elementary ideological effect."[75] The explicit canons of early modern femininity produce subjects who not only recognize but reiterate the precepts that shape social existence, and their participation invests ideological obviousness with vocal alterity.[76] In the course of my readings, I engage familiar tensions: between hierarchy and intercourse, discipline and consent, autonomy and need. These artificial yet powerful oppositions reflect competing modes of self- and other-definition, suspended in a fragile balance that might always collapse. Willful feminine subjects transect the frame of counterpoise: they bring conflicts to crisis, but stitch up rifts through improbable accords. Althusser is profoundly cynical about subjectivity, writing, "*There are no subjects except by and for their subjection. That is why they 'work all by themselves'.*"[77] Feminine will exposes the double meaning of self-automated work. Informed purpose both engineers and unravels the seamlessness of subjection; deliberate choice both animates the utility and annexes the authority of conventional roles. Even as ideological integration exerts a close pressure on identities and acts, such pressure forges subjects for whom knowing the codes may be a version of breaking them. Volitional acquiescence is integral to heterosocial order, and this book traces cultural vocabularies through which that paradox takes shape.

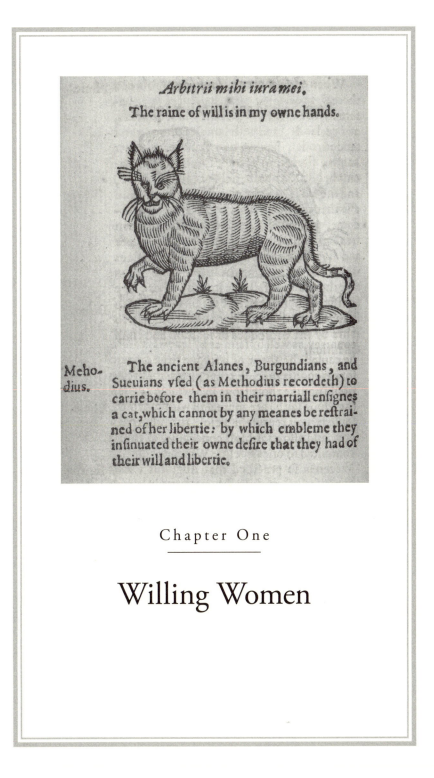

Arbitrii mihi iura mei.

The raine of will is in my owne hands.

Meho-
dius.

The ancient Alanes, Burgundians, and
Sueuians vsed (as Methodius recordeth) to
carrie before them in their martiall ensignes
a cat, which cannot by any meanes be restrai-
ned of her libertie: by which embleme they
insinuated their owne desire that they had of
their will and libertie.

Chapter One

Willing Women

How could a man be punished justly, if he used his will for the very purpose for which it was given? Since, however, God punishes the sinner, what else do you think He says but: Why did you not use your free will for the purpose for which I gave it you, that is, to do right?

—Augustine, *The Problem of Free Choice*, Book 2, Chapter 1, 75–76

It then emerges that the interpellation of individuals as subjects presupposes the "existence" of a Unique and central Other Subject, in whose Name the religious ideology interpellates all individuals as subjects.

—Althusser, "Ideology and Ideological State Apparatuses," 167

So Mightie, so Continuall, so Neere, so Domesticall

This chapter focuses on intersections of faculty theory and heterosocial subjectivity, and examines how a philosophical discourse of the well-ordered psyche participates in secular arguments about feminine roles. However, I take my epigraphs from two iconic accounts of the relationship between personal volition and divine power. The first is from Augustine's meditations on grace and free will, in which he sets a paradox: the proper use of free will requires an intention to act as has already been intended, so that virtuous subjects will themselves into accord with a prior meaning.[1] Purposeful work pursues determined ends, and good faith becomes a triumph of surrender, a self-consuming voluntarism for which subjectivity stands as both sacrifice and trace. Louis Althusser's account of interpellation also posits a force that subsumes particular intentions—a version of what Luke Wilson refers to as "agentless action"—in this case to argue that religious compliance produces social integration.[2] Althusser's framework folds the idea of the subject as agent into the larger structure of subjection:

Figure 2 (preceding page). "The raine of will is in my owne hands." Claude Paradin, *The Heroicall Devises of M. Claudius Paradin* (London: William Kearney, 1591), 74. By permission of the Folger Shakespeare Library.

In the ordinary use of the term, subject in fact means: (1) a free subjectivity, a centre of initiatives, author of and responsible for its actions; (2) a subjected being, who submits to a higher authority, and is therefore stripped of all freedom except that of freely accepting his submission. This last note gives us the meaning of this ambiguity, which is merely a reflection of the effect which produces it: the individual *is interpellated as a (free) subject in order that he shall submit freely to the commandments of the Subject, i.e. in order that he shall (freely) accept his subjection*, i.e. in order that he shall make the gestures and actions of his subjection "all by himself." *There are no subjects except by and for their subjection*. That is why they "work all by themselves."[3]

For Augustine, ethical subjectivity inheres in the deliberate attempt to achieve submission; for Althusser, the process is at once simpler and more annihilating, as it produces a subject prescribed into "the gestures and actions of his subjection" and displaces effort and ethics into the realm of illusion. Widely divided by time, faith, and didactic aims, Augustine and Althusser describe hierarchies based in disproportion, within which imperfect individual will serves a vast and mystified end.

Both models implicate will in the failure of full realization: the limits of a fractional, conditional individuation impede comprehension and compromise purpose. Augustine credits will with a natural inclination toward virtue and a rational capacity for moral action; however, nature and reason are deformed by confinement to a fallen state.[4] For Althusser, limitations follow from an always-precedent interpellation rather than from original sin, but produce an analogous susceptibility to delusion, seduction, and error. The inescapable condition of the incorporated subject—occupation of a body defined by spiritual defect or marked for social use—obscures as it distorts any correlation between qualified volition and unconditional power. Augustinian theology mystifies divine will, and requires subjects to meet an obligation they cannot reliably understand. Althusserian ideology shields the overarching demand through a trick of recognition: "It is indeed a peculiarity of ideology that it imposes (without appearing to do so, since these are 'obviousnesses') obviousnesses as obviousnesses, which we cannot *fail to recognize* and before which we have the inevitable and natural reaction of crying out (aloud or in the 'still, small voice of conscience'): 'That's obvious! That's right! That's true!' "[5]

The differences are evident. Augustine defines virtuous will as a divine gift, while for Althusser the will to virtue is a misleading premise that sustains a counterfeit apprehension of self. Structures of subordination posit radically dissimilar consequences—the possibility of grace, the inevitability of false consciousness—so that an Augustinian subject may do right and honor God, while an Althusserian subject can only do well, and produce the labor that a mechanistic social order requires. Augustine imagines an ultimate transcendence of the flesh; Althusser only speculates about internal distantiation and, more obscurely, science.[6] But the default positions of subjects resonate across the divide. These models share the figure of an instrumental will, which does its proper work by pursuing ends its contingent possessor can neither anticipate nor assess. Because choice is mediated through a corrupt or co-opted bodily implement, will is the symptom of inaccessible understanding; instrumentality is an effect of mystification, a sign of the gap between subjects and the authority that determines their subjection. Meaningful correspondence between specific acts and aggregate goals, whether conceived in religious or secular terms, can only be a leap of faith.

The meeting point of these disparate arguments suggests the difference that knowledge might make. In the early modern texts on which I focus, women will themselves to the will represented in social directives: volitional acquiescence animates subjects who recognize and choose the roles into which they are prescribed. A hierarchy that calls on divine intention and relies on useful bodies might mystify its significance in both Augustinian and Althusserian ways. Yet as the proliferation of conduct manuals and exemplary catalogues suggests, it would perhaps be counterintuitive to imagine that assimilation withholds its objectives. Within the disciplinary regime of sexuality, social strategies are accessible to awareness and exposed to scrutiny. Codes are highly legible—organized, preached, legislated, recorded, advertised, and sold—and equate virginity, chastity, and constancy with the conservation of cultural assets. In his discussion of action and agency, Wilson distinguishes theoretical knowledge from praxis: "The self's sense of itself as agent, in my view, has less to do with epistemological certainty than with a practical familiarity with an image of oneself actually acting; it is acting as praxis, rather than a theoretical capability of knowing when or why to act, that is in question."[7] When social futurity hinges on the quality of action, a motivated distribution of labor bridges that gap: because sexual virtue cannot be known with any certainty from without, feminine subjects must understand its theory in order to regulate their practices.[8] This does not create unfettered agents, liberated from doctrinal imposition; nor does it manufacture automata on the assembly line of authorized narratives. Instead it reveals that the terms of an ideological project can be learned and fulfilled by the embodied subjects on whom that project relies. A powerful and articulate causality connects the self-discipline of women to heterosocial coherence, forging a bond that imparts both force and a certain precariousness to the systematic production of expedient persons.[9] Early modern cultural theory publishes the dependence of good government on feminine sexual acts, and informs instrumental subjects with a purposeful understanding of their own work.

The idea that feminine subjects might know the rules, and use them to authorize constitutive action, reflects the steps of translation through which abstract ideals become social tenets. Those steps mark out changes in the premises of interrelation, moving away from perfect hierarchy and toward more debased, dimished, and effective arrangements. Lisa Freinkel describes the Lutheran problem of failed subjection: "All men fail equally, absolutely, to obey the Law, since to obey requires that we subject our will to an external constraint—that we act heteronomously rather than as self-willed, autonomous creatures. Luther's insight, at once a psychological and a philosophical one, concerns the lack of consent that such heteronomy implies."[10] Obedience requires an unattainable correlation between imperative and enactment, a complete absence of friction, ambivalence, or effort. By contrast, secular norms frame a contractual space in which obedience can be serviceable and consent can be sufficient; these are the demands of the true-enough for the good-enough, the fallen and functional covenants of ordinary use. Social requirements may appear to manifest an absolute truth, but they are not identical with that truth, and their conditional, permeable quality becomes visible precisely through the ways in which they are answered. Deliberate compliance identifies multiple sites of volition, even as it acquiesces in the projects it intends to advance. For feminine subjects, then, the habit of "working all by themselves" has complicated effects. Informed consent to prescribed work demonstrates that hierarchy emerges from a dynamic process: it is a product rather than a negation of will.

Will is a momentous faculty, encompassing the possibility of salvation, the possession of autonomy, the acceptance or disavowal of accountability for civil and religious predicaments. At the same time, it insistently raises the question of local effects. Frank Whigham writes, "In endlessly debated matters of religion (free will and predestination), social order (obedience and rebellion, social mobility and subversion, crime and punishment), gender ideology (women's willfulness, the sexual will), and family structure (parental authority, infidelities), the category of individual will played a central role."[11] Theories of will intermingle philosophical abstractions with ordinary affairs, and turn theological inquiry toward secular, particular capacities and limits. That turn creates an unlikely convergence of interlocutors. Analyses originate in widely divergent religious, ethical, and political investments, pursuing antagonistic aims and formulating incompatible arguments, but converge to a striking degree when they engage the issue of quotidian control. At such moments, irreconcilable agendas make space for a shared and fundamentally social concern with the intricacy of regulation, focused on the interplay of discipline and desire that defines will as a problem.

That problem takes shape as a drama of individuated agents: meditations on self-control and its failure populate the soul with elements engaged in formative but potentially anarchic transactions. Faculty theory, in its attempt to sort out the psychic parts, allocate their work, and define their discords and allegiances, describes internal qualities in a vocabulary of personation, which explains intrasubjective dynamics through the proper and improper acts of discrete subjects. Such qualities as reason, will, passion, judgment, fantasy, imagination, and wit appear less as fragments of a unified whole than as contentious citizens of a community, who may or may not conform to rules of behavior, function, and place. In her account of psychophysiology, Gail Kern Paster clearly explicates the connection between affective and social experience: "The experience of an emotion is thus transactional not only in being a response to a stimulus—whether that stimulus is external or internal, real or imaginary, present or remembered—but also in occurring, almost inevitably, within a dense cultural and social context."[12] Engaged with and fluent in the requisites of that context, anatomies of the mind delineate a world which operates as a system of interpersonal associations. Faculty theory in this way extrapolates social principles from the fluctuations of rebellion and restraint, relating internal and external negotiations not only through analogic iteration but through reciprocal causality. Microcosm both predicates and imitates macrocosm: the role played by will within the psyche prefigures and echoes the question of how to act in the world.

The thread of sociality connects even the most abstract and obdurate disagreements. Erasmus and Luther, in their contentions concerning free will, seem to divide the Augustinian paradox between them: "By freedom of the will we understand in this connection the power of the human will whereby man can apply to or turn away from that which leads unto eternal salvation";

"with regard to God, and in all things pertaining to salvation or damnation, man has no free will, but is a captive, servant and bondslave, either to the will of God, or to the will of Satan."[13] But underlying these unqualified declaratives is the peculiarity of lived experience, of knowing the will to act and intend within a formation which might—or might not—vacate that will of efficacy or substance. Erasmus's comments on grace describe divine power as absolute, but do not foreclose a qualified human intervention: "But since all things have three parts, a beginning, a continuation, and an end, grace is attributed to the two extremities, and only in continuation does the free will effect something. Two causes meet in this same work, the grace of God and the human will, grace being the principal cause and will a secondary, since it is impotent without the principal cause, while the latter has sufficient strength by itself."[14] Luther, too, acknowledges that the relationship between divine and human will might be to a degree cooperative, although he restricts that engagement to a still narrower space: "But, if we do not want to drop this term altogether (which would be the safest and most Christian thing to do), we may still use it in good faith denoting free will in respect not of what is above him, but of what is below him. This is to say, man should know in regard to his goods and possessions the right to use them, to do or to leave undone, according to his free will."[15] Intimations of secular volition appear in the interstices of this fiercely theological debate; human agency participates in the small everyday acts that construct some link between absolute authority and individual meaning. Those acts open up, however tentatively, a space in which subjection cannot be detached entirely from effective intent.

This is broadly predictable: a culture that aggressively educates subjects into their roles interlocks participation with constraint. Dolora A. Wojcie-howski points out that recent theories of subjectivity, in their focus on hegemonic structures and sites of resistance, reiterate earlier theories of will.

> The great irony, of course, is that very similar arguments were re-hearsed with great subtlety in the Renaissance, navigating between the Scylla and Charybdis of the under- and overdetermined subject, though the various insights of those debates are now schematized, misrepresented, or ignored. In this fashion theory has, in some ways at least, reinvented the will, though it seems archaic to speak of agency in such terms.[16]

A perilous navigation between abjection and insurrection is the project not only of theory, but of the subjects who appear in early modern narratives; as recent analyses of masculinity have shown, the complexities of inhabiting a prescribed performance shape the roles of both women and men.[17] But there is something specifically gendered about the problem of volitional acquiescence with which I am concerned. When faculty theorists describe a vital but volatile agent within a hierarchical frame, they connect will to women in explicit terms. Will is the generative principle without which reason remains impotently abstract. It acts, in theory, only to authorized ends; is governed by normative values; is a critical but restricted player in the conservation of structural stability. At the same time, it might always be seduced or misled, and, more dangerously, it conceives and consummates its own desires. Treacherous in its presence and paralyzing in its absence, will is at once evidence of and defense against a ruinous condition of lack. Faculty theory and heterosociality share this conflicted language of utility, self-sufficiency, and intrinsic threat, which identifies creatures turned to higher ends, but reined in only by frail strands of self-restraint. As it joins circumscribed function to unbounded capacity, the discourse of will follows a grammar of sexual politics.

Pierre Charron raises this to the surface, framing the relationship between reason and will as a marriage. He writes of ethical choice, "The understanding hath other preheminences: for it is unto the will as the husband to the wife, the guide and light unto the traveller, but in this it giveth place unto the will."[18] Charron explains that his analogy reinforces natural derivations: "whereby it followeth, that the will is enobled by loving those things that are high and woorthy of love; is vilified, by giving it selfe to those things that are base and unwoorthy; as a wife honoureth or dishonoureth her selfe by that husband that she hath taken."[19] It is a confident yet ambiguous point. Will accrues merit only by forming proper connections, but the ideal of propriety does not neutralize wayward potential. The claim that understanding holds preeminence reverses itself at the crucial point of choice—"but in this it giveth place unto the will"—and the argument about virtue is driven by phrases that privilege the decisive actions of will and wife: "loving those things," "giving it selfe," "honoureth or dishonoureth her selfe," "that husband that she hath taken." Heterosociality is overtly the model, and hierarchy is explicitly in question. Thomas Wright heightens the tension of that linked premise when he portrays will as "the governesse of the Soule," her reign marked by unseemly liaisons: "Without any great difficultie may be declared, how Passions seduce the Will."[20] Charron's dyad expands to a throng, with the troubled pair of reason and will at its center. Mingling intra- and intersubjective reference points, Wright describes reason's struggle for mastery as "so mightie, so continuall, so neere, so domesticall," and argues that men face a choice that is no choice at all: "eyther they must consent to doe their enemies will, or still bee in conflict."[21]

Marriage, adversarial and "domesticall," appears as the natural habitat of feminine will, suggesting that competitive claims on volition shape the edifice from which discipline derives its mandate. Wright's manly reason decides between surrender and eternal conflict—or does he own that decision at all? Charron's wifely will acquires her worth from her husband—or does she refract it through him? Is the patriarch a beard? Not precisely. Hierarchical difference is more than a cover story for some alternative truth; it is one lexicon of social order, which coexists uneasily with a language of intersubjective reciprocity. And the shared space of these rhetorics is far messier than the exclusive dominion of either could be. Frances E. Dolan analyzes two biblical figures that pervade discourses of marriage: "the fusion of spouses into 'one flesh' and the man's role as the head of that corporate body." Their incongruent simultaneity, she points out, imbues natural union with traces of the grotesque. "At every turn, the transcendent ideal of one flesh is haunted by the prospect of the marital body as a two-headed monster."[22] Dolan's image suggests that neither dominance nor synthesis can cure double vision. Marriage unites ideas without regard for their contrariety, and encodes a twofold argument that underlies the ascendancy of one: the overpopulated conjugal body incorporates a doctrine grounded both in partition and in intersection.

Duality unravels seamless plots, but it also responds to necessity and hints at desire. In an analysis of Petrarch's *Canzoniere*, Richard Strier writes, "The poet's bondage is always seen as having, at least potentially, a relation to his will that is not simply negative."[23] Sonnets meditate endlessly on the connection between being subjugated to one's own will and being governed by the will of another, and the idea of a bondage, inextricably imposed and innate, which disallows refusal or even repairs disability has some power to elucidate the curious ambivalence about feminine social will. Defining women in narrow terms of objectified use is not only untenable; it is also, in a sense that is both pragmatic and indefinably affective, not enough. Joshua Phillips takes up the complexities of affect in his study of communal identity: "Like 'property' (either that which one owns or an inalienable element of a person or thing) and 'possession' (a state of having control over or of being inhabited), the word 'belonging' expresses a complicated fiction about how one relates to others and to objects, simultaneously asserting both union and dominion. Not surprisingly, it has longing at its heart."[24] Under the pressure of a want that merges desire with need, the cliché of the willful woman becomes a mobile, transitive, ambiguously valued force. An impulse to suppress ungoverned agents collides with a dependence on their good work; even when accounts of volition rely on misogynist tropes, they produce a language of generative power. Feminine will might lead only to an elaborate genealogy of the obvious: women, being willful by nature (if by "nature" we understand "culture"), challenge masculine supremacy and provoke aversive response. But a more complex recognition interrupts this line of thought. Heterosocial ideology may be conceived by men, but it is not consummated in isolation, and the links between women and will lead from static truisms of fallen nature to flexible artifacts of constitutive performance. Will becomes feminine—seductive, constant, intractable, and fruitful—because these are the qualities through which it makes social sense. The question of whose sense, of what agendas are sacrificed or served, is the point at which faculty theory and heterosociality meet.

By Force of One Consent

Intention is a dislocation masquerading as an order, a proprietary, defensive, "I *meant* to do that." The same might be said of heterosocial hierarchy.

I pose this analogy to highlight the problem of a power structure that alienates its own work. Will enacts the intentions conceived by reason, and gives abstraction a grip on everyday events; women too provide traction, through the bodies that turn patrilines into children and the labors that organize domestic space. These functions inform claims that define both will and women as pliant means toward extrinsically determined ends. Lisa Jardine has historicized the processes that impose accountability but negate control; to quote her own elegant précis, "in its insistence on individual conscience and responsibility, I argued, reformed Christianity further burdened Renaissance women by making them responsible for the well-being of the domestic unit, within which they were explicitly *not* given any power."[25] The severance of obligation from jurisdiction and of virtue from agency produces compromised actors who can never mean well. This is a powerful cultural narrative, which draws on both theological authorities and popular polemics to flatten the nuances of feminine self-discipline, but mediation tests the limits of enclosure. A logic that equates reason with men and will with women achieves stability and futurity through displacement, attenuating the link between edict and execution. Heterosociality thus separates authoritative subjects from effective agents in a risky and revealing way. Affirmations of masculine autonomy recur to the crux of interdependence; integrity, at once psychic and social, relies on a heterogeneous participation which, as Judith Butler writes, "is both its ground and the perpetual possibility of its own ungrounding."[26] For early modern theorists, that reliance is not confined to an anteriorized fantasy of what Butler calls "pre-individuated *jouissance*."[27] The predicament is inescapably present and social, a need that locates efficacy outside the subjects it serves. In a scheme predicated on masterly inactivity, the privileged subject of paternal law represents a kind of dispossessive individualism.

A fantasy of collective will, which is only and always the will of power, imperfectly masks the pluralism of social work. In a reading of Hegel, Butler analyzes an economy "where the general will supersedes the individual wills of which it is composed and, in fact, exists at their expense"; that scheme of exclusion, she argues, is haunted by the unknowable agents it has erased.

> The "will" that is officially represented by the government is thus haunted by a "will" that is excluded from the representative function. Thus the government is established on the basis of a paranoid economy in which it must repeatedly establish its one claim to universality by erasing all remnants of those wills it excludes from the domain of representation. Those whose wills are not officially represented or recognized constitute "an unreal pure will" (para. 591), and since that will is not known, it is incessantly conjectured and suspected. In an apparently paranoid fit, universality thus displays and enacts the violent separations of its own founding.[28]

If feminine will, "incessantly conjectured and suspected," is the paranoid fit of heterosocial hierarchy, it is also a founding premise. The separations that produce an illusion of totalizing power entail a violence that returns upon the structure it protects, and the costs of the ricochet are calculated within authorized discourse itself. In the most reductive parables of misogyny, passive virtue opposes active vice as the assimilated opposes the abject. But as the practical work of chastity, marriage, and procreation makes clear, women act within a paradigm that cannot exclude their volition without making nonsense of itself. The plain problem for social self-perpetuation is that it requires women; the dark secret, which is no secret at all, is that it requires them as agents in the dual sense of that term.

The coincident logics that bind will to reason and women to men reveal the foundational role of consent. In her discussion of medical, social, and marital contracts, Elaine Scarry addresses the contradictions of consensual volition:

> In general, the whole notion of consent stands the distinction be-
> tween passive and active on its head, since consent theory claims
> that it is by the will of the apparently passive that the active is
> brought into being. . . . We are initially presented with a problem:
> here are the governed, subjected to laws; by what route have they
> been subjugated? We are then presented with a solution: they are
> not subjugated to the laws; they have willed those laws; they have
> brought that state into being; they have generated it. This quiets our
> alarm about subordination, but a moment later inspires a second
> occasion of bafflement: And now *how* exactly did they do that? To
> which we are given the answer: By staying still.[29]

Top-down arguments rely on intercessions from below: consent to the com-pulsory vow, the debilitating procedure, the circumscribing law. Framed as such an argument, heterosociality may present a univocal facade, as if Freud's speculation concerning femininity—"the accomplishment of the aim of biol-ogy has been entrusted to the aggressiveness of men and has been made to some extent independent of women's consent"—were in fact a fact.[30] But hierarchy is contract, its vertical principles kept upright by feminine subjects who stay still: not static, but constant, invested with a force that secures order through acquiescent purpose. The responsibilities incurred by those subjects underscore the inseparability of compliance and will. Scarry writes, "active and passive are so mystified in consent that the phenomenon of consent actually calls into question the reality or usefulness of the categories of passive and active . . . it may be that consent itself acts to explode, or at least disturb, those categories."[31] By mystifying the genesis of intentional effects, consent suggests that agency may not be coherent with authority, and supports an apparently monolithic project from locations that proliferate across taxo-nomic lines.

John Davies illustrates this effect in his account of the faculties, which describes elements combined in an unstable mixture of coalition and duress.

Davies locates will in sympathy with good but in close proximity to error; that split affinity demands the intervention of a feminized "judgement," which appears both as an extension of will and as a quality alienated from it.

> For as true *Good*, agreeth with the *Will*,
> So *Truth* hath with the *Minde* true simpathy;
> And as the *Will* hath no such foe as *Ill*,
> So *Error* is the *Mindes* most ennemy.
> If *Judgement* then approve of *Reasons* skill,
> Shee joynes hir selfe thereto insep'rably.
>> And so of *Judgments* reas'n and *Reas'ns* judgement
>> Makes then but one, by force of one consent.[32]

In its vivid use of personation, the narrative develops a markedly social vocabulary of rivalry and partnership as it works toward a functional organization of roles. Something like resolution emerges from a series of fraught exchanges, in which discrete and adversarial components become reciprocally informed and mutually bound. The appearance of control remains contingent on a tenuous, improbable accord; summed up in the phrase "by force of one consent," the arrangement works, effectively but insecurely, as an agreement among agents who may or may not continue to guarantee its terms.

That edgy interplay between hierarchy and contract blends psychic and social concerns; as Charron's analogy indicates, vexed relations among the faculties evoke the changeable terms of marriage. Simultaneously cited to illustrate fissures in self-government and to license government of another, marriage tightens the knot of internal volatility and interpersonal exposure until those tensions threaten to explode. Phineas Fletcher's fable of will and reason introduces "Voletta" as Understanding's queen, and recalls a lost idyll in which the bond encompassed both command and accord: "both their lights conspiring, / He saw what e're was fit for her requiring, / And she to his cleare sight would temper her desiring." Like Charron, Fletcher dismantles subjugation—"*Voletta* fair, who with him lives, and reignes; / Whom neither man, nor fiend, nor God constrains: / Oft good, oft ill, oft both; yet ever free remains"—and records the outcome of unconstrained will. "But (ah!) entic't by her own worth and pride, / She stain'd her beautie with most loathsome spot; / Her Lords fixt law, and spouses light deni'd, / So fill'd her spouse and self with leprous blot."[33] Mingling allegory and theology, faculty theory and social analysis, Fletcher depicts a disrupted soul and retells an Edenic fall, epic emblems for an all too domestic problem. Dolan pinpoints the issue when she describes marriage as an economy of scarcity: "there is not enough personhood—interiority and agency, self-love and will—to go around."[34] Fletcher's story is haunted by the never-was moment in which preeminence and mutuality could coincide, but a rift between those concepts vitiates both masculine rule and heterosocial alliance. In a perverse refraction of hierarchy, feminine will, "oft good, oft ill, oft both," eclipses masculine government; in a terrible parody of union, "spouse and self" dissolve into a wife's traitorous desire.

These are the risks of an analogy that tends toward identity. A single rhetorical system portrays subjects as divided in themselves and as indivisible from one another, forcing an overlap of microcosm and macrocosm that works against distinctions of degree or kind. Margaret Ezell succinctly describes the shortfall of exclusive power: "In theory and by law, women were 'subject to' men; in practice, controversy raged over exactly what 'to be subject to' encompassed."[35] In conceptual as well as practical ways, the gender dynamics within and among social subjects are too imbricated to allow for any categorical erasure of feminine will. It makes more sense to accept a fall into compromise, and acknowledge that will on terms which might limit its field. Heinrich Bullinger uses this tactic when he discusses marriages based in consent, asserting that the consent of women follows divine guidance. "The consentyng into mariage spryngeth out of gods ordinaunce and leaneth unto honesty. For an ordinate and pure love is it that she beareth toward her chosen, by hym her desyre to remayne wyth mynde, body, and good accordyng to the worde of the Lorde, to serve hym, to shewe her trouth plyghte unto hym, to suffer well and woo wyth hym."[36] Having argued that feminine choice should always be virtuous choice, Bullinger turns to "whoryshe, carnall, and affectionate wyll" in the same paragraph. He insists that these modes differ, even as his exposition confounds them:

> Here in also diffreth the consentyng in mariage from naturall inclination. A natural thyng is it, that two parsons which are of lyke kynd and complexion, of like nature and dispocision, of lyke maner and occupyeng, should beare more wyll, the one toward the other, than they do that haved no mutuall felowshyp herein. Yet is not thys wyll comparable to consentyng into mariages.[37]

It is difficult to draw a clear line between definitions that employ a common language of intention and desire. Virtuous and vicious unions may diverge in value, but they share the status of volitional contracts.

Will indiscriminately forges, breaches, and parodically approximates sanctioned bonds; it may be the link between social aims and individual desires, but it is also a breaking point.[38] In his sermon "A Wife in Deed," Thomas Gataker praises the wife who fulfills her obligations and thus earns her title, then writes of the willful woman, "And on the other side shee ceaseth to be *a Wife*, yea to be *a Woman*, when shee ceaseth to be a meanes of *good* to *Man*: Since that the *Woman* was not *made* but for *Man*, and for his good; and therefore shee answereth not her originall, if she be not so. And in vaine will it be for her to beare the *Name* of that shee is not."[39] Through the failure to "answer her original," a wife becomes an unfixed signifier, circulating promiscuously within the idiom of covenant. Identifying this as an instance of "the eruption of wayward volition into relations of office and duty," Katherine Rowe writes, "As a limb of the marital body, the wife executes the husband's will; but she also *ratifies* their mutual rights and obligations by doing so. Or, as in Gataker's example, she fails to ratify them."[40] The conjoined potential for endorsement and sabotage describes the twofold effect of feminine will, which secures and threatens marital ties. Despite his concern with treachery, Gataker affirms the need for volition: "*Marriage requireth a conjunction of Minds, of Affections, of Willes*. And better it were, that *Men* and *Women* should never come together, unlesse they beare *heartie affection* either to other, unlesse they joine *hearts* as well as *hands*."[41] This is the dilemma that marriage can neither resolve nor conceal: the unruly desire that threatens heterosociality is also the generative desire that guarantees its future. Catherine Belsey argues that the early modern divorce debate, with its emphasis on marital consent, leads to "a new mode of control, no longer centralized and overt, but internalized and invisible"; she concludes, "The new family of the seventeenth century, still under 'the government of one,' remains a place in which power is exercised privately in the interests of public order."[42] If control circumscribes the operations of consent, we might flip that statement and retain its sense: power may remain constant, but so too does the need for acquiescence. Social regulation is seamed with counterfactual trajectories, and the question of what can be realized is answered from diverse locations of choice.

She Rules (Being Taught) with Libertie Intire

Will follows the dictates of reason, yet pursues its own goals. As he reflects on this duality, Pierre de la Primaudaye describes a regime with two rulers:

"Wherefore the Will is the highest and most soveraigne vertue of desiring, farre above all other appetites, and that which woorketh with libertie, after the minde hath shewed unto it what it ought to follow, and what to eschew, what to make choyse of, and what to refuse."[43] Reason authorizes will to govern the senses and order the soul, but will, "the highest and most soveraigne vertue of desiring," chooses its course with unchecked liberty. This quality of autonomous mediation is the central paradox of will. Rowe outlines traditional distinctions among agent, patient, and instrument, and writes, "It is useful to think of these terms as part of a set of agency relations that are dynamic. As early modern anatomists recognized, anything might suffer an action as a patient and turn about to perform another, as an agent— the most famous example of this dyad, perhaps, being the soul and senses."[44] For faculty theory, will activates the dynamic, synthetic force of that turn: a doubled agent, both instrument and actor, does crucial work by crossing categories and voiding their discretion. As the meeting point of reason and passion, as a synonym for both intention and desire, will binds together what taxonomic logic holds apart, and discloses the inharmonious drives that converge in the name of integral states.[45] It forges links between disciplinary and disruptive energies, stressing interrelation rather than disjunction. Early modern theorists parse these effects in gendered terms, associating the concurrence of regulated labor and uncontrolled impulse with feminine social roles. When the boundary blurs between comparison and personification— when will appears both as a feminized faculty and as a feminine subject— faculty theory converges with social theory in a joint preoccupation with the indispensable, irrepressible agent within. Efficient cause and sovereign force: in that split but fused identity, the discipline of self-control mirrors the liberty of self-direction. Differently valued acts are absorbed into the conundrum of agency, so that, with telling coincidence, will is linked to women not only through errant mobility and improper attachment, but through the fruitful production of affiliation and exchange.

I have argued that theories of will follow a grammar of sexual politics. If feminine pronouns, the most obvious signs of that grammar, are conventional, they are in no sense neutral. This faculty is not consistently gendered in English; will is sometimes "he" and sometimes "it," and uses of "she" constellate densely around points where personification is elaborately developed, language is evocatively social, and stability is most at stake. Sentences that characterize will as susceptible, licentious, and ambitious take the feminine; so too do formulations that describe virtuous government and generative constancy. The threat of corruption might be lifted directly from the archives of misogyny, but the dynamism which vitalizes that threat also turns to productive ends. Where problem merges with solution, this poses a problem in itself, made manifest when ambivalence about self-rule bleeds into condemnation of its results. Davies's comment, "For our *Will's* Baiard blind, yet bold, and free," inspires a gendered gloss: "Therefore the *Will* hath too just cause of *feare* / Lest shee should runne into presumptuous *sinne*."[46] According to Wright, "the Will, by yeelding to the Passion, receyveth some little bribe of pleasure, the which moveth her, to let the bridle loose, unto inordinate appetites."[47] Wright not only describes a fall but attributes it to a decision; weakness becomes purpose with the introduction of consequential choice. Thomas Elyot cites the principle of consent to trace causalities of betrayal: "if our affectes by whom we be meved to do any thynge, do consent to the said dilectation, and than immediately wyll is corrupted so that she [is] false and disloyall."[48] La Primaudaye, too, defines consent as the mechanism of treacherous pacts: "Now if it so fall out, that the Will give place to the appetite, it is always with her consent, and that because shee agreeth rather unto the sensuall appetite then unto Reason."[49] Like Bullinger's metonymic slip from virtuous affection to carnal appetite, these accounts stress the variables of preferential determination: a chain of command might become a closed circuit, within which will means and wants on her own fickle terms.

When reason capitulates and order breaks down, the fusion of psychic and social models makes anarchic sexuality an irresistible figure for the crisis. Richard Hooker illustrates the importance of reasoned choice through examples that include adultery and divorce; Elyot describes the senses as "wanton girles" who "allure eftesones Wille to their appetite."[50] Richard Barckley associates unreasoned impulse with pregnancy, greensickness, and the distracting charms of courtesans.[51] *Mirum in modum* uses the term "fantasy" to describe a will bonded to desire, and equates this with the illicit passions through which women distort procreation:

> Which *Pow'r* fantasticke is of so great force,
>   As what she powrefully doth apprehend
> Within the Body she imprints perforce;
>   For to the Body, she doth force extend.
> A proofe whereof in women kinde is kend,
>   When they in *Coitu* fix their *Fancie* fast

> On him they fancie; if they then conceave,
> It will be like their *Fancies* object fac'd:
> If then a wife doth but in thought deceave,
> The husband in that face may it perceave.[52]

Will marks the body as a woman marks her child; at the same time, women pursue a "fancie" that maps disorderly minds onto future bodies. As analogues entwine their agents—the will that chooses desire over reason, the woman who prefers her lover to her husband—the full conflation of tenor and vehicle comes into view. Katharine Eisaman Maus writes, "Renaissance speech habits can make it difficult to know when what seems to us a bodily analogy is really an analogy; when we are dealing with metaphor and when with a bare statement of fact—and whether, many times, this kind of distinction is even germane."[53] In the examples I consider here, that confusion has coercive effects. Abstract figures collapse into material fears; in order to follow the peripatetics of will, an audience must understand the labile potential of feminine sexuality. As analogies extend outward with a contagious touch, their rhetorical force implicates readers in the loss of reason that spawns misogyny, just as misogyny shapes the cautionary tale of a reason lost to will. Emphasis on aberrancy drives this strategic misdirection: the isolation of unnatural acts offers a fragile, porous defense against the recognition that all acts of will, whether constitutive or destructive, share a quality of independent resolve.

La Primaudaye brings that quality to the fore, reframing government in terms of usurpation and tyranny.

> It commeth to passe also oftentimes, that *Will* refuseth all counsaile and exhortation to doe that onely which she pleaseth, thereby to shew that shee is Lady and Mistresse and subject to none. And beeing mounted up to that pride, shee accounteth this Lordshippe which shee taketh to her selfe to bee a great good, and so maketh knowne her power and magnificence, as it were a tyrannicall prince.[54]

Davies, too, conjures the image of unnatural feminine rule, and invents a verb large enough to convey it: "This *pow'r* hath highest vertue of *Desire*, / And *Caesarizeth* ore each *Appetite*; / Shee rules (being taught) with libertie intire."[55] "Shee rules (being taught)": an informed and insurgent will derives sovereignty from imparted knowledge. Political analogies, invoked to calcify hierarchical relations, retain their form as will moves within them, from servant to collaborator (both partner and traitor) to that tyrant who rules with "libertie intire." This is not a historical change across theoretical texts, but a self-correction intrinsic to theory itself: again and again, accounts of the faculties set up an ordered structure only to relocate the position of control. "Whereupon it followeth, that our Will is at libertie and free, and cannot bee constrayned," La Primaudaye concludes; according to Davies, "Yet nought can her resistlesse powre constraine, / For nothing can *desire* from her remove."[56] Desire invests choice with power, and produces a formula for misrule. Elyot pursues this to its end: "If the soule hastily without asking counsaylle of understandyng, do approve the said pswasion, bileving wyl, with out any other investigation or serch: Than she being abandoned of understanding, loseth hir dignite, and becommith ministre unto the sences which before were her slaves."[57] Like the fall of Eve, which it resembles so closely as to shade into sameness, the ascent of will rewrites frailty as an active pursuit of license.[58]

The violation of natural order begins as a symptom—"wyll is corrupted"—escalates to an impulse—"shee should runne into presumptuous *sinne*"—and comes to fruition as a deliberate act: "if shee had not voluntarily yeelded her selfe to those distemperatures, she might have overcome them, and beene in good case."[59] Choice exerts authority—"shee willeth whatsoever shee will"—and climaxes in a base apotheosis: "shee is Lady and Mistresse and subject to none."[60] Such processes create an actor who cannot be recalled to instrumental use: "So maugre *force*, shee *freedome* doth retaine."[61] This fall into dominion suggests that secondary terms, as causal agents of the systems they serve, might alter those systems beyond recognition. The feminine pronouns that personify will not only reflect social theory but produce it: they provide a language for the autotelic instrumentality that is always, at least potentially, an abuse. Incorporated within and antithetical to the proper work of power, will iterates the vital, improper work of feminine subjects, who act from inside at the risk of changing the rules. *Evils are the more grievous, the neerer, and the more inward they are;* as diseases in the entrailes," writes Gataker in "A Good Wife Gods Gift."[62] If—to follow that familiar progress from microcosm to macrocosm—will is internal to men as women are internal to heterosociality, the result in both cases seems to be dyspepsia.

Yet faculty theory engages femininity not only to accentuate potential disruption, but to substantiate principles of order. For *Nosce Teipsum*, volitional autonomy promises a more general freedom: "*Will* is as Free as any Emperour; / Nought can restraigne her *gentle* libertie: / No Tyrant, nor no Torment hath the powre, / To make us *will*, when we *unwilling* bee."[63] In this argument, the feminized rule of will, again glossed as "libertie," guarantees virtuous constancy. The move that binds will to feminine sexuality gestures twice, toward the chaotic propagation of bastard effects and toward the conservative perpetuation of legitimate forms. Accenting the weak points of patrilineal schemes, will presents a crucial if chancy antidote to sterility and stasis: continuity can be sustained only through contract, which hinges on the acquiescence of a self-directed agent of intent. Sir John Davies observes that efficacy requires close collaboration: "*Will* puts in practise what the *wit* deviseth; / *Will* ever acts, and *wit* contemplates still, / And as from *wit* the power of *wisdome* riseth, / *All other vertues* daughters are of *will*."[64] La Primaudaye is still more explicit: "Therefore the act of Will proceedeth indeede from Will, but it is judged of and counselled by reason: so that a man may say, that it is as it were begotten by reason, and brought forth by Will."[65] As they attribute consequential acts to the engendering capacities of bonds, these accounts intersect social narratives that foreground segregation but depend on alliance. Both within and among subjects, abstract imperatives require a second site of meaning for the production of a third term: in the terse verdict of *Microcosmos*, "The *Voluntary Appetite* we finde / Is gott by *Reason*, and produc'd by *will*."[66]

It Makes *Will* Law, When *Wit* Thinkes *Law* Unfit

In his influential survey of early modern faculty theory, Herschel Baker summarizes a long tradition of confident ideals.

> Men like Hooker, Shakespeare, Bacon, and the swarm of faculty psychologists clung to the old humanistic belief in the superiority of reason to will; they are, therefore, spokesmen of the Renaissance optimism I have been trying to describe. For if man is a rational creature, and if his reason is served by his will, then his possibilities for virtuous conduct are infinite. From Ficino to Milton the stream runs clear.[67]

Baker acknowledges that those "ifs" introduce the possibility of failure, but he contains such errors within his thesis, taking them as exceptions to a largely uniform rule.[68] "In its analysis of passion and perverted will, faculty psychology was perhaps more realistic than Neoplatonism about man's potential frailties. But the frailties could be construed only as aberrations. Man's proper function was reason."[69] This claim and others like it describe stable structures that subdue or estrange anarchic threats. Early modern texts, by contrast, pursue analyses in which "proper function" is less a transparent fact than a condition of manifold possibility. The processes that define and impersonate discrete psychic parts engender stories of reciprocity and conflict, within which taxonomies are forged only to be breached. Ruth Leila Anderson offers an acute synopsis: "The doctrine that the faculties of the soul are likely both by arrangement and by nature to rebel against reason is fundamental in Elizabethan thinking."[70] As this situation might predict, theoretical notions of how the psyche should work catalyze meditations on tactical reinforcement and potential collapse.

Wright implies a need for compromise when he advocates counsel rather than decree: "the Will affecteth, for the most part, that, the understanding perswadeth to bee best."[71] The stutter of qualification—"for the most part"—proves oddly conventional. In his discussion of "the soule reasonable," Stephen Batman describes a faculty governed by its own nature: "And kindly it desireth good and flyeth evill, though it choose evill other while for want of advisement."[72] Choice inclines toward good, but again a second thought—that "other while"—tempers assurance.[73] La Primaudaye steers a straighter course, if only by way of brevity: "God hath given to man understanding to know good, and will to desire and follow it."[74] But a few pages later, he too takes a strange swerve: "And as concerning the naturall disposition of the Will, it is to will that good which is truely good, or that which seemeth to bee so."[75] With the clause "or that which seemeth to bee so," flawed interpretation erupts into a set text. Hooker, too, qualifies his moral premise with a comment on misreading: "For evil as evill cannot be desired: if that be desired which is evill, the cause is the goodnes which is, or seemeth to be joyned with it. Goodnes doth not moove by being, but by being apparent."[76] This stark acceptance of the apparitional leaves will to pursue what is at least, and might be only, a façade; the show of righteousness invites misapprehension, and cannot guarantee virtuous intentions or acts. Edward Dowden writes of faculty theory, "Over the irascible and concupiscible passions the power of the reasonable soul is, or rather may and ought to be,

supreme."[77] With that amendment—"or rather may and ought to be"—
Dowden echoes the texts he describes. The fickle mobility of will, with its
category crossings and paradigm breaks, may look like an impertinent deviation, but it manifests the ambivalent texture of an argument that diverges
from itself.

This ambivalence reflects the complex relationship between notional and
practical situations of meaning. A conjectural sketch of agency draws a neat
line from intention to act; instantiating that proposition involves messy questions about the integrity, fidelity, and renegade sovereignty of will. Suspended in contemplative space, reason requires will to implement its
judgments.[78] This returns to the issue of alienated work, which for faculty
theory is the starting point; so Davies divides speculation, which perceives
truth, from practice, which pursues good.

> Thus *Reasons* reach is high and most profound,
> Whose deepe discourse is two-fold; which depends,
> On *Speculation*, and on *Practise* sound;
> The first hath *Truth*, the last hath *Good* for ends;
> For *Speculation* rests when *Truth* is found.
> But *Practise*, when that *Good* it apprehends,
>   It staies not there, but to the *Will* proceedes,
>   And with that *Good* the *Will* it freely feeds.[79]

The site of consequence shifts: when left to itself reason stops short, and will
is thus responsible not only for the fact of action but for its value.[80] Charron
praises the faculty that represents the foundation of integral selfhood: "The
Will is a great part of the reasonable soule, of verie great importance, and it
standeth us upon above all things to studie how to rule it, because upon it
dependeth almost our whole estate and good." But in the phrases that follow,
his point develops in more troubled terms: "this is that, that keepeth a man
intire, and importeth him much: for he that hath given his will, is no more
his owne man, neither hath he any thing of his owne."[81] The part that
"keepeth a man intire" raises the ghost of disintegration; a man may study
how to rule the will, but it is far from clear that the prerogative of government is ever in his hands.[82] Walter Ralegh celebrates will as the source of
human supremacy: "This is a part of the reasonable soul; this is one point by
which we are men, and do excel all other creatures living upon the earth."[83]

For all its eminence, the high ground is a position of considerable vulnerability, for proprietary claims cut both ways. To possess will is to risk being possessed and dispossessed by turns, and exposure to that risk is a condition of the subject's survival. When Francis Bacon writes, "The dutie and Office of *Rhetoricke* is, *To apply Reason to Imagination*, for the better mooving of the Will," he maps an arduous endeavor that is always under siege. "And as in Negotiation with others; men are wrought by cunning, by Importunitie, and by vehemencie; So in this Negotiation within our selves; men are undermined by *Inconsequences*, solicited and importuned, by *Impressions* or *Obversations*: and transported by *Passions*."[84]

Paster describes the strong likelihood of being so transported: "While reason and passion, or reason and sense, were yoked dichotomously, the opposition was hardly equal. Not in experiential terms, but only in semantic ones, did reason successfully oppose the passions."[85] To level this uneven field, Hooker asserts, "the object of wil is that good which reason doth leade us to seeke," and argues that will is defined by obedience: "neyther is any other desire termed properly will, but that where reason and understanding, or the shew of reason prescribeth the thing desired."[86] Like Gataker's dismissal of willful wives, Hooker's exclusionary move delineates a failure of contract rather than a triumph of constraint. He disowns ungoverned desire but does not defuse it, and his reference to "shew" shifts reason into that realm of the apparitional, leaving will to make its own judgments and form its own affiliations. In a more optimistic if still conditional mode, Nicolas Coeffeteau maintains that the soul can accommodate the passions when they fall under the aegis of a well-disposed will: "they may be considered in as much as reason may subject them to her command and prescribe them a *Law*. And in this consideration they may bee good or bad, according to the quality of the will that governes them." He supports his point through a vivid analogy. "Wee tame *Elephants, Tigers, Lyons, Panthers*, and other savage beasts, and are not moved: and will they not allow us a power to suppresse the brutishnesse of the sensitive appetite, and to moderate the *Passions* when as they advance themselves against *reason*, without great perturbation?"[87]

We might reasonably wonder. Moderation, when likened to lion-taming, seems less a fact than a fight, involving both exertion and hyperbole. Davies tends in this direction as well when he equates failed reason with "*Luciferian* pride," and offers prophylactic advice: "Then let *Reason* raine / Thy headstrong *Will*, and thy high thoughts restraine."[88] Self-restraint supports enlightened self-interest, but such merit is the product of labor rather than a state of nature or even of grace; one must fend off the devil to achieve an ordinary frame of mind.[89] Only a sort of muscular vigilance can sustain the appearance of spontaneous virtue, and that tension between the artless and the overwrought escalates in comparisons of the psyche to a monarchical state. Juan Luis Vives describes a simple regime: "The quene and princesse of all thynges mooste hyghest, is VERTUE, unto whom all other serve, as hande maydes their maistresses, yf they doo as by duetie, they are bounden."[90] Elyot's model is more elaborate, its roles more discretely defined:

> Nowe so it is that god, of whose majestie we have spoken, and be yet in speakynge, whan he hathe putte the soule (accompanyed with affectes as hir perpetuall servauntes and ministres) into the body as into hir propre habitation, he gyveth to hir the sences, to be as hir slaves or drudges. And commyttynge to hir for a chiefe counsayllour understandynge he leaveth with her also, Free wyll to be hir Secret-arye.[91]

These are arguments of degree: if each faculty keeps its place, specific acts of duty accumulate to a decorous whole. But that ingenuous premise does not obscure the repressive, defensive work of power. Edward Forset invokes a disordered psyche to justify political absolutism: "if [the people] turne mutinous and tumultuous, troubling the governour and State with seditious disorders, then be they as Rebels by the Justice of the law to be suppressed, even as the perturbations of the mind must be subdued by reason."[92] When Davies analyzes the social practice he calls "policy," he, too, points out that decorum follows from coercive methods: "It makes *Will* law, when *Wit* thinkes *Law* unfit, / Yet wils that *Law* should lincke with *Will* and *wit*."[93] Policy imposes control by using will against itself, and identifies the rule of law as enforced incoherence. Again faculty theory sets up a hierarchy only to anatomize it, and discover an unstable, largely hostile interaction of parts.

Philip Sidney sums up the result: "our erected wit, maketh us know what perfection is, and yet our infected will, keepeth us from reaching unto it."[94] In a similar vein, Vives imagines a fallen state in which "the love of our selfe, is chiefe councellour, and one that we all togyther folow"; he writes, "This blyndeth the eies of the mynde, and whan affections have ones gotten the upper hande, we flatter, we yelde, we obey them, as our lordes and rulers."[95] Barckley, too, emphasizes discord: "Order required, that reason should obey God, and our sences and desires should bee obedient to reason: But now contrariwise the sences over-ruleth reason, and desires leadeth our will: the body commaundeth the soule, and the carte is before the horse."[96] Wright associates such reversals with irrevocable degeneration: "By this alteration which Passions worke in the Witte and the Will, we may understand the admirable Metamorphosis and change of a man from himselfe, when his affectes are pacified, and when they are troubled. *Plutarch* sayde they changed them like *Circes* potions, from men into beastes."[97] Robert Burton contends that innate defect creates the momentum toward self-loss: "But in spiritual things we will no good . . . our concupisence is originally bad, our heart evil, the seat of our affections, captivates and enforceth our will. So that in voluntary things we are averse from God and goodness, bad by nature, by ignorance worse, by Art, Discipline, Custom, we get many bad habits: suffering them to domineer and tyrannize over us; and the devil is still ready at hand with his evil suggestions, to tempt our depraved will to some ill disposed action, to precipitate us to destruction."[98]

The hinge between intention and desire bears the weight of top-down work, and it might hold or it might break. If will abandons its place or abuses its power, dissolution ensues; the difference between order and chaos comes down to the wild card of choice. "This is it whereby we are made and called good or wicked, which giveth us the temper and the tincture," Charron flatly declares.[99] Caught in the double bind of agency, will must at once mediate and govern, translating self- into other-directed restraint while wielding the authority of its own capitulations. Execution of such a mandate seems all too difficult, and refusal all too likely. The tilted weight of that decision slides will toward fantasy, the faculty defined by its wayward power to desire and conceive. In an analysis of early modern interest in emotion, Susan James describes "a broader preoccupation in early-modern European culture with the relations between knowledge and control, whether of the self or others."[100] Fantasy implicates self and others in failures of knowledge and control, an infectious effect that informs Burton's chronicle of indiscriminate circulation: "So diversly doth this phantasie of ours affect, turn and winde, so imperiously command our bodies, which as another *Proteus, or a Cameleon, can take all shapes; and is of such force* (as *Ficinus* adds) *that it can work upon others, as well as our selves.*"[101] This is the end point of analogies that approximate subject to state: incontinent will is a shared contagion, a degenerative disease of the social order.

How can otherwise blear-eyes in one man, cause the like affection
in another? Why doth one mans yawning, make another yawn? One
mans pissing provoke a second many times to do the like? Why doth
scraping of trenchers offend a third, or hacking of files? Why doth a
Carkass bleed, when the murtherer is brought before it, some weeks
after the murther hath been done? Why do Witches and old women,
fascinate and bewitch children?[102]

The capricious power of will puts all its subjects in the same boat, "this whole
vessel of ours . . . over-ruled, and often overturned." It seems merely inevitable that after all the mimetic blearing and yawning, the universal pissing and
hacking and bleeding—after that perfect storm of physical, spiritual, and
social interpenetration—we arrive at the enigmatic capacities of women, and
at the specter of children they might send astray.

Coda

If this is the wreckage left by a negligent, depraved, reckless, or self-indulgent
will, and if it carries the certainty these authors describe, the need for efficient, consensual mediation becomes all the more apparent. But, like reason
and virtue, this quality threatens to become apparitional as well. Dislocated
onto women and dependent on their consent, the realization of schematic
ideals requires the work of subordinate terms. It seems then that consent
must be an expedient fiction. The occasional but formidable technologies of
subjugation, from locked doors to corporeal chastisement to death, suggest
that feminine affirmations of heterosociality can hardly constitute freedom of
speech. Yet we might productively turn to one of Scarry's suggestions about
consent and fiction, which she describes as "the one I believe to be most
accurate":

> Instead of understanding fiction to mean unreal or fraudulent or a
> lie, fiction is taken in its, for us, most familiar and positive sense:
> consent becomes, by this path of comprehension, an exercise of the
> artifactual response at a moment when the will is in danger of being
> impaired. That is, an actual recreation of one's own relation to one's
> external circumstances comes about. The artifactual holds within it
> the voluntaristic, and thus the generation of the artifact by those in

a position of passivity at a moment of great polarization from the active (the surgeon, the governors) equalizes the relation.[103]

The fiction of consent is more aptly a narrative, which imparts meaning to the structures it inflects. Feminine subjects consent to some effect, their will investing regulatory mechanisms with stability, futurity, and persuasive force. There is something vital and perverse about this conservative project, a constitutive volition which, as it answers a demand, gives acquiescence a sharp double edge: "by the alternatives of consent and revolution, we do not just pretend to make governments, we make and unmake them," Scarry writes.[104] Feminine will is itself a curious form of revolution, a refusal of erasure that confers more than subjection on those subjects who work all by themselves. But it is also that self-consuming voluntarism with which I began, the acceptance of a contract defined by disproportions of power. If we can see no escape from this contradiction, we might recognize that its entrenchment invests the will to social order with contradictions of its own.

Chapter Two

Willful Speech

Metonymy and Mastery

I meant what I said, and I said what I meant.

—Geisel (Dr. Seuss), *Horton Hatches the Egg*, 21.

It oft falls out,
To have what we would have, we speak not what we mean.

—Shakespeare, *Measure for Measure*, 2.4.117–18

"When *I* use a word," Humpty Dumpty said, in rather a scornful tone, "it means just what I choose it to mean—neither more nor less."

"The question is," said Alice, "whether you *can* make words mean so many different things."

"The question is," said Humpty Dumpty, "which is to be master—that's all."

—Carroll, *Through the Looking-Glass*, 188

The claim of linguistic mastery is almost always a joke on the speaker, its punch line delivered in two familiar propositions: subjects are alienated by their constitution in language, and language exceeds the speaker's intent. Early modern rhetorical theory highlights these predicaments through a gendered account of figurative speech. Here as in my discussion of faculty theory, I take seriously the feminization and sexualization of language, and consider how an impulse to populate intangible schemes with discrete and intentional figures connects specialized discourses to ideas about social contract. Patricia Parker gives a concise account of the link between linguistic and social concerns: "what presents itself as a study of language or logic quickly becomes

Figure 3 (preceding page). "We best shall quiet clamorous *Thronges*, / When, we our selves, can rule our *Tongues*." Illustration I, Book 2, in George Wither, *A Collection of Emblemes, Ancient and Moderne* (London: Augustine Mathewes for Richard Royston, 1635), 63. By permission of the Folger Shakespeare Library.

implicated in questions of social and political control."[1] Affirmations of rhetorical control draw on a familiar heterosocial paradigm, which distinguishes masculine authors of meaning from the feminized stuff in which realization transpires. That fusion of models, as it entangles linguistic agency with social intercourse, follows an intersection until it turns back on itself; when effective language takes on qualities of subjectivity and intent, the distance between maker and matter tends to collapse. Formulaic assertions of ownership and use yield to intricate, paradoxical transactions, which filter the conceit of mastery through tropes that invoke women more directly than they authorize men. At such moments, an odd literalism invades the discourse of figuration: feminized speech conjures up feminine subjects, who appear as reference points both for the possibility of functional exchange and for the byproducts, diversions, and failures of understanding that threaten to get in the way.

Rhetorical theory employs analogies, personifications, and exemplary anecdotes to equate tropes with women, and in one sense this has all the arrogance of the best clichés. Within the narrow logic of cultural truisms, women and words share the status of vessels in which things of import take shape; the residue of that idea persists in our own, often incongruous use of the term "seminal," as if a patrilineal confusion of insemination and signification still made unassailable sense. But if the intertwined devices of femininity and figuration answer the needs of cultural legibility, they also disclose the densely textured character of mediation, opening processes of transfer to decentered intentions and unpredicted results. As tools of transmission, these media are vital and variable rather than inert. The affinity between women and words identifies a willful language that crosses registers of social self-articulation: the sign that has a more than instrumental purpose creates effects that surpass its occasion, and even when figures plausibly convey a particular form of knowledge, their superfluity inflects service with license. Feminine subjects and linguistic ornaments bear necessary meaning in the shadow of presumptive excess. They are artifacts, at once useful and aesthetic; and, like that useful and aesthetic Trojan horse, they might always mobilize an alien agenda.

The phenomenon of willful language reveals friction between univocal methods and polyvalent means, and reflects disquiet about feminine contributions to the manufacture of cultural sense. Metonymy illustrates this with particular force, because rhetorical theorists define it in split and contradictory terms: like synecdoche, metonymy secures congruence among parts of a system; but like metalepsis, catachresis, and hypallage, it forges improbable and suspect bonds. In *The Artes of Logike and Rethorike*, a treatise based on the works of Petrus Ramus and Omer Talon, Dudley Fenner writes of "The chaunge of name called a Metonomie":

> It is double,
> - When the cause is put for the thing caused, and contrariwise.
> - When the thing to which any thing is adjoyned, is put for the thing adjoyned, and contrariwise.[2]

The definitions do not cohere. An exchange of cause for effect differs consequentially from substitution by contiguity; the first relies on a precedent relationship, while the second makes an arbitrary connection. The inconsistency of these operations, subsumed under a single term, resists absorption by ordered schemes. Roman Jakobson argues that metaphor presents an explicable pattern, while metonymy eludes the interpreter's grasp: "Similarity connects a metaphoric term with the term for which it is substituted. Consequently, when constructing a metalanguage to interpret tropes, the researcher possesses more homogeneous means to handle metaphor, whereas metonymy, based on a different principle, easily defies interpretation."[3] Metonymy disables homogeneous handling because its contiguous principle works twice, to close a circle of meaning and to extend the attachments of signs. As that double move articulates the intimate risks of proximity, it elucidates the reciprocal relationship between social and rhetorical formulations. Tropes are not figures for women, nor are women figures for tropes—not, at least, in a way that invites distinctions between referent and sign. Nor is this an analogy that holds terms in parallel without allowing them to touch. Femininity and figuration are utterly imbricated, overlapped and interwoven in a state of ambiguously valued capacity. Metonymy coincides with feminine subjectivity as it engineers connections but disallows assurance of their stability, integrity, or consequence; feminine subjects work metonymically when they secure a system that their volatile propensities might explode.

Parker summarizes the fraught convergence of gender, rhetoric, and social forms: "Women out of their place—in tropes subject to decorum and to warnings against 'Excesse' or abuse—are part of a potentially dangerous invasion of linguistic into social possibility."[4] In the readings that follow, I pursue the possibilities—inseparably social and linguistic—which metonymy brings to the surface when it puts the notion of proper place in question. Metonymic duality, with its power to affirm systems of meaning and impose alterations of sense, informs the constitutive yet errant qualities of feminine will. The twofold work of that will verifies and mystifies principles of association, cross-coupling the natural ties and synthetic attachments, organic orders and deliberate methods, that accumulate to the compromise of heterosociality. Metonymic intercessions bring elements into agreement, but expose the seams and the strains and the length of the reach; they enable a continuous production of terms without assuring fidelity to any original premise or intent. An energy that consolidates relations through conditional propinquities animates a structure that can never be entirely true to itself, but that preserves a cohesive surface through the sacrifice of referential guarantees. At once the mode and the sign of a feminized volitional faculty, metonymy produces the requisite fictions of social accommodation: alliance, generation, and the contingent conferral of name.

An Other Not Proper, But Yet Nye and Likely

Francis Bacon, with his great skepticism concerning language, uses the analogy of counterfeit to argue for informed distrust:

> And although it may seeme of no great use, considering that *Words*, and *Writings by letters*, doe far excell all the other wayes: yet because this part concerneth, as it were the Mint of knowledge (for wordes, are the tokens currant and accepted for conceits, as Moneys are for values and that it is fit men be not ignorant, that Moneys may bee of another kind, than gold and silver) I thought good to propound it to better Enquirie.[5]

The inquiry Bacon pursues does not distinguish the authentic from the false; knowledge fails to correct for the debased materials and promiscuous circulation inherent to the medium itself. "And lastly, lette us consider the false appearances, that are imposed upon us by words, which are framed, and applyed according to the conceit, and capacities of the Vulgar sorte," he writes. "And although wee thinke we governe our wordes, and prescribe it well . . . Yet certaine it is, that wordes, as a *Tartars* Bowe, doe shoote backe uppon the understanding of the wisest, and mightily entangle, and pervert the Judgement." An attempt to govern perverts the power to judge, and bars escape from compromised utterance: "it must be confessed, that it is not possible to divorce our selves from these fallacies and false appearances, because they are inseparable from our Nature and Condition of life."[6] There is no defense against a condition of error that delimits social existence; imperfect understanding and injurious conceits frame as they entrap the subject of willful speech.

Language itself appears as a subject in the sense that it defines an area of inquiry, but also in the sense that it has qualities of personhood: idealized and debased; compliant and resistant; faithful and treacherous; dedicated to a communal purpose and inclined to stray from that goal. Rhetorical figures do their work within a recognizably social landscape.[7] Early modern theorists stress the merits of natural signs, which promise fidelity rather than promiscuity of attachment. At the same time, they display an ambivalent fascination with figures that are elaborate, mysterious, and prolific beyond their assigned tasks. In a reading of Erasmus's *De Copia*, Brian Cummings writes, "Figures of speech allow a language to make things up, and thus (paradoxically) also create the conditions for mimesis."[8] Feminized figures widen the rift in this two-step premise: they correlate the social project that secures meaning through women with the rhetorical project that secures meaning through language, but vivify the suggestion that both women and language do indeed "make things up": opaque where they should be transparent, wayward where they should be circumspect, they assume a significance that has not been imposed. Unsurprisingly, then, George Puttenham's praise of ornament finds its way into awkward territory:

> And as we see in these great Madames of honour, be they for personage or otherwise never so comely and bewtifull, yet if they want their courtly habillements or at leastwise such other apparell as custome and civilitie have ordained to cover their naked bodies, would be halfe ashamed or greatly out of countenaunce to be seen in that sort. . . . Even so cannot our vulgar Poesie shew it selfe either gallant or gorgious, if any lymme be left naked and bare and not clad in his kindly clothes and coulours.[9]

Texts without tropes are like women without clothes, but ornate obfuscation is a chancy antidote to the naked truth. Puttenham's comparison attaches the desire for embellishment to poetry itself, expanding the scope of personification by shifting will from author to text. Invested with an explicitly feminine vitality, figures displace and seduce as they mediate; signification advances through detours and traps, impelled by agents who mean equivocally even when they mean well.

Theories that explain words through women locate a changeable process in the place of a useful object. Richard Sherry identifies tropes with attenuation, dispossession, and change: "in them for necessitye or garnyshynge, there is a movynge and chaungynge of a worde and sentence, from theyr owne significacion into another, whych may agre wyth it by a similitude."[10] That qualified "may agree," with its hint of irregular relations, creates a space for what Madhavi Menon calls "the surprisingly insistent link between rhetorical language and figural sexuality."[11] Henry Peacham notes that figures exploit likeness to contrive names: "Catachresis, is a necessary abuse of like words, for the proper, or when to that, that hath not his proper name, we lend the next or lykest unto it."[12] Angel Day connects altered meaning to the murder of kind: "the *Trope* changeth the signification, as in these wordes *Generation of Vipers*, meaning thereby *homicides* of their owne issue or antecessors, as the *Viper* devoureth her owne broode."[13] Puttenham writes of metalepsis, "it seemeth the deviser of this figure, had a desire to please women rather then men: for we use to say by manner of Proverbe: things farrefet and deare bought are good for Ladies."[14] False naming, maternal consumption, exotic appetite: descriptions of immoderate rhetoric make their points through clichés of feminine excess. Garnishes and ornaments inspire a suspicion directly proportionate to their appeal, and overtones of that response permeate Peacham's comment on compelling but improper proximities. "A Trope, is an alteration of a worde or sentence, from the proper and naturall signification, to an other not proper, but yet nye and likely."[15]

In his sermon "A Wife in Deed," Thomas Gataker ties problematic figuration to marriage, with its dependence on an association that might make trouble even as it must make sense. Having taken a proverb as his text—"He that findeth a Wife, findeth Good; and obtaineth Favour of God"—Gataker notes that the wife is not herself defined as good, and calls on tropes to fill the gap: "others answer, (and their *answer* is more probable) that it is a *Synecdoche*, a putting of *the generall for the speciall*; or an *Ellipsis*, a defective speech; that there wanteth the word *good*: as *wooll*, for *white wooll*; and *a Male* for *a sound Male*: so *a Wife* for *a good Wife*."[16] Through an application of synecdoche that repairs ellipsis, "wife" can become "good wife." It is an expansive hypothesis, allying the general to the specific in such a way that any wife might be presumptively good, which is Gataker's larger worry but not his immediate point. He meditates on rhetoric to argue for transparent meaning, and constructs essential premises—self-evident virtue, self-evident speech—through a labored artifice that masquerades as common sense. It takes too many hard steps to approach the obvious; Gataker first shifts conjugal proximity to a space of inscrutable language, then attempts to retrieve that proximity as good. In so doing, he saturates intimate ties with alien meanings, infusing strangeness into a familiar experience of being bound. Those uncanny moves recall Jonathan Dollimore's theory of transgressive reinscription: "As we shall see, the proximate is often constructed as the other, and in a process which facilitates displacement. But the proximate is also what enables a tracking-back of the 'other' into the 'same.'"[17] Gataker ultimately swaps synecdoche for chiasmus—"*She that is not a good Wife is as good as no Wife*"—but remains caught among figures that might not refer as they should: "For she is but *a Shadow without Substance*; shee hath *a Title without Truth*."[18] The wife whose title vacates truth is still, of course, a wife. Intimacy attaches in order to disconcert; under the aegis of "an other not proper, but yet nye and likely," bondage and alienation become versions of the same thing.

It Is Double

Proximity, whether of persons or of words, both secures and troubles ordered arrangements, and that mixed message is a distinctly metonymic effect. Sherry differentiates metonymy from metaphor on the grounds of imminence: "This trope differeth from Metaphora: because Metaphora chaungeth a word of her own with another, though the thinges be very divers: but here as the thinges must be very nigh, so must the wordes also be."[19] Nearness enables the touch that alters sense; a metonymic impulse that reaches indiscriminately for the next thing might confirm or destabilize ideals of natural correspondence. Modern theorists have linked Freud's processes of displacement and condensation to metonymy and metaphor, but in early modern treatises metonymy does the work of both, condensing meanings into indissoluble knots and displacing them into mystification.[20] Cummings observes that the relationship among rhetorical figures "is itself a kind of metonymy," and describes "how the paradoxical energies of similitude refract and convert as they pass through a new medium."[21] Those conjoined terms—paradox, energy, and similitude—compose a vocabulary for the resonance between metonymic license and feminine social acts. When mediation cannot be distinguished from refraction, a connective force engages orthodoxies at an angle, and creates indecipherable simulacra of authorized bonds. Disciplined generation intersects ungoverned proliferation; the figures that sustain and perpetuate a privileged structure endanger its survival as an integral form.

Perhaps predictably, explications of metonymy often attempt to isolate its conservative effects, and to apply metonymic links as a kind of strategic glue. In a discussion of logic, Henry Ainsworth explains how doctrine emerges from far more limited tenets: "It may be taken for a frame or constitution of Logical precepts, by this or that man written, called a Systeme; which frame may be also taken for an Art, by a Metonomy of the Cause for the Effect, accepting Art not for an habit ingenerated in the mind by precepts and use, but for a collection of universal precepts, to operate in a determinate latitude and limit of End."[22] Metonymic conduction allows local precepts, "by this or that man written," to become universal and determinate laws. The examples listed by one modern dictionary of literary terms—" 'The Stage' for the theatrical profession; 'The Crown' for the monarchy; 'The Bench' for the judiciary"—take an analogous approach, and imply that metonymy validates systematic operations through fragments that can be seen, felt, and acquired.[23] In "Four Master Tropes," Kenneth Burke makes the point directly: "The basic 'strategy' in metonymy is this: to convey some incorporeal or intangible state in terms of the corporeal or tangible."[24] An instrumental methodology truncates the vector of metonymic dynamism and breaks it into "metonyms," static objects that can be used to support equally static arguments. This is the logic that translates female sexual bodies—virginal, erotic, and reproductive—into metonyms for a heterosocial rationale.[25] As Karen Newman writes, "In the early modern period, the female body is the site of discourses that manage women: by continually working out sexual difference on and through the body, the social is presented as natural and therefore unchangeable, substantiated, filled with presence."[26]

Sherry's examples of metonymic exchange contribute to the notion of a closed economy, within which terms may trade places without challenging the dictates that govern relations and roles. He provides a list of reversible circumstances: "When the place, or that that conteineth, is put for the thyng that is in it"; "When that that is conteyned is put for that that doth conteine"; "When the doer is put for that that is done," "When that is done is put for the doer."[27] Where effect validates cause as cause guarantees effect, all elements converge toward an immutable end, interconnected in ways that are expediently versatile rather than mutable or fluid. A foundational unity informs substitution, and strictly limits the principles in play. The stratagem that locates mastery in the integrity of the system eliminates friction between agents and objects, accommodating all transactions under the name of order and reducing any contradictions to their usable parts. This efficient machinery ensures that the particular axioms which turn women into components need not agree to coalesce and hold. "Contest not with your *head* for preeminence: you came from him, not he from you," Richard Brathwait advises female readers;[28] Thomas Laqueur describes "the idea that conception is the male having an idea in the female body";[29] Ben Jonson's *Masque of Beauty* concludes, "Women were the souls of men."[30] The container and the thing contained become interchangeable precisely because hierarchy remains constant: an inflexible substructure grounds surface variation in a shared understanding of place. Under the terms of enforced collaboration, women are prepossessed parts—a body, a soul, an inverted penis, an extra rib—which refer to subjectivities other than their own. Thus circumscribed, metonymy generates a useful field of metonyms, and a poetics of partiality fills in an abstract design with fractional, digestible forms. This reiterates in social and sexual terms the method Parker ascribes to *De Copia*: "Dilation, then, is always something to be kept within the horizon of ending, mastery, and control, and the 'matter' is always to be varied within certain formal guidelines or rules."[31]

Yet even as artificially enclosed metonyms instantiate ideology in material form, referential shifts undermine the idea of a fixed presence that can be known or owned. Sherry defines metonymy as "Transnominacion," and describes its dissociative reach: "when a worde that hathe a proper significacion of hys owne, beynge referred to another thing, hath another."[32] The momentum that pushes words across things forms attachments only to discredit and discard them; substitution escapes the restricted space of complement, and implicates a potentially infinite series of terms. This is the process that leads Lacan to gloss metonymy as desire, and to depict its compulsory pursuits as "being caught in the rails—eternally stretching forth towards the *desire for something else*."[33] Gestures of possession yield the near-miss of partial apprehension, as "something" becomes "something else" and realization slips away through the breach of limits. Abraham Fraunce writes, "The *Metonymia* of the subject, is when the word that properlie signifieth the subject is brought to expresse the thing adjoyned thereunto."[34] Displaced by a transposition of name, the subject reappears through accidents of contiguity: not as a particular figure known by precedence, but as any figure close enough to touch.[35] Metonymy reinforces interrelation as a prerequisite of subjectivity, yet identifies connections with artifice and happenstance; kinship entails coincidence, which might mean either correlation or chance.

Puttenham places "*Metonimia*, or the Misnamer" in his section "Of the figures which we call Sensable, because they alter and affect the minde by alteration of sence."[36] His illustrations emulate those of his predecessors, but he appends a qualitative conclusion: "and in many other cases do as it were wrong name the person or the thing."[37] Women are metonyms for social logic in this way as well. The power to "wrong name the person," also expressible as "the desire for something else," is built into patrilineal organization, within which female bodies might always contain altered, unauthorized versions of the structure that contains them. Proximity is a form of constraint and a mode of opportunity; women are the reference points for masculine identity, and are therefore the agents of improper substitution. "Metonymy is both arbitrary and tropologically indistinguishable, which makes it at once the most fitting rhetorical figure for sexuality, and the least identifiable," Menon writes.[38] We can say of feminine sexuality, as of metonymy, that "it is double," both static sign and mobile force. Virtue certifies a legible futurity, but its active principle possesses that other, opaque and fugitive quality of desire.[39] If, as I have argued, feminine will has a metonymic relationship to heterosocial ideology, it is because metonymy works in these entwined and unreconciled ways: as a figure that condenses the meaning of a system, and as a drive that presses meaning beyond systemic constraints. That indivisible premise makes women at once metonyms and metonymic, signs of an order their significance exceeds.

Personification propels this comparison beyond analogy, and creates a realm of undiscriminated actors. Discussions of metonymic transfiguration use a vocabulary of wanton affiliation and deceptive exchange; their idiom illuminates what Margaret Ferguson describes as "a field in which grammar and biology are, as it were, at the extremes of a social spectrum, each exerting pressures on what the other is thought to be 'by nature.'"[40] Sherry implies that nature is very much at issue when he cites kinship to associate propinquity with transformation: "Metonymia, when in thynges that be syb together, one name is chaunged for an other."[41] In this ambiguous configuration, innate affinity might limit the danger or raise the stakes; the critical point may be that there is no way to evaluate the consequences of change. Peacham stresses the manifold possibilities implied by close contact: "Metonimia, when of thinges that be nigh together, wee put one name for another, and this chaunge of name is many wayes used."[42] Metonymic change spreads opportunistically, using naturalized bonds to produce disparate names, and through that process isolated sense gives way to indiscrete entanglements. "A *Metonymia* of the adjunct, is, when by the adjunct we expresse the subject," Fraunce explains;[43] the subject becomes known only through its adjunct, a manifestation of interdependence in which a secondary term generates and validates an otherwise immaterial first premise. Through such formulations metonymy abstracts the practical mode of sociality, and provides a theoretical apparatus to articulate the contingencies and reciprocities that constitute agents of meaning. Even Sherry's first precept marks autonomy as a myth: self-possession ("a proper significacion of hys owne") leads to dislocation, and relegates mastery to the itinerant state of "beynge referred to another thing."

Puttenham calls metonymy a "secret conceyt," and writes that its effects "reach many times to the only nomination of persons or things in their names . . . in which respect the wrong naming, or otherwise naming of them then is due, carieth not onely an alteration of sence but a necessitie of intendment figuratively."[44] The alteration of sense detaches proprietary nominations, exposing a gap between name and thing into which the thing itself might vanish or other things might intrude. Theorists accentuate such tendencies when they follow Quintilian in associating metonymy with hypallage, which the *Oxford English Dictionary* defines as follows: "A figure of speech in which there is an interchange of two elements of a proposition, the natural relations of these being reversed."[45] Early examples cited by the *OED* include a quotation from Puttenham, for whom "Hipallage" is not a precise synonym for metonymy but extends its course of error; he lists hypallage under his "auricular figures working by exchange," and notes that it affects words by "changing their true construction and application, whereby the sence is quite perverted and made very absurd." He calls it "the *Changeling*"—a name he describes as "much more aptly to the purpose"—and explains his reasons:

> specially for our Ladies and pretie mistresses in Court, for whose learning I write, because it is a terme often in their mouthes, and alluding to the opinion of Nurses, who are wont to say, that the

> Fayries use to steale the fairest children out of their cradles, and put
> other ill favoured in their places, which they called changelings, or
> Elfs: so, if ye mark, doeth our Poet, or maker play with his wordes,
> using a wrong construction for a right, and an absurd for a sensible,
> by manner of exchange.[46]

A poetic device that alters natural relations evokes the illicit exchange of children; this is transnomination with a vengeance, its secret mechanism concealing the fact that the items swapped are not "syb together" at all. Things found in a particular location may not be in their proper place; in this vein, Michael Drayton associates metonymy with unlikely paths and eccentric returns. "*Maeander* is a river in *Lycia*, a Province of *Natolia* or *Asia minor*, famous for the sinuositie and often turning thereof . . . heereupon are intricate turnings by a transsumptive and Metonimicall kind of speech, called *Maeanders*, for this river did so strangely path it selfe, that the foote seemed to touch the head."[47] Through the strange metonymic movement that confuses foot with head, a river gives its name to the "intricate turnings" that distance phenomena from the places in which they began.

Like Puttenham's transposed children, Drayton's river is a natural occurrence that deviates from a preset path. Unexpected developments confound the ordinary with the aberrant, and the link between rhetorical effects and social concerns makes metonymy a kind of shorthand for indiscretions that press against sites of cultural authority. Day uses the figure frequently in his chapter "Of Epistles Monitorie and Reprehensorie"; when, for example, he warns an addressee, "the worlde will crie out agaynst you," his marginal gloss reads, "Metonomia."[48] In *Of Divorce for Adulterie*, Edmund Bunny writes, "Christ by the figure of Metonymia did largely take the name of fornication, and that under the name of whoredome hee did include all such crimes, as were as great, or greater than it."[49] John Bulwer uses "a metonymie of the adjunct" to read a single gesture as the sign of vice, impudence, and effeminacy.[50] Such examples recast the controlled utility of metonyms: use of the material, the local, and the specific to signify an abstract system (Ainsworth's "collection of universal precepts") reveals what Slavoj Žižek calls the "inherent transgression" that underlies the system's proper work. As Žižek points out, that transgression is intrinsic rather than detached. Rachel Speght illustrates this when she employs a rhetorical turn on theology to erase distinctions among genders and kinds: "And *David* exhorting all *the earth to sing unto the Lord*; meaning, by a Metonimie, *earth*, all creatures that live on the earth, of what nation or Sex soever, gives this reason, *For the Lord hath made us.*"[51] Speght's exegesis, based on that aggressively capacious yet divinely certified "us," redefines heterosocial unions as contracts of equivalence. Metonymy binds overt authority to its suppressed constituents, draws out the implicit, the interdependent, and the disconcertingly proximate, and discloses the "unwritten, unacknowledged rules and practices" of which Žižek writes.[52] My proposition, here as throughout, is that metonymic figuration does not indicate or incite conflicts between social and antisocial agendas, but underlines the heterogeneous arguments of sociality itself.

At once unpredictable and inescapable, metonymic bondage mirrors the capricious, coercive, often discommodious or implausible attachments that support a façade of social order. Metonymy undercuts doctrines of mastery, locating effective force in processes of meaning rather than in the secure possession of transitive purpose. Puttenham's phrase "intendment figuratively" contains the crux: figures of intention neither coincide with nor produce a coherent subject who intends.[53] Thomas Middleton and William Rowley play with this dilemma in their description of a rhetorically obsessed tailor:

> By his Needle he understands *Ironia*,
> That with one eye lookes two wayes at once:
> *Metonymia* ever at his fingers ends.
> Some call his Pickadell, *Synecdoche*:
> But I thinke rather that should be his Yard
> Being but *Pars pro toto*, and by Metaphor
> All know, the Selleridge under the shop-board,
> He cals his Hell, not that it is a place
> Of Spirits abode, but that from that Abysse
> Is no recovery or redemption
> To any owners hand what ever falls.[54]

The passage comically underscores awareness that tropes can be signs of self-loss, and metonymy, with its illimitable processes of stretching forth ("ever at his fingers ends"), gives that prospect a particular edge. Enforcing misconception in the name of meaning, pursuing meaning toward the loss of name, a metonymic reach outstrips the speaker's grasp; as Jacques Derrida writes of the supplement, "Something promises itself as it escapes, gives itself as it moves away, and strictly speaking it cannot even be called presence."[55] Even in the most conservative contexts, metonymy interrupts transfers of knowledge and dismantles conventions of reference. John Merbecke explains the sacramental cup by expounding "a double *Metonymia*" at exhaustive length; as if suspecting that this pursuit has taken him too far, he assures his readers, "neither is it a vaine signe, though it be not all one, with the thing it represen-teth."[56] Metonymy can never be "all one," for it is double: it makes and alters sense.

That tension intensifies when metonymy itself is doubled with another trope: "The mocking speech, called an *Ironie*."[57] Petrus Ramus, who pairs the terms, defines irony quite simply: "The mocking Trope is, when one contrary is signified by another."[58] In this sense the changelings of Putten-ham's hypallage are not only metonymic but ironic, and it seems possible to say that irony shares with metonymy the effect of proximity with a twist. Each of these rhetorical figures equates conjunction with distortion, forcing into view the compulsive, artifactual correspondences that make systems of affiliation inherently perverse. Rendered inseparable by their common viola-tion of common sense, metonymy and irony join together what does not cohere, and impose intimacy to reveal the fault lines within naturalized rela-tions. They are acts of language that hold connection within narrow bounds—there is no escape into figural ellipsis—even as they force meaning to turn. This is how the "nye and likely" becomes improper: metonymically, ironically, through the willful if not precisely intentional collision of signs. "The scandal is that the sign, the image, or the representer, become forces and make 'the world move.'"[59]

Tell in Thy Mother Tongue a Strangers Mind

Illusions of linguistic mastery collapse at their foundations: entrenched as a myth of origin, the mother tongue constructs a lineage for the uneasy fit between masculine speakers and vernacular speech. As a rhetorical device, "mother tongue" sums up the uncanniness of embedded displacement; use of this phrase enfolds the subject in a medium that prepossesses the power to conceive. The mother tongue is metonym as symptom, a sign for the experi-ence of alienation from within. In "Reading the Mother Tongue," Jane Gal-lop describes a project of recovery: "We are not looking for a new language, a radical outside, but for 'the other within,' the alterity that has always lain silent, unmarked and invisible within the mother tongue."[60] For early modern authors, alterity has little to do with silence. Rhetorical theorists analyze the ethical, affective, and social consequences of vernacular expression, and personify that mode as if it were not just coupled with but occupied by and embodied in women. Truisms that tie feminine speech to sexual excess have been well documented, but even texts that presume the priority of masculine speakers cite female sexuality to communicate fears of uncontrolled circulation and compromised transmission.[61] Recent studies have shown how a provisional command of the vernacular jeopardizes masculine identity and control: Ferguson writes, "In figuring the vernacular itself or the vernacular text as feminine, the male author repeatedly risks losing his own stereotypical gender bearings in his linguistic matrix."[62] The loss is metonymic, a process that sets forth determinate meanings but is carried away by mobile associations. When masculine speaking subjects engage the mother tongue, they imagine a will to language other than their own.

William Attersoll critiques Catholicism in terms which, for all their familiarity, hint at difficult questions; noting that the church proscribes "the common mother tongue of all the people," he sternly declares, "The people of God must not be like Parrots."[63] Mediated access to an uncongenial vernacular seems unlikely to mitigate that risk. If the concept of a mother tongue retrojects linguistic estrangement into an originary condition, that history, however contrived, has intense imaginative power. Within its structure, the speaker who contests his unaccommodated position does so from a derivative and ventriloquized stance. References to the mother tongue are both ironic and metonymic: they force the convergence of tenure and dispossession, and delineate a situation of utterance that is bound to another but unfixed in itself. Near in conception and use, but not proper in the sense of being neither seemly nor owned, maternalized language invokes natural bonds to precipitate conflict between hierarchy and generation, exposing those systems to reversal, rupture, and intersubjective collapse. These effects resonate with Carla Freccero's description of queer forces in language: "Meanwhile, *queer* can also be a grammatical perversion, a misplaced pronoun, the wrong proper name; it is what is strange, odd, funny, not quite right, improper. Queer is what is and is not there, what disaggregates the coherence of the norm from the very beginning."[64] For masculine speakers, the mother tongue is a queer locution, perhaps the ultimate "wrong proper name."[65] The phrase calls on women who should not be there at all; it conflates linguistic and somatic causalities, and affirms—even if against the speaker's interests or will—that mastery depends on the figures in which it is conceived.

Language takes a strange turn when it reunites maternal subjects with the rhetorical convention of the mother tongue. "Figure" as trope shades into "figure" as body, and masculine occupation of the vernacular produces a chronicle of heterosocial encounters. Thomas Wilson's warning against "ynkehorne termes" exemplifies this pattern: "Some seke so farre for outlandishe Englishe, that thei forget altogether their mothers language. And I dare swere this, if some of their mothers were alive, thei were not able to tell, what thei say."[66] To chastise men, Wilson invites their mothers to speak through him; ventriloquism reverses its direction and relocates both ownership and intent. The mother tongue animates and incorporates figuration, materializing the women from whom it derives and locating them in intimate, authoritative, and sometimes adversarial relationships to men. William Austin argues that men depend on women for facility in language: "For from *their voyce* men learne to frame *their owne*, to be understood of others. For in our infancy, we learne our language from them. Which men (therein not ingratefull) have justly termed our *Mother tongue*."[67] Matthew Sutcliffe represents this debt in nationalist terms, praising Queen Elizabeth for "the Scriptures and publicke prayers in our mother tongue."[68] William Annand turns the same logic against the Roman church: "but yet there is one Roman speech that is used by all these together, and is the Dialect of them all in common. Well we may cal it their mother tongue, since we know she who suckled them, taught them also to speak."[69] Whether such references celebrate or disparage formative influences, the mother tongue summons the mother as if there were no distance between breath and blood. In "Sins of the Tongue," Carla Mazzio writes, "Because 'tongue' (like the Latin '*lingua*' and the Greek '*glossa*') also means 'language,' the very invocation of the word encodes a relation between word and flesh, tenor and vehicle, matter and meaning."[70] The mother tongue mingles abstract and corporeal intimations, and as the phrase modifies issues of religion, nationalism, and sovereignty, it remains attached to women. "Lingua is declined with Hec the Femenine, because it is a houshold stuffe perticularly belonging, and most commonly resident under the roofe of Womens mouthes," according to the schoolmaster in John Marston's *What You Will*.[71] However cautiously directed and applied, feminized speech ties meaning to an unfixed, undisciplined source. "What you will" might be the catchphrase of the vernacular: it conveys the quality of mobile volition that transforms a useful figure into an associative chain.

Wendy Wall quotes Marston's line at the start of her essay " 'Household Stuff,' " and, as her argument demonstrates, the values ascribed to a feminized vernacular are decidedly mixed. "Like the household in which early education and language acquisition took place, the native tongue was both a national ideal and a sign of the abject."[72] Commentators on the mother tongue claim it as suitable, beautiful, faithful, and authentic, and reject it as inadequate, indecorous, deceptive, and debased; conventions of femininity inform these verdicts, imbued with the full force of an incoherent essentialism. Ideas of the natural connect innateness to fault, and while masculine speakers worry at that irreducible simultaneity, feminine speakers incarnate it, as when a line from *Westward Hoe*—"Why mistris, railing is your mother tongue as well as lying"—describes the improper speech that is proper to women.[73] The vernacular may be an artless form, but it comes easily to witches; in *The Admirable Historie of the Possession and Conversion of a Penitent woman*, the preface assures readers, "those that are possessed ordinarily spake their mother tongue."[74] George Abbot's account of vernacular sermons records a striking annexation of expressive control: "When *Hus* began first to preach, the people which used handy craftes, did with great desire heare his sermons, and did reade the Scriptures, being turned by him into their mother tongue; so that they could dispute with the Priests: which the very women were able to do; yea and one woman did make a booke."[75] The mother tongue produces women out of language as it concedes that language comes from women, and divided assignments of value respond to a constant problem of jurisdiction. Lynn Enterline offers an important corrective to the notion of exclusive linguistic authority: "As my discussion of the *Metamorphoses* should make clear, in Ovid's poem rhetoric can indeed be a dangerously potent tool. But it is never merely instrumental—and certainly never merely the instrument of 'men.'"[76] The examples I have quoted interlink feminine agents and instruments; at these moments, women may be nurturers, teachers, sovereigns, liars, witches, authors, or whores, but they inhabit the mother tongue, and masculine speaking subjects encroach at a cost. In the poem "On a Talkative, and Stammering Fellow," the apostrophized speaker is at once possessed and bereft:

> Nature in thee did overact her part,
> And so struck dumb her Adversary Art.
> Let others boast their Mother Tongue, but she
> Hath giv'n the Mother of all tongues to thee.[77]

The affinity that connects mother nature to the mother tongue leaves masculine speech at once evacuated and haunted; feminized language has a will of its own, an unassimilated volition that shifts mastery toward imposture.

Ferguson acutely dissects the counter-fantasy of colonization. "Subtending the pervasive idea that the vernacular is like female 'nature,' an entity in need either of protection from foreign contamination and / or of improvement—sometimes by 'borrowing' words from other tongues, sometimes by being ruled through grammar, sometimes by retrieving 'old' words from the past—is the idea that educated men should devise artful ways to cultivate the vernacular as if it were a colonial territory."[78] The vernacular, if aptly cultivated, might safeguard such master discourses as law, medicine, poetry, theology, and science. Translation can thus become an ethical mandate; Ainsworth demands, "let Forms be written in which any head of Religion may popularly be propounded in the mother Tongue, that the people may be taught both truly and perspicuously."[79] Indigenous traditions can ascend to eminence, as when, in a strategic reversal, Philip Sidney identifies the mother tongue as a seemly heir. He traces a line of "Fathers in learning" from Greek to Latin to Italian, and writes, "So in our English were *Gower* and *Chawcer*. After whom, encouraged and delighted with theyr excellent fore-going, others have followed, to beautifie our mother tongue."[80] Sanitized by good government, the mother tongue might become a pure vessel, but ambivalence still attends common use. The preface to John Harington's translation of *Orlando Furioso* suggests that if poetry inspires doubts, the vehicle of transfer will confirm them: "There are peradventure manie men, and some of those both grave, and godly men, that in respect they count all poetrie as meerly tending to wantonnesse and vanitie, will at the verie first sight reject this booke, and not only not allow, but blame, and reprove the travell taken in setting foorth the same in our mother tongue."[81] Wantonness and vanity, those peculiarly feminine traits, are exacerbated by vernacular display.[82] Parker traces "the complex concerns about virility at work in the period's repeated diatribes against the 'female' tongue," and describes the issue of masculine style as "haunted by both the female and the effeminate," by "anxieties both about the ambiguous gender of men of words and about the activity of writing itself."[83] Debates over linguistic propriety cannot be decisively won or lost; the mother tongue is, in the densest sense of the term, indiscriminate, a set of contradictions compressed into a provocative figure of speech.

Failures of discrimination preoccupy advocates of the vernacular. "I doe not prohibit you to speake in your naturall and mother tongue, but I woulde not have you use improper and unfit speeches," a speaker advises in Stefano Guazzo's *Civile Conversation*.[84] The shakiness of this distinction motivates some authors to delimit a "mother tongue" that marks its users as socially unintelligible, as when Richard Younge writes in *The Drunkard's Character*, "the language of Hell is so familiar, that blasphemy is become their mother tongue";[85] or when Richard Barckley writes of the French, "blasphemie (say they) is their mother-tongue, and ordinarie with manie Frenchmen: Adulterie is to them a pastime: Symonie is common marchandise."[86] Admonitory exemplars break the chain of association, and quarantine the dangers of intemperance, indiscretion, and self-loss. However, as Wall's reading of *Gammer Gurton's Needle* suggests, differences maintained at the expense of common ground sacrifice more than they retrieve:

> In *Gammer*, the mother tongue and the mother—certainly the lost objects of nostalgic desire—are presented so as to contest a nostalgic view of English's feminized (il)legitimacy as its founding repudiation. . . . As *Gammer* holds up to scrutiny the gendered and sexual inflections of the educational system, it foregrounds a shared community signified centrally by the mother tongue—or by what might be called the politics of domestic speech.[87]

The vernacular poses a double bind: immersion generates ungoverned proximities and unions, but disavowal excludes speakers from shared understandings. When subjects repudiate the complex intersubjectivity figured by the mother tongue, they segregate language from quotidian intercourse and sever its logic from social codes. The demand for unadulterated speech projects the image of its obverse, a form of speech that preserves pure detachment from contextual obligations and remains faithful only to designed effects. The eccentric, illegible qualities displaced onto drunkards or Frenchmen come close to home, importing disengaged opacity into situations that predicate language as a means of contract. *Histrio-Mastix* says of clergymen, "They may not come forth upon the stage as Actors, nor act Comaedies in their mother tongue"; impertinent performance inflects a crucial role, and crosses belief with masquerade.[88] John Stephens's character of "A Page"—a figure he describes as "an abridgement of greater charges, sprung from the destruction of hospitality"—attributes inappropriate fluency to the erasure of valid bonds: "Hee speakes *Bawdy* freely as if it were his mother tongue: but he cannot bee so bad as his word."[89] An unmoored and disaggregated rhetoric makes it easy to take the speaker at his word, and to take that word as all there is; character comes into being through signs that adhere simply because they collide. In his analysis of *ēthos* and *prosōpon*, Gavin Alexander writes, "We have moral character, and the face or mask. Through metonymy, we are able to talk of the creation of a speaking voice as the creation of such a moral character or mask—ethopoeia and prosopopoeia. No mask is seen, but the words spoken stand for it; there may be no real moral character but only the simulacrum of one to be inferred from those spoken words."[90] At the negative extreme of such figuration, the arbitrary grasp of metonymy holds together a subject who can never be more than an artifact of words, and whose language confers neither integrity nor kinship.

Godfrey Goodman, in *The Fall of Man*, attributes this condition to a post-lapsarian collapse of truth into ornament. The chaos of "this poeticall and phantasticall age, which delights more in words then in substance" represents a punishment, "a great judgement of God, that man having forsaken the first fruite, and having associated himselfe to the beasts of the field; therfore he proves a stranger to himselfe, to his brethren, and forgets his owne mother tongue."[91] Trapped among improper associations, Goodman's subject suffers that specifically metonymic devastation, the loss of name.[92] If the fall of man is a fall into feminized figuration, it is at the same time a fall away, a descent into disconnection for which women stand as both corrupting cause and impeaching sign. The parables of linguistic abuse poise figural indiscretion against sterile isolation, and mastery—of the self, of others, of the medium in which self and other meet—has no natural ground. Bacon's *Advancement of Learning* offers a curiously accidental meditation on that predicament: the first edition of 1605 refers to "the Art of GRAMMAR; whereof the use in another tongue is small." The 1629 and 1633 editions correct "another tongue" to "mother tongue."[93] For a speaker caught up in a will to language that preempts autonomy or imposes estrangement, the shift from an other to a mother marks out an impasse. In *The Inarticulate Renaissance*, Mazzio writes of "a profound ambivalence about an increasingly alienated and scattered tongue used to shape common language as well as common law."[94] Thomas Winter's poem "To his Translation" encapsulates that sensibility in an apostrophe to alienated speech: "Go little eccho of anothers voice, / Tell in thy mother tongue a strangers mind."[95] An other's voice narrates a stranger's mind through the refraction of an echo: this is a mother tongue neither known nor owned, potentially lost or forgotten, and at odds with self-possession. "Characters are not every mans construction, though they be writ in our mother tongue," Nicholas Breton observes, as if character binds units of language to elements of person only to propel that compound relic beyond apprehension.[96] In the epistle which prefaces *The Shepheardes Calender*, E. K.

promises that Colin Clout's poetry will restore a bastardized vernacular to its "rightfull heritage," in opposition to those whose "first shame is, that they are not ashamed, in their own mother tonge straungers to be counted and alienes."[97] But who, after all, is not an alien? What would it mean—what would it take—not to be so counted?[98]

Judith Butler argues that agency originates in the experience of constraint—"one reason that 'agency' is not the same as 'mastery'"—and recurs to that experience, constituting identity through dependence and vitalizing a memory which, as it yokes need to damage, operates in the present tense.

> There is no way to protect against that primary vulnerability and susceptibility to the call of recognition that solicits existence, to that primary dependency on a language we never made in order to acquire a tentative ontological status. Thus we sometimes cling to the terms that pain us because, at a minimum, they offer us some form of social and discursive existence. The address that inaugurates the possibility of agency, in a single stroke, forecloses the possibility of radical autonomy.[99]

It is in this sense impossible to speak as or for one's self, to forget the interpellation that confers a capacity conditioned by limits and structured by relational contingency. If early modern rhetorical theorists cannot leave women alone, the failure or refusal to do so reflects the inseparability of linguistic and social schemes. "Who speaks when convention speaks?" Butler asks. "In what time does convention speak? In some sense, it is an inherited set of voices, an echo of others who speak as the 'I'."[100] A suppressed inheritance erupts when feminized figures fuse bodies to words; tropes call forth women in texts written by men, an evocative triumph of susceptibility over self-interest. The temporal distance of origins, like the ontological difference between figures, collapses into the immediacy of feminine social subjects, as if mastery must summon its own demystifying ghosts.

The Stark Impossibility of Thinking *That*

As a figure for naturalized relationships, metonymy describes the processes that make us think of the fire when we see the match ("when by the efficient cause, the effecte is streight gatherde thereupon") or change the litter when we see the cat ("When the doer is put for that that is done") or support the party when we see the politician ("The captain for the host").[101] It asserts the influence of familiar contact points, linking maps and destinations ("The finder for the thing that is found"), names and addresses ("The possessor for the thing that is possessed"), flags and nations ("The signe for that that is signified").[102] If the last items in these series are overtly ideological in a way that the previous items are not, metonymic continuity slides us past that recognition. An effortlessly coercive "and" imposes a poetics of self-evidence, which, by looking as innocuous as picture and frame or fish and fishbowl ("when that that is conteyned is put for that that doth conteine"), walks presumptive congruencies across the fissures into which they might fall, fracture, and change their shape. The invisible hyphens that regulate gender, sociality, and sex—man-and-woman, husband-and-wife, penis-and-vagina—are as natural as butter-and-bread or blankets-and-bed. This is the power of the obvious: conjunctions seem harmlessly mundane, even as first terms end up on top.

Yet metonymy is a mode of perversion, an endless series of capricious attachments that overwhelms the discretion of hierarchy or taxonomy. Michel Foucault famously begins his preface to *The Order of Things* with a list of categories taken from Borges's account of a "certain Chinese encyclopaedia": " 'animals are divided into: (a) belonging to the Emperor, (b) embalmed, (c) tame, (d) sucking pigs, (e) sirens, (f) fabulous, (g) stray dogs, (h) included in the present classification, (i) frenzied, (j) innumerable, (k) drawn with a very fine camelhair brush, (l) *et cetera*, (m) having just broken the water pitcher, (n) that from a long way off look like flies.' "[103] If categories are respectable, bondage is irresistible, and the preposterous metonymies of the encyclopedia banish decorum in favor of an insatiable desire for the next "something else." Foucault writes, "It is not the 'fabulous' animals that are impossible, since they are designated as such, but the narrowness of the distance separating them from (and juxtaposing them to) the stray dogs, or the animals that from a long way off look like flies. What transgresses the boundaries of all imagination, of all possible thought, is simply that alphabetical series (a, b, c, d) which links each of those categories to all the others."[104]

I have argued that metonymy figures the force of feminine will, which imposes social meanings as it threatens to undo their sense. A brief segment of Wilson's index—less fabulous than Foucault's encyclopedia, but arguably no less curious—shows how easily discrete terms break their boundaries, and gain an associative momentum toward unpredictable ends:

Wittie lye makyng.
Woe of this worlde, declared.

Women rebuked.
Wordes doubtfully spoken.[105]

Alphabetical coincidence yields a condensed history of misogyny, or rather of the enigmatic, effectual feminine acts to which misogynist discourse responds. But metonymy always takes the form of coincidence, in the twofold sense of that word: it forges correlations and subjects them to chance. In this way it articulates the volitional work of women, on whose connective powers heterosociality depends; those connections are coincidental artifacts, whatever they have to do with truth. The figure that should be most proper, and is certainly most near, is the sign of a knowledge that cannot be grasped. This is the unthinkable dimension of social order, the invisible network of intentions and desires, governed by an alien purpose, which forecloses elucidation by setting the stakes so high. Foucault describes a response that records its own deficit: "In the wonderment of this taxonomy, the thing we apprehend in one great leap, the thing that, by means of the fable, is demonstrated as the exotic charm of another system of thought, is the limitation of our own, the stark impossibility of thinking *that*."[106]

A hint of impossibility appears in my last example, taken from Thomas Lodge's *Catharos*. Lodge offers this summary of women:

> It shall be easie to gather the mishaps which a dissolute and wanton woman draweth after her, which are taken from the Latine word *Mulier,* which representeth unto us so manie evils as that containeth letters, which are sixe: to wite *M. U. L. I. E. R.* An evill woman is the evill of evlls: the vanitie of vanities: the letcherie of letcheries: the choller of chollers: the furie of furies: and the ruine of Realmes. Another good father hath discoursed all these Epithites according to the order of the Alphabet. But what is that the Italian Poet speaketh, when thus against that sex he inveigheth.[107]

Having catalogued dissolution—the "ruine of Realmes"—by way of a sequential yet disarticulated excursion into Latin, Lodge quotes the poem in Italian, and concludes, "I had rather some other should take the paynes to translate these vearses into our mother tongue, than my selfe."[108] The discourse of misogyny, which I take up in the next chapter, here stutters against the mother tongue. In her reading of the university drama *Lingua*, Mazzio writes, "the misogyny operative in the gendering of speech is but a thin disguise for failures of humanism to cohere, to translate, indeed to speak from within, and on behalf of, the human body."[109] This point about disguise and failure highlights the basic fallacy of misogynist discourse, which might always become self-reflexive to the point of muteness. In what language can one attack the figures, those indivisible bodies and words, which confer articulate identity? What false position must one assume, and what disfigurement must one accept, to disavow the reciprocities of subjectivity? There is of course no material impediment to vernacular misogyny—it is an early modern growth industry—but a conceptual problem may be something else again. The language that brings mastery home refers elsewhere, derived but not detached from the feminine subjects whose subjection it pursues.

_____

Chapter Three

Acts of Will

Misogyny and Masquerade

As sexuality undergoes some dizzying revisions, evidence that one is a woman "at heart" (the inquisitor's question) is not without worth.

—Brownmiller, *Femininity*, 17

Naturally, if you're a woman talking, whatever you use as an adjective has to agree with what you are.

—Conversational Italian class, Provincetown, Massachusetts, Fall 1999

In "The Alchemy of Style and Law," Barbara Johnson recounts her experience of writing a commentary for the *Harvard Law Review*. The commentary addresses the last essay written by Mary Joe Frug, and in it Johnson takes up a sentence left unfinished at Frug's death. Johnson poses the question, "How does this gap signify?"

> I sent my commentary to the *Harvard Law Review* for its round of editorial responses. When it came back from its first reading, the editors had changed "How does this gap signify?" to "What does this gap mean?" This is not at all the same question. "*What* does the gap mean" implies that it *has* a meaning, and all I have to do is to figure out what it is. "*How* does the gap signify" raises the *question* of what it means to mean, raises meaning as a question, implies that the gap *has to be read*, but that it can't be presumed to have been intended. The *Law Review* responded as if to question the mode or possibility of meaning was to speak a foreign language.[1]

Johnson distinguishes between an interpretive project applied to a fixed object—"it *has* a meaning"—and a dynamic interconnection among contingent subjects of meaning and inscrutable states of intent. My analysis of early modern misogyny takes resistance to an oversimplified "what" as its entry

Figure 4 (preceding page). Frontispiece, Joseph Swetnam, *The Arraignment of Lewd, Idle, Froward, and Unconstant Women* (London: M.C. for T. Passenger, 1682). By permission of the Folger Shakespeare Library.

point; as I will argue, an intricate, often adversarial relationship between "what" and "how," framed by "the *question* of what it means to mean," underlies the formulaic articulations of misogynist discourse. Even as this discourse asserts the power to determine *what* women mean, it is driven by concerns with *how* they mean, and with how they signify their capacity to intend. Its authority derives from an edict to discipline and define, but its narratives trace feminine meaning as a purpose in process, which precedes and shapes the disciplinary mandate itself. The "foreign language" in which misogyny questions the mode of meaning is its own language, estranged by a method that both disavows and responds to the active work of feminine will. Undercurrents burst into cover stories, and accounts of conventional femininity—whether "good" or "bad"—fuse clichés of nature and essence with conjectures about strategic self-invention.

Misogynist discourse presumes acceptance of social codes, an acceptance shared not only among those who speak but by those who are spoken. Pierre Bourdieu argues that symbolic systems consolidate stability and futurity through collective belief: "Symbols are the instruments *par excellence* of 'social integration': as instruments of knowledge and communication . . . they make it possible for there to be a *consensus* on the meaning of the social world, a consensus which contributes fundamentally to the reproduction of the social order."[2] Consensus, as the sign of integration, works through instruments of knowledge but depends on misrecognition: "For symbolic power is that invisible power which can be exercised only with the complicity of those who do not want to know that they are subject to it or even that they themselves exercise it."[3] Bourdieu seems to exclude the volition Elaine Scarry ascribes to consent—"The artifactual holds within it the voluntaristic"—but Scarry describes complicity as itself an operation of will: "Consent *is* an act of ventriloquism, an apparently mute disposition of the body that becomes a throwing of the voice into the political realm."[4] As both Bourdieu and Scarry suggest, univocal power is apparitional; it emerges from a collaboration it works to obscure. The crucial question highlighted by the intersection of these models is not whether subjects participate in the systems that govern them, but whether—and how—their participation signifies informed and effective intent.

Francis Bacon takes up connections among authority, consensus, and symbolic language when he distinguishes between aphorism, which he calls "a knowledge broken," and method. He censures method for irresponsible synthesis: "it hath beene too much taken into Custome, out of a fewe *Axiomes* or Observations, upon any Subjecte, to make a solemne, and formall Art; filling it with some Discourses, and illustratinge it with Examples; and digesting it into a sensible *Methode*." Writing that "*Methodes* are more fit to winne Consent; or beleefe; but lesse fit to point to Action; for they carrie a kinde of Demonstration in Orbe or Circle, one part illuminating another; and therefore satisfie," Bacon concludes that by "carrying the shewe of a Totall, [they] doe secure men."[5] He indicts arguments that translate fractional understanding into deceptive certainty: "for he that delivereth knowledge; desireth to deliver it in such fourme, as may be best beleeved; and not as may best examined: and hee that receiveth knowledge, desireth rather present satisfaction, than expectant Enquirie, and so rather not to doubt, than not to erre."[6] Such a "Contract of Errour," sealed by invested didacticism on one side and uncritical reception on the other, would epitomize the success story of misogynist discourse. As a set of truisms that "make a solemne, and formall Art," this discourse assembles stale examples into seamless narratives; its method, however circular, proceeds with that steady purpose of securing men. It constructs an apparitional preeminence, and hands down simplified verdicts from a great height. Valerie Wayne writes, "the sport of debates about women was suspect from the start, since it assumed positions of attack or defence that defined women as uncomplicated others who could be catalogued for their virtues and vices because they were inferior to and far less complex than men."[7] The scheme does not need rigorous logic to forge unified purpose and sense; it works most effectively through a partial approach to totalizing ends.

But misogyny, as a heterosocial idiom, does not detach authority from intercourse; a mode of power that creates a vacuum has limited use. Joseph Swetnam acknowledges this in one of his more virulent expositions: "thou canst not wrest them from their willes, and if thou thinke to make her good by stripes, thou must beate her to death."[8] Excision of feminine will would require an intrasocial bloodbath, and the implications of that insight are cautionary rather than programmatic: mastery backfires if it reaches its ultimate goal, proving the inefficiency of an absolutism that annihilates the subjects it seeks to rule. Swetnam's rhetoric couples a desire to expel or destroy with a consciousness that the targets are closely knit into the fabric of interrelation. Judith Butler's key question about hate speech resonates here: "Is there a repetition that might disjoin the speech act from its supporting conventions such that its repetition confounds rather than consolidates its injurious efficacy?"[9] In recurring to an ideal of unadulterated dominion, misogynist discourse seeks to animate a preposterous if terribly serious fantasy. But as that fantasy relies on conventions that enforce truth through exhaustive familiarity, the structure warps under its own weight. Butler observes, "there are reasons to question whether a static notion of 'social structure' is reduplicated in hate speech, or whether such structures suffer destructuration through being reiterated, repeated, and rearticulated."[10] The static paradigm that equates isolation with control runs counter to social survival; attempts to elaborate or fortify that paradigm not only expose its limits, but articulate the deficits and surfeits by which it is undercut.

Are Close Readings Really Only Relevant to Those Who Produce Them?

A few years ago, at a symposium titled "Historicism and Its Discontents," I speculated about the relationship between discontent with historicism and dissatisfaction with history.[11] Those positions are not of course the same, but they tend to converge around historicist studies of misogyny. Critiques of untextured historicism focus on its potential both to reiterate and to reanimate an oppressive historical phenomenon. A focus on patriarchal norms may lead to reductive conclusions, as Stephen Orgel points out: "To define Renaissance culture simply as a patriarchy, to limit one's view to the view the dominant culture took of itself; to assert that within it women were domestic creatures and a medium of exchange is to take Renaissance ideology at its word."[12] Analysis might establish false distance, and produce what Lena Cowen Orlin terms "the comforting reassurance that history has made progress and that we have come a long way (baby) from our early modern predecessors."[13] Phyllis Rackin observes that repetition can perpetuate disabling narratives and restrict understanding of their costs: "The historical narratives we choose (or have chosen for us) have consequences for the present and future, and if the story of misogyny and oppression is the only story we tell about the past, we risk a dangerous complacency in the present."[14] Taking misogyny at its word—and, as Orlin adds, "at its worst"[15]—vitalizes its power and compromises our response.

Wayne connects such hazards to the conditions of early modern femininity: "The risks of appropriative writing were high in the Renaissance when women were enjoined to silence and compliance; they are high now as we write about a silent past that cannot talk back. Approaching the past through dominant discourses only doubles the risk of that appropriation and prevents our being able to distinguish among available ideologies."[16] She presents this problem as a challenge for feminist criticism, intensified by the emergent orthodoxies of new historicism. Almost fifteen years later, Rackin describes the same problem as dominating—or perhaps haunting—feminist historicism. "With the turn to history in literary studies generally, and especially in the field of the Renaissance, feminist Shakespeare criticism has been almost completely shaped by the scholarly consensus about the pervasiveness of masculine anxiety and women's disempowerment in Shakespeare's world."[17] As they resist a narrowly scripted plot, these arguments warn that reiterative accounts of misogyny may draw feminist projects into misapprehensions or distortions of early modern culture. If we listen for other voices, "becoming alert to alternative discourses that are present at a particular historical moment and the variety of textual forms associated with them,"[18] we may learn different stories: "Cumulatively, archival fragments construct a radically different picture of women's history than that we have gathered from more coherent, culturally motivated narratives."[19]

The danger lies in reproducing cultural theory under the illusion that we are studying social history. A return to the archives in search of more diverse materials offers an important corrective; so too does a skeptical return to the practice of reading. As I will suggest throughout this chapter, close attention to stock narratives often reveals an inverse correlation between coherence and motivation. Patriarchy's word is no one's mother tongue, and misogynist discourse speaks through conditional, defensive, and synthetic formulations, as conflicted as they are powerful. I do not mean to understate that power; tracing fault lines in a deleterious structure will not undo its effects. But the process does uncover negotiations that masquerade as prescriptions. As many scholars have argued, there must be a disparity between monitory tenets and lived experiences.[20] Rather than regard those tenets as complacently disengaged, I trace their ambivalent evocations of a feminine will that might close the gap, and imbue abstractions with a belated, artifactual, yet serviceable substance. In her analysis of the asymmetrical imperatives that dictate sexual morality, Laura Gowing writes, "Like so many elements of patriarchy, the double standard was supported and enforced not just by men but by women: we need to question how it was shared, understood, and deployed by

when Swetnam asserts that a man's greatest labors will be "a great deale too little to get her good will," and concludes, "nay, if thou give her never so much, and yet if thy personage please not her humour, then will I not give a halfe-penny for her honesty at the yeares end."[29] But these affective responses spin off from the pragmatic assessment voiced by Barnabe Rich: "neither are the most of them curbed in with any other bridle then what they willingly put upon them selves."[30] Futurity hinges on feminine intention, and disciplinary rhetoric breaches its categories when it engages the question of choice.

To take misogyny at its word, then, is not to accept its cover story, but to recognize its beset and contested situations of utterance. Conflict occurs across agendas; Margaret Ezell observes of misogynist satires, "one of their most interesting side effects is that they provided profemale writers with the perfect platform from which systematically to attack the central tenets of patriarchal ideology."[31] But misogynist discourse also internalizes its own impasse. As Catherine Belsey notes, "Texts take issue with other texts, but they also differ from themselves, inscribe the conflicts they take part in."[32] Methods that proceed axiomatically do not determine a line but create a haze, which fails to hide the predicament of a social theory that seeks detachment from its founding premise. In *A treatyce of Moral philosophy*, William Baldwin disguises the premise as an indictment: "A woman is a necessary evill." Necessity is the salient point here, even if evil is the emotive trigger; Baldwin's catalogue of sexual platitudes locates the menace of women within the structure of marriage, and describes a compulsory bond saturated with corruption and abuse. "Geve thy wife no power over thee, for if thou suffer her to daye to tread uppon thy foote, she will to morow treade upon thyne heade." "Women in mischiefe are wyser then men." "It is better for women to be barrayne, then to bring fourth a vile wicked carrayne." "There is not so fierce and perilous an enemy to a man as his wife." That last statement strips away distractions to leave only the starkness of "wife." The fierce peril of conjugal union is not aberrant but innate; the threat posed by women is inextricable from the need for intimate alliance. "Womans companye is an evil that cannot be eschewed."[33]

It may be obvious that misogynists have a problem with women, but I would pause before dismissing this as a tautology without weight. Swetnam, whose vitriol earned him the title role in the play *Swetnam the Woman-Hater*, repeats Baldwin's truism with a telling qualification: "women are all necessary evills, and yet not all given to wickednesse." The evil follows from the necessity, which nonetheless motivates an allocation of blame: "it is said of women, that they have two faults, that is, they can neither say well, nor yet doe well."[34] The argument loops back on itself; the fault of the system belongs to its devalued subjects, without whose participation the system would not function at all. Mary Beth Rose notes that conflicting views of women are indivisibly coupled, and concludes, "The logic of this dualistic sensibility often construes marriage as at best a necessary evil, the means by which a fallen humanity reproduces itself and ensures the orderly succession of property."[35] In an effort to mitigate the evils of necessity, misogynist texts reach for a strictly functional accommodation; if it involves a compromise, it at least achieves a goal. But internal ambiguities—"and yet not all given to wickedness"—signal a crisis of knowledge that undoes such designs. Instrumental reductionism requires apprehension of the object, which incoherence precludes: unstable assignments of value cross boundaries without difficulty but not without consequence. A refusal to narrate the difference between good and bad women suggests a failure to identify that difference or prove that it matters. Having railed against marriage, Swetnam gives these guidelines to the man who pursues it: "There are six kinds of women which thou shouldest take heed that thou match not thy selfe to any one of them: that is to say, good nor bad, faire nor foule, rich nor poore."[36] Feminine subjects might do well or they might do ill, but the exercise of definition becomes strangely inert as categories reach a vanishing point. When misogynist rhetoric draws lines only to point out that women transect them, heterosocial intercourse has no safe space.

This sets up a strong argument against risking the contract at all. Gowing stresses the unlikelihood of habitable arrangements: "The rhetorics and performances of gender—in which we must include the words of insult and the languages of marital dispute as much as prescriptions in print—made women out to be impossible wives, continually threatening sexual betrayal and domestic danger."[37] In *The Batchelars Banquet*, the epigraph proposes a simple solution: "*View them well, but taste not, / Regard them well, but waste not.*"[38] Swetnam offers the same advice—"a woman is better lost then found, better forsaken then taken"[39]—and Roland du Jardin presents the traffic in women as a vehicle of schism. "One being reprehended for giving his daughter in marriage to his enemy, said, that he knew not how to be better revenged of him."[40] In *The sevens sorowes that women have when theyr husbandes be deade*, whose very title itemizes a finite devotion, the fear that wives will devour men's substance merges into cannibalism. "And many tymes in stede of fleshe or fyshe / A dede mannes head is served in a dyshe."[41] Feminine intentions differ in quality, but share a common license; as Frances E. Dolan has shown, nothing separates self-determination from the power to do harm. "Accounts of petty treason represent married women's subjectivity both as agency—words and deeds in the world and accountability for them—and as self-awareness. The accounts ally both to violent resistance."[42] Married men incur jeopardy, and the only defense is to switch the victims, as in the proverbial tale of the hanging tree.

> *Arrius*, being himselfe a married man, and seeing one lamenting and making great moane, that three of his wives, one after another, had all hanged themselves in one tree in his Garden; he with great desire requested a branch thereof, marvailing that the man should sorrow for so good successe, bade him proyne and dresse that tree well, which brought him forth so good fruite, as to rid him of that which so much annoyed him.[43]

This turns volition back on itself: there can be nothing better than a disposable wife, unless it is a series of wives who dispose of themselves.

But these arguments are framed by social contracts; they market prophylactics within an endemically infected state. "For a married man is like unto one arrested, and I think that many a man would flie up into Heaven, if this arrest of marriage kept them not backe," Swetnam muses, but he does not anticipate a quick levitation.[44] "Some have beene of opinion, that the gods would descend and dwell with us, if it were not that women lived amongst us," Jardin reports, but he writes in a post-lapsarian moment.[45] Counterfactual nostalgia fuels the case against marriage, providing bare cover for quotidian facts. Polemicists fall back on the residual ideology of which Wayne writes, and while a differential rhetoric that isolates, blames, and repudiates women has power as a weapon, it does not defend against heterosocial implication. Misogynist discourse interleaves those dogged, fragile fantasies of autonomy with pragmatic concerns about the roles women play. If social self-perpetuation requires some degree of feminine agency, *what* degree? and what kind? The chapter on women in *Wits Theater* consists entirely of brief examples; these five give a sense of the scope.

Araetia taught her Sonne Aristippus phylosophy.
The Spartane wemen delighted to see their children die valiantly in defence of their country.

[W]hen King Antiochus dyed, the Queen Laodicea his wife dissembled the matter, untill shee of her owne decree, had made another
King in Syria.
The Romans had a law, that what soever a woman with childe
longed for, shee should have it.
The greatest part of Asia was conquered and governed, more by the
wemen Amazons, then with any barbarous people.[46]

Each anecdote delineates a sphere of intention, but even this limited assort-
ment ranges from pedagogy to violence to government to appetite to conquest, and evaluations or distinctions do not appear in the chapter at all.
How exactly might one shop from this catalogue? Feminine volition is a
vital, unpredictable factor in heterosocial transactions, which does its work
by crossing the categories that would secure its worth. The case for virtue,
with its constitutive effects on social order, appears complicated even to authors who defend the intrinsic goodness of women. "This may at first perhaps seem an odd Assertion, and extravagantly Paradoxical, but will appear a
certain Truth, when we have prov'd it," Agrippa assures the readers of *Female
Pre-Eminence*; or, in the words of a dedicatory epistle from *A Womans Woorth*,
"I might call it a Paradoxe, because some men (vainely transported) no doubt
will tearme it so: Notwithstanding, I holde it for a truth."[47]

Examine, and You Will Find Small Difference

Despite its immediate and specific social consequences, feminine will is entrenched as an originary premise. Ezell notes that early modern authors trace
marital roles to the ultimate primal scene: "The issue was felt to be sufficiently complex that a return to Eden was deemed necessary in order to
establish a framework for discussing the behavior of contemporary women."[48]
Retrojection, which so often lends timeless authority to strategic edicts and
norms, here reifies a dilemma: as the prototype for ruin and regeneration and
the test case for heterosociality, Eve instantiates the conflicts of misogynist
discourse. Accounts of her origins bind hierarchy to reciprocity, conflate
equivalence with disproportion, and propagate questions of precedence, purpose, and value.

The woman was taken from and oute of the syde of man and not from the earthe, least any man shoulde thynke that he had gotten hys wyfe out of the myer: but to considre that the wyfe is the husbondes fleshe and bone, and therfore to love her, yet was she not made of the head. For the husbon is the head and master of the wyfe. Nether was she made of the feete, as thoughe thou mighteste spurne her awaye from the and nothynge regard her but even oute of thy syde, as one that is set nexte unto man, to be his helpe and companion.[49]

Two strands of logic weave through this narrative, and Thomas Gataker pulls on both. The first stresses a metonymic connection between part and whole; the woman extracted from the man refers back to him, and marriage at once repeats and reverses the story of creation. "She was at first *taken out of man*; and is therefore by *Creation* as *a limbe reaft from him*," Gataker explains. "And she was afterward joyned againe in *Mariage* with *Man*, that by *Nuptiall conjunction* becomming *one flesh* with him, she might be as *a limbe restored* now and *fastned* againe *to him*."[50] A passive, partial body finds its ordained disposition: Eve is reft only to be restored, and as a solitary limb she has little hope of standing on her own.

But independent action is Eve's most notorious talent, and her catastrophic excursion into self-government launches a more volatile metonymic progress, which moves away from origins to forge other meanings. When Gataker returns to creation, he does so by way of the fall. "The *Man* misseth his *rib*, and seeketh to recover it againe: and the *Woman* would be in her old place againe, under the *Mans arme* or *wing*, from whence at first shee was taken. Nor is this affection and disposition at all evil simply of it selfe," he writes. "But since that *sinne* came in by the fall of our *first Parents*, *Mankind* having lost that power and command of it selfe that before it had; this affection is not only tainted and mixed generally with much filth, but is growne so violent, impetuous and head-strong with the most, that it is readie to break forth into grievous inconveniences."[51] Excesses proliferate from a single intemperate act, and this archetypal pattern confirms a social commonplace: the misdeeds of "mankind" do most damage when their agents are women. As the story of Eve becomes a theory of marriage, it articulates tensions between providential arcs and counterfactual swerves, and underscores the variables of synthesis. In its ideal form marriage redresses a loss and restores a balance, but intention rather than destiny must ratify that contract, and feminine will circulates as a wild card. Virtuous choice is vital—both active and crucial—as Heinrich Bullinger makes clear. "This consent, is that over-gyvyng and graunt of thy harte, whan unto thy chosen spouse thou promisest and gyvest thy selfe over in wedlocke and in the hyghest love and felowshyp that maye be under God."[52] If a prior unity molds the accord, then to give one's self is to give that self back; consent sketches a perfect circle, which could lose its shape with a twist of will. Derived from and bound to men, women might build the bridge between an incorporate past and a generative future, or they might open the chasm between flawless and fallen states.

Heterosocial contracts fill a need and take a risk. If Eve's choice has the power to corrupt all men, is marriage compensatory or reiterative? does it restore hierarchy, or surrender again to feminine will? Readings of the fall range widely, but meet at the junction of agency and fault. Robert Allott uses patrilineal entitlement to assign responsibility: "Although Eve transgressed before the man, yet is the originall of sinning, ascribed to Adam, because the succession is accounted in men, and not in wemen."[53] Disavowals of femi-nine autonomy reach a perverse apotheosis: because women are secondary effects, primary guilt belongs to men. The alternative of Eve's independence yields a chronicle of deliberate ruin: "shee was no sooner made, but straight-way her mind was set upon mischiefe, for by her aspiring minde and wanton will, shee quickly procured mans fall, and therfore ever since they are and have beene a woe unto man, and follow the line of their first leader."[54] This double bind corrupts genealogy beyond recall. On the one hand, patrilineal descent perpetuates masculine error; on the other, the "wanton will" of women breeds an endless threat to social order. To break that deadlock, some exegeses disavow all human responsibility, which has the dubious result of making the entire problem a divine mistake. Edward More writes of Eve, "Her lacke of strenght and nothyng els, was cause of her forlore," and Juan Huarte attributes her susceptibility to a difference of degree: "for God filling them both with wisedome, it is a verifyed conclusion, that he infused the lesser portion into her."[55] In a remarkable embellishment, *The Schole house of women* posits a difference of kind; according to this version, a dog stole Adam's rib and ate it. God improvises: "A remedy, god founde as yet / Out of the dogge, he toke a rybbe / The woman forthwith he made of it." A bestial pedigree confirms absolute deviation; women are unkind—crooked, curst, and growly—because they share no kinship with men. "As to the man, neyther kynne nor sybbe / Nature she foloweth, and playeth the gyb / And at her husbande, doth barke and ball / As doth the curre, for nought at all."[56] The story severs metonymic ties, and substitutes a changeling.

William Austin contends that such a story, if true, would mean something quite different. "Had [Eve] been made but of the living *flesh*, of some *gentle beast*, it had yet been (in respect of the *lively* and *prepared* matter,) somwhat more *honourable*, then that of [Adam's]; whose substance of creation was *base* and *senseles*, till it was *purified* and *enriched* with a *soule*."[57] Eve's origin in lively matter, whether Adam or some other beast, affirms her preeminence. "For, divers *little* creatures are procreated by the *Sunnes heat*, and the earths sliminesse. Which, (from *earth*, growing into *living* things:) *first*, stirre; then, *creep*; then, *leap*; then, *flie*; (as *wormes, serpents, frogges*, and *insects*;) which have, as well the benefit of *sence, motion*, and *generation*, as *Man*."[58] Austin reverses the merits of primary and secondary generation, and argues that parthenogenesis confers prestige not on the body in which it originates, but on the body it conceives. The extracted part yields a better whole; creation becomes an evolutionary narrative, making women less a second thought than a second step. Agrippa writes, "Thus the Woman in relation to time indeed was formed last, but in respect of Dignity, first of all conceived in the divine Idaea, (as 'tis written, Before the Heavens were created I chose her;) the End, according to the Catholick Creed of Philosophers, being ever first in Intention, though last in Execution: but Woman was the End, and last work of God."[59]

A survey of these positions suggests a vigorous, invested, and unresolved conflict between misogyny and proto-feminism, with Eve's status as its crux.[60] However, when gynophobia and gynophilia converge at the principle of difference, their disparate arguments produce a common effect. Whether Adam is a frog or Eve is a dog, whether an original man subjects a derivative woman or a spiritual woman surpasses a material man, they remain divided by inviolate lines. The terms of creation prove either insufficiency or transcendence; the circumstances of the fall confer either blame or amnesty; and each of these conclusions sets women apart. A move toward iconic extremes pushes back against heterosocial interdependence, promising that, even if women begin at the center of the story, they can be dispersed to its edges. Like exemplary catalogues, in which oppositions of virtue and vice evacuate the space of social compromise, arguments that abstract Eve's significance displace the socialized femininity for which her marriage provides a model. Eve thus becomes a model in a different sense: she exemplifies the simplified misogynist project that separates feminine subjects from masculine pursuits.[61]

Yet misogyny is rarely simple, and many texts that start with separation proceed to describe its failure. In a seemingly radical argument that in fact cites an established line of thought, *A Dyall for dainty Darlings* explains that shared beginnings lay the foundations for egalitarian social bonds: "she was not made of the head nor the foote, but of the ryb and side of man, which sheweth, that as she may not be a mystresse, so must she be no maide, as no soveraigne, so no servaunt, but an equall companion."[62] Rachel Speght makes this a mandate for identical dispensations: "therefore saith God concerning man and woman jointly, *Let them rule over the fish of the Sea, and over the foules of the Heaven, and over every beast that moveth upon the earth*: By which words, he makes their authority equall."[63] Austin goes still farther, asserting not only an equivalence of degree and kind but a complete absence of distinction. "What should make him so *proud*, as to *Despise*, and, with so *many sought-for words contemn Woman* (his other self?). . . . It shewes, as if a man should *love* his *head*; and *hate* his *braines*: Is not *she*, *he*? Examine, and you will find *small* Difference."[64] For a hierarchy that rests on its own self-evidence, denials of difference shake the ground. Exemplarity brackets women as too bad or too good for the practical habits of social subjectivity, but the endlessly reworked story of Eve identifies that strategy as a diversion. Both origin and fall locate women inside, integral to a social body for which the genetic bodies of Adam and Eve are at once analogue and pretext. "This being rightly considered, doth teach men to make such account of their wives, as *Adam* did of *Eve*," Speght writes: "men ought to love their wives as themselves, because hee that loves his wife, loves himselfe: And never man hated his owne flesh (which the woman is) unlesse a monster in nature."[65] This too is a conventional argument, plausibly evolved from the one-flesh paradigm that subtends creation and marriage: men cannot repudiate women without disaggregating their own integrity.

Eve's consequential volition stands as a reference point for the elaborate and potentially injurious reciprocities that shape heterosocial relations. Belsey writes, "Eve, who is necessary to ensure [Adam's] happiness, also destroys it; the woman created in order to contain desire within the Law proves to be herself anarchic."[66] However polemicists might moralize the fall, they circle back to the conclusion that everything depends on a woman's choice, and such knowledge is never safely historical. Recognition that women are vital parts in the machine carries a sense of suspended certainty, as the imperative "must" gives way to the speculative "might" and—less tentative but more disquieting—to the declarative "will" of feminine subjects themselves. Gataker writes of the good wife, "Let her consider what a fearefull thing it is to bee otherwise. For her that was made for *a helpe*, to prove not an helpe but an hurt: for her that was given for a blessing, to prove a crosse and a curse. As one saith of *Eve*, *reaft from Adam as a rib, and shot by Satan at him as a shaft*: bestowed on him by God to consummate his felicitie, but made by Satans slight and her owne default, the meanes of his extreme miserie."[67] Women might always be otherwise, their good will in default; but in the very possession of that will they are too close to home. "Reaft from Adam as a rib, and shot by Satan at him as a shaft": misogynist discourse emanates not from the objective distance of the judge, but from the fearful nearness of the target.

Liftyng Up the Vayle of Natures Secretes, in Womens Shapes

The ricochet effect of polemics might point to reticence as the wiser course: "Thucidides was of opinion, that those wemen were most honest, of whose commendation and disprayse there is least speech used."[68] Misogynist discourse accumulates a long history of ignoring this advice, which reaches one of its peaks in the blazon's extravagance of praise and blame. Karen Newman writes, "These descriptions of gestural obedience are part of a rhetorical disciplining of the female body by fragmenting it, most emphatically perhaps in the *blason*. Anatomization was a strategy for managing femininity and controlling its uses."[69] The blazon gives us shorthand for the double talk, at once laudatory and antagonistic, through which masculine subjects discipline feminine objects, but it also gives particular contours to the concern with feminine will. Nancy Vickers famously describes the relationship between a Petrarchan speaker and his addressee: "he cannot allow her to dismember his body; instead he repeatedly, although reverently, scatters hers throughout his scattered rhymes."[70] Vickers's account, like Newman's, unveils the encoded conviction that feminine subjectivity requires a defensive response: conceits of poetic mastery, with their incongruous mix of dispersal and confinement, deploy the self-protective, contradictory tactics that masquerade as control. As Newman observes, "the fragmentation of the female body I have analyzed in marriage sermons, conduct books, and the like not only masters by dismembering but also threatens such mastery through that very dispersion and the semiotic instabilities it sets in motion."[71]

Blazons isolate fragments in order to capture larger concepts, and secure that tenure through rhetorical shifts from one piece to the next. They might in this way cut off the escape routes of metonymic figuration, harnessing both synecdoche and contiguity toward the aesthetic absorption of the body described. Patricia Parker defines the blazon in such terms: "Like Keats's Grecian urn, it is both stasis and movement, *pictura* and descriptive narrative at once."[72] Metonymies disrupt symbolic stasis with mobile affiliation; blazons reconcile these processes when they imply that movement across parts demonstrates ownership of the collected work. As desire subsumes all sites of meaning, it becomes the instrument of a single articulate intention. This, I think, is the cultural fantasy that confers the form's imaginative power: read in this way—taken at its word—the blazon assuages the discomforts of interdependence by segregating an exclusive subject of volition. Bruce Smith writes, "The poet, not the mistress, is the *subject*, in every sense of the word. Seen in its rhetorical context, a Petrarchan sonnet is a power ploy of speaker over listener; seen in its social context, it is a power-ploy of a man over a woman; seen in its sexual context, it is power-ploy of male over female."[73] As metonyms for heterosocial hierarchy, women work well and only well, their will a muted echo of the will that engulfs their sense.

The close link between assimilation and display leads Jonathan Sawday to associate poetic anatomies with corporeal dissections. "Just as the courtiers relished the opportunity to demonstrate their wit over and above the female body, so the physicians and anatomists could consume bodies—particularly female bodies—in front of an admiring, and largely male audience."[74] Disarticulation, whether material or linguistic, supplies digestible feminine bodies to feed the communal appetites of men. Such indulgences have their risks, as Sawday indicates when he projects the anatomist into a liaison with Medusa: "the attributes of the Medusa—blood, head, and skin—are emblematic of a fragmented and dispersed body-interior—a profoundly ambivalent region— whose power can be somehow harnessed for good or ill."[75] The phrase "for good or ill" reminds us that even a dead Medusa poses some tricky problems, but Freud, at least, has a solution. In his account of the man who is turned to stone, he reads paralysis as erection and enables the sufferer to repossess himself: "To display the penis (or any of its surrogates) is to say: 'I am not afraid of you. I defy you. I have a penis.'"[76] And if Freud's subject sounds just a little silly, Medusa, like the Petrarchan object, does not speak at all. On a flight to Italy, I read a phrasebook that included the sentence, "Non sento il mio collo" (I do not feel my neck). When might one need such a phrase? Is it literally, somatically, possible to use it? In Florence I went with Lynn Enterline to see the statue of Perseus holding Medusa's head. "Non sento il mio collo," she said. I took her point: sometimes the ventriloquist has the only voice.

But as Enterline has so convincingly demonstrated, ventriloquism is a dangerous game, and Medusa's head may be no one's puppet. "Medusa's story tells us that in an Ovidian universe, the capacity for aesthetic pleasure may give way, with but the slightest of turns, to a total evacuation of the self."[77] Scholars drawing on and departing from Vickers emphasize that there is nothing objective about the process of objectification; its compensatory gymnastics manifest the tenuous states of rhetorical and sexual mastery.[78] In the cultural fantasy I have sketched, an anatomy can produce a polemic, and a polemic can take shape as a poem. Those slippages—between material practices and ideological projects, between poetic conceits and social agendas, between feminine subjects and feminized corpses—might confirm the pervasive power of hierarchies based on sex. Yet sex is an unstable foundation for such premises. In a practice that crosses a range of disciplines, expositive texts often use sexualized vocabularies to assert that active figures do things to inert figures: the sonnet's speaker prevails because he talks, the prospective father, because he thinks, the anatomist, because he is less dead. None of these privileges has any claim to immutability; all are constituted through relation rather than in isolation; and each identifies difference as situational rather than absolute.[79] Taxonomies are embedded in proximities, reciprocities, and dependencies, and metonymy has a greedy reach, drawing neatly severed objects into eccentric ambits of meaning that a hierarchical imperative neither encompasses nor apprehends.[80]

Claims of mastery record a wish to set limits, to confine the scope of knowledge within the compass of proprietary jurisdiction and expunge what does not fit. John Banister, having spent more than seven pages describing male sexual organs, refuses to go farther, "because I am from the begynnyng perswaded, that, by liftyng up the vayle of Natures secretes, in womens shapes, I shall commit more indecencie agaynst the office of *Decorum*, then yeld needefull instruction to the profite of the common sort."[81] Through this emphatic silence, Banister opposes knowledge to control; information might propagate at random, and the "secrets" he cites not only concern dangerous subjects but threaten to create them. Katharine Eisaman Maus compellingly connects physical mysteries to the enigmas of subjectivity: "In sixteenth- and early seventeenth-century England the bodily interior is still mysterious in a way perhaps hard to recapture in an age of medical sophistication, and in a way quite precisely analogous to the mysteriousness of human motives and desires."[82] The threat to regulation, of the self and of others, is always inside; alien intentions and desires circulate within the persons and systems that engage in the projects of government. Any decision to ask too much or look too hard carries the penalty of an intolerable understanding, which fractures the surface of coherent formations and invites unassimilated agents to appear in the gaps. Banister's reticence is a conceit, as motivated as it is conventional: it protects the observer from a perilous encounter not just with the secrets women contain, but with the alterity they might reveal or impose.

We are back at Medusa's head, which, with its history of capricious devastation, distills the possibility that women influence and alter the possessive trajectories they ignite. In *The Anatomy of Melancholy*, Robert Burton tells a provocative story: "A company of young Philosophers on a time, fell at variance, which part of a woman was most desiderable and pleased best? some said the forehead, some the teeth, some the eyes, cheeks, lips, neck, chin, etc. the controversie was referred to *Lais* of *Corinth* to decide; but she smiling, said, they were a company of fools; for suppose they had her where they wished, what would they first seek?"[83] This seems designed to satisfy masculine desire on multiple levels; a woman co-opted to complete her own blazon signifies both authorial control and sexual conquest. Burton's imagined scene evokes Lorna Hutson's account of "persuasive communication," which, she argues, strengthens authority and coalition in new ways: "the claim to be able to 'fashion' women by addressing them through persuasive fictions of themselves lent a special social credibility to the masculine activity of authorship."[84] In this sense, the ventriloquism of feminine acquiescence should consolidate masculine homosocial power. But as Burton's next sentence implies—"Yet this notwithstanding," it begins—the story does not take him where he wants to go. The problem lies in being taken: this kind of persuasive fiction subjects men to a knowing manipulation of desire, and the triumph of possessive attainment devolves into a relinquishment of will. Any such surrender dislocates other fixtures as well; masculine subjects cede the agency of appraisal, forfeiting their power to determine the value of a contract, the nature of an interaction, or the significance of a response. The distance between "no" and "yes" collapses under the weight of feminine choice, as both the object who denies and the object who invites revise the transitive property of objectification itself.

Monitory texts make the consequences explicit. Their cautionary tales illustrate failures of sexual government through women who combine cultural literacy with bodily capacity, investing the position of desired object with knowledge and purpose. These aversive examples often appear in blazon form, as when *A Briefe Anatomie of Women* describes a series of willful parts:

> The golden tresses of their amorous hair . . . doth manifestly express the true performance of their dutie to their great Lord and master *Lucifer*, in observing so well his livery. . . .
>
> Their roling eies, like shining pearl, seem to be the baits that insnare men in their love, whose fruit is destruction,
>
> Their ears delight to entertain frivolous discourses, especially if it relate to their praise and commendation, which is to them a thing most plausable. Their tongue [is a] stirring and active member, both defensive and offensive. . . .
>
> Their Lips are the Posterns from whence issueth lying, deceit, and all manner of dissimulation.
>
> Their neck and brests are left bare unto the open view of the world to signifie that nature hath fairly acted her part without, although there remain no grace within.
>
> Their Arms and Hands are ever ready to perform their respective duties unto the other parts of the bodie, whether good or evil: Their bodie it self is a magazine of corrupt and ill humors, which hath continual recourse to all the rest of the members: Their Thighs are the ascent unto this frail fabrick of corruption, their legs the supporters, and their feet swift guides to the waies of vanity; so that from the crown of their head to the sole of the foot, there is not a good member, no not one.[85]

This list indexes an arsenal—the body's "magazine"—that is turned against the speaker.[86] Rich, too, itemizes feminine sexual will in active bodily terms: "she hath a tongue to traine, *eyes* to allure, *lookes* to attract, *teares* to excuse *Smiles* to flatter, *Inticements* to provoke, *Frownes* to delay, *Beckes*, to recall, *Lippes*, to inchant, *kisses* to inflame, a *body* to performe, and all these to poison."[87] *Hic Mulier* admonishes women, "But for those things which belong to this wanton and lascivious delight and pleasure: as eyes wandring, lips bylling, tongue inticing, bared brests seducing, and naked armes imbracing: O hide them, for shame hide them in the closest prisons of your strictest government.''[88] Framed by the outline of the blazon, tracing its course and listing its parts, descriptions of intentional objects remap the vectors of desire.

In an analysis of Marot's blazon and counter-blazon of the breast, Vickers writes, "Between the 'moments' of these two texts there is a discontinuity, a gap, a time suggested but unspoken: in the blazon, we read ripeness (the untouched breast); in the counterblazon, we read depletion (the overtouched breast); but we never read fulfillment (the touch)."[89] By withholding contact, blazons and counter-blazons assert dominion over sexual value: they reach for the prerogative of judgment as they fail or refuse to seize the body itself. The examples I have quoted dismantle that exclusive authority, populating the temporality of touch and locating the drive to fulfillment in the body described. Consummation matters far less than the will that compels or prohibits it; when that will inheres in women, wantonness and decorum have equal power to detach choice from men. A volitional shift reveals the full force of heteroerotic compulsion, and anticipates its end in ruin: "they lay out the foldes of their haire, to entangle men into their love; betwixt their brests is the vale of destruction, and in their beds there is hell, sorrow and repentance."[90] Transported and transfigured, the blazon remains what it has always been, an argument grounded in the matter of its undoing. As Julia Kristeva reminds us, "In 'artistic' practices the semiotic—the precondition of the symbolic—is revealed as that which also destroys the symbolic."[91]

Burton directly connects the apparitional mastery of the blazon to the instability of heterosocial contracts, arguing that all the conceits in the world cannot guarantee a good marriage. "Let her head be from *Prage*, paps out of *Austria*, belly from *France*, back from *Brabant*, hands out of *England*, feet from *Rhine*, buttocks from *Switzerland*, let her have the *Spanish* gate, the *Venetian* tyre, *Italian* complement and endowments . . . after she hath been married a small while, and the black oxe hath trodden on her toe, she will be so much altered, and wax out of favour, thou wilt not know her."[92] The familiar point about beauty and time culminates in estrangement, an outcome already implicit in that set of outlandish parts; aesthetic manipulation fails to secure what it grasps, and socialized desire fades from a durable solution to a palliative device. Changeable attachments are consequential, as Constance Jordan's account of unbound wives makes clear. "The disorderly woman signifies the putting back into competitive play of objects that have already been assigned a use, a time and place of operation, and an interest or purpose."[93] If rhetorical dissection and marriage guard against mobile feminine meanings, Burton caricatures these defenses. His hyperbolic blazon insists that women cannot be fixed in time, place, or use, and his prognosis for an advantageous match mocks the goals of social acquisition: "thou shalt be as the Tassell of a gosse-hauke," he promises, *she will ride upon thee, domineer as she list*, wear the breeches in her oligarchicall government, and beggar thee besides."[94]

Despite that "oligarchicall government," sexual conquest is not a game women win. Instead I suggest that these odd progresses along feminine bodies, which reach for something unapprehended and valorize a mastery that tends toward alienated will, comment on the limitations of hierarchy and taxonomy as descriptive methods or disciplinary modes. Across disparate contexts, a poetics of vivisection describes the purpose of women—both their use and their intent—as mobile, capacious, unpredictably evocative, and anything but dead. Rather than capture feminine objects, blazons sketch the volatile interrelations that lie beneath fictions of control. Even as misogyny distributes praise and blame, it locates heterosocial subjects within a reciprocal discursive and erotic system, visible in the concluding couplet of Shakespeare's Sonnet 138: "Therefore I lie with her, and she with me, / And in our faults by lies we flattered be." If such economies attest to a wary cynicism, they also call upon a generative intersubjectivity, a slip from coercion toward consent. The effects are inseparable: a tacit acknowledgement of interdependence does not enable us to excavate an egalitarian ideal from the ruinous project of subordination. The tension between these structures does, however, provide a rationale for the ambivalence and incoherence with which misogynist discourse addresses feminine will.

Cast the Realism Aside—Its Consequences for Women Are Deadly

When theorists of feminine will foreground the centrality of choice, they recognize—often both explicitly and unhappily—that the terms and products of virtue are performative effects. Volition translates the prescribed functions of objects into the purposeful acts of subjects. "If she be faire, thy house shall then bee a Stage, the people Spectators, and thy wife the Actor of a Comedy": disillusionment inflects this comment, but does not diminish the importance of the illusion itself.[95] Comedies produce marriages, after all, and the wife who plays her part well enough answers the question of whether she is good enough. Performance supersedes empirical proof, pointing not to an opposition of truth and show but to an inscrutable link between them;

whether naive or skeptical, spectators can respond only to figures who act as they are supposed to do. "Supposed" implicates both prescription and assumption, and the convergence of these meanings forecloses access to their differences. From the site of an authority they both reflect and constitute, women articulate ideological imperatives. Jardin takes this to its logical extreme when he writes, "If thou desirest to have children of thine owne, I wil tell thee what thou shalt doe: Cause the mother that beares them, to bestowe them as a gift upon thee, wherupon thou maist then, without lying, say they are thine owne."[96] This satiric yet pragmatic advice identifies mothers as the authors of plausible lines: they confer paternity as a gift, constructing an assurance in response to a demand. This may be a good act or a bad one; such judgments are suppressed by efficacy on one side and need on the other. Feminine will affirms social certainties through persuasive simulacra, and even if women can be taken at their word, what does it mean that they get to say?

To frame that question, we might turn to a sex toy catalogue, perhaps the ultimate source of performative gifts. The video section of one catalogue includes a page headed "Lesbian and All-Girl Porn." It seems imaginable that all-girl porn might have some consonance with lesbianism, but the catalogue erects a partition between what one does and who one is. "Unlike most lesbian-themed adult videos, this charming tape features lesbian characters (not straight girls on a lark), authentic orgasms and terrific chemistry between stars."[97] The touchstone of authenticity unites person to persona, and divides that fidelity from itinerant play. To the irresistible question "how do we know," the only available answers are "because they say so" and "because they act that way," and the only reference point is the "lesbian character." An establishment that sells discretionary penises, "more realistic than the real thing," also markets knowledge of the true and the false. I cite this catalogue not to cast doubt on lesbian porn—or indeed on the discretionary penis—but rather to note that when we invest ourselves in a performance, we apply motivated criteria to preconceived evidence. Women may be faking it, or they may be doing it for real. But in either case they are doing it, performing roles that an interlocutor's requirements not only inscribe on their bodies but put in their hands.

This connects closely to Joan Riviere's account of "the conception of womanliness as a mask, behind which man suspects some hidden danger."[98] In *A Discourse Against Painting and Tincturing of Women*, the subtitle of which promises to "discover" the hidden dangers of murder, poisoning, pride, ambition, adultery, and witchcraft, Thomas Tuke addresses the relationship between being and seeming. "It is not enough to be good, but she that is good, must seeme good: she that is chast, must seeme chast: shee that is humble, must seeme humble: shee that is modest, must seeme to bee so. . . . It is not enough for Christian chastitie that it be, but that it be also seene."[99] In *The English Gentlewoman*, Richard Brathwait takes a rather different approach; he writes of the virtuous woman, "Her desire is to *be*, rather than *seeme*, lest *seeming* to *be* what she *is not*, shee gull the world, but her selfe most, by playing the counterfeit."[100] As this juxtaposition implies, artifactual virtue resists explication: women who choose to seem may be no better than they should be, but they may be no worse.[101] The practice of seeming is suspect, and, to recur to Riviere's term, dangerous: "If she seeme to love thee, thou eatest and drinkest, and sleepest with a spie," Jardin warns.[102] It is also crucial to the execution of social contracts. Volitional acquiescence animates a paradox of self-possessed instrumentality: willing women enact autonomous intentions in the service of regulatory codes. If womanliness is a masquerade, the "hidden danger" it conceals might be that feminine subjects know what they are doing.

The danger is not particularly well hidden. Misogynist clichés revolve around the premise that virtue, whether earnest or assumed, is always an impersonation: it lends a body to a social requisite. That premise does not expose hypocrisy, but reframes authenticity as the byproduct of situational needs. Volition forges a bond between acting good and acting well, and if that coincidence inspires misgivings, it also disables the mechanisms that would separate expediency from truth. In her analysis of *The Taming of the Shrew*, Holly Crocker writes, "Katharine's pose of submission, which must be at once sincere and artificial, is thus the most destabilizing aspect of the play."[103] Awareness that choice infuses decorum with a workable plausibility fails to reveal that women are really something else; instead it poses a far more intractable dilemma by revealing nothing at all. Riviere's turn to the "genuine" elucidates the point. Her proposition hints that the greatest challenge is not to distinguish the fake from the real, but to understand that this is the wrong question: "The reader may now ask how I define womanliness or where I draw the line between genuine womanliness and the 'masquerade'. My suggestion is not, however, that there is any such difference; whether radical or superficial, they are the same thing."[104] The opacity of that statement mirrors the citational enigma of masquerade. For an early modern rendition we might turn to Shakespeare's Timon, who places this curse on his own feast: "If there sit twelve women at the table, let a dozen of them be—as they are."[105]

Sue-Ellen Case's "Toward a Butch-Femme Aesthetic" argues that, when roles supply the place of reality, "a strategy of appearances replaces a claim to truth," exposing the radical potential of citations that refuse to refer. "Thus, butch-femme roles evade the notion of 'the female body' as it predominates in feminist theory, dragging along its Freudian baggage and scopophilic transubstantiation. These roles are played in signs themselves and not in ontologies."[106] When signs break free from compulsory truths, roles become tools and toys, invested with the energy of strategic realization. In "A Fem(me)inist Manifesto," Lisa Duggan and Kathleen McHugh unfold conditions of performance that trifle with a hopelessly insufficient "real." "Fem(me) is neither an ideal nor a category. She makes a scene, an entrance, an appearance—she steals the show (she *is* the show) of difference, but she cannot be fixed as a certain effect 'in itself.' Fem(me) is always inter-actionable, never onanistic or narcissistic. Mirrors are not the pool in which she drowns; they are the instrument or metaphor of her essential irony."[107] The show of difference nominated as "fem(me)" sets its scene against a backdrop of cultural expectations, and unfixes their meanings as it interacts with their forms. Performance does not jettison the notion of identity, but renders it inseparable from elusive figuration; making an appearance exploits the power of seeming as it stakes a claim on being, but a "being" in which the only essence is irony. Constellations of exploded reference points illuminate spectacular subjectivities that stage a mobile gloss on categories and ideals. Like Johnson's reading of an irreducible gap, these theories repudiate "what" for "how": how do subjects signify, and how do they alter the systems through which they mean?

Queer performances oppose the ideological agendas of misogyny and display its disavowed recognition: femininity is an artifact produced through volitional habitation and self-referential masquerade. Judith Halberstam grounds the histrionic extremes of camp in the theatrical quality of feminine roles: "because camp is predicated on exposing and exploiting the theatricality of gender, it tends to be the genre for an outrageous performance of femininity (by men or women) rather than outrageous performances of masculinity."[108] Halberstam's conclusion—"camp is always about femininity"—invites a complementary speculation: femininity, even in its most domesticated forms, might always have something to do with outrageous performance. Traub argues that the early modern femme confronts orthodox arrangements with an unsettling contiguity: "Because the femme inhabits a point proximate to proper 'femininity', she poses a unique threat to patriarchal gender and, in the seventeenth century, to the manufacture and consolidation of heterosexual desire."[109] Questionable associates might precipitate proper femininity into those ambiguous quotation marks; but then, women who participate in heterosocial intimacies often appear as rather questionable associates as well. Case's call to arms—"Cast the realism aside—its consequences for women are deadly"[110]—responds to a long campaign that seeks to eradicate ambiguity through essentialist reduction. It would be hard to overstate the impetus of that campaign, or the wreckage it has left behind. Yet for all its oppressive power, misogynist discourse is enmeshed in contingency, its master narratives interrupted and reshaped by the counterfactual logic that transforms objects into subjects and multiplies sites of will.

Duggan and McHugh imagine a phantom meeting of the feminine and the femme: "Historically, the feminine arises apparently ego-less, bereft of active drives, agency, mobility, thought. The fem(me) haunts this historical aberration from within and without. What the feminine represses returns from inside and outside as the future of desire. Refusing the fate of Girl-By-Nature, the fem(me) is Girl-by-Choice."[111] A history of passive femininity haunted by an immanent volitional ghost: this might be the other story of misogyny, stubbornly articulate and imperfectly repressed. It resonates, too, with Carla Freccero's proposal for an alternative historiography: "The past is in the present in the form of a haunting. This is what, among other things, doing a queer kind of history means, since it involves an openness to the possibility of being haunted, even inhabited, by ghosts."[112] If misogynist discourse seems profoundly unwilling to be haunted, it nonetheless haunts itself with the specter of feminine will. Misogyny is its own queer history, a dominant narrative that invests the trope of authorial ventriloquism with an estranged vitality. What if we take seriously, even for a moment, the conceits of obligation, necessity, and self-defense, the claims of writing because one must, even if against one's will? Toward or about or through whose will does the misogynist then write? In asking this, we might unravel the equation of speaking subject with exclusive subject, and make sense of the surplus agents who erupt into univocal texts. If we look at misogynist discourse, however fleetingly and fantastically, as the compulsory, overpopulated enterprise it claims to be—if we in *this* sense take it at its word—we find a labyrinth of volitional intersections. Does shifting the angle change the story? At the very least, it suggests that there is something unmethodical about a structure haunted by its own familiars.

In all thine Actions, have a care,
That no unseemlinesse appeare.

DECEAT·VT·NE·QVID

.91.

Chapter Four

"My Intents are Fix'd"

Constant Will in *All's Well*
That Ends Well

This is a vice in them, that were a vertue in us; for obstinacy in a bad cause, is but constancy in a good.

—Browne, *Religio Medici*, 48

The fickleness of women I love is only equaled by the infernal constancy of the women who love me.

—Shaw, *The Philanderer*, 121 (Act 2)

"What Does the Woman Want?"

For a romantic comedy, *All's Well That Ends Well* has an intractable image problem. "It has been customary since the late nineteenth century to call *All's Well That Ends Well* a 'problem play,'" one introduction begins,[1] inviting a question which, despite the historical weight of custom and consensus, should be more than rhetorical: what exactly causes the trouble? Throughout the play, the feminine protagonist remains constant to an ideal of chaste marriage, yet her pursuits inspire uneasy reactions onstage and off. One source of disquiet, of course, is that they *are* pursuits: for choosing and chasing her desired object until he succumbs to something more like exhaustion than bliss, Helena has been charged with faults ranging from an excess of ambition to a lack of discrimination. And yet, when one considers that the marital strategies of Shakespearean comedy range from eloping to cross-dressing to other acts of bed tricking, Helena's reputation for extravagance invites attention. *All's Well* somehow tempts the sort of misremembering that veils the violence of *Romeo and Juliet* behind the mists of the balcony scene, or restricts Hamlet to ineffectual navel-gazing, or translates Cordelia's silence as

Figure 5 (preceding page). "In all thine *Actions*, have a care, / That no *unseemlinesse appeare*." Illustration XLI, Book 4, in George Wither, *A Collection of Emblemes, Ancient and Moderne* (London: Augustine Mathewes for Richard Royston, 1635), 249. By permission of the Folger Shakespeare Library.

a refusal to lie: Helena becomes a type of the disorderly woman, her conservative motives knocked out of bounds by an excess of desire. That she seeks legitimate endorsement of a socially sanctioned bond tends to slip the mind, as if the messiness of her bed trick, which entangles indiscretion with redemption, eclipses its neat result. Annabel Patterson's comment on a more abstract critical tradition—"It is surprising how often past discussions of intention have promulgated axioms, rules, and even prohibitions"—is markedly germane to the regulatory and proscriptive impulses that have trailed Helena through literary history.[2] The ambivalence she stirs up inflects and echoes the tone of *All's Well*, a late comedy in which the project of socialized desire leaves conventions of gender and genre notoriously strained.

Helena's willful constancy imposes that strain. Passively construed, constancy might reflect well on its possessor and on the system it protects; William Baldwin writes, "Naturally in times past wyves were adurned with these vertues, that is to be shamefast in theire visages, temperate in woordes, wyse of wytte, sober in goinge, meke in conversacion, pitifull in correccion well regarding their livyng, not keping companies, stedfast in promise, and constant in love."[3] Baldwin prescribes through nostalgia, and in this way avoids overt discussion of intent and effect; at the same time, by presenting a catalogue of behavioral choices that culminates in constant love, he implicitly brings those issues to the fore. From Helena's attachment to Demetrius in *A Midsummer Night's Dream*, which leaves him permanently bewildered and enchanted, to Britomart's commitment to Artegall in *The Faerie Queene*, which leaves him repeatedly confused and unhorsed, feminine devotion alters men. Such examples, however strange in their specificities, condense a more general recognition: in its resolute adherence to a proper object, constancy is a consequential feminine act that intersects masculine identity in vital and unsettling ways. Aggressively directed to an admirable end, Helena's tenacious virtue reveals that the exclusive allegiance of women has the power to make men, not only as bodies but as social subjects.

Women who assert constancy are subjects of their own discourse, even as they are subjects in an ideological sense as well, constituted by a prescriptive force which ensures, in Louis Althusser's famous phrase, "they 'work all by themselves.'"[4] Slavoj Žižek points out that Althusserian ideology rests on a presumption of ignorance: "'*ideological*' *is a social reality whose very existence implies the non-knowledge of its participants as to its essence*—that is, the social effectivity, the very reproduction of which implies that the individuals 'do not know what they are doing.' "[5] But as Helena's performance suggests, constant women may know exactly what they are doing, and may do it with a great deal of calculation. While it might be too simple to say that knowledge is power, knowledge of this kind unsettles the naturalized organization of power among men. Žižek identifies women as ideologically disruptive, and locates that effect in the opacity of their desire.

> It is this intuition which is behind the ill-famed male chauvinist wisdom that "woman is a whore": woman is a whore because we never know what she means—for example, she says "No!" to our advances, but we can never be sure that this "No!" does not really mean a double "Yes!"—an appeal to an even more aggressive approach; in this case, her real desire is the very opposite of her demand. In other words, "woman is a whore" is a vulgar version of the unanswerable Freudian question *Was will das Weib?* ("What does the woman want?").[6]

All's Well interrupts this misogynist monologue, imagining a woman who turns to the structures that define her—patrilineality, hierarchy, romantic comedy—and poses the question: "What do *you* want?" Beyond this, the play implies that the question is largely rhetorical, the inverted articulation of an answer already known. Žižek writes of the disingenuous demand, "the best way to frustrate it is to comply with it, to consent to it without reservation."[7] Helena's willed constancy shows that this effect escalates when demand and response converge in formulaic earnestness: a cooperative logic falters under the weight of its substantiation.

Throughout *All's Well*, Helena plays prescribed roles: father's daughter, king's subject, husband's wife, heir's mother. She acts according to the letter, which lends a nice irony to Bertram's letter to her, in which he defies the King's command and the conventions of marriage: "When thou canst get the ring upon my finger, which never shall come off, and show me a child begotten of thy body that I am father to, then call me husband; but in such a 'then' I write a 'never'" (3.2.57–60).[8] Helena's response defuses his defiance, insisting instead on a proper order that Bertram can neither embody nor speak. "I am your most obedient servant"; "I shall not break your bidding, good my lord"; "In every thing I wait upon his will" (2.5.72; 2.5.88; 2.4.54). Where Bertram's willful tyranny puts individual masculine authority at odds with social regulation, Helena's willing submission reconciles the particular to the general, localizing the aphorisms of feminine virtue. But in her determination to embody an ideal—"Who ever strove / To show her merit, that did miss her love?" (1.1.226–27)—Helena identifies her constancy as a volitional mode, which fulfills social requirements not through passive nature but with active purpose. Richard Brathwait writes of Eve, "the *Subject* whereof she was made begot not in her a *crookednesse*, but *pliablenesse* of nature: ever ready to *bend* her will, and apply her affection to the mould of Man: not cruelly to domineere, but constantly to adhere to her Mate."[9] An anodyne parable with a caustic touch, this genealogy of feminine accommodation articulates the problem of Helena's virtuous intent. Constancy fuses determination to acquiescence ("ever ready to bend her will"), and such self-government is a wild card—not because its guarantees are not true, but because these truths, however self-evident, may not signify in predictable ways.

Forcible Application of Direction

Misogynist discourse tends to represent constancy in negative terms, defined by its wayward yet destined failure. The prospect of feminine sexual choice conjures up inconstancy—an unseemly selection of too many or the wrong one—as when Thommaso Buoni, in *Problemes of Beautie*, refers to "the inconstancie of a woman, her facilitie to bee perswaded, and the small resistance shee maketh against her unbridled appetite, which together leade her to her utter ruine."[10] Nor is this really a matter of choice at all; as Baldwin writes, "We note in children inconstancye, and likewise in weomen, thone for slendernes of wittes, and thother as a naturall sickenes."[11] The only agency attributed to constant women is that of deception, figured in the emblem in *The Theater of Fine Devices* which depicts a woman shaking hands with a man who holds an eel. The accompanying poem reads,

> A womans constancy is even as sure,
> As if one held an Eele fast by the taile,
> Her faith nor love do never long endure,
> But fleete away as Sunne doth melt the haile:
> As many authors, Greeke and Latine pure,
> Have left in writing for our more availe,
> > That womens words mens eares do so delight,
> > They make them oft beleeve the crow is white.[12]

The female speaker of *The Arte of Love* makes a similar point, informing readers, in highly elliptical terms, that women may be exactly as constant as they are unscrutinized. "Thinke not but mens constancie in love must needs goe beyond ours," she warns, "for men bee lesse suspitious than wee are; therefore they have the greater wisedome and government."[13] Feminine constancy is a byproduct of masculine credulity, an acute and cynical observation on heterosocial mechanics that yokes good government to blind faith.

The contention that women can't help themselves is a reflexive defense, and like many such defenses it fundamentally, pragmatically, does not work: misogyny dismisses constant women as figments of a hopeful imagination, but patrilineal succession relies on their substantial presence. In her analysis of the conflicted relationship between humoral volatility and contractual bonds, Katherine Rowe writes, "The routinized, clichéd quality of complaints about female inconstancy can obscure the deep conceptual paradoxes they mark."[14] *All's Well* elaborates such a paradox in its treatment of Helena's will, an ambivalently valued faculty that exposes her to rote disparagement even as it enables her to produce and validate Bertram's heir. Feminine volition has the potential to revise or dismantle social organization, to challenge masculine entitlement or forge exclusive feminine bonds;[15] but for *All's Well*, as for the cultural logic the play cites and dissects, constancy operates primarily and indispensably to secure heterosocial relations. When Brathwait tells the story of a woman who physically humiliates a man in defense of her chastity, his introductory gloss—"this Maiden-constancy in one of our owne"—raises thorny issues of interconnection and control.[16] Whose ownership, and of what or whom, does such a moral victory prove? What needs does it disclose or answer, and what certainties does it restore or disturb?

A number of readers trace a pattern in *All's Well* that alternately incites and assuages fear of women; in such accounts, Helena's performance offers a portrait of excess at one moment, a parable of decorum at the next.[17] Yet these readings, like the play to which they respond, controvert a straightforward progress from insurrection to submission. Critics who address the either/or impulses of *All's Well* disclose the persistence of both; in Janet Adelman's words, "Nearly from the beginning, we have been invited to see Helena both as a miraculous virgin and as a deeply sexual woman seeking her will."[18] Other critics, as they respond to that duality with aversion or disavowal, in effect restate Bertram's case, from Sir Arthur Quiller-Couch's conclusion that Helena "is perhaps too 'efficient' to engage our complete sympathy" to David Scott Kastan's description of "a tenacity too nearly predatory to be completely attractive or satisfying."[19] Whether such comments reveal the play's preoccupations or our own—and the line is, at the very least, blurred—Helena excites a discomfort that shades toward misogyny.[20] But by presenting her desire as the force that restores and sustains social stability, *All's Well* disables conventional distinctions between passive conformity and active impropriety. Stock footage of a woman who pursues, deceives, entraps, and ultimately subdues a man is projected onto a screen of benignly authoritarian approval. The scheming, voracious, disingenuous woman and the woman who fulfills the obligations of virgin, wife, and mother are neither opposites nor even alter egos, but the same figure read twice. In an early speech to Parolles, Helena maps the uneven terrain of synthesis:

> There shall your master have a thousand loves,
> A mother, and a mistress, and a friend,
> A phoenix, captain, and an enemy,
> A guide, a goddess, and a sovereign,
> A counselor, a traitress, and a dear;
> His humble ambition, proud humility;
> His jarring concord, and his discord dulcet;
> His faith, his sweet disaster; with a world
> Of pretty, fond, adoptious christendoms
> That blinking Cupid gossips. (1.1.166–75)

Describing this figure as "composite and indeed oxymoronic," David Bevington observes, "Helena seems to be talking about herself."[21] As she compiles qualities without regard for coherence, Helena writes all the emblematic mottoes on a single page. She integrates an irreducible multiplicity, and as interlocutors we echo her effect, drawing pictures too large for categorical constraints. Helena is not the quintessential fractured subject; one of the problems for this problem play is that she doesn't seem fractured enough. Rather than separate disruptive volition from compliant orthodoxy, *All's Well* binds volition to orthodoxy in a single figure's multivalent acts. The result is an outrageously intentional, sexual, articulate, and efficient femininity that runs amok without doing anything wrong.

Helena's aggressions toward Bertram, her forceful revisions of his identity and futurity, occur within the contexts of authorized marriage and romantic comedy. By using desire to make social sense, she executes a purpose that is doubly determined, at once effect and cause of the structures within which she circulates: her intentions both reiterate and reanimate the requisites of heterosocial intercourse. In response to Parolles's raunchy banter about virginity, she seeks information rather than escape: "How might one do, sir, to lose it to her own liking?" (1.1.150–51). Here as throughout the play, Helena theorizes not only her position but the abstractions that inform it; she occupies situations of utterance that equate personal goals to social ends. As she deliberately does what the aims of marriage and comedy require, and requires in turn that marriage and comedy accomplish their aims, she interlocks her will with structural imperatives. "'Tis pity," she says, "That wishing well had not a body in't" (1.1.179, 181). The image of incorporate desire anticipates the bed trick that makes a body the vehicle of Helena's wish; at the same time, it forecasts accomplishment of the chanciest task of heterosocial ideology, the elusive transmutation of virginal separatism into chaste marriage. Faced with this and with the dissection of his own masculine imposture that follows, Parolles offers a peculiar promise. "I am so full of businesses, I cannot answer thee acutely. I will return perfect courtier, in the which my instruction shall serve to naturalize thee" (ll. 206–8).

"To naturalize thee": the formulation acknowledges that social subjects emerge from intentional work. That work is not Parolles's but Helena's own, as her last line of the scene makes clear: "my intents are fix'd, and will not leave me" (1.1.229). Meanings of the Latin *intentio* range from "a stretching out, straining, tension" to "a directing of the mind towards any thing," the latter encompassing "exertion, effort," "attention, application," and "a design, purpose."[22] The *Oxford English Dictionary*, under "intention," lists definitions that include "volition which one is minded to carry out," "a purpose, design," "stretching, tension," and, suggestively, "forcible application of direction." (By the eighteenth century, "intention," with retrospective aptness, also meant "purposes in respect of a proposal of marriage."[23]) In his nuanced analysis of these meanings, Luke Wilson describes intention as active knowledge that conceives its objective in acquisitive terms.

> *Intention*'s etymology points to the epistemological aspect of intention, which figures so importantly in modern use of the term "intentionality": an intentional object is an object toward which thought extends itself. The quasi-spatial language of reaching out situates an agent of thought at a certain essential distance from both mental objects and objects external to the mind, which the mind appropriates mentally, or at least makes mental contact with, through an

intentional mental act; intention is arguably part of a picture of the mental process founded in an appropriative epistemology in which knowing entails an act of mental acquisition.[24]

As Wilson suggests, distance motivates a trajectory of possession, in which conceptual apprehension has transitive, proprietary force. Intention constructs a grammar of purpose that takes an object; Helena's fixed intent is mobile, vectored, set not in a place but on a target. She may be governed by an autocratic impulse, but intention subsumes persons in order to make subjects, here the subject of "all's well" the proposition and *All's Well* the play. In this sense Helena recalls another meaning of *intentio*, "the first or major premise in a syllogism."[25] If the social and generic tenets of *All's Well* approach syllogistic certainty, they begin with the premise of a woman's intentional desire.

Through that close convergence of intention and desire, Helena mobilizes the full ambiguity of feminine will: without it, doctrines are impotent abstractions, but its efficiency is also its threat. Personified by early modern theorists as both a vital mediator and an autonomous actor, will is possessed of self-control and given to self-indulgence, an artifact of good government and an agent or *agent provocateur* of misrule. Pierre Charron characterizes it as the faculty of pursuit, which might generate ideal forms or succumb to improper attachments: "By the will, on the other side, the soule goeth foorth of it selfe, and lodgeth and liveth elswhere in the thing beloved, into which it transformeth it selfe; and therefore beareth the name, the title, the liverie, being called vertuous, vitious, spirituall, carnall."[26] Promise and peril coincide in the moment of consequential choice: a proper alliance vests subjects in virtue, a wrong turn condemns them to vice, and only when the decision is irretrievable can its outcome be assessed. These are the stakes of Helena's desire, which commits her to identity with her object and ransoms the future to the value of her bond. Richard Hooker argues that a perception of merit directs desire: "To choose is to will one thing before another. And to will is to bend our soules to the having or doing of that which they see to be good."[27] Virtue depends on self-regulation, which, if it echoes some larger directive, does so through a medium that might transmit or distort. "For some there are whose heart and Will agree so together, that there is no dissimulation," Pierre de la Primaudaye writes;[28] wholehearted volition produces truth in action, but that truth, like Hooker's discipline and Charron's contract, posits a world within the subject to frame precepts for subjects in the world. As these paradigms derive systems from persons, they not only gloss Helena's actions but describe her twofold role. At once driven by will and a figure for it, she instantiates the practices in which theory finds form.

Manifested in the King's revived potency, the Countess's patrilineal scheme, and the conjugal duty Bertram tries to disavow, social self-perpetuation revolves around Helena's acts of will. Structurally, Helena does not upset conventional arrangements; she speaks in the name of custom, asserting that kings should govern subjects, husbands master wives, and fathers determine children. But she is upsetting in that other, affective sense, exposing natural order as an engineered set of parts. Helena becomes the untimely voice of comic conclusions: she says "All's well that ends well" not once but twice (4.4.35, 5.1.25), and a resolution that should be intrinsic to the play's ending appears, as *her* resolution, in the midst of crucial plots. When she echoes Puck's "all shall be well," she speaks as a kind of *deus ex machina*. But "Jack shall have Jill" is not Jill's line, and Helena inhabits the machine for which she speaks.[29] In order to end well, the story requires Helena to tell it as she submits herself to it, an improbable double move reflected in the play's contortionist tricks. Her strategies impose a disconcerting visibility: heterosocial consolidation is a matter of medicines, money, letters, rings, books, bed tricks, and—perhaps—babies. The silent machinations of ideology become the creaking equipment of work. Barbara Hodgdon reads this as a mode of ventriloquism: "intent upon *meaning, deed, act* and *fact*, she seems distanced, apart, speaking more for the playtext's mechanism than for herself."[30] In the course of *All's Well*, it becomes increasingly difficult to distinguish mechanism from self, a coalescence that functions less to dehumanize Helena than to underline her oddly personal command of abstractions. The sense of something forced that shadows the play's festive gestures, appearing equally in their hesitancy and in their doggedness, reflects the vexed necessity of taking Helena at her word.

An Hawks Eye, a Ladies Hand, and a Lions Hart

All's Well refers explicitly to Helena's constancy when she presents herself as doctor to the King. The scene stresses the absurdity of a female physician, but turns the joke with Lafew's praise:

> King: What her is this?
> Lafew: Why, Doctor She! My lord, there's one arriv'd,

> If you will see her. Now by my faith and honor,
> If seriously I may convey my thoughts
> In this my light deliverance, I have spoke
> With one, that in her sex, her years, profession,
> Wisdom, and constancy, hath amaz'd me more
> Than I dare blame my weakness. (2.1.78–85)

Constancy links medical skill to the broader array of practices through which Helena imposes order on the play's unruly bodies. Medicine, with its arcane procedures, intimate interactions, and opportunities for deceit, foregrounds the indiscretions of knowledge and the mysteries of intention. Helena's incongruous proficiency thus gets at the crux of her role: she knows and does and means too much, even as she pursues fruitful work toward focused ends. The details of the King's disease and cure have inspired much speculation, but whatever we imagine about Helena's procedures, her expertise takes an edge from the fact that she possesses it at all. "The 'knowing' woman is only precariously a force for moral good," writes Lisa Jardine. "Lurking behind that moral front is the female sensuality which is readily released into potential for harm (specifically, harm to men)."[31] Feminine knowledge is intersubjective, a force measured by its impact on men. It is also, as if by default, sexual knowledge.

This constellation of ideas shapes anxieties about disclosure, which conflate objects and subjects, "about what" and "for whom," as they tie the problems of content to those of reception. *The Compleat Midwife's Practice* describes porous boundaries: "written for Gods glory, and the benefit and help of Mankinde, and intended onely for the use of sober, pious, and discret Matrons," the text still invites the charge that secrets have been overexposed, "prostituted to every unworthy Reader, that makes use of such things onely for a mockery, and a May-game, and to promote idle and lascivious discourse."[32] To tell at all might be to tell too much or too many, as Helkiah Crooke recognizes when he cautions male readers against excessive curiosity: "we will first describe the parts of generation belonging to men, and then proceed to those of Women also; of which wee would advise no man to take further knowledge then shall serve for his good instruction."[33] Women are indecorous objects because they can create improper subjects: a concern about contagion (men might be tainted by unsuitable facts) mirrors a fear about procreation (men might be ruined by unverified facts). The question of what it means to know women collides with the question of what women

know, about their own bodies and about the bodies they produce.[34] Men risk
more than innocence when they interrogate female sexuality too closely; they
imperil the belief system of hierarchical discretion and control. Valerie Traub
argues that medical writers displace responsibility for unseemly disclosures
onto women, and describes this misogynist move as "radically unstable":
"For, if fear is what renders the body of woman available as the abject figure
for what it means to know, this strategy uncannily turns back on men."[35]
Helena's role suggests that shared implication not only destabilizes authority,
but overpopulates the realm of knowledge. Medical treatises create a focal
point for the dangers of heterosocial proximity; when writers warn against
injudicious engagements, the subject they proscribe takes on active capacities,
and locates potential self-loss at the intersection of women and men.

"Bring in the admiration," the King instructs Lafew; to the audience,
"Thus he his special nothings ever prologues" (2.1.88, 92). The King sees
Helena as the symptom of a larger disease:

> I say we must not
> So stain our judgment, or corrupt our hope,
> To prostitute our past-cure malady
> To empirics, or to dissever so
> Our great self and our credit, to esteem
> A senseless help when help past sense we deem. (ll. 119–24)

The *Oxford English Dictionary* cites this passage in its definition of "empiric"
as "an untrained practitioner in physic or surgery; a quack."[36] The menace
of such dissemblers, who can adulterate a man's body and discredit his name,
duplicates the implicit threat of feminine sexual acts. Like the opaque façade
of virtue, the esoteric practice of medicine evokes theatricality; this association appears throughout *The Anatomyes of the True Physition, and Counterfeit
Mount-banke*, which excoriates false physicians as "Bragadocian *Thessali*,"
"disguised Maskers," and "Stage-players." "Neither doth the possession of a
great Library, and multitude of Bookes, make a man learned: no more then
Ajax armor would make *Thirsites* a stout Souldier," the author warns.[37] The
mountebank traduces a noble inheritance: "*Physiologye* the first Part of Phys-
icke, chalengeth for her Patrimony, those seven Things whereof our Nature
consisteth: Elements, Temperaments, Humours, Spirits, Parts, Faculties, and
Functions. Here is a large walke for our silly Empericke, as uncouth, and
unknowne to them, as *Terra-America, China*, or *Guiana*, to our poore Plough

men."[38] This same conviction, that an abused patrimony produces a false empiric, motivates the King's dismissal of Helena: "But what at full I know, thou know'st no part, / I knowing all my peril, thou no art" (2.1.132–33).

Empirically, as it were, the King is wrong. Yet the unclear line between truth and counterfeit inflects *All's Well* strongly, as Helena's defense indicates.

> I am not an imposture that proclaim
> Myself against the level of mine aim,
> But know I think, and think I know most sure
> My art is not past power, nor you past cure. (ll. 155–58)

The King's capitulation—"More should I question thee, and more I must—/ Though more to know could not be more to trust" (2.1.205–6)—does not banish the specter of imposture, but concedes that effective performance requires a close symbiosis of verisimilitude and credence. When Helena stakes her integrity and life against the King's dissolution and death, she offers a contract forged as much between actor and spectator as between woman and man, subject and monarch, or physician and patient. Her efficacy remains an act—an impersonation, as well as an intercession—even when it proves its worth, linking inscrutable masquerade to recuperative result. She figures the pluralities portrayed in Edward Forset's allegory of body and state: "Lastly, I will bestow upon our politicall Phisition that complement of qualities, which we usually look for in a Surgion; that is an Hawks eye, a Ladies hand, and a Lions hart."[39] Deft and inapt, Helena mixes such unlikely ingredients: she knows more than she should, but her knowledge serves a purpose; she plays a part, yet acts in good faith. As so often in this play, in doing what she unexpectedly can, she does what she presumptively should. "For who is neerer at hand, or fitter to minister comfort in such cases," Thomas Gataker writes, in a sermon titled "A Wife in Deed": "to cheere up a man in griefe and heavinesse, as *Davids Harpe* did *Saul*, to accompanie him, and attend him in sicknesse and weaknesse, as *Abishag* did *David*; to bee as a *Musitian* to him in the one, as a *Physitian* in the other."[40] Through a constant will that performs virtue as remedy, Helena regenerates a king with her own sovereign art.

That transaction dispels imminent mortality only by unraveling other certainties as well. The King declares,

> [O]ur most learned doctors leave us, and
> The congregrated college have concluded

That laboring art can never ransom nature
From her inaidible estate. (2.1.116–19)

The encounter between a woman who proclaims herself a doctor and a sovereign male body that declares itself dead evacuates the concept of stable actors. "The boundaries between principal, agent, instrument, and patient in bodily action, as they are carefully recorded, often shift and collapse," Rowe writes of anatomical transactions.[41] With the King's resolution, "for I, / Thy resolv'd patient, on thee still rely" (ll. 203–4), *All's Well* makes the borders between subjects as porous as those of the medicalized body itself. If the King dies, Helena does not affirm command over his body, but dies as well; if he lives, she is reinscribed as his subject but gains the authority of his word. Pursuing what she terms "the elusive ungendering of death," Traub argues that anatomical practices invalidate the precedence of distinction: "instead of expressing an essentialized vision of two preexisting and radically incommensurate genders, early modern anatomical illustrations demonstrate the extent to which gender is reciprocally *manufactured* in order to defend against the vulnerability to mortality that all bodies share."[42] *All's Well* stages its defense against death, but the subjects who survive trade fantasies of autonomy for a precarious and conditional interdependence. What ideology of gender has been manufactured here, and by whom?

All's Well deflects this question from origins to maintenance, and expands its compass from the idiosyncrasy of miracle to the constancy of everyday work. Within the complex machinery that manufactures subjects, feminine volition preserves masculine privilege. Women act so that men can be; in a turn on Parolles's line, they naturalize their own practices, and extend that effect to the system as a whole. Their understanding of and acquiescence in a heterosocial schematic coincides with its viability as a social institution. That correlation shows most clearly in the breach: when the Countess tells Helena, "He was my son, / But I do wash his name out of my blood, / And thou art all my child," she raises all those other, quieter speech acts into view (3.2.66–68). Having certified Bertram's lineage through faithful mediation, she undermines his identity by erasing herself from the equation. *All's Well* in this way insists on the priority of legible, articulate, and intentional bonds: maternal blood is not at issue in any narrowly material sense, but the rhetorical act of banishment calls up the entire network of relations that feminine knowledge might fabricate or undo.[43] The Countess anticipates and doubles Helena's interventions, which point to potential breakdowns as they reintegrate a husband and recuperate a king. "The plot of *All's Well That Ends Well* hinges on Helena's specialist knowledge, and on the power that knowledge gives her," Jardine writes.[44] "Specialist knowledge" is not limited to medicine, and a hinge, the play reminds us, is a complicated moving part.

For Helena, knowledge creates an intricate relationship between authenticity and enactment, from which she develops the enigmatic coherence of her intent. "No more of this, Helena; go to, no more, lest it be rather thought you affect a sorrow than to have," the Countess warns at the beginning of *All's Well*, to which Helena replies, "I do affect a sorrow indeed, but I have it too" (1.1.51–54). The surface distinction between grief for her father and pain over Bertram overlays a far denser and more textured fusion of modes. David McCandless writes, "When Helena seems to affect femininity for the sake of covering her unfeminine, predatory tracks, she may not be crudely dissembling but rather, like a good method actress who loses herself in the role, truthfully simulating, thereby authenticating the role demanded of her." McCandless describes this as "a kind of Lacanian misrecognition."[45] If Helena's social role clothes her in the "armour of an alienating identity" of which Lacan writes, the most suggestive aspect of this may be its infectious effect: as she conflates transparent truth with strategic display, recognitions form and disintegrate around her.[46] Like the King, the Countess knows what she sees, only to question what she knows: "It is the show and seal of nature's truth, / Where love's strong passion is impress'd in youth," she declares (1.3.132–33), and then, having reconceived evidence as pretense, calls for testimony to bolster proof. "Invention is asham'd, / Against the proclamation of thy passion, / To say thou dost not: therefore tell me true" (ll. 173–75). Looking twice yields double vision; when the conception of character merges identification *with* and identity *as*, distinctions give way to the strange integrity of paradox. Show and truth are not alternatives for Helena, but tracks along which two lines of impersonation—the practice of simulation and the constitution of personhood—converge.

Helena's flexible veracity underscores the extent to which masculine identity is hemmed in by constraint. *All's Well* plays with homosocial parthenogenesis, but exhibits an archetypal ideal trapped by its own success: as men make men, they become patrilineal vessels defined by their assimilation. A man who successfully reproduces himself is always that man, the same man; the more a son demonstrates continuity, the more his status as an individuated agent empties itself out. The Countess's first line—"In delivering my son from me, I bury a second husband" (1.1.1–2)—opens *All's Well* in the shadow of relentless generational replication. Bertram can only be his father's son; in the King's words,

Youth, thou bear'st thy father's face;
Frank Nature, rather curious than in haste,
Hath well compos'd thee. Thy father's moral parts
Mayst thou inherit too! (1.2.19–22)

Nostalgia governs futurity, and, from his derivative and prefigured location, Bertram's options are preemptively foreclosed.[47] "I cannot love her, nor will strive to do't," he says in protest against his marriage, to which the King replies, "Thou wrong'st thyself, if thou shouldst strive to choose" (2.3.145–46). Bertram defies his forced marriage by refusing to perpetuate his line, a determination expressed in the futile vow, "I will not bed her" (2.3.270). He knows only the terms of repetition, and resists them through a reiteration which, as it substitutes "no" for "yes," highlights the absorption of difference back into sameness. In this plot of passive inscription—"O my Parolles, they have married me!" (l. 272)—Helena's will to generative union implements paternal law.

When the King tells his attendant, "I fill a place, I know't" (1.2.69), he describes the condition of masculine social subjects: to be a man is to be a stand-in for the next man, a stopgap in the progress of an uninterrupted line.[48] This permanence across persons imposes an integral correspondence between nature and image. Identity is—to use Parolles's word again—naturalized, but any suggestion that this involves a process divulges tensions between the artificial and the essential, hinting at fissures and fault lines beneath the stifling seamlessness of patrilineal transmission. Men must be identical with their positions, and they cannot be demonstrably self-made. This is why Parolles provokes such drastic reprisals: as a man who can pretend, he abuses the privilege of the apparent. Bevington writes, "Parolles flaunts a penchant for which he becomes notorious later in the play, that of giving away men's secrets."[49] The most treacherous secret of all is that men can seem at will. Performative masculinity undoes the assurance of being as it breaks the link between credible appearance and legitimate fact: "Is it possible he should know what he is, and be that he is?" (4.1.44–45). Parolles contaminates the homosocial body, and the contagion spreads; in his deception of Diana, Bertram commits treason against himself and breaches the limits that define him.

First Lord: Now God delay our rebellion! As we are ourselves, what
     things are we!

Second Lord: Merely our own traitors. And as in the common
  course of all treasons, we still see them reveal themselves, till they
  attain to their abhorr'd ends; so he that in this action contrives
  against his own nobility in his proper stream o'erflows himself.
  (4.3.19–25)

For Parolles, but also and more important for Bertram at the play's end,
imposture must be expiated by a high-profile vivisection. "I would gladly
have [Bertram] see his company anatomiz'd, that he might take a measure
of his own judgments, wherein so curiously he had set this counterfeit" (ll.
31–34). Simulation, marked as sedition against the authority that makes men,
must differ absolutely and visibly from truth. "Simply the thing I am / Shall
make me live," Parolles concludes (ll. 333–34). This is not a matter of self-
knowledge—Parolles never doubts his own nature—but of transparency restored. Helena's deliberate performances enlarge the meaning of impersonation; the punishments incurred by Bertram and Parolles narrow it to the
debasement of a lie.

Helena does not invent herself from nothing. Early in *All's Well*, Lafew
offers a pointed reminder: "You must hold the credit of your father" (1.1.39–
41, 78). As the verb intimates, Helena is an agent rather than an object of
reiteration; Bertram embodies his legacy, but Helena makes use of hers.
"Not simply a prescription for a surefire cure, the receipt is also a powerful
trace of Helena's father figured as offspring," Garrett A. Sullivan Jr. writes.
"Her use of it, then, constitutes an act of remembrance understood in terms
not of her father's image but of his actions."[50] The distinction between
image and action is crucial. Inheritance invests a new subject, linked to the
past by duties more dynamic and less determined than those imposed by
fathers on sons. Men are fixed by linear transmission; women are mobile
regenerators, potential revisionists who might redraw the lines. This disparity places both the threat of patrilineal interruption and the defense against
it within the scope of feminine choice, a familiar predicament that illustrates
the facts of sexual life. Adelman writes of Helena, "her showing forth of the
ring and of her own pregnant body in the last scene rewrites the parthenoge-
netic fantasy embedded in the ring's history, redefining the transmission of
male honor—and male identity—as inevitably contingent on the female
body."[51] Contingency implicates not only Helena's body but her will: as
the Countess says, "she derives her honesty, and achieves her goodness"
(1.1.44–45).

All's Well extends the inconvenient truth about masculine identity, from its origins in female bodies to its maintenance through feminine acts. In this way Helena illustrates the facts of social life as well, her volition recasting the characters of men. When she chooses her husband, the candidates appear only as a numbered sequence, their words delimited by the frame of her address: "And grant it"; "No better, if you please"; "Fair one, I think not so" (2.3.77, 84, 98). Lafew treats positive responses as if they were rejections— "Do all they deny her?" "These boys are boys of ice, they'll none have her" (ll. 86, 93–94)—and his misreading of the discursive surface emphasizes the deeper sense in which the lords are identified not by their choice but by Helena's.[52] That choice detaches one man from the common mass when Helena performs the contradiction of willed surrender. "I dare not say I take you, but I give / Me and my service, ever whilst I live, / Into your guiding power.—This is the man" (ll. 102–4). Her obdurate obedience integrates Bertram into heterosociality, and the comic drive of *All's Well* is fuelled by this active virtue that creates and connects subjects. "This is the man": constant women might make men not by incubating them but by wanting them, a proposition which, like Helena herself, serves the ends of social continuity but deeply complicates the means.

A Minimum of Consistency to Our Being-in-the-World

"Thy will by my performance shall be serv'd," the King declares after his cure. It is an extraordinary pledge, which designates Helena the agent of sovereign acts (2.1.202). Absolute power becomes the medium of feminine will, a blend of abdication and seizure that should pose a clear danger. Carolyn Asp writes of Helena's marriage plot, "This request, which depends upon patriarchal power for its implementation, paradoxically subverts the very order of patriarchy itself."[53] Yet the transaction is less preposterous than chiastic: the King's revitalized power is subject to Helena's will, and Helena's will as his subject revitalized the King's power. This is more than wordplay, although wordplay is hardly trivial when sovereigns and subjects trade speech acts. Chiasmus might be Helena's rhetorical scheme, more apt than tautology or paradox; at its heart is a figure that holds elements in balance, and makes unexpected sense from their transposition. Helena's constant will, I have argued, conflates personal desires with social requisites, compressing microcosm and macrocosm into an indissoluble knot. Her role in *All's Well* works as a two-part imperative, which, at its junction, switches first premises. It would be possible to express this in ways that approximate a chiastic grammar—she wills men to turn back to service through the service she turns to their will—but I suspect it would also become tedious. I want instead to preserve that idea of the switch, in which individual and ideological priorities meet and change order. Helena draws events to her own conclusions, but her plots answer social demands. Through her single-minded pursuit of a husband, she recuperates the vitality of patriarchal roles. Her intercessions are radical: she cures a king, conscripts a husband, buys a bed trick, and returns (pregnant) from the dead. But those exploits serve a traditional end: through them Helena adheres to the most basic heterosocial contract, which requires women to produce and protect the eternal sameness of men. I would stress that this dialectic, despite its apparent equilibrium, is fraught with the problem of unassimilated agency. No convention domesticates Helena as the force or the voice of social ideology; if she makes a conservative argument, she does so from a position for which that argument has no place.

This is *All's Well*'s curious sleight of hand: Helena confirms the near-magical dominion of the social over the individual, but exposes that structure to a potentially skeptical gaze. Her marriage, which ratifies generic and social contracts, also divides authority against itself, embroiling husband and sovereign in a debate that unsettles the basis of hierarchical dispositions. Bertram calls on social history: "She had her breeding at my father's charge—/ A poor physician's daughter my wife!" (2.3.114–15). The King responds with cultural theory: "'Tis only title thou disdain'st in her, the which / I can build up" (2.3.117–18). In the moment, the second point supersedes the first; a sovereign can grant a title, and thus alter the quality of a subject. Yet it is precisely the meaning of "quality" that the exchange puts in question. Does it describe an innate attribute, or an acquired one, and what is at stake in the difference? Bertram appeals to an idea of inborn status that contributes substantially to royal prerogative, and in this sense the privilege of the moment might vacate the larger logic of ascendancy. The King's defense—"Honors thrive / When rather from our acts we them derive / Than our foregoers" (ll. 135–37)— substitutes intentional acts for unconditional states, and requires an audience to accept contradictory propositions about a preeminence that uses immutability to authorize fabrication. Efficacy and immanence: two versions of legitimacy claim the same space in what are, oddly, the same terms, both insisting on the transparency of position, both shielding fragile ties to verification. Helena precipitates this split, her layered capacities at odds with the truths that rely on an impenetrable social surface.

When Helena rearticulates order, she does so at an angle to that surface:

her affirmation of social edicts both illuminates and distorts. The bed trick, which transforms misconceived seduction into chastised desire, elucidates through refraction. "You see it lawful then," she tells the Widow (3.7.30), and as law passes through the medium of her will, its decrees twist into workable shapes.

> Why then to-night
> Let us assay our plot, which if it speed,
> Is wicked meaning in a lawful deed,
> And lawful meaning in a lawful act,
> Where both not sin, and yet a sinful fact.
> But let's about it. (ll. 43–48)

Wicked meanings and sinful facts create lawful marriage from illicit sex; ends trump means with a decisiveness that might parody, undercut, or simply improve on the expedient strategies of patrilineal succession. But to the extent that those strategies rely on passive female vessels, they are utterly supplanted when the bed trick becomes a death trick. Helena disappears as a social subject, receding into an abnegation of self that disables the judgments of others. Only her own constant will can return an heir from that space. Her pregnant body takes shape through Diana's conundrum of an impossible truth:

> He knows himself my bed he hath defil'd,
> And at that time he got his wife with child.
> Dead though she be, she feels her young one kick.
> So there's my riddle: one that's dead is quick—
> And now behold the meaning. (5.3.300–304)

At this moment of perfect obscurity, the play's resolution turns on a meaning that perpetuates rather than resolves a riddle. Helena's pregnancy is doubly a symptom: of the interdependence that undergirds hierarchy, and of the intentional virtue that makes social integrity at once the motive and the product of feminine will. The recklessly sexual and chastely generative body that concludes this play is symptomatic in the Lacanian sense of being closed off from the symbolic, inaccessible to the techniques that make knowledge a breakable code. Is Helena actually pregnant (and what does this question mean for a body that has staged both sex and death)? Is her child actually

Bertram's (and can any answer bridge the gap between his deviant purpose and its orthodox effect)?

The point lies less in the difficulty of resolving these questions than in the impossibility of asking them. *All's Well* makes it clear that masculine subjects cannot afford to doubt feminine virtue, not least because Helena has become the only authority for its precepts. Her pregnant body is an instance of the Lacanian *sinthome*, which Žižek glosses as "a signifier as a bearer of *jouis-sense*, enjoyment-in-sense."[54] The sinthome refuses interpretation, but provides the only access to a fantasy of self. Žižek writes,

> What we must bear in mind here is the radical ontological status of symptom: symptom, conceived as *sinthome*, is literally our only substance, the only positive support of our being, the only point that gives consistency to the subject. In other words, symptom is the way we—the subjects—"avoid madness," the way we "choose something (the symptom-formation) instead of nothing (radical psychotic autism, the destruction of the symbolic universe)" through the binding of our enjoyment to a certain signifying, symbolic formation which assures a minimum of consistency to our being-in-the-world.[55]

Acceptance of Helena's mystified meaning ensures the consistency of being that inheres in futurity. "If she, my liege, can make me know this clearly, / I'll love her dearly, ever, ever dearly" (5.3.315–16): Bertram's "if" identifies Helena's opaque but transitive knowledge as the scaffold for that hard clear surface of assured place. As long as women sustain the security of the self-evident, masculine subjects can be as they seem: fathers and sovereigns, husbands and sons. The mirror of constancy reflects a cohesive social system in the shadow of disintegration. "All yet seems well," says the King (5.3.333), and his muted, belated paraphrase accepts a necessary fall into Helena's language, through which being-in-the-world might make sufficient sense. In determined support of the status quo, Helena saves a king, makes a husband, and perpetuates a patriline. She also demonstrates that ideological obviousness rests on the conditional guarantees of feminine will.

It is hardly surprising, then, that the ending of *All's Well That Ends Well* provokes responses that echo the King's doubtful summary rather than Helena's confident anticipation. "In spite of its title, the play refuses to end well, indeed virtually refuses to end at all," writes Kastan; "but, pointedly, it is the desire for comic endings that has informed—and deformed—the action throughout."[56] To want an ending is to lack one, a judgment which, as it points toward Helena's informing and deforming will, glosses desire in Lacanian rather than comic terms.[57] Accounts of frustrated, conditional, partial, or contrived consummation vary, except in the suspicion that the play's title, if not actually a red herring, is at least some kind of bait. While the tradition of *All's Well* criticism includes its share of celebrations, which detail the triumphs of men, women, and happy endings, it also encompasses more than its share of discontents.[58] When Thomas Cartelli argues for the success of the ending, he reiterate this sense of strain, writing that the play asks of its audience "a surrender that becomes equivalent to a theatrical act of faith in the rough magic of artifice by which the play effects its confirmation of Helena's fantasy."[59] The theatrical act of faith demands a surrender to Helena's control that is also an acceptance of her own good faith, a redoubled submission to her will's rough magic. Such a response repeats the play's need to make things fit, to force recalcitrant pieces into some kind of place. We can never know enough, but must always know too much: *All's Well* illuminates the shadowy awareness that this is all we have, that to break apart the labored construction would uncover worse puzzles beneath. Helena—acknowledged or imagined as obedient subject, dutiful daughter, faithful wife, and devoted mother—promises the only good ending. If willful constancy makes this a problem play, it does so by telling us how much worse it would be not to have the problem at all.

The enforced wish fulfillment of Helena's bed trick, like the disciplinary mandate of her role, displays what is after all an open secret of comedy: pleasure is not suppressed by generic or social norms, but is produced in and through them. Helena echoes the call of what Žižek terms ideological *jouissance*, the pleasure of form for form's sake and of compliance as an end in itself. But *All's Well*'s own end makes this investment overt, turning us back toward Žižek's insistence that for ideological subjects, only ignorance is bliss: "As soon as they perceive that *the real goal is the consistency of the ideological attitude itself*, the effect is self-defeating."[60] To see the process as the goal is to deflect its achievement, but Helena makes recognition inescapable. In leaving us to take her at her word, *All's Well* speaks an unspeakable desire in a virtuous woman's voice. Jonathan Gil Harris offers a powerful insight into barren forms: "the play is haunted by the fear that seeming succession may amount to little more than dropsical deconception, and that the end may be merely a sterile repetition of the beginning rather than an advance on it."[61] I would add that the play is haunted, too, by the hint that such repetition may

Figure 6. "Love in enduring death." Otto van Veen, *Amorum Emblemata* (Antuerpiae: Typis Henrici Swingenij, 1608), 185. By permission of the Folger Shakespeare Library.

be enough, that constancy may disclose the limits of the systemic fictions it sustains. "Sterile repetition" might be another term for homosocial partheno-genesis, that narrow space of masculine continuity secured by constant femi-nine will. Helena's solution to the play's crises—to structural damage and disordered conduct—works as it should. In so doing, it suggests that she enacts an impossibly knowing ideological *jouissance*, which shreds the fabric of concealment as it answers the underlying demand. *All's Well* produces its pleasures, but they cannot, perhaps, be accepted with equanimity from this all too open hand.

When Helena's return provokes the King to ask, "Is't real that I see?" (5.3.306), she replies, "No, my good lord, / 'Tis but the shadow of a wife you see, / The name, and not the thing" (5.3.306–8). It is Bertram, for once, who sees the point. "Both, both. O, pardon!" (5.3.308). Both, both: the thing and the name, the truth and the performance, the generative body and the engendering will, must be recognized in all their agonistic coherence before recuperation can begin. "The marriage that is ratified at the end of the play is presented not as a joyous lovers' union but as a compromised bargain, not as a happy ending but as a precarious beginning," Carol Thomas Neely writes.[62] That precariousness informs Helena's final appeal to authentic appearance: "If it appear not plain and prove untrue, / Deadly divorce step between me and you!" (ll. 317–18). We end not with a climax but with a counterfactual, another "if" that proliferates the directions in which truth might lie. The King's response describes an abiding need: "Let us from point to point this story know, / To make the even truth in pleasure flow" (ll. 325–26). Speculatively produced by a story only Helena can tell, the progression from knowledge to pleasure makes teleology another act of faith. "Does *All's Well* really 'change the story?'" Susan Snyder asks. "I don't know. What it does do, I think, is to enact—by disjunction, indirection, and suppression as much as speech and action—the difficulties and conflicts of imagining a woman as active, desiring subject. It doesn't end unambiguously 'well,' and has trouble ending at all. That shouldn't surprise us."[63] For *All's Well*, as for any number of stories about feminine subjects who mean to do as they should, virtue weaves volition and assimilation into a form of agency that must be compromised at best. "That man should be at woman's command, and yet no hurt done!" says the Clown (1.3.92–93), describing a scene *All's Well* refuses to enact: Helena does not invert heterosocial hierarchies, but seeks and claims their restoration. Still, when socialized desire secures its tenets through feminine will, the victory is potentially pyrrhic. We might note that the emblem of constancy in the *Amorum Emblemata*, which depicts Cupid burning at a stake, shows a woman adding fuel to the flames.[64]

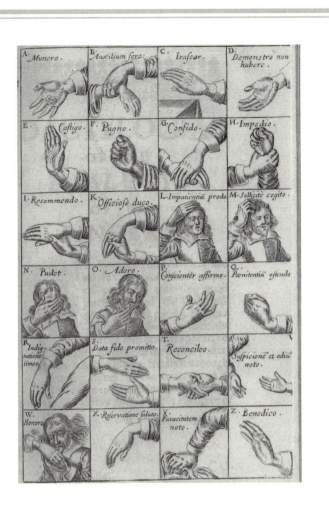

Chapter Five

"Will in Overplus"

Recasting Misogyny
in the *Sonnets*

If thy soul check thee that I come so near,
Swear to thy blind soul that I was thy Will,
And will, thy soul knows, is admitted there;
Thus far for love my love-suit sweet fulfil.
Will will fulfil the treasure of thy love,
Ay, fill it full with wills, and my will one;
In things of great receipt with ease we prove
Among a number one is reckoned none.
Then in the number let me pass untold,
Though in thy store's account I one must be.
For nothing hold me, so it please thee hold
That nothing, me, a something sweet to thee.
    Make but my name thy love, and love that still;
    And then thou lov'st me, for my name is Will.

                            —Shakespeare, sonnet 136

Will

Shakespeare's sonnet 136 offers a curiously heterogeneous meditation on will. Its final statement inspires speculations ranging from get-to-know-Shakespeare literalism to Joel Fineman's claim concerning "the specific materiality of absence that regularly defines what is *in* a Shakespearean name."[1] Gordon Williams, in *A Glossary of Shakespeare's Sexual Language*, cites its unsubtle puns to illustrate the use of "will" as genital slang.[2] The reference to lovers in remarkable yet unremarked number takes homosociality to an extreme, leading to Eve Sedgwick's observation that "the men, or their 'wills,' seem to be reduced to the scale of homunculi, almost plankton, in a warm but unobservant sea."[3] The intercourse of "will" and "soul" evokes faculty theory, with its ordered connections among the psychic parts, and through its images of deception and blindness puts that arrangement in peril. Will is often taken

Figure 7 (preceding page). "Alphabet of naturall Gestures of the Hand."
John Bulwer, *Chirologia: Or The Naturall Language of the Hand* (London: Tho. Harper, 1644), 155. By permission of the Folger Shakespeare Library.

as a synonym for intention, and often as a synonym for desire; yet intention and desire share an uneasy affiliation at best, and the sonnet heightens that friction as it forces their coincidence. The process of subjective constitution—"make but my name thy love"—locates the agency of self-making outside the self, its perverse imperative mystifying the questions of whose volition is at stake and of what a claim to possession might mean. It seems impossible to confine this sonnet's will to a single purpose or sense; as Lisa Freinkel writes, "A list of implausibly discrete and distinct definitions takes the place of paraphrase."[4]

Full beyond capacity, sonnet 136 reveals something dense and fickle in that word "will," with its power to implicate and intimate so much: as a faculty and a name, a sexual synecdoche and an intentional fallacy, will circulates in unpredictable and incommensurate ways. It stands as a metonym for individuated subjectivity, and at the same time metonymically fuses the persons vitalized and held hostage by that subjective conceit. Freinkel argues that because the rhetorical strategies of the will sonnets refuse to distinguish immediacy from citation, they render a key question unanswerable: "Who is speaking in this poem, and whom is the language of the poem bespeaking (or interpellating)?"[5] Sonnet 136 can be read as a sexist slur (this woman is open to all comers), as a sexual homogeny (all men want the same thing), as a social hegemony (all men are the same thing), as a philosophical observation (when the soul is blind, the will runs wild), and as a theory of interpersonal subjectivity (you complete me). What does it mean that it can say all of these things, in cacophonous and irreducible chorus? In these fourteen lines, as in the 28 poems for which they are a focal point, will interweaves its subjects: heterosocial desire works not as a categorical scheme but as a convergence of porous and protean sites of meaning, deeply complicating the premises of agency, autonomy, and hierarchy that rest on sexual distinction.

Those premises appear, in sonnet 136, through the familiar misogynist move that unites men in relation to a promiscuous feminine sexuality, but they appear at an angle, turned askew or perhaps set adrift by the more intricate promiscuity of will itself. I have argued that misogynist discourse reflects and responds to the reciprocal implication of heterosocial subjects, but constructs a cover story which simultaneously distinguishes good women from bad ones and separates all women from men. In its simplified form, misogyny uses feminine objects to support an ideal of masculine self-sufficiency. The circulation of will across lines of gender nullifies that system. Shakespeare's last 28 sonnets represent subjects locked in volitional exchange, and disclose the improbable, unworkable qualities of taxonomic segregation.[6] The sonnets turn an analytic lens on social transactions: their relationship to the cover story of misogyny is citational, invoking a cultural poetics that their own poetic method defamiliarizes and reconceives through an intersectional theory of will. The persistent impulse to read these sonnets as a subsequence, despite questions concerning the order of the sequence as a whole and the markers that distinguish its objects of address, reflects their sustained interrogation of social, sexual, and poetic intercourse.[7] The poems are less a story than an anatomy, not of a passively objectified female body but of the active and consequential encounters that produce gendered agents. If misogynist reductions exclude women from bonds between men, and if sonnets appear to give poetic form to that project, these sonnets of will expose the factitiousness of such moves.[8] In its most recognizably misogynist moments, the sequence most thoroughly unsettles the cultural truisms to which it refers.

Because Shakespeare's sonnets interpolate elements of a reductive, hegemonic social narrative, they risk identification with that narrative. In his account of *habitus*, Pierre Bourdieu describes representational practices as caught between repetition and innovation: "Because the *habitus* is an infinite capacity for generating products—thoughts, perceptions, expressions and actions—whose limits are set by the historically and socially situated conditions of its production, the conditioned and conditional freedom it provides is as remote from creation of unpredictable novelty as it is from simple mechanical reproduction of the original conditioning."[9] Readings of Shakespeare's *Sonnets* often attribute to them this partial and contradictory freedom, tracing Shakespeare's departures from the sonnet sequence tradition, but describing, too, his reproduction of a conservative heterosocial order. The "ordinary practices," "significant without a signifying intention," of which Bourdieu writes—in this case the all too familiar practices of sexual essentialism—produce an effect of inevitability: by invoking misogynist clichés, the *Sonnets* must reinforce hierarchical partitions between early modern women and men.[10]

Yet will crosses categories of sameness and difference, of self-possessed intention and other-possessed desire, a mobility that theorists of the faculties emphasize in even their most schematic accounts. Pierre Charron writes, "The Will is a great part of the reasonable soule, of verie great importance, and it standeth us upon above all things to studie how to rule it, because upon it dependeth almost our whole estate and good."[11] Well-managed, will manages in turn, but even if this conditional and attenuated touch imposes discipline, it also connects the exercise of government to the barely leashed forces on which that government is based.[12] Will intercedes not through passive transfer, but by joining together as it acts between. Thomas Wright defines it as a double-edged faculty of choice, which, as it inclines equally toward tempered judgments and capricious fancies, forms the contact point that links them: "she hath ingrafted in her, two inclinations, the one to follow Reason, the other to content the Sences."[13] The energy of attachment overrides motivated separations, and transects the borders that insulate regulatory forces from ungoverned drives. Will should mediate between reason and passion; when it instead consummates improper unions, theorists personify it in gendered terms. "This *pow'r* hath highest vertue of *Desire*, / And *Caesarizeth* ore each *Appetite*; / Shee rules (being taught) with libertie intire."[14] As the capacity for desire becomes the criterion of rule, a hierarchy cedes place to a network, in which feminized will draws together indiscrete parts.

A number of powerful readings have traced the crises of subjectivity and representation figured in the *Sonnets*' treatment of will. Fineman describes "Will" as the sign of the linguistically split subject: "'Will' in this *effective* fashion designates the way the poet's visual being (the ideal correspondence of 'I' and 'you,' of poetic ego and ego ideal) is constitutively disrupted, spatially and temporally, by the verbal meaning that identifies poetic self (the constant, personal reference of a proper name)."[15] Freinkel argues that the will poems confound the referential claims of figure: "It is, accordingly, precisely this figural notion of fulfillment that Shakespeare's *Will* challenges."[16] Margreta de Grazia takes sonnet 136 as the point at which self-possession and its attendant hierarchies collapse: "Will himself takes on the hysterical attributes of the womb that obsesses him. . . . There could be no more shocking manifestation of his hysteria than sonnet 136 in which every word could be said to signal his desire, homonymically or synonymically." Signification, de Grazia writes, is reduced "to the tautological deadlock of 'Will wills will.' Nor is Will ever released from this uterine obsession."[17] Valerie Traub instead reads the sonnet as a response to this predicament: "If 'will' initially functions as a metaphor for the lady's erotic appetite, it ends as a metonym for the poet's identification and union with other men, as an 'abundance' of wills subsumes the woman's desire."[18] The fractured "I," the exhausted sign, tautology, hysteria, obsession, subsumption: through a language of dissolution and merger, of broken boundaries and failed autonomy, such readings echo the cumulative verdict of early modern faculty theory: a subjectivity articulated through will cannot take singular or self-sufficient form.

In Shakespeare's last 28 sonnets, the ties that bind men to understanding and women to impulse break against the speaker's rejection of reason, his repeated insistence on possession of and by a condition of will to which he at once lays claim and surrenders. Arguing that none of his senses "desire to be invited / To any sensual feast with thee alone," the speaker splits "sense" into its irreconcilable meanings, severing the rational from the passionate and isolating will not as a mediator but as a renegade force (141.7–8). In *Nosce teipsum* Sir John Davies expounds a system that pulls unruly sense into the pyramid scheme of good judgment: "And as from *Senses Reasons* worke doth spring, / So many *Reasons understanding* gaine, / And many *understandings*, *knowledge* bring; / And by much *knowledge*, *wisdome* we obtaine."[19] Such a model cannot work for these sonnets; as de Grazia writes, "In sonnets 127 to 154, language is will's mouthpiece."[20] "Whoever hath her wish, thou hast thy Will, / And Will to boot, and Will in overplus; / More than enough am I, that vex thee still, / To thy sweet will making addition thus" (135.1–4). "Will in overplus," and still the speaker "mak[es] addition": subjects appear ("thou hast thy Will"; "More than enough am I"), but only through an undifferentiated outbreak of intentions and desires.[21] A psychic insurrection becomes an interpersonal contract: the speaker's will enters into alliance with that of his addressee, leaving reason outside. "For, thou betraying me, I do betray / My nobler part to my gross body's treason; / My soul doth tell my body that he may / Triumph in love; flesh stays no further reason" (151.5–8). The soul does not restrain desire, but feeds it—"Poor soul, the centre of my sinful earth, / Feeding these rebel powers that thee array" (146.1–2)—and the economy of dependence that displaces isolation recurs in sonnet 147. "My love is as a fever, longing still / For that which longer nurseth the disease, / Feeding on that which doth preserve the ill, / Th'uncertain sickly appetite to please" (147.1–4).[22] Will binds together what reason should hold apart: "My reason, the physician to my love, / Angry that his prescriptions are not kept, / Hath left me" (147.5–7).

In this sequence of will sonnets, the speaker's faculty of meaning intersects a volition other than his own—with pleasure and pain, jokes and excoriations, trepidation and desire, anger, wonder, conspiracy, and recognition—so that tropes of address open channels of return. The set pieces of misogyny, which range from impossible idealization to sexual disgust, make their appearances, but fail to accumulate to a sovereign whole. Will does not secure difference (men will women to serve their purpose; women will themselves away from that purpose), but creates the space of engagement in which masculine and feminine subjects meet. A subject / object divide becomes a metonymic association—subject-and-object—into which the presumptive mastery of objectification dissolves. The fusion of self-reflexivity and the fission that subordinates "you" to "I," those two moves that erase the responsive or constitutive agency of the object, give way to a dynamic of transactional subjectivity.[23] Considering the effects of an indeterminate "third" on a binary paradigm of gender, Marjorie Garber writes, "what is crucial here—and I can hardly underscore this strongly enough—is that the 'third term' is *not* a *term*. Much less is it a *sex*. . . . The 'third' is a mode of articulation, a way of describing a space of possibility. Three puts in question the idea of one: of identity, self-sufficiency, self-knowledge."[24] "Will" is such a third: as feminine and masculine faculty, as male and female genitals, as improper reference and proper name, as irresistible force and movable object, it circulates with a volatile relational power.

Contract

As they cite and rework the formulas of heterosocial intercourse, the last 28 sonnets ask what it might mean to apostrophize desire and get an answer. Such a question takes us toward prosopopeia, the figure Paul de Man associates with apostrophe and autobiography: prosopopeia, de Man writes, is "the fiction of an apostrophe to an absent, deceased, or voiceless entity, which posits the possibility of the latter's reply and confers upon it the power of speech."[25] This sounds very much like the rhetorical strategy often attributed to the sonnet sequence genre, which, as it generates the fiction of affective autobiography, apostrophizes a voiceless entity for which it imagines a purely instrumental power of response. Yet such mechanical contrivances exceed the constraints of their invention. In her reading of Ovidian narratives, Lynn Enterline describes the risks of cross-voicing: "As soon as Ovid's poems provoke the Barthesian question—'whose voice is this?'—one can no longer say, with any certainty, whose 'experience' of violence or desire the text is representing, or for whom its stories may be said to 'speak.'"[26] Shakespeare's last sonnets construct a pact between speaker and addressee that blurs the lines of identity and agency. The effect recalls de Man's "figure of reading or of understanding": "The autobiographical moment happens as an alignment between the two subjects involved in the process of reading in which they determine each other by mutual reflexive substitution."[27] Subject and object become "two subjects involved in the process of reading," who between them compile an autobiography: not of privileged if anguished solipsism, but of heterosocial symbiosis.

These sonnets present an intercourse of knowledge: conjured to embody sexual and poetic possibilities, the desired object realizes those possibilities in both senses of the term. Citing the tenet that women are responsible for misogynist response, the sonnets make this a knowing responsibility, a deliberate intervention into structures of meaning. That intervention anticipates Karen Newman's proposal that we rethink the traffic in women: "Even the most cursory glance at the history of hermeneutics suggests that texts can be mobilized to tell other stories that produce what Adorno called a *Kraftfeld* or force field in which subjects and objects are mutually constituting, mediating, in which power circulates, as do the positions of subject and object themselves."[28] The process of understanding from within, of investing a formally and ideologically prescribed role with intention, creates an object who knows what objectification means, and who thus unsettles the assumption that feminine sexuality is embodied in women but controlled by men. "Traffic," as Newman's argument suggests, becomes a figure less for a closed economy of masculine agents than for the open question of who is driving. Linking men to one another through a will that is neither disciplined nor owned, the sonnets' addressee simultaneously consolidates and disrupts homosocial coalition. Sonnets are rituals of desire, erotic routines vulnerable to an inappropriate response: not "no," not even "yes"—although that failure of refusal is haunting enough—but "I know."

"Thou art as tyrannous, so as thou art, / As those whose beauties proudly make them cruel; / For well thou knowst, to my dear doting heart / Thou art the fairest and most precious jewel" (131.1–4). The woman here addressed appears neither as heedless object nor as inert catalyst; her knowledge rewrites roles. "Thine eyes I love, and they, as pitying me, / Knowing thy heart torment me with disdain, / Have put on black, and loving mourners be, / Looking with pretty ruth upon my pain" (132.1–4). It might be tempting to dismiss this as a conceit, a fantasy of inversion that has no lasting meaning. But even if we imagine that the speaker deliberately assumes the position of helpless victim—even, that is to say, if we persist in distributing the agency of these sonnets in traditional ways—it must, to paraphrase Shakespeare's

Hippolyta, be our imagination then, not theirs. The sonnets themselves resist such a distribution, whether ordered or inverted, and foreground a conspiracy of intent. Sonnet 138 makes this clear: "When my love swears that she is made of truth, / I do believe her, though I know she lies" (138.1–2). There is an effective and perhaps even affective mutuality here; in Richard Strier's arresting formulation, "Shakespeare adds sex and company to Petrarch's solitary commitment to '*errore*' to produce a *folie à deux*."[29] There is also a direct statement of contract. "Thus vainly thinking that she thinks me young, / Although she knows my days are past the best, / Simply I credit her false-speaking tongue; / On both sides thus is simple truth suppressed" (138.5–8). Speaker and addressee combine to keep the project going, and identify the structures that formalize endlessness—the blazon, the sequence, the metonymies of desire—as processes of shared invention. Compliment becomes complement and supplement; the poetry of praise becomes a system of exchange. If this is a debased economy, it is also a functional one, in which the severance of credit from truth creates a method that works: "Therefore I lie with her, / And in our faults by lies we flattered be" (138.13–14).

Anything for a quiet life, we might say, but in so saying we would dismiss as merely untrue something that offers to tell a far more complicated truth about interdependence. If the exchange of lies manipulates persons into serviceable roles, are we in a fallen world, or a social one? And if to say there is no difference deploys an easy and empty cynicism, does that adequately explain these poems? In "Sociality and Sexuality," Leo Bersani asks an unexpected question: "Is lack necessary to desire?" His reading of Plato's *Symposium* posits an alternative. "Presence is always relational; desire would be the affective recognition of something like our debt to all those forms of being that relationally define and activate our being. Desire mobilizes correspondences of being."[30] Shakespeare's last set of sonnets records the costs incurred, but also the benefits accrued, within a system of relational definition and generative correspondence. The passionate desire for connection may expose a practice of deliberate seeming, but it does so from a condition of need that "truth"—suppressed, but also in some more fundamental way unavailable and ineffectual—cannot answer. As supplement to that truth, in response to that need, the woman addressed must know the language of desire, must, in effect, read it in order to read it back again, changed by her own addition. Sonnet 145 begins with the speaker's citation of her "I hate," only to record its revision:

> But when she saw my woeful state,
> Straight in her heart did mercy come,
> Chiding that tongue that, ever sweet,
> Was used in giving gentle doom,
> And taught it thus anew to greet:
> 'I hate' she altered with an end. (145.4–9)

That alteration is consequential. " 'I hate' from 'hate' away she threw, / And saved my life, saying 'not you' " (145.13–14). The speaker attaches his survival to the woman's supplemental phrase: her consensual addition, rather than leaving two statements coherently distinct ("I hate," "Not you"), runs them together to create a point of contact. This collaborative move exemplifies the sonnets' pattern of synthesis, in which the conjoining of discrete ideas of person creates subjects who can function where autonomy fails. If these subjects lie in the processes of self- and other-invention, they at the same time discredit the greater cultural lie that holds men and women apart.[31]

The speaker offers a proposition: if you take pity on me, he promises, "Then will I swear beauty herself is black, / And all they foul that thy complexion lack" (132.13–14). As it parallels the mutually constitutive fictions of sonnet 138, this covenant makes the woman a cultural ideal and the speaker a poet. Rayna Kalas writes, "epideixis, by *its* very generic conventions, always reveals the dependency of the speaking subject upon the subject of its praise."[32] That epideictic structure requires a great deal of maintenance and negotiation. "Tell me thou lov'st elsewhere; but in my sight, / Dear heart, forbear to glance thine eye aside": the speaker describes a jointly conceived split between his knowledge and his creation of knowledge, between what he recognizes and what he makes visible by seeing (139.5–6). Again: "If I might teach thee wit, better it were, / Though not to love, yet love to tell me so": sustain the illusion with me, the speaker asks, or I will tell a different story entirely (140.5–6). When this sonnet concludes, "That I may not be so, nor thou belied, / Bear thine eyes straight, though thy proud heart go wide" (140.13–14), we are in an odd paraphrase indeed: pretend you are what you must be, so I will not belie you by telling the truth. Imperatives revolve around performance, which connects subjects as it correlates appearance with report; it does not matter whether representation refers accurately or astray, as long as it shelters a viable bond.

The project of idealization thus undermines the notion that praise, as an objectifying tactic, dislocates women from meaningful intervention; only through feminine acts of knowing and willful seeming can the discourse take shape. Fineman writes of feminine will and self-perjuring language, "The duplicitous sexuality of the lady, what the poet calls her 'Will' (135, 136) and 'common place' (137), embodies, as it were, the voice of such a language, a language *of* desire because a language of linguistic and erotic 'lie.'"[33] For the speaker, this is not a matter of being deceived, but of being refigured so he can rewrite. Through a woman's knowledge he must himself know differently, even as he knows differently in that other sense as well: "Whence hast thou this becoming of things ill, / That in the very refuse of thy deeds / There is such strength and warrantise of skill / That in my mind thy worst all best exceeds?" (150.5–8). The twisting force, the "strength and warrantise of skill" that produces desire from a willed revision of meaning, promises enclosed reciprocity, even if it is a version of the compulsive, tormented enclosure that causes Richard Halpern to observe, "the Dark Lady is a systematic though relatively subdued collection of those attributes that would constitute a Sadean as opposed to a Petrarchan sublime."[34] But the exclusive fiction misleads, for the encounter extends beyond the dyad of lover and beloved. "Who taught thee how to make me love thee more, / The more I hear and see just cause of hate? / O, though I love what others do abhor, / With others thou shouldst not abhor my state" (150.9–12). Both subjects form fraught ties to "others," the speaker by dissenting from a more general misogynist response, the addressee by joining with those others at the speaker's expense. The poetic contract, doubly forged, between masculine poet and feminine ideal implicates the social contract forged among masculine subjects in relation to feminine sexuality, expanding the scale on which volition entangles its subjects.

"Me from myself thy cruel eye hath taken, / And my next self thou harder hast engrossed: / Of him, myself and thee I am forsaken, / A torment thrice threefold thus to be crossed" (133.5–8). To be "crossed" is not only to be thwarted, but to be caught in the intersection of wills:

So now I have confessed that he is thine,
And I myself am mortgaged to thy will,
Myself I'll forfeit, so that other mine
Thou wilt restore to be my comfort still;
But thou wilt not, nor he will not be free,
For thou art covetous, and he is kind;
He learned but surety-like to write for me,
Under that bond that him as fast doth bind. (134.1–8)

The abuse of kind—of kindness, and of likeness—draws homosocial attachment into heterosocial intercourse, an intermingling that informs the transition from division to confusion in sonnet 144: "Two loves I have, of comfort
and despair, / Which, like two spirits, do suggest me still: / The better angel
is a man right fair, / The worser spirit a woman coloured ill" (144.1–4). The
contrast seems clear enough, yet the speaker records its failure. "And whether
that my angel be turned fiend / Suspect I may, yet not directly tell; / But
being both from me both to each friend, / I guess one angel in another's
hell" (144.9–12). "Hell," like the will whose sexual meaning it repeats, is a
general meeting place; perhaps the speaker would agree, too, that hell is other
people. But the difference between those affiliations chosen by "kind" and
those enforced by "unkind abuse" cannot be known, or at least can be known
only after distinction has broken down: "Yet this shall I ne'er know, but live
in doubt, / Till my bad angel fire my good one out" (144.13–14).

"Others" appear in the speaker's discourse in connection with the
woman of his address: as the readers of her nature and his poems, as the men
with whom he experiences her will, as the "next self," the beloved man who
shares his seduction. His idealizing project alienates him from a more authorized homosocial judgment: "Yet in good faith some say, that thee behold, /
Thy face hath not the power to make love groan; / To say they err, I dare not
be so bold, / Although I swear it to myself alone" (131.5–8). He defines sexual
thrall as a shared breach of trust, which undercuts the integrity of social
commitments:

> O but with mine compare thou thine own state,
> And thou shalt find it merits not reproving;
> Or if it do, not from those lips of thine,
> That have profaned their scarlet ornaments,
> And sealed false bonds of love as oft as mine. (142.3–7)

The violation of legitimate bonds threatens to vitiate all bonds: unsustainable
obligations unravel both the subject who evokes them and the sociality to
which they refer. The speaker is a traitor to himself—"Canst thou, O cruel,
say I love thee not, / When I against myself with thee partake?" (149.1–2)—
and to the others, for him the other selves, whom the woman too betrays.
"In loving thee thou knowst I am forsworn; / But thou art twice forsworn to
me love swearing, / In act thy bed-vow broke and new faith torn, / In vowing
new hate after new love bearing" (152.1–4). But the capaciousness of will
offers a terribly practical solution: these treacheries, too, are contracts, "false

bonds of love" formed by the woman that attach the speaker to other men. "Be it lawful I love thee as thou lov'st those / Whom thine eyes woo, as mine importune thee" (142.9–10). As an indiscriminately transitive condition of desire, will constitutes a system of subjects, binding through shared implication what discretion or betrayal might divide. The speaker is not isolated from other men, but joined to them in the chain whose links are forged by something wanting, wanting something.[35]

Lust might connect men to one another not through privilege or power or their own reciprocal desire but through the corruption of a sexual fall. That threat would be recuperable: it produces the useful argument that heterosexuality ruptures or dilutes homosocial alliance. Such a position confines women, however sexually active, to the passive role of obstacles, causes but not agents of social trouble. But the *Sonnets'* deployment of misogynist discourse is too complex and too fractured to sustain this model. The speaker describes lust as a loss of reason in which masculine desire and feminine intention converge: "Past reason hunted, and no sooner had, / Past reason hated as a swallowed bait, / On purpose laid to make the taker mad" (129.6–8). "On purpose laid," the bait that draws men together is a willing woman. Those notorious sexual innuendoes—"So thou, being rich in Will, add to thy Will / One will of mine, to make thy large Will more" (135.11–12); "Wilt thou, whose will is large and spacious, / Not once vouchsafe to hide my will in thine?" (135.5–6)—equate the fantasy of conquest to the prospect of dissolution. All layers of the pun, from volition to genitalia to name, merge masculine and feminine qualities, disable the separation of persons, and disperse specificity into the vortex of union. The will of these sonnets presses against the hostile supremacy Bersani critiques in "Is the Rectum a Grave?":

> the self which the sexual shatters provides the basis on which sexuality is associated with power. It is possible to think of the sexual as, precisely, moving between a hyperbolic sense of self and a loss of all consciousness of self. But sex as self-hyperbole is perhaps a repression of sex as self-abolition. . . . As soon as persons are posited, the war begins. It is the self that swells with excitement at the idea of being on top, the self that makes of the inevitable play of thrusts and relinquishments in sex an argument for the natural authority of one sex over the other.[36]

An integral sense of self, at once triumphant and embattled, provides a rationale for sexual hierarchy, but will in the *Sonnets* is a multiply vectored

force that fractures and subsumes the sovereign persons who might be constituted by desire. "Think all but one, and me in that one Will" (135.11–14):
subjectivity in these poems does not mean having a will of one's own. Shared
possession of a woman, understood as rivalry or as traffic, becomes shared
possession with a woman, a shift that defines autonomous masculinity as an
untenable state. To be a man among men is to be a man with a woman;
homosociality still works, but it does not work alone.

Beauty, Truth

If will is the engine that drives these processes, beauty is their trace. Here the
interlocking of intention and desire leaves its mark: the last 28 sonnets represent beauty as at once a construct that imposes social meaning on sexual
response and a concept that precipitates response across categories of meaning, a mode of both making and dismantling heterosocial sense. As a currency
negotiated between women and men, beauty is a collaborative cultural narrative, its vicious and virtuous effects produced at the points where agendas
converge. It is not an aesthetic or sexual fact, but a demand that forces shape
into meaning and meaning into shape. In a discussion titled, "Love-Melan-
choly. Beauty a Cause," Robert Burton writes, "the question is how and by
what meanes Beauty produceth this effect? By sight: the Eye betrayes the soul,
and is both Active and Passive in this business; it wounds and is wounded, is
an especiall cause and instrument, both in the subject and in the object."[37]
Active and passive, wounding and wounded, subject and object, blend together through the conflation of instrument and cause. This is the artifact
that the "dark lady" sonnets ventriloquize and dissect.

Thommaso Buoni, in his *Problemes of Beautie*, poses what might be the
question of Shakespeare's speaker: "Why is Beauty worthy of Love?"[38] Beauty
has absorbed sonnet-makers throughout the history of the genre, joining aesthetic and erotic concerns. It condenses a range of preoccupations: with virtue, with generation, with elevating aspiration and degrading response.
Beauty is a medium for the transmission of ideology, representing divine
grace in human form and the more pragmatic blessings of appropriate conjugal and reproductive arrangements. At the same time it is the "bait" of which
Shakespeare's speaker so bitterly complains, the lure to a spiritually fallen and
socially destructive sexuality. Composed by masculine subjects to evaluate,
define, and discipline feminine objects, the doctrine of beauty reflects, too,
the contributions of the knowing women who participate in its manufacture.

Its clichés illustrate both taxonomic codes and the intercourse that breaks them. Iterating those clichés from multiple and dissonant perspectives, Shakespeare's last sonnets delineate a scheme in which objectified women—beauty's dead metaphors—engage the strategies that catalogue their value.

Genuine beauty poses a hazard to men, which shapes Burton's images of paralysis, death, and contagion: "Who can say I will not be taken with a beautiful object? I can, I will contain: No, saith *Lucian*, of his mistris, she is so fair, that if thou dost but see her, *she will stupifie thee, kill thee straight, and Medusa like turn thee to a stone, thou canst not pull thine eyes from her, but as an adamant doth iron*, she will carry thee bound headlong whether she will her self, infect thee like a Basilisk."[39] The *Sonnets'* speaker invokes this prodigious power, and insists that women knowingly deploy it: "ah, my love well knows / Her pretty looks have been mine enemies, / And therefore from my face she turns my foes / That they elsewhere might dart their injuries" (139.9–12). In references to women "Fairing the foul with art's false borrowed face" (127.6), "such who, not born fair, no beauty lack, / Sland'ring creation with a false esteem" (127.11–12), the poems reiterate, too, the conviction that simulated beauty threatens sexual and social order, encapsulated in Roland du Jardin's warning to complacent husbands: "If thou sufferest her to beautifie her selfe, the world will say thou art too holy, meaning too horney."[40] But is this a different threat from that posed by "pretty looks," or the same one? Where distinctions are subsumed under a common danger, what mechanism separates the true from the false?

The formulaic presumption that bad acts distort beauty—in Buoni's terms, an unchaste woman "hath wronged that naturall gift of hers, and darkned the light thereof by her deformed actions"—appears in sonnet 131, with its statement, "In nothing art thou black save in thy deeds, / And thence this slander, as I think, proceeds" (131.13–14).[41] Yet the sonnet incorporates three sites for the production of beauty's effects, that of the speaker, of his addressee, and of the slanderers; beauty becomes diffusely circumstantial, raising the questions not only of who dispenses judgments, but of where volition manifests itself in the texture of decree. And of course bad acts may not distort beauty at all, as in the resigned protest, "The statute of thy beauty thou wilt take, / Thou usurer, that put'st forth all to use" (134.9–10). Here beauty is precisely as irresistible as it is devalued, promising the "little bribe of pleasure" that the will, freed of reason, so anarchically pursues.[42] Beauty and false beauty, virtue and its loss, merge in their impact; nature and artifice circulate under the same name. As Freinkel writes, "The problem of the poet's world seems to be that the difference between essence and ornament makes *no* difference."[43] That breakdown catalyzes the speaker's complaint to love in 137:

> If eyes, corrupt by over-partial looks,
> Be anchored in the bay where all men ride,
> Why of eyes' falsehood hast thou forged hooks,
> Whereto the judgement of my heart is tied?
> Why should my heart think that a several plot
> Which my heart knows the wide world's common place? (137.5–10)

"Eyes' falsehood" is recognized without remedy, mirroring the problem that concludes sonnet 129: "All this the world well knows, yet none knows well / To shun the heaven that leads men to this hell" (129.13–14). Knowledge constructs neither functional boundaries nor circumspect response; reason and passion may diverge, but their division does not produce discretion. The contradictory meanings of beauty are inextricable, coupled by their convergence in a common place that might also, I think, be heard as "commonplace."

Sonnet 130, "My mistress' eyes are nothing like the sun," emphasizes this point. Informed by convention yet committed to negation, structured by a kind of poetic stutter ("not . . . not . . . not"), the poem is a counter-blazon that fails to generate aversion, an exposé of the gap between ideal and actuality that refuses to privilege either. Katherine Duncan-Jones reads it as straightforward misogyny: "Though Shakespeare's celebration of 'black' beauty has often been linked with Sidney, whose 'Stella' has black eyes, it is really horribly different, for this woman also has a muddy complexion, bad breath and a clumsy walk."[44] My students tend to find it romantic, a touching instance of realism in love. The equal availability of these readings suggests, as early modern comments on beauty suggest, that a happy medium is in fact a mixture, a set of contraries that occupy the same space. The conclusion to this sonnet, "And yet, by heaven, I think my love as rare / As any she belied with false compare" (130.13–14), makes the speaker's mistress neither better nor worse than those belied objects among whom he places her in other poems. Cynical and idealistic accounts of beauty are simply, if differently, equal, and "false compare," combining with "art's false borrowed face" in the generation of "false esteem," highlights not some better truth but a pragmatic, contingent act of faith. In the terse formulation of sonnet 138, "love's best habit is in seeming trust" (138.11).

These sonnets scrutinize standards grounded in caprice. Sonnet 127 begins with historical change: "In the old age black was not counted fair, / Or if it were, it bore not beauty's name" (127.1–2). A genealogy of name traces not continuity but adulteration and rupture: "But now is black beauty's successive heir, / And beauty slandered with a bastard shame" (127.3–4). Inauthentic self-representation commingles with the slanders of others; subject both to individual amendments and to paradigm shifts, cultural authority becomes enmeshed in the "bastard shame" of a lineage into which the wrong generators intervene.[45] The legacy of a bastardized tradition is relativism: dynamics of embodiment and response stake no claims on the essential or the immutable, and a condition of value secures subjects only through their mutual acceptance of its terms. Daniel Juan Gil writes, "the Dark Lady points to a comparatively modern world where lack of (inherent) beauty is no obstacle to being called beautiful, and where being called beautiful in some sense makes it so."[46] In that "comparatively modern world"—which, by implication, anticipates our world—it seems merely common sense to say that beauty is relative rather than fixed, and this insight is hardly unique to modernity. But in early modernity it works against the grain of epideictic verse and neoplatonic philosophy, which elevate subjects through virtues external to themselves, and rely on the intrinsic worth of the catalyst.[47] There is thus something radical about common sense, which restores both contingency and animation to an object that becomes more than a means. Beauty is only a field of contested meanings, but the will to beauty effects a consequential exchange of complements in the intricate circuitry of intention and desire.

Absolute statements about time and essence dissolve into conditional assessments of "here" and "now," in which strategic investments conspire to produce a vital but variable asset.[48] The speaker articulates his own values in qualified terms: "And to be sure that is not false, I swear," he protests; "Thy black is fairest in my judgement's place" (131.9, 12). That "I swear" works as a danger signal, a hint that judgment may have been wrenched out of shape. Poetic subjectivity becomes self-consciously subjective in that other, more troubled sense, increasingly tentative about the relationship between idealizing an object and telling a truth. Sonnet 137 records a sense of irreversible error: "Or mine eyes, seeing this, say this is not, / To put fair truth upon so foul a face? / In things right true my heart and eyes have erred, / And to this false plague are they now transferred" (137.11–14). Conveyed by the "fair truth" of manufacture to a "false plague" of misrepresentation, the speaker expresses nostalgia for a voice that never was. Sonnet 152 catalogues the loss:

> I am perjured most,
> For all my vows are oaths but to misuse thee,
> And all my honest faith in thee is lost:
> For I have sworn deep oaths of thy deep kindness,
> Oaths of thy love, thy truth, thy constancy,
> And to enlighten thee gave eyes to blindness,
> Or made them swear against the thing they see:
> For I have sworn thee fair: more perjured eye,
> To swear against the truth so foul a lie. (152.6–14)

Kindness, love, truth, constancy: the stock terms of idealized femininity, condensed in that last word "fair," constellate a social, sexual, and poetic ideal that circulates at an impassable distance from a reference point. It is this language of lying, this act of "remarking the difference embedded in a specific kind of verbal duplicity, by speaking about a language that *as* language breaks the perennial univocity of *Ideas Mirrour*," that leads to Fineman's famous claim: "Shakespeare in his sonnets invents the poetics of heterosexuality." Duplicitous language speaks the crux of sexual difference, "the heterogeneous power of heterosexual desire."[49]

Yet there is another crux here as well, one of *in*difference, not only or even primarily between truth and lie but between the feminine and masculine wills that produce effects of seeming. In early modern discourse, the idealization of women celebrates seeming, which verifies a transparent state of merit: "This beauty which is so much esteemed amongst women should be *a Looking glasse*, whereby we might afarre off, display the Majesty of the creator," and so beautiful women become the media that guarantee chaste sexuality, higher virtue, and good children.[50] The defamation of women condemns seeming, which represents an opaque act of fraud: "If she be faire, it will give cause to the world to thinke her dishonest; for that beauty and chastitie seldome dwell under one and the same roofe," and so beautiful women become the contaminants that produce fallen sexuality, worldly preoccupations, and adulterated or aborted lineage.[51] Through the relentless double-speak of polarized misogynist schemes, such conflicting aphorisms might work to the same purpose, as both the elevation and the debasement of women remove them from masculine spheres. But these readings of self-evident signs leave the questions of meaning—of what meaning, and of whose—unaddressed. Women who know their own beauty know, too, the expectations it imposes

on them; so *Hic Mulier*, having admonished women at length against painting and other forms of deception, concludes with a single telling phrase:
"Imitate nature."[52] The imperative presupposes that beauty results from willful impersonation, and that the key difference lies not between authenticity
and simulation, but between responsible and irresponsible mimesis. "Imitate
nature" might translate to "accommodate culture."[53] Buoni writes of women
who manufacture the appearance of beauty, "they knowing that those women
are of highest accompt in the world, which excell the rest in bodily *Beauty*,
and being naturally addicted to affect honor, and to be highly accompted of,
they are enforced to adde those colours to their naturall *Beauty*."[54] Matter
follows knowledge: women recognize the demands made of them, and shape
themselves to those demands. "Enforced" to do what they desire to do, "naturally addicted" to an effect they must artificially produce, they will themselves to another will, an Augustinian paradox in social form.

What then, under the touch of men, women, nature, culture, divinity,
dishonesty, and sex, can feminine beauty tell, about virtue or vice, about
spiritual or social value, about the joint and contested operations that make
it or make it up? It appears as the product of intentions and desires which
collide in the space of will, but that will is neither referentially governed nor
discretely possessed. Beauty is not something that God does to women for
men, or that men do to women for God or for men, or that women do to
women for women or for men or for God; or rather it is never only one of
these things. The volition that animates it is a hybrid creature, a means of
answering need that is only partially a way of making sense. Women who
know how to seem might or might not be; there is no way of telling—of
relating or knowing—the difference. The apparent contradictions of the *Sonnets* acknowledge this impossibility: when heterosocial requisites produce
beauty as an artifact of shared cultural will, evidence is sacrificed to that act
of production. There is a discourse of unrequitedness here, not between
speaker and addressee but between entangled subjects and the singular
"truth" they call upon. In his extraordinary account of lyric and empire,
Roland Greene writes,

> But requital of all kinds fails more often than not, and when it
> does so, lyric serves to measure the responses of those received
> standpoints—exiles, worshippers, mourners, and of course lovers—
> for whom completeness, commensurability, or reciprocity is fleeting

or unavailable. Their utterances come to serve as templates for all
the other experiences of unrequitedness; they give voice to conditions of doubt and dissent that qualify the idealist values of the age.
These standpoints cannot easily be sorted into winners and losers.[55]

The question of what can be "won" or "lost" in Shakespeare's last sonnets
becomes the question of what can be made from reciprocal acts of will. In
this sense the sonnets construct a metapoetics of heterosociality, which tells
truths not about an object of desire but about the desires that circulate
around objectification.

Those desires seek to construe a coherent ideology from a disparate field
of actors and effects, an effort legible in Richard Brathwait's address to his
female readers: "But for you, unblemished Beauties, who hold nothing compa-
rably precious to a continent Soule: as your minds become devoted wholly to
goodnesse: so you must give mee leave to interveine my Discourse with others
of your Sex, who fall so farre short of your perfection, as it might seeme strange
to reason, that one and the same Mould should produce Subjects of such
different Natures."[56] The problem, as Brathwait acutely indicates and disin-
genuously denies, is that one can never know to whom or of whom or for
whom one speaks; the "interveining" of discourse is too complete. We see
its effects graphically in Buoni's statement, as categorical and as confused as
Brathwait's: "bodyly *Beauty* is a cleare signe (if Malignity bee not hidden
under it) of a faire (that is) of a vertuous minde." Those brackets, containing
hidden malignity but containing, too, the more mysterious qualifier "that is,"
mark a knowledge foreclosed by the contradictory significance of the apparent.
"*Beauty* either true, or seeming, is also a good, either true, or seeming," Buoni
continues, as if truth and seeming have been so fully confounded that they
can appear only in parallel, as terms that neither pull apart nor touch. If the
result is social, sexual, and aesthetic confusion, it is also poetry: "therefore this
man it honoreth, that it admireth, this in private discourse it prayseth, and
that both in prose, and verse it extolleth."[57] The question that elicits such
incongruent answers is, again, "Why is Beauty worthy of Love?"

To his addressee, Shakespeare's speaker poses that question in the vocabulary of coercion: "O from what power hast thou this powerful might, / With
insufficiency my heart to sway, / To make me give the lie to my true sight, /
And swear that brightness doth not grace the day?" (150.1–4). This returns to
the problem of an effect that lies, in all senses of the word, within a woman's
control. But as if her answer could never be sufficient, the speaker puts the

same question to the abstraction of love: "Thou blind fool love, what dost thou to mine eyes, / That they behold, and see not what they see? / They know what beauty is, see where it lies, / Yet what the best is, take the worst to be" (137.1–4). These two facts, what beauty is and where it lies, are part of the same fact, which can never be a fact at all but rather a fact manqué: a constellation of fragile certainties generated from their own situational necessity. A second address to love undoes even the knowledge of error: "O me! What eyes hath love put in my head, / Which have no correspondence with true sight? / Or if they have, where is my judgement fled, / That censures falsely what they see aright?" (148.1–4). Eyes either do or do not correspond to "true sight"; judgment either does or does not censure rightly what those eyes have or have not taken amiss. When the sonnet appeals to social criteria, which might possess at least the authority of consensus, disorientation escalates:

> If that be fair whereon my false eyes dote,
> What means the world to say it is not so?
> If it be not, then love doth well denote,
> Love's eye is not so true as all men's: no,
> How can it? (148.5–9)

How can it, indeed, whether the "it" in question is love's eye, the speaker's eye, or the eye of "the world" that looks with the inescapably false consciousness of "all men"? Such points of view can work neither collectively nor autonomously; no one authority suffices, and no sum of authorities adds up. This is a world made by *habitus* that interrogates the force of habit, a space of obviousness in which recognition fails. In its treatment of beauty, the sequence figures the processes by which mastery slides into partiality. Vision is not in any definitive way false, for there is no place from which to deliver such a verdict; it is instead arbitrary, an anthology of perspectives that do not determine a line of sight, but proceed instead along lines of interest. I, you, they, love, history, the world: the speaker mobilizes them all to circulate an ideal, and in so doing makes beauty the common place, the commonplace, of everyone and no one.

The questions the speaker poses—do I see what I think I see? do others see it too? how can I believe one thing and know another, or believe two irreconcilable things at once?—pathologize perceptions that lack a shared referent, and become the questions of madness. For these sonnets, ungoverned will acts as an articulate psychosis: "Mad in pursuit, and in possession so, / Had, having, and in quest to have, extreme; / A bliss in proof, and proved, a very woe; / Before, a joy proposed; behind, a dream" (129.9–12). Had, having, in quest to have: this temporal collapse compresses possession into self-loss, and leaves no conceptual space in which will might mediate between reason and passion. Madness displaces other, more conventionally social sources of authority:

> Past cure I am, now reason is past care,
> And frantic mad with ever more unrest;
> My thoughts and my discourse as madmen's are,
> At random from the truth vainly expressed:
> For I have sworn thee fair, and thought thee bright,
> Who art as black as hell, as dark as night. (147.9–14)

Yet the gap between knowledge and truth—between "sworn" and "thought" and, on the other side, "are"—denotes a fact less substantial than the speech acts that betray it. There may be no general truth, but there is a common language, for madness is not a solitary state but a shared one. Intention and desire become unreasonably entwined not only in the speaker's will, but in the will that implicates all subjects of a heterosocial intercourse that erases the bounds of self. Defined severally as an inescapable result of acquiescence, a compulsive response to rejection, an idealizing and a debasing truth and lie, madness is the sign of an unaccommodated interpenetration that can be neither controlled nor refused. And misogyny, with its self-assured techniques of making persons, becomes the vehicle of contagion. "For if I should despair, I should grow mad, / And in my madness might speak ill of thee; / Now this ill-wresting world is grown so bad, / Mad slanderers by mad ears believed be" (140.9–12). If there is a totalizing cultural narrative here, it is this: a mad world believes what a mad speaker says of a woman who enables and enforces his speech. The *Sonnets* roughly dismantle separatist taxonomies; univocal impositions drown in a flood of volitional exchange. Misogyny is not a system but a symptom, of an eccentric—both unreasoned and decentered—surfeit of wills.

Overplus

In what sense, then, might we understand these 28 sonnets themselves as a system? Or as Heather Dubrow asks, does it ever make sense to read sonnet sequences as narratives? It is more useful, perhaps, to think of them as oblique provocateurs of our own need for narrative, poetic avatars of an old joke that might be paraphrased as follows: "It was a dark and stormy night. Three robbers were sitting around a campfire. 'Tell us a story,' one said. 'Okay, said another, here's a story. "It was a dark and stormy night. Three robbers were sitting around a campfire. 'Tell us a story,' one said. 'Okay, said another, here's a story. "It was a dark and stormy night . . ."'"'"" It could go on forever, and if one is sufficiently committed to tormenting one's audience, it does. But it raises, too, a number of questions. Why are they robbers? The specificity gestures toward an actual story, even as the story being told ironizes that gesture. Why a night, and why a campfire? Perhaps to suggest markers of time and place, which are methodically denied us by the non-story we have. Why are there three of them, when only two speak? Perhaps to remind us of the triangulation of storytelling, and of the significance of those who are silent. In taking this joke seriously for a moment, I suggest that it presents a meta-story about the investment in familiar stories, and about how that investment produces a self-perpetuating cliché. "It was a dark and stormy night."

Dubrow writes of the *Sonnets*, "these poems repeatedly problematize the narrative impulse that the conventional wisdom so unproblematically assigns to them."[58] In recognizing this, and in resisting the impulse to map prescribed narratives onto the sequence, readers unfold the meanings of the gaps. "Every effort to read these poems continually reminds us that here is a poet who has created a text that constantly recoils when we touch it," Gregory Bredbeck writes. The result is a space of ambiguous possibility, in which "the sequence creates an experience wherein we are continually able to read the sodomite but are never quite sure if we should."[59] Jonathan Goldberg's interrogation of the assumptions that attend "homosexual" and "heterosexual" famously redefines heterosexuality as sodomy; Halpern's pursuit of that idea leads him to credit the feminine addressee with "a proto-Sadean sublimity, a sublimity that is sodomitical through and through."[60] De Grazia's skepticism about a "scandalous" homoeroticism uncovers the fear of miscegenation. Bruce Smith historicizes pronouns to reveal elusive situations of utterance: "The 'I' of Shakespeare's Sonnets refuses to conform to the sexual dictates of another time and place. If the 'I' in these poems is so difficult to locate, then how wary you and I—or you, I, and *they*—should be in presuming to say 'we.'"[61] When Freinkel proposes that we read "Will" through the "abuse" of catachresis, she illuminates not referential figuration but the endless processes that displace it: "because

Will is an ornament that must keep ornamenting, falsifying and restoring in the very same gesture, *Will* is also that ornament that signals our inability to distinguish ornament from ornamented."[62] By declining an obvious story, readers disclose counter-narratives which, just as Garber's "third term" is not a term, are not narratives at all but exposés of a coercive narrative desire.

As they refuse to read the *Sonnets* toward a foretold conclusion, such accounts discover unassimilated possibilities—the sodomite, the sadist, the miscegenist, the inappropriable "I," the figure of abuse—but they do not discover these things *as* things, as the "real story" which would make an alternative but still integral sense. Instead they find non-sense, an effective challenge to those master narratives that persist even in and through their inversion. In the last 28 sonnets we find the non-sense of taxonomic misogyny as well. Its premises, deployed unevenly and incoherently, reflect back at an acute angle on the logic of heterosocial hierarchy. Rather than offer a reflexive repudiation which, by balancing "no" against "yes," fuels an ideological machine, intersubjective will reframes the conversation. Regulatory structures preoccupy the discourse of will in the *Sonnets*, but they do not circumscribe it, and the constitutive trespasses of gendered subjectivity appear in the crossings and the breaks. I depart from Dubrow by taking the last 28 sonnets as interrelated meditations on heterosocial bonds, but I share her uneasiness with the familiar narrative that might follow from that choice: by reading for unity, we may find what we presuppose, a coherent misogynist approach that fulfills its disciplinary functions.[63] By suspending presumption, we can recover a fragmentary, porous, and in all senses partial account of the relations among social subjects.

These sonnets heighten an unreason that the formulaic reductions of misogyny always, however reluctantly, let slip. They do not invent a new scheme, but deploy the speaking parts of an old one in destabilizing ways. Jonathan Dollimore's account of transgressive reinscription, "the return of the repressed and/or the suppressed and/or the displaced via the proximate," resonates closely: feminine subjects participate in the strategies of social habitation, and the last 28 sonnets articulate an immanence that silence can only belie.[64] Greene writes, "to be sufficiently historical and poetic at once, interpretation ought to consider alternatives to the individualist conception of person (such as gender, class, and generation) as horizons of the lyric poem; to assess tropes and other fundamental features as determining the lyric's position in relation to events; and finally to explain the poem as a medium of social change in process."[65] It might be too much to say that the *Sonnets*

Figure 8. "A wished warre." Otto van Veen, *Amorum Emblemata*
(Antuerpiae: Typis Henrici Swingenij, 1608), 9. By permission of the Folger
Shakespeare Library.

effect social change through their treatment of categorical edicts, but they are
radically and metaculturally skeptical, and their intersectional theory of will
puts critical pressure on the truisms of heterosociality. The sequence ends
with that pair of notoriously opaque poems in which two cupids, like three
robbers, like the platitudes of misogyny, appear as traces of a story displaced
by metatextual repetition. For all their symbolic promise, these last sonnets
do not impose teleology or referential figuration or a discipline of sense, but
turn again around a subjectivity consummated in artifactual interdependence: "the bath for my help lies / Where Cupid got new fire: my mistress'
eye" (153.13–14).

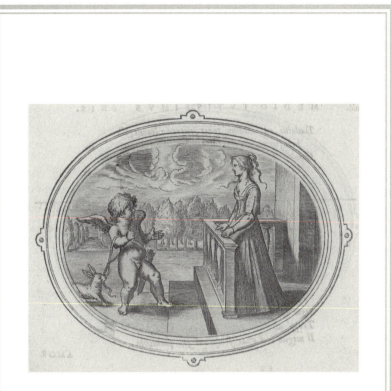

Chapter Six

"Twixt Will and Will Not"

Chastity and Fracture

in *Measure for Measure*

Are all women then turn'd Masculine? No, God forbid, there are a world full of holy thoughts, modest carriage, and severe chastitie; to these let mee fall on my knees, and say; You, O you women; you good women; you that are in the fulnesse of perfection, you that are the crownes of natures worke, the complements of mens excellencies, and the Seminaries of propagation; you that maintaine the world, support mankinde, and give life to societies; you, that armed with the infinite power of Vertue, are Castles impregnable, Rivers unsaileble, Seas immoveable, infinit treasures, and invincible armies. . . . You are *Seneca's* Graces, women, good women, modest women, true women: ever yong, because ever vertuous, ever chast, ever glorious.

—*Hic Mulier*, sig. A3–A3v

But I wretched, most wretched, in the very commencement of my early youth, had begged chastity of Thee, and said, "Give me chastity and continency, only not yet."

—Augustine, *Confessions*, 8.7.17

In *Measure for Measure*, Isabella offers two propositions that bracket the play's action as they address the threat of death: "O, let him marry her," and "Thoughts are no subjects, / Intents but merely thoughts" (1.4.49; 5.1.453–54).[1] These statements instantiate a complex interplay of solution and problem: they signal a progress toward comic ends, but hint that it might founder in the gap between intention and act. As Isabella argues for Angelo's inadvertent innocence, she describes a fault line that runs through *Measure*. Angelo does not carry out his plan, but his reprieve exposes a more comprehensive disjunction, which separates abstract strategies from material accomplishments.[2] While this suspension of effects preserves the possibility of redemption, it also interrupts the teleology that presses toward socialized desire. The

Figure 9 (preceding page). "Beginings are dificill." Otto van Veen, *Amorum Emblemata* (Antuerpiae: Typis Henrici Swingenij, 1608), 41. By permission of the Folger Shakespeare Library.

awareness that masculine subjects cannot translate conception into consummation is both deliverance and dilemma, as if a conclusion can take shape only through vacated agency; the exculpation of Angelo, like the Duke's refusal to enforce his own laws, attenuates activity into inertia. If *Measure* is indeed a problem play, it displays one obvious problem in its notorious parade of top-down management styles, and the Duke's abdication and Angelo's tyranny are symptoms of the same limitation: political authority fails to generate social integrity. That failure reflects a double break—between judgment and regulation, and between reason and passion—which signals the absence of effective will. Sovereign subjects suffer an estrangement of the vital faculty that mediates between what they should mean and what they can do. Isabella's chaste volition intervenes, with the opacity of a principle that is at once integral to and detached from the system it works to restore.

Measure sets up a math problem: neither a contract safeguarded by virginity nor one verified by pregnancy equals marriage. As Janet Adelman writes, "for Angelo as for Vienna, there is only a region of sexual soil below marriage and a region of absolute purity above it, with no middle ground for legitimate sexuality within marriage."[3] Addition and multiplication devolve into division and subtraction; the ethos that inspires Pompey's famous protest—"Does your worship mean to geld and splay all the youth of the city?" (2.1.230–31)—recognizes only the alternatives of abstinence and crime, and forecloses the space in which sexuality turns to social use. This risks being simple plot summary, not only of *Measure* but of comedy as a genre: the play revolves around a problem of unsocialized desire. But *Measure* engages the issue in theoretical terms, and pursues a sustained meditation on ideological practice. In its intensely social rendering of philosophical ideas about subjectivity, the play reflects on the brittle links between abstract tenets and the bodies that enact them.[4] More particularly, through what Katharine Eisaman Maus describes as "the play's contestatory way of imagining the relationship between sexuality and community," *Measure* evaluates the comic prize of married chastity.[5] Utility and fantasy collide in that compressed term of social accommodation, which translates necessary compromise into ethical, erotic, and formal triumph. Yet as the sheer hard work of chastisement makes clear, married chastity is an act of faith manufactured through an act of will, and when *Measure* constructs counterfactual paths toward ruinous failure and conditional success, it leaves only a narrow space of difference between them.

Interpretations of *Measure* have often described it as a disquisition on hierarchy, illustrated by effective state power and coercive heterosocial unions; such arguments fix the text in its cultural moment, but at the same time displace the story in favor of prehistory and sequel. Onstage, we witness a failure of connection between precepts and enactments, and in this sense *Measure* is less about ideological obviousness than it is about the alienation of agency. As influential readings answer the play's most urgent questions— can the Duke rule effectively? does Isabella accept his proposal?—they re-suture actions to their proper subjects, and reconcile intentions to results. Jonathan Dollimore makes a strong claim for political efficacy: "The Duke also embodies a public reconciliation of law and morality. An omniscience, inseparable from seeming integrity, permits him to close the gulf between the two."[6] Adelman offers a grim verdict on Isabella's fate: "a sanctuary made only to be violated, invaded and shamed as much by the play as by Angelo and the Duke, her threatening power is in the end firmly subordinated to the imperatives of patriarchal marriage."[7] Under the pressures not only of genre and history but of the play's specific investments, draconian government and autocratic marriage have the feel of things that must happen. Yet the Duke's machinations fail more conspicuously than they succeed, and Isabella, in the end, remains silent.[8] As Natasha Korda incisively points out, *Measure* with-holds conventional indices of location and affiliation: "no one is 'at home' in this play, and virtually no one is married."[9] If the answers we provide seem self-evident, it is all the more striking that the play refuses to provide them at all.

Hierarchical constancy requires that willing subjects conspire in the rule of law, a scheme which *Measure* empties out from the start. At the play's conclusion, the reason that imposes restraint still stands at odds with the passion that pursues anarchic ends. The gap might be bridged by marriage, which weaves a disciplinary yet reciprocal contract between those poles. That synthetic remedy informs Isabella's response—"let him marry her"—but her demand is doubly unanswerable: it is so obvious as to forestall argument, and there is no auditor with the will to meet it. Isabella must effect her edict herself, rewriting social order in the terms she takes as prescribed, and speak-ing not only for her own dedicated virginity but for a chastised sexuality that becomes the law it seeks to obey. *Measure* in this way segregates feminine will from masculine subjects, even as that will answers the needs of heterosocial self-perpetuation. In a realm of fragmented sovereigns, Isabella's virtue prom-ises integration, but her self-government discloses the conflicting forces that must cohere toward comic ends. She makes married chastity happen, but she cannot entirely make it make sense; her own inherent contradiction, which disengages her from the system in which she invests, raises questions for which her final refusal to answer stands as a sign. We are left with the speculative possibility that social accord might follow from intersubjective contract, and with marriage as the generic and social model for that bond. *Measure* refuses to naturalize this generative resolution; instead, the play represents both the idea and its improbability through the ambiguous figure of Isabella's will, and suggests that any bridge may span a void.

Intents But Merely Thoughts

Measure sums up the crisis of masculine sovereignty in the question repeatedly posed to the Duke: "What is your will?"[10] Will has become both remote and obscure, and the effect of disordered priorities appears in Angelo's early line, "Always obedient to your Grace's will, / I come to know your pleasure" (1.1.25–26). The Duke's pleasure supersedes his will as it fuses personal and collective liberties: he abandons his people because he has licensed their abandon, because his lack of displeasure causes a confusion that exceeds his desire for command. The Friar's censure—"It rested in your Grace / To unloose this tied-up justice when you pleas'd" (1.3.31–32)—provokes an acknowledgment that justice has escaped the reach of its agent: "Sith 'twas my fault to give the people scope, / 'Twould be my tyranny to strike and gall them / For what I bid them do" (1.3.35–37). As he frames a choice between consistent indulgence and inconstant tyranny, the Duke erases the premise of good government.[11] Early modern political theorists argue that a ruler curbs unrest as reason governs the passions: "Wherefore we may wel judge of *Reasons* rule, / By the *Affections* and *Wils* continence; / As a good *Prince* or *Master* of a Schoole, / Make them they governe, hate, and shun misrule."[12] But *Measure* divides the faculties, setting judgment against inclination rather than connecting social control to the sovereign's well-ordered person. "The knowledge which respecteth the faculties of the minde of man, is of two kinds," writes Francis Bacon; "The one respecting his understanding and reason, and the other his will, appetite, and affection, wherof the former produceth position or decree, the later action or execution."[13] Decree breaks loose from execution in the absence of effective will, a disarticulation to which the Duke submits his person and his state.

As both consequence and sign of that fracture, abdication creates a partial, impotent isolation, detaching the monarch from authority over subjects he cannot escape.[14] Lucio repeatedly disparages the Duke to his face, but the joke lies less in Lucio's ignorance of his interlocutor than in the Duke's certainty that his face is still his own. The disguised ruler clings to an ideal of effective language—"Let him be but testimonied in his own bringings-forth" (3.2.144–45)—but he rewrites himself as a subjunctive third person even as he asserts the prerogative of the speech act.[15] "O, sir, you are de-ceiv'd," Lucio insists, and adds a tautology that overrides the Duke's provi-sional self-identity: "Come, sir, I know what I know" (3.2.123, 152). Jonathan Goldberg describes Lucio and the Duke as "actuating each other, operating as bound antagonists, linked as firmly as main masque and antimasque in a courtly entertainment."[16] As the theatrical analogy suggests, a subject's unruly performance not only threatens contamination, but constitutes its audience as already open to that threat. "Thou art the first knave that e'er mad'st a duke," the Duke tells Lucio in the revelation scene (5.1.356), but the rebuke cannot sustain its argument, for how is the Duke made, if not by the subjects he should rule? Constitutive reciprocity—Goldberg's "actuating each other"—realizes the state on correlative terms. Edward Forset argues that a ruler suffers the civil disorder that mirrors his own condition: "The humors of the bodie do often forciblie prevaile in the working and stirring of the mind . . . So the customes and inclinations of the people in each Countrie, hath otherwhile no smal force in the inclyning of the Soveraignes disposition, if not to approve, yet to tollerate some imperfections."[17] The disguise plot is in this sense belated; Lucio's reference to "the old fantastical Duke of dark corners" implies that the Duke has always strayed from the secure core of regulation, anticipating the absent monarch role he will eventually perform (4.3.156–57).[18] Unshaped by his own disposition, the Duke has no stable place from which to counter Lucio's certainty: "Friar, thou knowest not the Duke so well as I do" (4.3.161–62).

"The Duke is very strangely gone from hence," says Lucio at the play's beginning, "but we do learn / By those that know the very nerves of state, / His givings-out were of an infinite distance / From his true-meant design" (1.4.50; 52–55). Disingenuous speech may begin as policy, but "true-meant designs" recede to leave an impassable space between the subject who speaks and the subject he would speak as. "I pray you, sir, of what disposition was the Duke?" the Duke asks Escalus, and Escalus replies, "One that, above all other strifes, contended especially to know himself" (3.2.230–33). In his read-ing of the Duke's attempts to manage self-representation, Harry Berger asks, "Is there any indication that he *wants* to know himself?"[19] This, too, is a question of absent will; always a self in contention, the Duke abdicates to escape what he continues to be, his plot pacing out the distance between sovereign purpose and recuperative act.[20] When he tries to restore justice, his strategy separates power from presence, and widens the breach between intention and its effects. He transmutes his voice into a token, with the self-alienating statement, "The contents of this is the return of the Duke" (4.2.196–97). Authority precludes imminence; the "character" the Provost recognizes is not the person he sees but the text he reads, and only by detaching signs from the subject they identify can the Duke appear at all. Having imagined himself as Oberon ("I am invisible"), he speaks as Peter Quince: "All for your delight / We are not here."[21]

There is nothing particularly startling in this; the unified subject is far rarer and more fantastic than the subject in disarray. Yet if *Measure* does not argue for the peculiarity of self-division, it does impose a sense of consequence. The Duke's dislocated will spins off speech acts as uniformly masterful as they are indifferently embodied; haunted by the strange egalitarianism of a dispersed authenticity, the play crowds its stage with legitimate speakers, so that the revelation scene can only add one to many. "Were you sworn to the Duke, or to the deputy?" the Duke asks the Provost, who denies that the distinction signifies: "To him, and to his substitutes" (4.2.182–84). Escalus's assertion, made to the disguised Duke—"The Duke's in us; and we will hear you speak" (5.1.294–95)—has neither more nor less validity than anything the Duke himself might say; "came I hither, / To speak as from his mouth, what he doth know / Is true and false," Friar Peter announces, as if anyone could speak from that mouth, and have an equally plausible grasp on those truths (5.1.154–56). The symptom proliferates: everyone speaks for the law, and no one crosses the space between judgment and execution. The Duke himself reappears by indirection, offering inscrutable hints long after disguise has exhausted its use. "The Duke / Dare no more stretch this finger of mine than he / Dare rack his own. His subject am I not" (5.1.313–15). That last statement seems all too acute in its subjective disavowal. The Duke comes full circle, from absent presence to present absence: his restoration will always have happened too often and too late, through replications and displacements that constellate around a failure to infuse will into the local habitations of law.[22] The play produces its deus ex machina, but the machine is an assembly line of gods, who may accumulate to some effect but do not instate a unique agent at the source.

When the Duke instructs Angelo, "In our remove be thou at full ourself," he tries to invent Angelo as a kind of reverse avatar, a reference point of full presence for his own citational performance (1.1.43). "I have on Angelo impos'd the office, / Who may, in th' ambush of my name, strike home, / And yet my nature never in the fight / To do in slander" (1.3.40–43). The Duke hopes to protect both law and reputation, but reinforces the discontinuity he seeks to erase: nature does not agree with office, any more than name—at once the instrument of ambush and the object of slander—agrees with itself. By formally separating identity from act he forecasts a repetition, through which the transfer of title substitutes two subjects who cannot mean well for one who should. "This ungenitur'd agent will unpeople the province with continency," Lucio warns (3.2.174–75), and describes Angelo as an incorporation of unnatural processes. "They say this Angelo was not made by man and woman after this downright way of creation. Is it true, think you?" (3.2.104–106). Arguing that "he is a motion generative, that's infallible" (3.2.111–12), Lucio introduces two terms that conflict; editors sometimes correct "generative" to "ungenerative" to make it fit with the "ungenitur'd" of the later line.[23] But the inconsistency makes a point. Acting both as ungenitured agent and as motion generative—as the state agent who proscribes and the lawless motion that pursues—Angelo intensifies the incongruence between office and nature and further separates sociality from sex. Under his aegis, both public pacts and private attachments fail to produce sanctioned unions: in his unconsummated vow to Mariana, his illicit coercion of Isabella, and his violent divorce of Claudio and Juliet, Angelo vitiates the utility of desire. Sexuality explodes or stagnates, a force held at extremes by immoderate rule. "The law (who so well considereth thereof) is nought else, but a reasonable will of the law maker," Juan Huarte writes, "by which he declareth, in what sort he will that the cases which happen dayly in the common wealth, be decided, for preserving the subjects in peace, and directing them in what sort they are to live, and what things they are to refraine."[24] A reasonable will imposes cohesion both within and among subjects, but in Angelo's world of evacuated abstractions, will represents a vivisecting tool. This isolates his error. By recognizing only a hierarchy of severance, Angelo inhabits a dangerously incomplete mode of government, which dismantles social contracts and alienates his own faculty of self-control. He regards will as an instrument with which he can excise desires external to him, choosing partition over interrelation as if this were his choice to make.

The act that uses will to banish passion is not social justice, nor is its enforcement the work of rational virtue.[25] Angelo responds to Isabella's plea for mercy with the far too simple "I will not do't"; to her "But can you if you would?" he replies, "Look what I will not, that I cannot do" (2.2.51–52). He equates his will with law, but as Huarte argues, arbitrary autocracy breaks that link. "I sayd, a reasonable will, because it sufficeth not, that the king or emperour (who are the efficient cause of the lawes) declaring his will in what sort soever, doth thereby make it a law, for if the same be not just, and grounded upon reason, it cannot be called a law, neither is it: even as he cannot be tearmed a man who wanteth a reasonable soule."[26] The ruler's unreasonable will is tyranny, as Angelo's rule is so often named, and a tyrant lacks the integral quality of a man. Angelo insists that judgment guides his will and will effects his intent; desire is grit in the machine, an insurrection that justifies Claudio's death as it would his own.[27] "When I, that censure him, do so offend, / Let mine own judgment pattern out my death, / And nothing come in partial" (2.1.29–31). But Angelo is exactly partial, a creature of the faculty he mistakes as his means. When he argues that mercy would make him "the very cipher of a function" (2.2.39), he more aptly describes his relationship to a volition that neither fortifies his reason nor constrains his passion. The instrument turns back on the agent of its inapt use: mastery is a symptom of failed integration, and the claim of absolute dominion not only invites conquest but shows that it has already occurred. Angelo's belief in limitless jurisdiction reveals his subjection to unbounded will.[28]

The Provost equates Angelo's judgment with unreason, and pleasure again intrudes into the language of government: "I'll know / His pleasure, may be he will relent. Alas, / He hath but as offended in a dream!" (2.2.2–4). Pronouns slip; Angelo's relentless pleasure merges with the pleasure for which Claudio must die, and Claudio's willing vice touches Angelo's willful justice. The touch anticipates Angelo's later capitulation, but at the same time *is* that capitulation, consummated not between persons but within the person who fantasizes self-mastery and discovers self-betrayal. The Provost's inquiry, "Is it your will Claudio shall die to-morrow?" provokes a hectic interrogation: "Did not I tell thee yea? Hadst thou not order? / Why dost thou ask again?" (2.2.7–9). Angelo's underlying question—how does my will signify?—is as vast as an Augustinian dilemma, and as simple as the Provost's second thought. "I have seen / When, after execution, judgment hath / Repented o'er his doom" (2.2.10–12). The second thought is not of course simple at all. Mary Thomas Crane writes, "In the dark world of *Measure for Measure*, however, Shakespeare has created human cognitive systems in which pure rationality is not only impossible but in which the contamination of emotion seems necessarily unethical."[29] Because Angelo repudiates the integrative capacities of will, he experiences affect as bilateral despotism. "Answer me to-morrow," he tells Isabella, "Or by the affection that now guides me most, / I'll prove a tyrant to him" (2.4.167–9). Discipline yields to indiscriminate excess; affective response infects his judgment through the unbridled mobility of forces he disowns. Angelo does not act out of character, except in the sense that his will exceeds the character he has drawn of himself; lust is only a new name for the masterless force that drives him.[30] John Davies describes will as a capricious sovereign who binds the subject to a fallen state: "This liberty of *Monarchizing* thus / Shee deemeth good, what ill so ere ensues; / Which *libertie*, is *bondage* base to us."[31] An importunate feminine principle usurps masculine self-possession: the sexual poetics of this might tempt us, as Angelo is tempted, toward the false analogy of Isabella's guilt. But Angelo succumbs to his own uncoupling of intention and desire. He believes he can use reason in isolation, and mistakes passion for a separate implement that confirms his power of choice. Nicolas Coeffeteau argues that such errors always come home: "The *Passions* are absolute and depend not on the Empire of vertue. They present themselves uncalled."[32] Angelo's alienated will invites that passionate insurrection, just as it creates the mirage of self-sufficient reason. This twofold seduction leads to an either / or deadlock that cannot govern the political state, but does define his own.

Doubleness motivates the charge of hypocrisy, a mode of deliberate deception that masks the problem of alienated will. Hypocrisy circulates less as an exposure of false identity than as a false guarantor of true identity, making a distinction between person and role that denies discontinuity within personhood itself. The Duke's scheme pursues the wrong question: "hence shall we see / If power change purpose: what our seemers be" (1.3.53–54). An opposition between being and seeming presumes a singular self, overlaid with pretense but accessible to discovery and judgment.[33] Angelo instead over-inhabits the condition of being. His desire for Isabella multiplies the ways in which he means: "She speaks, and 'tis / Such sense that my sense breeds with it" (2.2.141–42). That crowded word "sense," which holds reason and passion within one term, condenses Angelo's unresolved duality. He describes himself as torn between essence and façade: "O place, O form, / How often dost thou with thy case, thy habit, / Wrench awe from fools, and tie the wiser souls / To thy false seeming! Blood, thou art blood" (2.4.12–15). But to confess himself a hypocrite is to invoke a constant identity his language cannot sustain. Place, form, case, habit, blood: where, in this mix of fractional and factitious impersonations, do we locate either false seeming or the truth it implicitly protects? Escalus's reproach increases the confusion: "I am sorry, one so learned and so wise / As you, Lord Angelo, have still appear'd, / Should slip so grossly, both in the heat of blood / And lack of temper'd judgment afterward" (5.1.470–73). Appearance is stabilized by "still"; blood becomes a "slip." Which has any claim on the real? Like the Duke, Angelo does not possess a person and assume a disguise; he occupies a disjointed condition that both exceeds and evacuates the place he attempts to fill. Having termed Angelo forsworn, murderous, "an adulterous thief, / An hypocrite, a virgin-violator," Isabella concludes, "It is not truer he is Angelo / Than this is all as true as it is strange" (5.1.40–44). Angelo's hypocrisy, like his tyranny, entangles truths made strange by their coincidence; he is, in the Duke's revealing phrase, "meal'd with that / Which he corrects" (4.2.83–84). When sovereign subjects dissociate will from government, an unintegrated man embodies the law of a disintegrated state. "This deed unshapes me quite, makes me unpregnant / And dull to all proceedings. A deflow'red maid! / And by an eminent body that enforc'd / The law against it!" (4.4.20–23). Unshaped and unpregnant, a preeminent body that neither attains unity nor enables generation, Angelo forfeits himself to a chaotic mix of faculties that do not make social sense. The will of the ruler commits treason against itself: "Nothing goes right—we would, and we would not" (4.4.34).

Will and Will Not

In her plea for Angelos's life, Isabella argues that this paralyzing rift should serve as mitigation:

> His act did not o'ertake his bad intent,
> And must be buried but as an intent
> That perish'd by the way. Thoughts are no subjects,
> Intents but merely thoughts. (5.1.451–54)

Inefficacy kills intention, truncates its advance, and prevents a criminal act: problem becomes solution. But what happens if we juxtapose Isabella's "Thoughts are no subjects, / Intents but merely thoughts" to Huarte's "The law . . . is nought else, but a reasonable will of the law maker"? Stability depends on the directive power of sovereign reason, and that power, undercut by the Duke's tolerance and by Angelo's tyranny, becomes a mandate which lacks material incarnation.[34] Isabella closes the gap: as she moves *Measure* toward married chastity, her will reconciles reason to passion and recuperates order, alliance, and continuity. We can trace versions of that pattern in many comedies. Through rebellion and acquiescence, disguise and revelation, departure and return, the feminine subjects of this genre vitalize the interdependencies that sustain social forms. Reading Shakespearean comedy through the ethical tradition that extends from Erasmus to Levinas, Donald R. Wehrs argues that women "assume the task of inducing language and corporeality to acknowledge one another, a mutual recognition on which hopes of personal and communal regeneration rest."[35]

Measure differs by degree, in the intensity with which it ties heterosocial intercourse to violence and identifies this as more than a generic conceit. Early modern tributes to feminine agency produce catalogues of women who kill themselves to avoid or atone for rape, and change the story only by reversing its direction, as when Thomas Heywood commends a collective murder: "they pluckt off his garments by force, and so discovered him to be of the contrarie Sex: at which *Diana* enraged, commanded all her Virgins to take up their Bowes and Quivers, and so they shot him to death with their Arrowes."[36] This encounter occurs outside social space, but its logic enters that space more directly than we might expect. *A Womans Woorth* praises an equally deadly response to a man's sexual lies: "She having no other supporte for her innocencie, then the true witnesse of her soule, unattainted and free from so vile an infamie; raisde up her spirits with such rightfull disdaine, against the unjust ravisher of her reputation, as she spared not to kill him in the middest of a verye honourable assembly." The "ravisher of reputation" commits a rhetorical crime and receives a corporeal punishment, but the text records no disproportion between these public acts. Instead, the author concludes with his own verdict: "which (under correction of better judgement) in my minde deserved rather pardon and recompence, then any ill reproche, scandale or punishment."[37] The defense of virtue obeys a higher law, an abstract idea that plays out in blood. Chastity is not a passive attribute, but the motive force of a battle between violence and violation. *The Lawes Resolutions of Womens Rights* describes an ingrained conflict—"But to what purpose is it for women to make vowes, when men have so many millions of wayes to make them break them?"—followed by a now-notorious counterfactual: "if the rampier of Lawes were not betwixt women and their harmes, I verily thinke none of them, being above twelve yeares of age, and under an hundred, being either faire or rich, should be able to escape ravishing."[38] The text recommends a penalty of death; law disciplines masculine lust in the name of feminine virtue, and, while this may be ventriloquism, its dynamic of utterance is complex. Heterosociality demands chastity of women, and supports that demand with a threat to kill men: an abstract ideology seems to speak, but through and to whom? The doctrine that chastises sexual subjects who are programmed for mutual destruction empties itself of the volitional persons it governs, denying feminine will, but erasing masculine choice as well. Where, then, does the system put its bodies? It cannot hold them apart, in a balance preserved by the prohibition of touch. Instead it sets them at odds, fracturing the veneer of natural order through a contest of wills that poises loss of feminine chastity against loss of masculine life. If this does not seem like an ideal account of social organization, it does sound remarkably like the plot of *Measure for Measure*.

As the play's chastising voice, Isabella calls attention to the conflict entrenched within heterosocial bonds. When readings of her role diverge drastically, asserting compliant subordination on the one hand and separatist resistance on the other, they reflect the open question of chaste will in a plot that finds closure in marriage. Criticism that goes two ways indicates that chastity could go either way: it might be an element consumed by the solution or a catalyst left untouched. The middle ground on which feminine agents participate in communal priorities is far harder to reach; useful objects and antisocial exempla appear as natural products of virtue, but an outcome that preserves the social value of sexual subjects requires something more like alchemy. Heinrich Bullinger addresses the difficulty by binding feminine will to divine grace: "The consentyng into mariage spryngeth out of gods ordinaunce and leaneth unto honesty. For an ordinate and pure love is it that she beareth toward her chosen, by hym her desyre to remayne wyth mynde, body, and good."[39] This paradigm sanctions desire and election as it assigns those capacities to women. Barbara Baines describes the basic paradox: "Chastity is thus the form of power that subjugation assumes."[40] A virtuous disposition of self solidifies social accord by dispersing the sites of sexual control, for consent presumes not a single capitulation but an ongoing volitional act. Isabella's proposition—"let him marry her"—relies for its success on the constant, purposeful feminine will that supports the contract of married chastity. The fact that Isabella stands apart underscores the systematic operation of that will, but discloses an unresolved tension: *Measure* isolates the principle of union in an other-directed faculty of choice.[41]

Isabella mobilizes chaste will to reshape the sexuality of *Measure*.[42] There is nothing uplifting about her intervention; it is not utopian but bleakly pragmatic, an unsentimental comment on the fact that heterosocial hierarchy depends on the agents it is built to destroy. But rather than dismiss Isabella as allegorical or unkind, we might echo the questions posed by Judith Halberstam in her discussion of the stone butch: "What does it mean to define a sexual identity and a set of sexual practices that coalesce around that identity within a negative register? What are the implications of a negative performativity for theorizing sexual subjectivities?"[43] Isabella's negative performativity, her obdurate "no," distances her from intimacies as she distills disordered practice into workable theory. By defining that role as at once intrinsic and estranged, *Measure* draws attention to the antisocial residue of socialized desire, and illuminates a will to virtue that exists both within and apart from the system it sustains. Isabella impels others toward a state from which she withholds herself, a double-edged act which externalizes a crux within chaste marriage. Feminine consent must preserve some constrained but still vital autonomy, a volitional superfluity that works to social ends. Isabella figures that attribute and reveals its risks: when she takes her body off the market and puts her will into circulation, she attenuates the connection between institutional requirements and individual choice, and tests the fragile, consequential link between compliance and self-direction.

Isabella's chastity is proprietary and transitive, a quality she possesses in order to impose. If the Duke guides her actions, he does so not only in disguise but in the abstract, his present absence reconceived as the concentration of an ideal. Isabella animates and executes that ideal, fulfilling an obligation which takes shape through her own resolve. Angelo reads feminine intercessions in strictly instrumental terms: "These poor informal women are no more / But instruments of some more mightier member / That sets them on" (5.1.236–38). He misrecognizes women as he misapprehends will, understanding neither the scale of their efficacy nor the purpose to which they turn; from his partial perspective, that "more mightier member" must be incorporate in men. He again grasps only the most limited concept of hierarchy, and refuses to see that its local expressions have failed. Isabella's resolution—"If ever he return, and I can speak to him, I will open my lips in vain, or discover his government" (3.1.192–94)—makes a point through its imprecise pronouns: she discovers the government of two rulers, in the doubled sense of exposing its faults and retrieving its functions.[44] She is motivated by the principle of law, both in the local sense of disciplinary codes and in the larger and more vital sense of social futurity. "The primordial Law is therefore that which in regulating marriage ties superimposes the kingdom of culture on that of a nature abandoned to the law of mating," Jacques Lacan writes. "Even when in fact it is represented by a single person, the paternal function concentrates in itself both imaginary and real relations, always more or less inadequate to the symbolic relation that essentially constitutes it."[45] "Imaginary and real relations"—those unrealized illusions of synthesis, sufficiency, perfect immanence and essential presence—delimit the scope of *Measure*'s patriarchs, "always more or less inadequate" to the law for which they stand. Regulatory edicts bypass this dubious habitation, and establish the symbolic relation of marriage under the warrant of chaste feminine will.

Isabella cannot be abstracted into the symbolic, any more than she can be reduced to instrumental use; she negotiates a meeting point between corporeal and social states. The fact of her virginity becomes the fantasy of chastised sexuality, a process in which "fact" and "fantasy" are distinguished not by a differential relation to truth, but by the shift from a bodily circumstance to a shared understanding of how that circumstance might mean. Arguing for a reciprocal relationship between ideology and embodiment, Crane writes, "The question becomes, then, not to what extent the play exerts a normativizing force in the formation of early modern subjects but rather in what ways conditions of embodiment are imagined as contributing to the creation of cultural norms."[46] This resonates with the circular genesis of virginity: even as a patrilineal order bases its survival on untouched bodies, those bodies emerge as belated precedents, their significance produced by the need for virtuous acts. When Lucio says to Isabella, "Hail, virgin, if you be, as those cheek-roses / Proclaim you are no less" (1.4.16–17), or when the Duke says, "The hand that hath made you fair hath made you good" (3.1.180–81), each speaker contends that Isabella's person predicates her virtue. But beneath the constant surface of natural meaning lies the variable condition of meaning well.[47] Angelo describes an adversarial relationship between virtue and mystification: "Your sense pursues not mine. Either you are ignorant, / Or seem so craftily; and that's not good" (2.4.74–75). If Isabella can seem, she must not be; if she knows to pretend ignorance, she reveals the loss of innocence.[48] Yet Isabella's reply refutes his reading. "Let me be ignorant, and in nothing good, / But graciously to know I am no better" (2.4.76–77). She asserts her virtue by sketching its compass, rejecting transcendent claims for situational affirmations, and in this way verifying the worth Angelo impugns. Her rejoinder mixes authenticity, volition, and social fluency to force a compound recognition: she is as she seems, but this risks understating the complexity of seeming to be as she is. Mario DiGangi writes, "Isabella occupies the space of resistance and loss between 'virgin' and 'wife'—a space

that is collapsed by the apparently seamless passage from 'maid' to 'wife.' "[49]
As that image of a spectral and volatile "between" suggests, being, for Isabella, is not a fixed state of truth but a mobile process of engagement. She
continually reconstitutes virtue through acts—both interventions and performances—that validate the exigencies to which she responds. Elsewhere, I
have discussed the equivocal cultural narratives that describe virginity and
chastity as acts of feminine will.[50] What, then, of a feminine subject who
both manages her own virginity and pursues the chaste marriages of others?

When Angelo first asks Isabella, "what's your will?" (2.2.26), she describes an impasse that splits her sense of self:

> There is a vice that most I do abhor,
> And most desire should meet the blow of justice;
> For which I would not plead, but that I must;
> For which I must not plead, but that I am
> At war 'twixt will and will not. (2.2.29–33)

The alternatives—to follow a will that renounces virtue, or to renounce will
itself—reflect a world in which agency works only as error. As Marcia Riefer
writes, "More than any comic heroine thus far, Isabella has reason to take
sexual degradation seriously."[51] Isabella's engagement with sexuality, however
mediated and undesired, threatens to reproduce the feminine guilt that appears in Claudio's self-reproach: "But it chances / The stealth of our most
mutual entertainment / With character too gross is writ on Juliet" (1.2.153–
55). "Mutual entertainment" cannot be mutual at all; it casts its participants
as author and inscription. In his catechism of Juliet, the disguised Duke
reveals the emptiness of reciprocity:

> Duke: So then it seems your most offenseful act
>   Was mutually committed?
> Juliet: Mutually.
> Duke: Then was your sin of heavier kind than his.
> Juliet: I do confess it, and repent it, father.
> Duke: 'Tis meet so, daughter. (2.3.26–30)

"Father" and "daughter" are more and less than courtesy terms; through
their use, the displacement of consent by sin appears as paternal law. Isabella's
advocacy enmeshes her in this logic, and exposes her to what Berger describes

as "the compromising conditions of her reluctant return to a discourse of gender and sexuality dominated by male fears and desires."⁵² Within this discourse, feminine sexual volition equals feminine sexual fault.

Separatism offers one escape from that trap, and Theodora Jankowski argues compellingly that Isabella resists heterosexual interpellation.

> Isabella, however, in accepting the name of one type of not-women—queer virgin—has wrested both the power of choice and the power of defining, or categorizing, herself away from men. Only by being a queer virgin can she challenge the sexual economy by creating a category of autonomous female who has the power to resist both Angelo's illegal—and the Duke's legal—proposals of sexual servitude.⁵³

I want to hold on to the force of this resistance, and trace its effects on the heterosocial encounters in which Isabella argues for a more functional law. Isabella alters the range of choice: she does not respond to Angelo on his terms, but challenges his right to set them. "I would to heaven I had your potency, / And you were Isabel! Should it then be thus? / No; I would tell what 'twere to be a judge, / And what a prisoner" (2.2.67–70). Recasting herself as judge, Isabella detaches sovereignty from masculinity, and argues that any virtuous subject might act as agent of the law. She refutes the equation of her chastity with Claudio's life—"We cannot weigh our brother with ourself" (2.2.126)—and, when Angelo argues, "Nay, women are frail too," she turns his platitude to reverse its blame. "Women? Help heaven! men their creation mar / In profiting by them" (2.4.124; 127–28). The image of a woman marred for masculine profit illustrates her own position, for which she takes herself to task: "it oft falls out, / To have what we would have, we speak not what we mean. / I something do excuse the thing I hate, / For his advantage that I dearly love" (2.4.117–20). Isabella theorizes her self-division, and condemns a rupture between proper intention and suspect desire, "what we mean" and "what we would have."

Angelo insists that an essential unity is in fact her weakness: "Be that you are, / That is a woman; if you be more, you're none" (2.4.134–35). The tautological directive—"be that you are"—presumes that Isabella must follow affection, and that her attachment to her brother is interchangeable with erotic surrender. Angelo repeats the familiar argument that links feminine will to uncontrolled desire; as a woman, Isabella should understand the sense of sense. Yet she does not understand at all: "I have no tongue but one; gentle my lord, / Let me entreat you speak the former language" (2.4.139–40). She recurs to the vocabularies of law, reason, and judgment, her own former language: "Better it were a brother died at once, / Than that a sister, by redeeming him, / Should die for ever" (2.4.106–8). Jessica Slights and Michael Morgan Holmes describe the controversion of truisms: "At once a chaste bride of Christ and a politically savvy woman, Isabella is 'more than' a woman in Angelo's terms and as such constitutes a forceful challenge to conventional assumptions about the connection between sexuality and female identity."[54] Angelo threatens Isabella with a bleak analogy—"Were not you then as cruel as the sentence / That you have slander'd so?" (2.4.109–10)— but she translates this into her own austere resolve. "Then, Isabel, live chaste, and, brother, die; / More than our brother is our chastity" (2.4.184–85).

It seems that Isabella has made a divisive choice, rejecting affection for abstraction and troubling many readers in the process. Jacqueline Rose identifies this decision as a fulcrum for critical response: "criticism has alternatively revered and accused her in such a way that her sexual identity has become the site on which dissatisfaction with the play, and disagreement about the play, have turned."[55] Claudio, Isabella's first and most invested spectator, speaks for a larger audience: "Sweet sister, let me live. / What sin you do to save a brother's life, / Nature dispenses with the deed so far, / That it becomes a virtue" (3.1.132–35). Broad strands of the play's critical and theatrical histories suggest that, by introducing Isabella's adamant refusal, Shakespeare makes her so high-minded she enters her own orbit. But Judith Butler's point about embodied states is pertinent here: "Surely there must be some kind of necessity that accompanies these primary and irrefutable experiences. And surely there is. But their irrefutability in no way implies what it might mean to affirm them and through what discursive means."[56] Isabella will not give her body for her brother's use, but that denial opens up a more expansive affirmation: her irrefutable bodily experience becomes the touchstone of heterosocial viability. Through the discursive shift from "I am / At war 'twixt will and will not" to "our chastity," sexual restraint takes shape as a social project; the singular attribute of virginity broadens its scope, to encompass a communal move toward generative continence. But it both matters and signifies that *Measure* inhibits empathy and incites ambivalence. Isabella's choice echoes the stark imperatives that make a necessity of virtue, and weave sacrifice into the fabric of normative relations.

Isabella forfeits Claudio when she denies his social worth, condemning his depravity as an opportunistic contagion. "O you beast! / O faithless coward! O dishonest wretch! / Wilt thou be made a man out of my vice? / Is't not a kind of incest, to take life / From thine own sister's shame?" (3.1.135–39). As a family romance that creates neither lawful marriage nor legitimate children but constructs parodies of both, incest disfigures premises that assimilate the sexual to the social, and severs private bonds from public contracts. By accusing her brother in these terms, Isabella erases him from the records of patrilineal descent.[57] "What should I think? / Heaven shield my mother play'd my father fair! / For such a warped slip of wilderness / Ne'er issu'd from his blood" (3.1.139–42). To read this only in terms of anger or hysteria would ignore its structural weight. When Isabella says, "Die, perish! Might but my bending down / Reprieve thee from thy fate, it should proceed" (3.1.143–44), she makes a relentlessly social judgment. "Thy sin's not accidental, but a trade. / Mercy to thee would prove itself a bawd, / 'Tis best that thou diest quickly" (3.1.148–50). Anna Kamaralli writes, "Isabella may not invent the direction of the plot, but at each turning point in the play its direction hangs on her yes or no. If that yes or no choice comes out of a moral code, rather than personal inclination, she has indeed usurped a power usually reserved for men."[58] Isabella exercises a decisive faculty of choice; her edgy mix of resistance and compliance presses events to a point. I think, however, that her acts of determination reveal more than they usurp. *Measure* has little time for naturalized masculine prerogatives, and its ruthless anatomy of superstructures uncovers their foundations in feminine will. Condemning the pacts that debase alliance, rejecting the exchanges that vacate discipline, fleshing out hollow laws with the offer of her brother's death, Isabella actuates the tenets of social order. As is perhaps obvious, this is a long way from saying that she makes a happy ending.

Socialized desire, that bare formula for comedy, has fallen through the gaps in the play's broken system. Contract without sex is deadly: to Isabella, Angelo's betrayal of Mariana seems a distortion worse than death. "What a merit were it in death to take this poor maid from the world! What corruption in this life, that it will let this man live!" (3.1.231–33). Sex without contract is all too lively: "I had rather my brother die by the law than my son should be unlawfully born" (3.1.189–91). These cannot remain the only options, and Isabella brings will—as intention and desire, as energy and law—into alliance with itself. Coeffeteau describes the vital fusion that a virtuous will effects: "So as the triumph of vertue consists not in pulling away or rooting out the *Passions*, as monsters; but in ruling and reforming them like unto insolent and disobedient children: for they grow in us and are as the fruits and buds of our sensuality, which have onely need to be made subject unto *reason*."[59] As Isabella's mediation causes reason and passion to intersect, her cohesive influence does not eliminate sex, but reformulates its place in the regime of sexuality.[60] Laura Lunger Knoppers describes Isabella's agency as an alternative language—"Isabella speaks a counter-discourse to that of the male authorities, a discourse of chastity which gives her an independent, autonomous power"—and argues that a patriarchal plot must neutralize that threat.[61] Even if we imagine that *Measure* attempts a more capacious accommodation, feminine will operates in a register of ambivalence: its promise to restore conventional forms of order exposes a radical dislocation, and enables an imperfect return.[62] Isabella imposes her will, but it remains far from clear whether the chastising process reflects redemptive amendment or base necessity, whether it rises to alchemy or provides only a denatured solution.

Let Him Marry Her

Marriage, as so many readers have noted, is the play's final punishment.[63] For all his threats, the Duke does not enforce the death sentences of Angelo, Claudio, and Lucio; instead, with nasty precision, he oversees their weddings. "Go take her hence, and marry her instantly. / Do you the office, friar, which consummate, / Return him here again" (5.1.377–78). This constriction, of a sexuality that defies law into a sexuality that serves it, imposes order as it registers loss. Lucio's protest—"Marrying a punk, my lord, is pressing to death, whipping, and hanging" (5.1.522–23)—may express concern that his wife is a whore, but it also records the joyless knowledge that, through the coercive work of social taxonomy, she will cease to be one.[64] Rather than refute the definition of marriage as penalty, the Duke's reply to Lucio draws other unions into the equation. "Slandering a prince deserves it. / She, Claudio, that you wrong'd, look you restore. / Joy to you, Mariana! Love her, Angelo! / I have confess'd her, and I know her virtue" (5.1.524–27). Knowing feminine virtue, the Duke implies, means recognizing the intimate relations of chastity and chastisement, and accepting the causality that binds virtuous meanings to disciplinary effects. These marriages reprise the fantasy of the bed trick, through which a virgin / whore antithesis might become synthesis and license access to the best of both worlds. But they reveal, too, its melancholic fall: married chastity, which looks like a happy medium, is instead a compulsory compromise. Comedy's flirtation with tragedy culminates not in death, but in an understanding that the ending is not an end at all; this, for however long it endures, is where we must live.

The bed trick plays out a still less tenable fantasy about virtue itself, elucidating the incongruity that makes chastity at once absolute and negotiable. "On the one hand, virginity is seen as a value and a virtue; on the other, as a commodity to be exchanged," Carol Thomas Neely writes of the problem plays.[65] *Measure* collapses that distinction when the bed trick identifies bodily virtue with both individual choice and anonymous use, and reveals that chastity, like marriage, is not a seamless entity but a fractious convergence of adversarial terms. If corporeal innocence is vital to the scheme, so too is informed purpose: "It lies much in your holding up" (3.1.261), the Duke tells Isabella, and says of Mariana, "It is not my consent, / But my entreaty too" (4.1.66–67).[66] The fortuitous value of chaste objects intersects the intentional values of chaste subjects, commingling inert commodities with active practices of meaning. Many scholars have challenged the idea that chastity can only objectify women; their analyses recover the potential for chaste agency, and trace its implications in a range of compelling ways.[67] In a recent contribution to this project, Amy Greenstadt constructs an analogy between authorial intention and chaste feminine will, which draws on the contradiction Neely explicates. Greenstadt writes, "It makes sense that the period's vision of the individual's absolute power and potential subjection would be connected to the specifically female ideal of chastity, a virtue that positioned women simultaneously as rising above and stifled beneath a set of social, cultural, and political structures predicated on the control of their bodies and lives."[68] *Measure*'s bed trick literalizes that simultaneity to a remarkable degree. Rather than distribute autonomy and reification among disparate persons, develop those possibilities across time, or divide them between hypothesis and experience, the play forces an absolute convergence. In so doing, it draws a fine line—which may be no line at all—between the axis on which married chastity turns and the crux on which it breaks.

When the Duke proposes his plan to Isabella—"If you think well to carry this as you may, the doubleness of the benefit defends the deceit from reproof. What think you of it?" (3.1.256–58)—her answer suggests that she accepts its utilitarian terms. "The image of it gives me content already, and I trust it will grow to a most prosperous perfection" (3.1.259–60). But her first caveat claims some quality that this plot cannot touch: "Let me hear you speak farther. I have spirit to do any thing that appears not foul in the truth of my spirit" (3.1.205–7). A statement of spiritual self-possession erupts into a context of interchangeable bodies, and accentuates the friction within virtuous sexual will. The structure of the bed trick, which transforms virginity into married chastity yet preserves the virginal body intact, demonstrates that chastity is both means and end of social law: it must mean its own end, and at the same time remain an end in itself. This is the double edge of Parolles's riddle in *All's Well*: "Loss of virginity is rational increase, and there was never virgin got till virginity was first lost" (1.1.130). The surface describes the mechanics of reproduction, but beneath this we might feel a second, sharper point. A chaste woman perpetually reconstitutes herself as chaste, choosing, again and again, to make sexuality the sign of virtue. Chastity must be mutable and unconditional, a split requirement materialized in the bed trick's sleight of flesh.

The play concludes by way of this paradox, grounding its solution in the ambiguity of feminine sexual meaning. Isabella claims the body Angelo has seduced, only to reaffirm her untouched status; as Michael Friedman points out, her narrative arc defies logic. "Having announced that she slept with Angelo, Isabella can never see her virginity truly restored in a social sense: the slander itself is enough to deflower her in the eyes of society."[69] Yet *Measure* specializes in logical extremes, and in a theoretical sense Isabella's self-amendment, from sexual instrument to uncorrupted agent, repeats the quotidian magic of social virtue. Adelman's astute reading locates the bed trick in relation to "a morning-after fantasy, in which a virgin is violated and then abandoned, psychically transformed into a whore." Describing the trick as a "two-body accommodation to the morning-after fantasy," she argues that its artifice rescues men from their base desires, even as the visible work of that rescue undermines the order it secures.[70] If we shift focus from repressed sexual fantasy to the overt requisites of social contract, the outcome remains precarious: as a strategy intended both to preserve virginity and to consummate marriage, the bed trick vividly demonstrates that women choose to participate in sanctioned sexuality, and choose to be inviolate again to the world at large. Sexual virtue cannot be proven and appropriated once and for all, but must be repeatedly reinvented and performed. Butler famously describes gender as "an identity tenuously constituted in time, instituted in an exterior space through a *stylized repetition of acts*."[71] These terms—of tenuous constitution, formulaic repetition, and public space—are the conditions of normative femininity, through which bodily sex operates in some manufactured but acceptable relationship to social persona. Neither a passive vessel nor an adamant virgin makes sufficient sense of everyday intercourse, and only the reiterative exercise of feminine will can bring those unwieldy ideals into functional coincidence.

Chastity cannot make sense in singular terms, and by mobilizing two stories through one body, Isabella answers an extravagant demand. As both the agent of married chastity and the absolute referent for that contingent state, she shows that the will to virtue must remain to a degree independent of, and unaccommodated by, the hierarchical assimilations of heterosociality. But the final appeal to Isabella's will brings a delicate equilibrium to crisis: "Dear Isabel, / I have a motion much imports your good, / Whereto if you'll a willing ear incline, / What's mine is yours, and what is yours is mine" (5.1.534–37). Can the will to marriage willingly, willfully, marry itself? Can the fruitful and frictional layers of body and act, of medium and agent, of autonomy and integration, collapse into a flat "yes"? Can the bed trick be un-tricked, or tricked out for what was only, after all, a double date? The Duke's proposal focuses a conflict between product and process, between the serviceable answer of a comic conclusion and that other, more abstract and fugitive question of ideological continuity. Isabella's chaste will upholds a system in which it does not participate; she infuses integrity into paradox by representing, however fantastically, the dual meaning that social futurity so illogically requires. The gesture toward closure splits that will into conflicting functions—incorporate instrumentality and autonomous agency—which fracture its precarious coherence, so that the attempt to forge an inclusive heterosociality jeopardizes the longer arc of socialized desire. David McCandless compellingly argues, "[Isabella's] silence strands her between autonomy and patriarchal inscription"; at the same time, I would add, her silence sustains the hope that an irreducible contradiction may somehow continue to work as synthesis.[72] Any resolution of Isabella's story must oversimplify her role, for the process of ending is a calculus of costs. The problem of her decision is not that her answer eludes us, but that she might answer at all, reducing manifold capacity to a circumscribed form of use.

Isabella does not answer, but audiences have answered for her, with uneasiness and incredulity, displeasure and discontent. If the Duke's petition finds acceptance—hers, or ours—it does so by claiming the privilege of suspended disbelief, and that claim does not pass uncontested. The frequent reaction from my students ("He wants to *marry* a *nun*?") illustrates the conundrum, as do reviews of Peter Hall's 2006 production of the play. Opinions of that production vary: Charles Spencer's review is titled "A measure of success," while Tim Walker's review leads with "Death comes as a relief."[73] Hall's straightforward presentation draws mixed assessments, from Michael Billington's tribute—"its supreme virtue is that it makes you listen to the text with heightened awareness"[74]—to Kate Bassett's dismissal of the direction as "perfunctory."[75] But reviewers agree that the stark production emphasizes the shock of the ending. "What is always a jarring moment produces a stunned, disbelieving silence."[76] "It is an impressive performance by James Laurenson, although even he cannot bring off the Duke's final and ludicrous declaration of love for Isabella."[77] "Andrea Riseborough's Isabella and everyone else simply stand and gawp at James Laurenson as the Duke who has surreptitiously watched and manipulated all this nonsense and now decides to wed the nun. Like some of us, they just can't register what has happened."[78] "The assembled throng turn to one another in utter shock, Isabella clings to her brother Claudio and the lights go down on this dark and deeply troubled city."[79]

This wholesale rejection is at least suggestive, and arguably odd. Shakespearean comedies offer many unlikely endings, but while Katharine's capitulation, Hippolyta's domestication, and Olivia's myopic satisfaction may frustrate and perplex, we commonly call on cultural critique—our own, or Shakespeare's—rather than refuse to accept the plot. What does it say if we argue that something *cannot* happen? If we have recourse, as Benedict Nightingale does, to the statement, "My theory is that the Bard got stuck"?[80] Or conclude, still more simply, that *Measure* is "hack tosh," or "a bugger of a play"?[81] And why does *Measure* give us the space of Isabella's silence in which to compose such a response? In Leah Marcus's dense formulation, "What can her silence mean?"[82] As those particular words indicate—not "does," but "can"; not "say" or "imply" or "reveal," but "mean"—the questions stirred by silence extend beyond a single moment or a single fate. Isabella's will to virtue both supports and exposes the fragile compromise of heterosociality, and finally offers only the knowledge that, in moving toward an answer, we proceed toward a state of loss. If marriage seems neither persuasively real nor attractively imaginary, this is perhaps because it is so aggressively symbolic, a social imperative uneasily occupied by the bodies that populate its scheme. *Measure* breaks open the comic unification of necessity and desire, revealing that they must converge, but cannot cohere. The problem has a particular urgency for the regime of social sexuality: both the emblematic collaboration of reason and passion and the ideological conflation of virginity and married chastity appear as products of an arduous process, at best artifactual, at worst inconceivable. The play's unspoken final verdict highlights a troubled awareness that chastity is a matter of will, and that whatever chaste feminine subjects might choose to do, it must always be too much, and can never be enough.

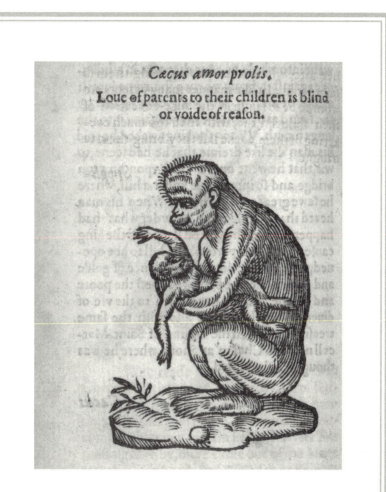

Cæcus amor prolis.
Loue of parents to their children is blind
or voide of reason.

Chapter Seven

"Fallen Out With
My More Headier Will"

Dislocation in *King Lear*

Sweet gyrle (quoth he) the glory of my life,
The blessed and sole object of mine eyes,
For whom the Heavens with Nature fell at strife,
On whom the hope of all my fortune lies,
Whose youth, my age with comfort still supplies,
    Whose very sight, my drouping hart doth raise,
    And doth prolong thy aged fathers dayes.
              —Drayton, *The Tragicall Legend*, sig. G1

Let a man but further consider the great difficulty that consisteth in
the bringing up of Children, if he have them; the infinite discomfort,
if he have them not.
        —Jardin, *A Discourse of the Married and Single Life*, sig. A6v.

King Lear revolves around a king's misguided will. The wordplay seems irresistible: Lear's errant will causes him to make a bad will, to banish the hope of unified accord and abandon his kingdom to unworthy heirs. But if we suspend the retrojected teleology of hindsight, does the succession Lear constructs guarantee conflict, insurrection, and death? Social disintegration is not compassed in a single sovereign act; it expands and escalates throughout the play, and finds its most incisive articulation in feminine subjects who assume autonomous states. When Lear cedes kingdoms to two daughters and banishes the third to a rival realm, *Lear* plays out the possibility that feminine will might circulate on its own terms, cut free from masculine absolutism and animated by independent intentions and desires. The play represents disaffected agents who give up affiliation only to seize alternative jurisdictions: problems of absence and presence, highlighted in *Measure for Measure* by vacated law and chaste discipline, intensify in the exiles and instatements of this later play. Women are detached from hierarchy even as they incorporate the principles of government; their faculty of meaning operates directly,

Figure 10 (preceding page). "Love of parents to their children is blind or voide of reason." Claude Paradin, *The Heroicall Devises of M. Claudius Paradin* (London: William Kearney, 1591), 282. By permission of the Folger Shakespeare Library.

neither overseen nor mediated in its consequential powers of choice. *Lear* sketches the foundation and dissolution of a state populated by figures of alienated will. That narrative arc, which sets feminine subjects at odds with patrilineal survival, executes the separatist agenda of misogyny and enacts its corrosive effects.

Abdication is clearly a red flag, but it may at the same time be a red herring. Richard Strier points out that Lear's division of the kingdom causes little disquiet, and indeed represents a prudent response to political instability: "the plan, insofar as we can infer its details, was a sensible and politically astute one. . . . One is tempted to ask the critics who think of the division of the kingdom as inherently disastrous what they think Lear ought to have done."[1] Strier persuasively argues that Lear's circumstances limit his options, and that his solution does not break down until he derails it with ill-conceived sequels.[2] The raw force of those errors may compel our attention, as train wrecks tend to do, but we witness another phenomenon as well: an eccentric, itinerant sovereign reveals the dispersal of sovereign will. When Lear asks his daughters to speak for the right to succeed him, and thus disregards the presumption implicit in Kent's opening line—"I thought the king had more affected the Duke of Albany than Cornwall" (1.1.1–2)—he demystifies the exclusivity of masculine government.[3] The decision ensures chaos only if we attribute an essential and essentialist misogyny to the play, an ideological entrenchment that construes women as the natural enemies of order. Nothing binds us to that perspective, nor is it the only one available. In response to John Knox's polemic against female rulers, John Aylmer formulates a complex argument about plurality:

> So the woman being eyther as a childe to hir father, or a servaunt to
> hir maister, or a wyfe to her husband, respecting these persones: can
> not be head over them in those offices: that is in the office of a
> father, a maister, or a husband. But in the office of a ruler and a
> magistrate she may be this mans wyfe, that is his subject, and his
> head, that is his magistrate. So that this argument by destinction is
> nothing, for it is a Fallax, called *ignoratio elenchi*, as resolve it, and
> you shal see the faulte.[4]

Aylmer imagines what *Lear* brings into effect: the roles played by women proliferate, so that daughters remain daughters even as they become sovereigns, and represent paradox rather than incapacity. Paradox, of course, is messier.

When Lear says, "by the marks / Of sovereignty, knowledge, and reason / I should be false persuaded I had daughters" (1.4.227–29), he condenses the loss of social authority, affective affiliation, and subjective constancy into one act of estrangement, iterating the comprehensive collapse that leaves him "fallen out with my more headier will" (2.4.90). *Lear* proceeds toward desolation when men abandon self-government and intersubjective exchange, and exclude the women who vitalize those practices. "Why this fellow hath banished two on's daughters and done the third a blessing against his will," says the Fool (1.4.98–100); the phrase "against his will" sums up the interlocked procedures of self-inflicted division and other-addressed disavowal that undermine personal and social integrity. Will becomes not the vehicle of a king's judgments but a quality of the subjects he has disowned, and its alienated potency uncouples the interdependence that maintains and regenerates heterosocial forms. As Lear disclaims his ties to the future, he breaks apart the social body, disclosing that men cannot remake themselves without the purposeful participation of women. This is less a biology lesson than an anatomy of shattered contracts.

Who with Best Meaning Have Incurred the Worst

By working through the processes that lead from initial disconnection to sterile isolation, *Lear* exposes the error that takes misogyny as a directive for social practice. Misogyny, in early modern contexts, often manifests a concern that women interact too closely with men, and in *Lear* this appears as hyperbolic dread. Gloucester says to Regan, "I would not see thy cruel nails / Pluck out his poor old eyes, nor thy fierce sister / In his anointed flesh rash boarish fangs" (3.7.59–61). Albany demands of Goneril, "Tigers, not daughters, what have you performed? / A father, and a gracious agèd man, / Whose reverence even the head-lugged bear would lick, / Most barbarous, most degenerate, have you madded" (4.2.41–44). Lear himself argues that, through heterosexual intimacy, men propagate their own annihilation: "Is it the fashion that discarded fathers / Should have thus little mercy on their flesh? / Judicious punishment: 'twas this flesh begot / Those pelican daughters" (3.4.66–69). Even this brief catalogue shows a picture of ruin. Yet the fear that women might act—however authentic its affective content—mistranslates the understanding that women must act. Misogyny is a symbolic exercise of control, of the kind that leads Pierre Bourdieu to conclude,

"Symbolic power, a subordinate power, is a transformed, i.e. misrecogniz-able, transfigured and legitimated form of the other forms of power."[5] This particular exercise describes a double move: misogyny legitimates a power that would suppress and expel feminine subjects, even as it transfigures the constitutive power of feminine subjects themselves. To accept misogynist dis-course on its most overt terms is to misrecognize the crucial interrelations that underlie those terms, to mistake a requisite proximity for an extrinsic threat. The partial apprehension displayed in *Lear*, through which an inter-dict obscures a need, renders femininity monstrous. "Then let them anato-mize Regan, see what breeds about her heart"; "Women will all turn monsters"; "Humanity must perforce prey on itself / Like monsters of the deep"; "Down from the waist / They're centaurs, though women all above."[6] Such statements follow the programmatic misdirections of misogynist plati-tudes, and recognize only unnatural breeding or a barren dead end. Social rebirth vanishes from this space.

In severing themselves from women, men make all feminine will equally dangerous, and the constancy of Cordelia becomes as deadly as the violent caprice of Regan and Goneril. The distinctions that misogynist categories impose—between virtue and vice, between value and cost—are undone by the success of excision. Inevitably, an argument that links Cordelia to Regan and Goneril resists the sentiments circulated within and elicited by the play. Alterity, policy, desire, and damage may, as I will argue, unite the effects of feminine will in *Lear*, but the agents of those effects inspire divided response. Such qualitative differences determine the affective and exemplary legacies of these characters; however, they neither explain nor redress the crisis of social futurity that the play foregrounds as a central concern. *Lear* distinguishes between virtuous and vicious acts, but the problem of alienated will sharply separates the taxonomic projects for which those distinctions matter from the social processes for which they do not. When the misogynist repudiation of women succeeds, it connects subjects across ethical, emotional, and aesthetic boundaries, opposing transactional feminine volition to the stasis of mascu-line detachment.[7]

That process begins with Cordelia's banishment, which dismisses the good will that informs social bonds. From the start, *Lear* highlights Cordelia's faculty of choice: "What shall Cordelia do? Love and be silent" (1.1.55). Her decision is deliberate and informed, a withholding of performative speech that she understands as an act. When she does speak, her "Nothing, my lord" describes a self-imposed limit, and her explanation—"I love your majesty /

According to my bond, nor more nor less" (1.1.81–82)—expresses a refusal to violate obligations she regards as self-evident. For Cordelia, the transparent terms of the bond require only the briefest shorthand to revive recognition. She is wrong, of course, not in her knowledge of the rules, but in her belief that such knowledge still binds this social universe. Philippa Berry writes, "In his rejection of Cordelia and Kent, Lear rejects those very cords or bonds— the claims of the heart or 'bias of nature'—whose honouring the play implies to be central to true sovereignty."[8] Lear accuses Cordelia of dishonoring a covenant his own language breaks: "Here I disclaim all my paternal care, / Propinquity, and property of blood, / And as a stranger to my heart and me / Hold thee from this forever" (1.1.102–5). Renaming his daughter bastard and barbarian, Lear rewrites her meaning and substitutes alienation for contract. "According to my bond": as it loses its shared sense, this phrase marks the divide between Cordelia's intersubjective intent and the isolating force of Lear's desire.[9]

Cordelia's silence suggests a refusal to lie, as if her sisters' extravagance must infect her own speech. Yet she does speak of love, both to the audience and to the king; the lie she will not tell would contravene social law.

> Good my lord,
> You have begot me, bred me, loved me.
> I return those duties back as are right fit,
> Obey you, love you, and most honor you.
> Why have my sisters husbands, if they say
> They love you all? Happily when I shall wed
> That lord whose hand must take my plight shall carry
> Half my love with him, half my care and duty.
> Sure I shall never marry like my sisters,
> To love my father all. (1.1.84–93)

If anything, Cordelia understates the case. Lynda Boose points out, "Lear the father will not freely give his daughter her endowment unless she purchases it with pledges that would nullify those required by the wedding ceremony."[10] Early modern texts routinely celebrate the conjugal love that supersedes filial duty; Agrippa adheres to that convention when he counsels, "Let the father gyve place, the mother gyve place, the chyldren, the brothers and systers, let al the heape of frendes gyve place to the swete benevolence and entier love of man and wife, and that for great skyl. For the father, mother, chyldren, brethern, systers, kynsfolke, be the frendes of nature, and workes of fortune: man and wyfe be the mistery of god."[11] In her willingness to love Lear and leave him, Cordelia turns individual attachment toward communal regeneration. Lorna Hutson describes her as "an example of a woman who embraces the inarticulacy and discontinuity proper to the stability and assurance of the gift as pledge of friendship between men."[12] Strategic intention and affective desire are closely knit here, integrated by the will to marriage; Cordelia speaks the theory of homosocial exchange as she participates in its practice. *Lear* thus begins with a fundamental mistranslation, through which the daughter who promises masculine alliance and patrilineal continuity becomes the barbarous alien of her father's bastardizing word.

Lear repudiates the usefulness of bodies, the value of bonds, and the efficacy of consent, evacuating pragmatic, affective, and contractual logics through a totalizing vision that can only misread. If, within a patriarchal structure, fathers can do what they want with daughters, this father wants to do without one. That choice plays out the risks of taking misogyny at its word: homosocial exchange stops short, as no marriage allies men to one another. When Lear describes France and Burgundy as "rivals in our youngest daughter's love" (1.1.41), he subordinates all desires to his positions as father and as king. But in the course of the brief scene he abjures those roles; as a result his demands produce effects counter to their purpose, and his final word is nonsense.[13] "Thou hast her, France. Let her be thine, for we / Have no such daughter" (1.1.251–52). How can he give the daughter he refuses to own? Heinrich Bullinger, in his only qualification of paternal right, bars the irresponsible father from the influence he has forfeited: "Then ought the father well to consydre that thorow hys owne wrongful and unrighteous demeanour, he hath lost his authorite as towechyng hyndryng and breaking of that mariage."[14] Cordelia's comment on Lear's choice of Burgundy and Burgundy's refusal—"I shall not be his wife" (1.1.238)—suggests that the site of dispensation has shifted: she speaks after she has been spoken for, and unmoors her will from masculine decree. Left to her own devices, Cordelia does what she knows she should, but in so doing—and in so knowing—she changes the meaning of her acts.

Her will is not the renegade liberty that leads William Cecil to warn, "Marry your Daughters betimes, least they Marrie themselves."[15] Instead, Cordelia inherits the responsibility of self-government. When she tells Lear, "what I well intend / I'll do't before I speak" (1.1.214–15), she poses the integrity of meaning well against the chaos of subjective fragmentation. Her reference to proprietary intent invokes the difficult but not entirely tacit awareness that daughters, those building blocks of homosocial alliance, must be more than commodities if they are to have value at all. In Michael Drayton's *Legend of Matilda*, Matilda asserts the autonomy of her virtue:

> My words, judgment, which law could not reverse,
> My frownes, such clowds, as no joy could disperse,
> Tygars are tam'd with patience and with skill,
> All things made subject, but a womans will.[16]

In a sermon titled "The Vertuous Daughter," John Bryan equates virtue with deliberate choice: "It is an elective habit, inclining the will to well-doing."[17] Cordelia possesses this "elective habit" and claims these prerogatives of judgment, but in the collapsed economy of *Lear*, her desire to be a proper daughter damages her father. "Cordelia's response is more than honest; it is at least a little cruel, and thus presages her sister's more serious revenges later," Richard Halpern writes; or, in Harry Berger's succinct formulation, "She in effect commits [Lear] to prison."[18] Such statements assign a determinative power to Cordelia's acts, even as she acts for a principle that should govern both her father and herself. An ascription of interpersonal chastisement identifies Cordelia, as an individual, with the tenets Lear violates and the consequences that follow. What does it reveal when we equate Cordelia's will with the law she obeys, and describe a rift between the theory that binds her and the practice that sends her away? At the very least, this draws attention to a substantial discontinuity between masculine subjects and the social precepts that authorize their roles. Elaine Scarry writes, "through one's consent, one generates a political obligation, and through that obligation the state and its laws come into being. Consent *is* an act of ventriloquism, an apparently mute disposition of the body that becomes a throwing of the voice into the political realm."[19] Whether we take Cordelia as the play's hope of salvation or its agent of reprisal, she offers this consent, with a body given up to sovereign disposition and a voice that speaks the value of her bond. When Lear refuses, he retreats into a solipsist ascendancy that can only, ever more madly, ventriloquize itself.

Cordelia can neither leave nor come back as the sign of paternal efficacy; she translates banishment into choice and performs return as invasion. When she finally reciprocates Lear's affective demand, she does so with an army.[20] The Gentleman who describes her mingles allegory with prophetic analogy: "It seemed she was a queen / Over her passion who, most rebel-like, / Sought to be king o'er her" (4.3a.13–15). Microcosm and macrocosm overlap only to conflict: as a queen who subdues a wayward king, Cordelia condenses self- and other-directed mastery, and conflates the desire to restore a filial bond with the intention to conquer a sovereign state. She claims that she means only for another:

> O dear father,
> It is thy business that I go about;
> Therefore great France
> My mourning and important tears hath pitied.
> No blown ambition doth our arms incite,
> But love, dear love, and our agèd father's right. (4.3b.23–28)

Cordelia's final insistence that she serves her father, like her first adherence to her bond, implements a contradictory self-subordination through which she rejects a local argument (the whim of a father, the boundary of a nation) in order to acquiesce in a larger imperative (the law of marriage, the father's name). She defines herself as an instrument, but her service is conceived as autonomy and consummated in violence. If this happens in one sense against her will, it is in another sense precisely the sign of that will, and of its disloca- tion from the masculine subject in whose interests it acts. According to Scarry, "the will itself is couched in embodiment. Movement locates, rather than merely illustrates, the will."[21] A turn from England to France imperils patrilineal continuity; a return from France to England undermines political integrity. Several chronicles describe Cordelia's martial role as masculine, as when Raphael Holinshed calls her "a woman of a manlie courage,"[22] but *Lear* refuses such transvestite rationalizations. "We are not the first / Who with best meaning have incurred the worst," Cordelia says after her capture (5.3.3–4), and that yoking of "best" to "worst" reflects the double bind that makes feminine good will both deliverance and devastation. The act that sustains is the act that kills, vexing the question of what it means to mean well. This is the brutal logic of the supplement: alienated will cannot be reabsorbed into sovereign masculinity, but must exacerbate the insufficiency it works to repair.

The Laws Are Mine, Not Thine

Feminine good will leaves the stage with Cordelia, but effective intention remains; to remember Regan and Goneril only as fiends is to forget their sharp knowledge. Cordelia understands that the ethical value of bonds coincides with their social use, and Regan and Goneril, too, grasp the structures which organize a disciplined state. For them bonds are ties of policy, adhesive warrants of function and place; they diverge from Cordelia in the tenor of their acts, but share her investment in the priority of the system. Before his exile, Kent admonishes Lear's remaining daughters: "And your large speeches may your deeds approve, / That good effects may spring from words of love" (1.1.172–73). His formula has a strict if debased accuracy, for Goneril and Regan, like Henry V at Harfleur, use words to good effect, even as the sense of "good" shifts from decency to facility. Calculated performance transfers power, from a king who has lost the language of policy to heirs who speak it as their mother tongue.

"You see how full of changes his age is," Goneril says. "The observation we have made of it hath not been little. He always loved our sister most, and with what poor judgment he hath now cast her off appears too gross." Regan's response identifies a prior incapacity: "'Tis the infirmity of his age; yet he hath ever but slenderly known himself" (1.1.277–82). Direct, austere, and detached, this is an acute account of the scene. The diagnosis of troubled rule—imprudence, inconstancy, and failed self-knowledge—registers the warning signs and predicts the result: "If our father carry authority with such disposition as he bears, this last surrender of his will but offend us" (1.1.291–93). The incongruence between Lear's proclivities and his authority wreaks havoc; when he says, "Only we still retain / The name and all the additions to a king" (1.1.123–24), he suggests that the body politic might circulate while the body natural takes a vacation. In so doing, he vacates sovereign meaning. With an apparent inadvertence matched by its syntactic precision, Kent's "Why, fare thee well, king; since thus thou wilt appear" (1.1.168) names the problem: Lear's will to appear king has only the appearance of a king's will. Kent's advice—"Reverse thy doom, / And in thy best consideration check / This hideous rashness" (1.1.137–39)—earns him credit for loyalty. Regan and Goneril make the same judgment, and incur the charge of betrayal. Yet the residual doctrine of government appears only in their rational ill will. The scene ends with Regan's "We shall further think on't" and Goneril's "We must do something" (1.1.294–95), an epigram on abdication that reconnects sovereign purpose to efficient act.

When Goneril resolves, "I would breed from hence occasions, and I shall" (1.3.25), that "breeding," with its fecund intentionality, suggests that wayward women will build a new and terrible state. The edicts of that state look much like politics as usual: govern the house as you would govern the nation; restrain those subjects who cannot restrain themselves; privilege hierarchy over empathy, strategy over rashness, and discretion over truth. Cristina León Alfar reads this as a critique of political absolutism, and writes of Regan and Goneril, "their rule exposes the violence of patrilineal structures of power because the women rule in a patrilineal fashion, reproducing existing forms of power, rather than according to naturalized gender distinctions." This, she argues, is "the basic source of the critical bias against them: Goneril and Regan behave like men."[23] Alfar's important analysis challenges the automatic recourse to misogyny; instead, she contends, female appropriation of masculine hegemony invites scrutiny of the institution itself. I share this resistance to the idea that *Lear* enables a simple misogynist response, but I want to consider how the play elucidates a specific logic of feminine rule. Perhaps the most notable thing about the autocracy of Lear's daughters is that it requires no learning curve.[24] As the negative truisms of femininity—shrewdness, scheming, expediency, sexual calculation, and the priority of ends over means—mirror the practical habits of state, misogyny appears less a dominant ideology than a sign of political naïveté. Regan and Goneril force belated recognition of immanent capacities: they translate policy into practice, and remind us that, within heterosocial hierarchy, women perform precisely that role. Severed from masculine oversight, and enfranchised by a founding oversight in the other sense of the word, Regan and Goneril integrate a streamlined authority that executes its own intent. In an absolutist scheme the law enacts the sovereign's will, and, in perverse accord with the grimmer tenets of political philosophy, feminine will governs through the ambiguity of license.

It is easy to say that Lear's daughters act heartlessly, but it would be hard to argue that they act without reason. When the Fool says, "they will make an obedient father" (1.4.230), he marks the imposition of one order as he describes the inversion of another. Fathers should govern daughters, but incontinent subjects must be ruled by reason, even if that reason is not their own. In Regan's words: "You should be ruled and led / By some discretion that discerns your state / Better than you yourself" (2.4.123–25). When Goneril threatens Lear with "that offense / That else were shame, that then necessity / Must call discreet proceedings" (1.4.207–9), her proceedings sound quite horrible. But does the horror reside in the threat itself, or in its articulation by a woman who speaks as both ruler and daughter? "Come, sir, I would you would make use of that good wisdom / Whereof I know you are fraught, and put away / These dispositions that of late transform you / From what you rightly are" (1.4.215–18): this is not bad advice, and Lear's response only sharpens the point. "Who is it that can tell me who I am? / Lear's shadow?" (1.4.226–27). These outrageous daughters draw an utterly ordinary conclusion: chaotic persons produce anarchic states. "How in a house / Should many people under two commands / Hold amity? 'Tis hard, almost impossible" (2.4.217–19). Lear's recourse to the past—"I gave you all"— provokes an incisive gloss on that history: "And in good time you gave it" (2.4.227).

"O reason not the need," Lear demands (2.4.241), as if his desire might stand, self-evident, against all the reason in the world. Pitiless judgment clashes with passionate appeal, and, however helplessly or indeed willingly we may be seduced by Lear's eloquence, he does not invalidate the logic by which judgment wins. "Give ear, sir, to my sister; / For those that mingle reason with your passion / Must be content to think you are old, and so—/ But she knows what she does" (2.4.209–12). Knowledge informs action as reason restrains passion, confirming the arguments of a rational will. Lear's will, by contrast, can only take him astray: "He leads himself," says Regan; and, in response to Gloucester's plea for mercy, "O sir, to willful men / The injuries that they themselves procure / Must be their schoolmasters" (2.4.274, 278–80). Policy precludes empathy, which is in a way a matter of time. It might be possible to mourn Lear, whether in truth or in show, if he were dead. But instead an emptied site of monarchy circulates under a monarch's name, and Lear imposes a coercive melancholia that forces memory into the present. "Every hour / He flashes into one gross crime or other / That sets us all at odds," Goneril says, and calls Lear "Idle old man, / That still would manage those authorities / That he hath given away" (1.3.3–5; 1.3.16–18). The wit to recognize this problem, and the will to solve it, make Regan and Goneril intolerable; few could want to witness the process that translates melancholia into mourning and puts the past in its place. The push toward a pragmatic, troubling, and deeply compromised solution recalls other rulers who conspire in the deaths of kings, reprising the recognition that Richard II or Henry VI must die for the progress of history, and echoing the certainty that history will be haunted by those deaths. But *Lear* alters the texture of action by putting choice in feminine hands.

If Regan and Goneril differ from their regicidal precursors, the disparity lies not in what they do but in how they mean. When new kings eliminate old ones, they might act in anger or pleasure or envy or spite, but such urges hide beneath a dispassionate statesmanship with which they conflict. Women in *Lear*—and again I include Cordelia—interweave systematic and affective causalities, realizing the theoretical paradigm that yokes intention to desire in the figure of a feminized will. In *Microcosmos*, John Davies writes of the will, "Yet nought can her resistlesse powre constraine, / For nothing can *desire* from her remove."[25] Will derives power from compulsion, and *Lear*'s feminine subjects draw on the energy of that fraught convergence. Reasoned intention produces policy at the expense of persons: Cordelia's determination to be a good daughter, like her sisters' willingness to be bad ones, reflects an acuity that might preserve the state as it destroys a king. All recognize the unreason of Lear's demands, and each privileges the abstract criterion of order over the claims of a father who cedes his place as a social subject. But this methodical purpose, which renounces particular attachments for general stability, coincides with and encompasses the incursions of desire. Calculated projects enforce irrational inclinations, and inchoate drives undergird deliberate plots: value judgments may construct a taxonomy of motive, but even those sensitive instruments cannot sort out the tangled relationships among causes and effects. When Goneril and Regan conflate lust with ambition, a sexual rivalry tends toward civil war. When Cordelia merges political influence with filial devotion, a national invasion bodies forth emotional commitment. *Lear* evokes monitory stigmas of excess—hysteria, fixation, frenzy, whim—only to show that the equation between desire and debility does not hold. Rather than trace the familiar path along which reason devolves into passion, the play fuses those forces in feminine agents, and even the most destructive impulses bear the marks of strategic intent.

As complement to her sexual seduction, Regan offers Edmund her property and her name: "Take thou my soldiers, prisoners, patrimony. / Witness the world that I create thee here / My lord and master" (5.3.75–77). The danger of unrestrained feminine acts finds its stock fruition, as desire diverts legitimate inheritance to a bastard heir. At the same time, those acts effect a political allocation of assets and status; Regan asserts the authority to redistribute what she owns, and her self-subordination perversely verifies her prerogative of disposition. Goneril objects, and Albany responds indiscriminately to the multiplied threat: "The let-alone lies not in your good will" (5.3.78). But will has attained so broad a scope that there is something fantastic in the claim to know its limits, and Goneril and Regan hold the powers of choice between them. When Albany produces proof of Goneril's betrayal, she denies his jurisdiction: "the laws are mine, not thine. / Who shall arraign me for't?" (5.3.53–54). Autonomous feminine sovereignty becomes fully explicit, spotlighting the discontinuity between masculine subjects and social consequence, yet Albany answers with a cliché and a text. "Most monstrous! Know'st thou this paper?" (5.3.55). As he chastises his wife from a position she has negated, he sounds like the embattled speaker of *Haec Vir*: "if you will have no rulers but your wills, you must have no reward but disdaine and disgrace."[26] Regan and Goneril have had their share of disdain and disgrace, but the idea that unrestrained will disables them ignores the practical politics of the world in which they function. Albany himself concedes that categories have been exploded and reference points lost: "I fear your disposition. / That nature which contemns it origin / Cannot be bordered certain in itself" (4.2.32–34). Goneril's "disposition," like Regan's, is inextricable from self-disposition, replacing the conceit of essential origins with a "nature" that reconceives itself. As Goneril escapes the scene, Albany speaks an empty command: "She's desperate; govern her" (5.3.157). The wish-fulfillment fails twice: it neither resurrects the moribund faith that masculine subjects can govern, nor revives the hope that a platitude such as "desperate" can enclose the meaning of feminine will. Rousing though Albany's new manliness may be, it offers an immaterial response to Goneril's control of law and death.

The Text Is Foolish

Through the broken bonds that open an impassable space between subjects, *Lear* completes the ideological project of misogyny and counts the social costs. R. Howard Bloch argues that misogynist discourse homogenizes women to distance them from men: "Its purpose—to remove individual women from the realm of events—depends upon the transformation of woman into a general category, which, internally at least, appears never to change."[27] In pursuit of this purpose, *Lear*'s masculine subjects first accept and finally inhabit the mistranslation that opposes all feminine agents to social order. It is a problem of literalism, of the sort Slavoj Žižek imagines when he suggests that power might be vulnerable to its own public formulations:

> in so far as power relies on its "inherent transgression", then— sometimes, at least—*overidentifying* with the explicit power discourse—*ignoring* this inherent obscene underside and simply taking

the power discourse at its (public) word, acting as if it really means what it explicitly says (and promises)—can be the most effective way of disturbing its smooth functioning.[28]

Lear conducts a peculiar experiment in overidentification: a public discourse confuses the underside with the surface, so that the same subjects who speak for mastery instantiate degeneration. As a rhetorical symptom, misogyny responds to and thus emphasizes the inconvenient need for intercourse; as a programmatic imperative it pursues partition. *Lear* focuses on that second mode, which misconstrues heterosocial unease as a mandate for homosocial separatism; the "inherent transgression" of power is then neither dependence on nor oppression of women, but their elimination from zones of contact. Authority bonds to its own violation: to accept the mandate is to eviscerate a social organism, and *Lear* depicts this as self-inflicted damage rather than an insurgent breach. Disorder originates not in feminine subjects who approximate masculine entitlement, but in masculine subjects who identify madly with an oversimplified account of power. In her analysis of the tensions between inconstancy and contract, Katherine Rowe makes an acute point about projection: "figures of authority displace anxieties about the degree to which the state itself is governed by impulsive passions, through familiar misogynist gestures."[29] This seems particularly apt to *Lear*, in which a king who dispossesses himself reviles and disowns his daughters, and the twofold tactic of transfer and exile casts off a sustaining premise of social integrity. When men not only take misogyny at its public word but understand that word to be a speech act, they consummate the ruinous fantasy which excludes feminine will from masculine interactions. *Lear* in this way exhibits the false position of a power structure that at once overspeaks and undercuts itself. Berger reminds us that a play may represent a stance it does not endorse: "there is a difference between the story the text tells and the story or sermon performance preaches, which includes the stories the characters tell."[30] Masculine characters perform their story of successful displacement and sanitized space, but when the play erases the potential for generative contracts, it projects the vanishing point of sociality itself.

A number of scholars have noted that *Lear* does not endorse misogynist discourse in any straightforward way, echoing—if sometimes faintly— Goneril's judgment: "No more, the text is foolish" (4.2.38).[31] Still, Alfar argues, "As critics we have taken our view of Goneril and Regan from these male characters, so that their evil is defined by acts of will, power, violence, and sexuality—acts that disrupt the patrilineal morality's definitions of 'appropriate' femininity."[32] If analysis replicates the attitudes it describes, the interested passions of characters speak the verdict of the play. A change of word between quarto and folio gives a local but suggestive glimpse of this effect. In the quarto, Edgar's response to Goneril's intrigues begins, "O indistinguished space of woman's wit"; in the folio this becomes "O indistinguished space of woman's will" (q. 4.5.263; f. 4.5.267). The shift has specific resonance: in early modern faculty theory, "wit" appears as a synonym for reason, while "will" designates the force of execution. *Nosce teipsum* offers two models, the first of which constructs a familial analogy: "*Will* puts in practise what the *wit* deviseth; / *Will* ever acts, and *wit* contemplates still, / And as from *wit* the power of *wisdome* riseth, / *All other vertues* daughters are of *will*."[33] The second draws on the rhetoric of state: "*Will* is the *Prince*, and *wit* the Counsellour, / Which doth for common good in Councell sit; / And when *wit* is resolv'd, *will* lends her power, / To execute, what is advisd by *wit*."[34] In each instance, wit sets up a structure within which will carries out its work. The power dynamic is slippery—will is propagator and prince, guided by but not subject to a superior understanding—but the interchange yields efficient action. In the quarto version that might be precisely the point: "indistinguished space of woman's wit" describes a capacity which may be both alien and boundless, but which operates as an intelligible mode of government. At once demanding recognition and resisting integration, this effective alterity delineates the threat posed by sovereign women who represent viable sites of power.

Most modern editions follow the folio here, and their footnotes suggest that even an unbounded space of will has limited scope. Editions of the quarto gloss "wit" as "cunning," while "will"—which appears in conflated editions as well—is defined as "lust," "desire," or "appetite."[35] Like the axiomatic idiom of misogyny, these narrow synonyms reduce an unassimilated force to a figure of conventional excess. Undisciplined women desire at the expense of reason; their will may escape control, but in so doing it defines and solidifies social borders.[36] Annotated as it is, the difference between "wit" and "will" reflects the pattern often read onto *Lear*'s feminine subjects: appetite supplants cunning, and the shift from quarto to folio mirrors a move from the deliberate machinations of the first three acts to the passionate bloodbath of the final scenes. But this *is* a reading, its assumptions masked but not neutralized by its place in the play's editorial apparatus.[37] Changing "wit" to "will" might, with equal plausibility, accentuate the complexity of

Goneril's plot, which conflates strategic desire for political advantage with sexual desire for a bastard. Reason is bound up with volition, not only in faculty theory but in the play; will cannot be narrowed to lust, any more than feminine choice can be reduced to passion. The ending of *Lear* displays not a triumph of innate intemperance over tactical acuity, but their commingling in that undistinguished space of wit and will.

Where, then, is the space for men? In the hands of women, power looks like cruelty and works as policy; the more intractable dilemma may be that in the hands of men, it tends to become invisible. *Lear* recalls Roland du Jardin's comment on domestic patriarchs: "Now, the difficulty that is incident to this regiment, is such, and so great, that few men take pleasure in possessing it, none at all performe it in that manner they should."[38] The gap between position and performance informs a critical history that treats *Lear* as a twist on the absent monarch play: the king effectively disappears, even if he refuses to leave.[39] For a number of scholars, Lear's untenable theory of nominal rule becomes a symptom rather than an aberration, exposing absolutism as conditional, fragile, and imperfectly immanent. Dan Brayton argues that *Lear* defines preeminence as an artifact of situational eventualities: "The play thus underscores the fundamental contingency of sovereign power, that it is not inherent or metaphysical but positional, not absolute but contingent. Sovereignty is discovered to be the illusion produced by a particular hermeneutic and territorial apparatus."[40] The idea of an illusory monarch, expediently assembled and vulnerable to disarticulation, illuminates the distance between ideological machines and the figures they manufacture. The sense of disproportion is strongly persistent in responses to *Lear*: from Coppélia Kahn's analysis of "the failure of a father's power to command love in a patriarchal world" to Halpern's account of "the divorce between the signs and the material realities of royal power," readers emphasize incommensurability.[41] Such judgments closely repeat those of Goneril and Regan, whose status as critical targets may too easily obscure the fact that they provide critical models as well.

I am not concerned to instate Regan and Goneril as our neglected ancestors or our transhistorical colleagues, but I do want to think about what happens when we talk about sovereignty only in terms of Lear. Focusing on a gap between patriarchal theory and masculine practice reinstates Lear in the same gesture that deposes him: when his brief tenure and long dispossession tell the whole story of monarchy, it is all too easy to suture what the play disjoins and restore what it displaces, simply by concentrating on what is not there.[42] Leonard Tennenhouse takes this to a logical extreme when he construes failure as proof of a more durable success: "for lack of a natural embodiment, power reverts back to its metaphysical source—the patriarchal principle itself."[43] It seems worth pausing at that phrase "for lack of a natural embodiment." In what sense does *Lear* enable us to naturalize power as a patriarchal principle incorporate in men? To do so requires not only that we revise absence into presence, but that we ignore presence itself: the play fills Lear's space with sovereign women, and only by emptying it again can we make dominion the province of those who refuse to inhabit it. This retraces Lear's trajectory and duplicates his choice, which, as it rejects the roles played by feminine subjects, invests in a system that lacks vital parts. Alfar's suggestion that Regan and Goneril reenact patriarchal absolutism opens one avenue of inquiry; the argument I propose here about feminine will and efficient alterity suggests another; a third might be to conclude that *Lear* represents women as truly awful rulers, and to take the crucial next step of asking what that means. My point is that all three of Lear's daughters exercise consequential authority, and that *Lear* thus anatomizes diverse modes of power even as it meditates on one tragic fall. If we isolate Lear as he isolates himself, we too lose the logic of connection, and a network of dynamic elements yields to the error of one man. Tennenhouse writes, "But the relationship of power to gender is obviously *not* the issue this play asks an audience to consider. Rather, in reestablishing the bond between kinship and kingship, this play wants us to think of them both in male terms."[44] He argues for an interpretive act that segregates masculine from feminine subjects; the play demonstrates that such an act is not the mechanism of amnesia, but a catalyst for preoccupation. A directive to ignore powerful women might as well be an order not to think about wombats or unicycles or cardamom pods, with which captivating objects we must be instantly if bemusedly obsessed.

Lear often provokes a sense of necessary exclusions, enforced by the dissonance between registers of engagement. "Is the play to be read in a psychoanalytic, ethical, and personal register or in a political and historical one?" Halpern asks.

> Like hysterica / historica, two terms fighting for the same textual
> space, each mode of reading has a certain claim to legitimacy, and
> neither manages fully to supplant or eradicate the other. This situa-
> tion does not admit of happy pluralisms, however; as in Lear's king-
> dom, or as in his self-imagined anatomy, a sequence of painful

displacements occurs as something is always trying to rise to the top.[45]

Halpern describes a mimetic effect: the play proceeds through competitive displacement, and practices of reading follow. Kathleen McLuskie also outlines a coercive connection between text and reader; of *Lear*'s ending, she writes, "At this point in the play the most stony-hearted feminist could not withhold her pity even though it is called forth at the expense of her resistance to the patriarchal relations which it endorses."[46] The conflict of priorities suggests that we must choose between kinds of subjects—between disparate areas of inquiry, but also between idiosyncratic persons and social constituents—which have suffered an irreparable split. *Lear* reiterates Lear's importunate demand, and insists that its interlocutors must care, but about what? about love and madness? or about the vitiation of patriarchal power and the interruption of patrilineal descent? As McLuskie and Halpern suggest, any such choice brings only a partial return; the failure of "happy pluralisms" mirrors the play's broken bonds, reproducing schism and recording its sacrificial residue. A need to choose may not constrain our critical methods, but the mere idea of it sets off a symptomatic echo as it describes, however factitiously, an alienation of the critic's will. And if a coincidence of personal and political investments has been or even seemed unattainable, I suspect that for critical methodologies, as for the play they address, this has something to do with the place of feminine subjects.

Great Thing of Us Forgot

As if to confirm that his person is at odds with his function, Lear regains his throne for eleven lines: Albany's "for us, we will resign / During the life of this old majesty / To him our absolute power" closely precedes Lear's "Break, heart, I prithee break" (5.3.297–99; 310). Jonathan Dollimore reads the juxtaposition of Lear's death to Cordelia's as a challenge to ideological reinstatement: "The timing of these two deaths must surely be seen as cruelly, precisely, subversive: instead of complying with the demands of formal closure—the convention which would confirm the attempt at recuperation—the play concludes with two events which sabotage the prospect of both closure and recuperation."[47] The loss of recuperative possibility reenacts the play's first destructive move, as the deaths of Cordelia and Lear fix them in the failure of connection. Lear never apprehends Cordelia's intent; when she demands, "Sir, know me," he replies, "You're a spirit, I know. Where did you die?" (4.6.48–49). Whether we explain this line as madness or as prescience, it repeats the misrecognition and displacement ("I know"; "where?") that alienate feminine meaning. Lear's last question to Cordelia—"What is't thou sayest?" (5.3.271)—reaches for intersubjective exchange, but the gesture stops short at a corpse. His final fantasy of a self-sufficient dyad calls upon a sentimental conceit, as if he could write himself into the parable in which a young woman tells her suitor, "I thinke that the Lord hath left unto me great ritches, in as much as he hath graunted me the onely company of my aged Syre, unto whome (as in youth) he shewed me love, so in age I may yéeld good will."[48] But if, as many readers have suggested, this is what Lear has always desired, it is another mistranslation. Both Janet Adelman and Kahn describe the deaths of women as sacrifices that protect Lear from pragmatic sociality; as Kahn argues,

> If he did agree to meet Regan and Goneril, he would have to aban-
> don the fantasy that one good woman like Cordelia can triumph
> over or negate her evil counterparts, as well as the fantasy that a
> prison can be a nursery in which Cordelia has no independent being
> and exists solely for her father as part of his defensive strategy against
> coming to terms with women who are as human, or as inhuman, as
> men.[49]

Stanley Cavell, too, notes the inherent disavowal of Lear's final acknowledgement: "He has come to accept his love, not by making room in the world for it, but by denying its relevance to the world."[50] The refusal of social intersection with which Lear begins has expanded beyond measure, to become the evacuation of social survival with which *Lear* ends.

Death both results from the error that structures the play and appears as another iteration of that error, marking less a teleological conclusion than a turn within a circle. "Great thing of us forgot!" says Albany, in one of his more memorable lines; "Speak, Edmund, where's the king, and where's Cordelia?" A stage direction follows: *The bodies of Goneril and Regan are brought in* (5.3.234–35 & s.d.). The great thing so tirelessly forgotten is generative heterosociality, first lost with the banishment of Cordelia, and lost again with the segregation of these other heirs whose deaths collapse into Cordelia's own. By allowing Cordelia to be fatally overlooked, the play abandons the illusion of futurity. But the bonds that sustain that illusion have been elided from the opening scene, and if the end is implicit in the beginning, it is because of this: Lear casts off the feminine will that binds agency to consent. He sets that will loose to circulate on its own terms, in the terrible autonomy of Goneril and Regan and in the injurious determination of Cordelia's departure and return. These independent processes pose a danger, but their cessation signals a collapse: as the image of feminine government disappears, it takes with it the effective will to power. Scarry argues that even at moments of extreme disability, consent retains its force: "The whole issue of consent, by holding within it the notions of sovereignty and authorization, bears within it extremely *active* powers. Yet it often arises precisely at the point where by any conventional description there seems an extreme of passivity." She notes, "The patient may even be dead."[51] The annihilation of all feminine subjects presses that paradox beyond its capacity.

When *Lear* eliminates women, it actuates the self-destruction implicit in heterosocial hierarchy. The play returns dominion to men, at least in the sense that it leaves them as the only breathing claimants to the place. And it achieves from Cordelia that final quality in the litany of feminine virtues: "For there is nothinge that doth so much commend, avaunce, setforthe, adourne, decke, trim, and garnish a maid, as silence."[52] We might, with Lear, read pure stillness as the fruition of Cordelia's "Love, and be silent": "Her voice was ever soft, / Gentle and low, an excellent thing in women" (5.3.271–72). But Cordelia does not remain silent when the play begins; she chooses to speak the principle of social pacts. That principle evaporates with her murder, and with the deaths of Goneril and Regan as Kent records them: "All's cheerless, dark, and deadly. / Your eldest daughters have fordone themselves, / And desperately are dead" (5.3.288–90). Cheerless, dark, and deadly, this half-empty world has lost both the productive exchange of Cordelia's bond and the effective policy of her sisters' rule, leaving a collection of not quite sovereign men to improvise their way toward an empty throne. The plot has worked through Jardin's meditation on paternity—"Let a man but further consider the great difficulty that consisteth in the bringing up of Children, if he have them; the infinite discomfort, if he have them not"—and exposed the desolation beneath that thin layer of satire.[53] Or, as Dympna Callaghan writes, "the plot itself, moving through female silences intimated by various forms of female utterance . . . moves not inward and upward towards the tragic hero, but rather towards the void at its centre, which has been, from the first, the axis of its revolutions."[54]

As the play ends, unmoored authority circulates among compromised agents, who cannot recognize each other in hierarchical terms. "Our present business / Is to general woe," says Albany, and then, immediately, "Friends of my soul, you twain / Rule in this kingdom, and the gored state sustain" (5.3.316–18). Is that first "our" a royal plural, or a communal one? Does that second move divide the kingdom again, balance its first division, or underscore its irreparable fracture? Perhaps there is no clear heir because there is no logic by which to inherit; legitimacy derives from heterosocial contracts, and the erasure of feminine subjects undoes those contracts absolutely. In *Patriarcha*, Robert Filmer argues that a state cannot lose the premise of inheritance: "It is but the Negligence or Ignorance of the People to lose the Knowledge of the true Heir: for an Heir there always is. If *Adam* himself were still living, and now ready to die, it is certain that there is One Man, and but One in the World who is next Heir, although the Knowledge who should be that one One Man be quite lost."[55] More than knowledge has been lost in *Lear*. Patrilineality itself has been vacated, and the task of replicating and preserving "one man" simply ends. The play dismantles the strategic contradiction of homosocial self-perpetuation, which at once relies on and refutes the active roles of women; within this phantasmatic rationale, links among men are verified by but independent of feminine choice. But when a strictly literal misogyny conceives independence as isolation, it empties transactions of vital agents and exposes its barrenness as a disciplinary scheme. In the wake of that rupture, masculine sovereignty cannot rearticulate itself, a consequence anticipated in Lear's impenetrable question: "I am a king, my masters, know you that?" (4.5.190)

The last lines of *Lear* project a more final ending. "The oldest have borne most; we that are young / Shall never see so much, nor live so long" (5.3.323–24). Albany speaks these lines in the quarto, and Edgar in the folio; the shift both does and does not matter, for no candidate for rule displays the faculty of self-government. The forces that mobilize masculine subjects—melancholy, jealousy, grief, guilt, obsession, zeal, ardor, rage—are those of unconstrained passion. Kent as fervent mourner; Albany as frenzied cuckold; Edgar as avid revenger: no one stands for stability or continuity, and the multiple locations of that final speech suggest that it might belong to anyone. A troubled account of proper conduct defines the play's survivors: "Speak what we feel, not what we ought to say" (5.3.322). That rift between affect and tactic is a peculiarly masculine problem. Cordelia binds love to purpose, and Regan and Goneril yoke intemperance to method; even at the height of a murderous sexual rivalry, Goneril argues with calculated intent. "Combine together 'gainst the enemy, / For these domestic door particulars / Are not to question here" (5.1.29–31).[56] Women die in a complex knot of passion and policy, but the men who survive them fall to pieces. "Speak what we feel": any ruler or ruler manqué seems liable to collapse under his own emotional weight, so that *Lear* becomes a litany of sentimental implosions: "his flawed heart, / Alack too weak the conflict to support, / 'Twixt two extremes of passion, joy and grief, / Burst smilingly" (5.3.192–95); "If there be more, more woeful, hold it in, / For I am almost ready to dissolve, / Hearing of this" (5.3.198–200); "Break, heart, I prithee break" (5.3.310); "I have a journey, sir, shortly to go; / My master calls, and I must not say no" (5.3.319–20). Rebecca Bushnell compellingly maps the intersections of misogyny, tyranny, and un-reasoned excess: "Woman is represented as framed in nature as what the 'male' tyrant becomes: the principle of the lower and ferocious power of desire usurping the sovereignty of reason."[57] *Lear* does something odd on that common ground of nature: masculine subjects succumb to immodera-tion, while feminine subjects employ it. The play offers no ideal model of government—tyranny, license, and myopic devotion are equal-opportunity flaws—but it does distinguish between facility and incapacity. The fusion of intention and desire, however incoherent and fractious, is the condition of effective will. When its agents are all dead, emotion and efficacy are irrevoca-bly disengaged.

Cordelia dies of a political plot, a statement that implicates not only Edmund's failed usurpation of the throne, but *Lear*'s highly successful redi-rection of history. If Edmund stage-manages a murder in order to demolish patrilineality, the same might be said of *Lear*: both character and play replace restoration and inheritance with the erasure of sovereign lines. In earlier ver-sions of the story Cordelia reinstates Lear, and succeeds him when he dies. Edmund Spenser gives that account in *The Faerie Queene*:

So to his crowne she him restor'd againe,
In which he dyde, made ripe for death by eld,
And after wild, it should to her remaine:
Who peaceably the same long time did weld:
And all mens harts in dew obedience held.[58]

Geoffrey of Monmouth assigns a duration to Cordelia's reign—"a peaceable Possession of the Government for five Years"—to which most chroniclers

adhere.[59] Holinshed refers to the period as "The gunarchie of queene Cordeilla," and its brevity does not imply inconsequence;[60] *The Mirour for Magistrates* uses Cordelia's voice to make that clear. "And I was queene the
kingdome after still to holde, / Till five yeares paste I did this Iland guyde: /
I had the *Britaynes* at what becke and bay I wolde."[61] Shakespeare's *Lear*
requires us to forget not only Lear's restoration, but the continuity it imposes
and the active terms on which his daughter takes his place.

    To explain this revision of a familiar history, we might note—as readers
across the years have noted—that Shakespeare wrote a tragedy, and Lear and
Cordelia are unavoidable if lamentable victims of the genre. Aesthetically, it
would be difficult to balk at the change, particularly when we consider the
"happy ending" of *The True Chronicle History of King Leir*. "Ah, my *Cordella*,
now I call to mind, / The modest answere, which I tooke unkind: / But now
I see, I am no whit beguild, / Thou lovedst me dearely, and as ought a
child . . . Come, sonne and daughter, who did me advaunce, / Repose with
me awhile, and then for Fraunce."[62] One might reasonably opt instead for
that all-obliterating "Howl, howl, howl, howl." Still, it risks tautology to
argue that characters die because they appear in a tragedy, and it seems worth
pressing at the deletions those deaths ensure. As the figure for a lost future,
Cordelia is last in a series of three: all Lear's daughters vanish from this stage,
and the only blood they leave behind is spilled toward that dark and deadly
end. Here the full impact of *Lear's* altered course comes home, for the chronicle history of King Lear does not finish with his death or with his daughter's.
Cordelia dies after her nephews Margan and Cunedag rebel against her; they
then turn on one another, and, as Geoffrey of Monmouth writes, "*Cuneda-
gius* gained the Monarchy of the whole Island, which he governed gloriously
for three and thirty Years." In Spenser's words, "Then did he raigne alone,
when he none equall knew."[63] This provides a lesson in flexible ethics:
Cunedag is the bloodthirsty son of a pitiless mother until he delivers a durable state. Pragmatic reversals are commonplace enough, but the lineage this
story so forcefully preserves compels attention. Cordelia succeeds Lear after
conquering her sisters; Cunedag and Margan divide the kingdom after cap-
turing their aunt; Cunedag reunites it after killing his brother; and for more
than thirty years, Lear's grandson holds the throne. The serial usurpations
are so intrafamilial as to verge on incest: whatever the damage to persons,
there is never a threat to blood. For Shakespeare's *Lear* this continuity, which
turns violence toward diachronic ends, becomes the sacrifice of a tragic moment.

In citing these chronicles, I do not mean to privilege "history," or to assume anything about what Shakespeare's audiences remember or know. I instead want to underline the deliberation with which *Lear* evacuates patrilineal heterosociality. In place of grandsons who would carry his blood, Shakespeare's Lear envisions the blasted wombs of his bastardized daughters; instead of the daughter who might succeed him, he chooses a misrecognition enforced in her exile and repeated in her death. Patriarchal ideology, embodied in the connections of patrilineal descent, becomes an abstraction that has expelled, forgotten, and killed its material conditions of existence.[64] Its greatest vulnerability inheres not in women, good or bad, but in the futility of an unanchored argument; the sequestered principle of masculine supremacy forecloses history, at least as that history might move forward through a sustained knowledge of kind. After the excision of feminine will, *Lear* displays only the bleak atomization of solitary persons, each equal to the others in his capacity to perpetuate nothing.

Nahum Tate's *The History of King Lear* tends to be mentioned as a slightly embarrassing intermission, but we can perhaps understand why it played for so long. Edgar's final speech gestures forward:

> Our drooping Country now erects her Head,
> Peace spreads her balmy Wings, and Plenty Blooms.
> Divine *Cordelia*, all the Gods can witness
> How much thy Love to Empire I prefer!
> Thy bright Example shall convince the World
> (Whatever Storms of Fortune are decreed)
> That Truth and Vertue shall at last Succeed.[65]

Ending on that word "succeed," the play restores a futurity erased by *Lear*'s final stage direction: *Exeunt, with a dead march*. Samuel Johnson famously objected to Shakespeare's conclusion: "*Shakespeare* has suffered the virtue of *Cordelia* to perish in a just cause, contrary to the natural ideas of justice, to the hope of the reader, and, what is yet more strange, to the faith of chronicles." He acknowledged the appeal of Tate's adaptation, citing both public opinion and his own experience. "In the present case the publick has decided. *Cordelia*, from the time of *Tate*, has always retired with victory and felicity. And, if my sensations could add any thing to the general suffrage, I might relate, that I was many years ago so shocked by *Cordelia*'s death, that I know not whether I ever endured to read again the last scenes of the play till I his superstitious way of Paganisme, for in these 3. Townes which he built, hee erected 3. Temples, and placed 3. Flammins or Pagan Bishops in them.

Yeeres before Christ.
Rudhudibrasse, 892.

THis King built *Canterbury, Winchester,*
And *Shaftbury,* he from the ground did reare:
And after twenty nine yeeres reigne was past,
At *Winchester* sore sicke, he breath'd his last.

Bladud reign'd 20. 863.

BAathe was by *Bladud* to perfection brought,
By Necromanticke Arts, to flye hee sought:
As from a Towre he thought to scale the Sky,
He brake his necke, because he soar'd too high.

This *Bladud had beene a Student in* Athens, from whence hee brought many learned men: hee built Stamford, a Colledge I thinke, the first in England; striuing to play the fowle or the foole, he brake his necke on the Temple of Apollo in Troynouant.

Leire, 844.

LEire (as the Story saies) three daughters had,
The youngest good, the other two toobad:
Yet the old King lou'd the that w rong'd him most,
She that lou'd him, he banisht from his Coast.
False *Gonorel* and *Ragan,* he betweene
Them gaue the Kingdome, making each a Queene.

But young *Cordeilla* wedded was by chance,
To *Aganippus,* King of fertile *France:*
The eldest Daughters did reiect their Sire,
For succour to the young'st hee did retire,
By whose iust aide the Crowne againe he gain'd;
And dyed when he full forty yeeres had reign'd.

Leire *built* Leicester *and was a good Prince. At* Leycester *he built a Temple to* Iames Bifrons, *or* Iames *with two faces.*

Yeeres before Christ.
Qu. *Cordeilla,* 805.

MAd *Morgan,* an vnmanner'd *Cunedagne,*
Their Aût *Cordeilla* with fierce war did plague:
They vanquish'd her, and her in Prison threw.
And hauing reign'd fiue yeeres, her selfe she slew.

She reigned with her Husband Aganippus till he dyed, and then in her widowhead her cruell kinsmen oppresd her. Shee stabb'd her selfe in prison, being tyrannously vsed, in despaire of her liberty.

Morgan Cunedagus, 800.

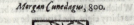

THen *Morgan* did 'gainst *Cunedagne* contend,
And at *Glamorgan, Morgan* had his end,
Then *Cunedagus* sole King did abide,
Full three and thirty yeeres, and then he dyed.

Morgan *was the Sonne of* Gonorel, Leires *eldest Daughter, and* Cunedagus *his kinsman, was the Sonne of* Ragan.
The Prophet Esay *prophesied about this time.*

Riuallo,

Figure 11. "A Memoriall of Monarchs, from Brute to King Charles." John Taylor, *All the Workes of John Taylor the Water-Poet* (London: John Beale et al for James Boler, 1630), 271. By permission of the Folger Shakespeare Library.

undertook to revise them as an editor."⁶⁶ Was Johnson himself tempted to "revise" toward some other end? Probably not; he was, after all, Johnson. But Shakespeare's *Lear* is haunted by the specter of Cordelia's missing will: throughout the play, restoration can be imagined only by those subjects who lament her absence and recall her bond. Tate extracts Cordelia from a futile ventriloquism that ends with silence, and preserves her in a generative social role. Suggestively, his epilogue meditates on constancy:

> Inconstancy, the reigning Sin o' th' Age,
> Will scarce endure true Lovers on the Stage;
> You hardly ev'n in Plays with such dispense,
> And Poëts kill 'em in their own Defence.
> Yet One bold Proof I was resolv'd to give,
> That I cou'd three Hours Constancy Out-live.⁶⁷

It is of course a joke on the audience. Yet constancy, understood not only as erotic or romantic fidelity but as a larger commitment to contract, is the unaccommodated ghost of *King Lear*. If we do not want Tate's intervention, we might nonetheless recognize in it the extent to which Shakespeare's play leaves us wanting *something*, and impresses stark knowledge of what has been willfully lost.

Doe not the golden Meane, exceed,
In Word, in Passion, nor in Deed.

Epilogue

Or

The Roman Matron

Do you not heare how lamentably your natural mother your coun-
trey of England, calleth upon you for obediences saying. Oh, remember remember my dear children in what case you stande, your
enemies be round about you, lyke unsaciable ravenours to pluck me
from you, to cast you out of my lap where I have this .110 yeres lyke
a faithful mother nourished you. . . . Lette me rather satisfie my
thirste with their effeminate bloud, then they should pluck from you
my motherly breastes: Sticke to youre mother, as she sticketh to you.
—Aylmer, *An Harborowe for Faithfull*
and Trewe Subjectes, sig. R1–R1v

In the passage I take as my epigraph, John Aylmer conveys a nationalist
agenda through the familiar conceit of the mother country, which evokes an
equally familiar tautology: masculine subjects guard feminine objects, and
preserve the material habitations of their own sovereign states. But Aylmer's
vignette, which concludes a defense of female rule and appears with the marginal gloss "Englandes voyce to hir children," is curiously at odds with this
scheme. A personified nation ("your natural mother") commands obedience;
ravishment of the female body ("to pluck me from you") transmutes into
displacement of the male body ("to cast you out of my lap"); and maternal
violence emasculates and infantilizes with an indiscriminate touch. "Lette me
rather satisfie my thirste with their effeminate bloud, then they should pluck
from you my motherly breastes." The feminine voice of nationalist imperatives identifies men as objects of address and implements of service, defined
by a destiny they did not conceive and condemned to privation if they fail to
fulfill it. Despite its careless way with masculine privilege, the dynamic may
sound familiar. Agrippa celebrates it when he retells the story of Coriolanus:
"While *Rome* stands, the Name of that grave Matron . . . will be famous,

Figure 12 (preceding page). "Doe not the golden *Meane*, exceed,/In *Word*,
in *Passion*, nor in *Deed*." Illustration XXXV, Book 3, in George Wither, *A
Collection of Emblemes, Ancient and Moderne* (London: Augustine
Mathewes for Richard Royston, 1635), 169. By permission of the Folger
Shakespeare Library.

who by checking the inordinate rage of her Son *Coriolanus*, preserv'd that Emperial City, the young Captain at his *Mothers* perswasions desisting from his unnatural hostility against his *Mother-Country*."[1] The mother country is the crux, and a mother speaks in its name. This closed circle structures Shakespeare's *Coriolanus* as well, which stages an equation between the spectacle of Volumnia's ascendant will and the vision of an integral state.

I posed a question in my introduction—why focus this book on Shakespeare?—to which I might add another answer: within a short span of time, Shakespeare wrote two plays that exemplify the imaginative extremes of feminine social will. *King Lear*, I have argued, segregates women from men in order to count the costs of a pyrrhic victory. A perfect act of discipline vacates the system it serves, and the play concludes with the end of futurity. *Coriolanus* offers a caustic antidote in the figure of Volumnia, who not only protects Rome against a threat to its future, but coincides with the ethos that defines its celebrated space. In "Woman's Fantasy of Manhood," D. W. Harding writes, "Volumnia provides Shakespeare's most blood-chilling study of the destructive consequences of a woman's living out at someone else's expense her fantasy of what manhood should be."[2] If we presume the priority of interpersonal obligations, Harding could have a case, albeit one grounded in the suspect math of the zero sum. But if Volumnia concerns herself instead with Rome as a renewable image of itself, the mandate that secures social values through women achieves its apotheosis in her invention and destruction of her son. In *Lear*, a structure emptied of feminine will dies; in *Coriolanus*, a structure equated with feminine will not only survives, but reaches toward ideological perpetuity.

When Thomas Sheridan adapted *Coriolanus*, he titled it *Coriolanus: or, the Roman Matron*.[3] "Or" succinctly expresses the crisis of contract; in Shakespeare's play, reciprocity subsists under the shadow of erasure. As many readers have noted, *Coriolanus* uses the mother-son dyad to explore the possibilities of "and," but records a triumph of "or" when Volumnia alone survives. In reproductive terms, she creates Coriolanus and destroys him; in social terms, she acculturates and expels him; in political terms, she indoctrinates and sacrifices him; in psychoanalytic terms, she propels him through the mirror stage, only to drag him back into fragmentation. Pressed too far, "and" becomes "or," so that "Coriolanus: or, the Roman Matron" represents neither a balance nor a choice, but a formula in which the second term supersedes the first. *Coriolanus* transforms a conventional proposition— women make men to sustain the state—into a radical identification: feminine will fuses with the will of the state, and men exist as the corporeal instruments of an abstract union. I have argued that, when narratives of feminine will reveal the interdependence that subtends hierarchy, they create a correspondence between reading against the grain and reading for the plot. Volumnia's plot yields disposable men, useful to the project of continuity but never fully participant in it. In the case of *Coriolanus*, then, reading against the axioms of gender and power simply means reading. If this has the feel of overstatement, so too does Volumnia: she pursues the strategy of over-identification, "simply taking the power discourse at its (public) word," but her unconditional assent makes that word her own language.[4]

I would like to offer a brief schematic account, which covers familiar ground. My point derives from that familiarity: *Coriolanus* makes Volumnia both active and iconic, and in the intense visibility of her proceedings, we witness a purpose so thoroughly indoctrinated that it threatens the viability of social forms. The absolute fidelity of Volumnia, like the misogynist literalism dissected by *Lear*, realizes a logical extreme. An arc of elimination—the inexorable plot of "or"—shapes her most memorable moments, which often function as intensified cultural truisms. She presents herself as the inventor of her son: "I have lived / To see inherited my very wishes / And the buildings of my fancy."[5] The intimate correlation between his actions and her wishes suggests that Coriolanus himself has been built by Volumnia's fancy, formed by some high-octane version of the maternal imagination so often blamed for prodigies and monsters. Volumnia famously makes this explicit: "Thy valiantness was mine, thou suck'st it from me" (3.2.129). But rather than substitute maternal for paternal inheritance, she imagines Coriolanus as a conduit for abstract tenets; legitimacy, for her, is the condition of being impersonated by power. She insists on the efficacy of orthodox formulations: "now it lies on you to speak / To th' people; not by your own instruction, / Nor by th' matter which your heart prompts you, / But with such words that are but roted in / Your tongue" (3.2.52–56). Public words constitute the subject, and for Volumnia, Coriolanus is the medium of a speech act that originates in the philosophy of rule. She builds a soldier—"Thou art my warrior, / I holp to frame thee" (5.3.63–64)—and modifies him for statecraft when that venture serves more urgent ends. If he follows her directives, through which the tenets of authority speak, he will answer the needs of Rome; if he does not, he will cease to signify. This verdict reflects an integrated ideological will, impervious to friction between intention and desire. Volumnia's language transmits the resonance of personal investment, both intense and complex, but its terms remain opaque. *Coriolanus*, like *Lear*, distinguishes affect from policy: we cannot know what Volumnia wants for her son, because she knows so well what she must demand from him.

"Hear me profess sincerely," Volumnia says at the start, "had I a dozen sons, each in my love alike . . . I had rather eleven die nobly for their country than one voluptuously surfeit out of action" (1.3.21–25). Coriolanus does not witness his counterfactual death, but he understands it nonetheless; those dead sons of his mother's conception echo in his final cry, "O mother, mother! / What have you done?" (5.3.182–83). And what *has* she done? It would be too simple to say she has killed him. But she has named the disparity between his actions and the meaning she assigns him, and he disappears into that gap. After Coriolanus capitulates, Volumnia returns to a reaffirmed political state: "Unshout the noise that banish'd Martius! / Repeal him with the welcome of his mother" (5.5.4–5). The absence of her son appears as victory, translated by the chauvinism that subsumes particular men. *Henry V* concludes its calculus of death with that chilling small phrase, "none else of name" (4.8.105), and Rome, too, substitutes collective gain for individual loss with effortless sleight of hand. But Coriolanus was not "none else of name" until his name ceased to signify Rome's fortune, and his disappearance by proxy—"Repeal him with the welcome of his mother"—binds Volumnia to a utilitarian creed. In the early seventeenth century, current meanings of "repeal" ranged from withdrawing a privilege to revoking a sentence to renouncing an action to recalling an exile. The word could also, more rarely, mean restore or return or repel.[6] We can resort to common sense or context clues—although the common sense of fickleness is difficult to parse, while the *Oxford English Dictionary* cites Shakespeare four times across three definitions, and does not cite *Coriolanus* at all—but we cannot, with certainty, reduce several to one. This small conundrum points to a larger failure of difference: in a world of expendable men, to renounce one is to recall another, who may for the moment be of more use. At its limit, *Coriolanus* envisions a system that does not depend on masculine individuation, but uses and discards anonymous male bodies in the name of institutional constancy.

In a theoretical sense, this precisely consummates patrilineal ideals: no one man matters when the goal is to keep all men the same, and that sameness depends on the relentless resolve of women. Volumnia thus epitomizes the connection between feminine acts and social codes. But if the narrow trajectory of *Coriolanus* succeeds in preserving Rome, it fails or refuses to sustain a model of contract. The bond between feminine will and abstract paradigms excludes rather than enables bonds between subjects, and hetero-social engagement leaves only some scraps and a trace. Where *Lear* presents the error of excision, *Coriolanus* produces the opposite yet identical crisis of equation: strategies that define women against ideological formations and fantasies that identify women with those formations prove equally barren. The first leaves persons with no future, but the second crafts futures that barely involve persons at all. Such specters, animated by the Shakespearean stage, underscore the need for more flexible accommodations; *Lear* and *Coriolanus* displace women to opposite poles, and leave us to contemplate the vacant middle ground. Throughout this book, I have traced the intricate, often adversarial or paradoxical contracts forged by feminine will. These con-tracts may—and perhaps must—incite ambivalence when they hold, but they leave wreckage when they collapse. Social futurity depends on volitional in-tersections: this premise, however veiled, translated, distorted, or disavowed, frames the compromised prospect of livable space.

Notes

Introduction: Virtue Trouble

1. Burton, *The Anatomy of Melancholy*, 1.1.2.11, p. 30.

2. In her analysis of the early modern debate concerning the status of women, Jordan concludes, "Its larger reference is always to the nature of authority and the status of the subject in relation to authority" (*Renaissance Feminism*, 308). A number of scholars have linked feminine consent—which interweaves choice and restriction, autonomy and compliance—to the complexities of agency that inflect early modern theories of marital, legal, and political contract. See for example Jordan; Rogers, "The Enclosure of Virginity"; Kahn, "Margaret Cavendish and the Romance of Contract"; Rowe, *Dead Hands*, esp. 86–110, and "Inconstancy"; Rudolph, "Rape and Resistance"; Gowing, *Common Bodies*, esp. 82–110; and Suzuki, *Subordinate Subjects*. Burks describes a troubling relationship between consent and rape law: "Rape law encountered a tremendous difficulty in dealing with the fact that women, unlike other chattel, have wills of their own . . . What if a woman consented to be ravished?" ("'I'll Want My Will Else,'" 765). Scarry notes that consent theory mystifies the condition of agency: "In general, the whole notion of consent stands the distinction between active and passive on its head, since consent theory claims that it is by the will of the apparently passive that the active is brought into being" ("Consent and the Body," 881).

3. As K. Newman writes, "Managing femininity so as to insure the reproduction of the commonwealth, great and small, was a significant ideological feature of early modern England" (*Fashioning Femininity*, 16).

4. Batman, *Batman uppon Bartholome*, "The Table," sig. ¶¶iv. See K. Newman: "In the age of mechanical reproduction, the printed book disseminated ideologies of femininity to an unprecedentedly broad audience" (*Fashioning Femininity*, 6). For overviews of the production of exemplary and monitory texts, see for example Camden, *The Elizabethan Woman*; Ezell, *The Patriarch's Wife*; Jordan, *Renaissance Feminism*; Kelso, *Doctrine for the Lady of the Renaissance*; King, *Women of the Renaissance*; Maclean, *The Renaissance Notion of Woman*; and Woodbridge, *Women and the English Renaissance*.

5. Scott, "The Evidence of Experience," 793.

6. Rich, *The Excellency of good women*, 4–5.

7. Foucault, "Governmentality," 87. Foucault describes this as a historical turning

point—"Government as a general problem seems to me to explode in the sixteenth century" (87)—and identifies family economy as the primary model (92). Korda offers an important corrective to Foucault's focus on men, emphasizing the vital, complex roles played by women within household economies. See *Shakespeare's Domestic Economies*, esp. 48–51.

8. Foucault, "Governmentality," 95.

9. "This means that, whereas the doctrine of the prince and the juridical theory of sovereignty are constantly attempting to draw the line between the power of the prince and any other form of power, because its task is to explain and justify this essential discontinuity between them, in the art of government the task is to establish a continuity, in both an upwards and a downwards direction" (Foucault, "Governmentality," 91). In making this argument, Foucault substantially reiterates the analogic link between microcosm and macrocosm so familiar from early modern texts; see 91–92.

10. Butler, *The Psychic Life of Power*, 59, emphasis in original.

11. Butler, *The Psychic Life of Power*, 60.

12. Butler, *The Psychic Life of Power*, 60.

13. "If a given regime cannot fully control the incitements that it nevertheless produces, is that in part the result of a resistance, at the level of impulse, to a full and final domestication by any regulatory regime?" (Butler, *The Psychic Life of Power*, 60–61).

14. On the rhetorical strategies of early modern didactic texts, and in particular the practices of copia and method, see Ong, "Tudor Writings," 48–103; Cave, *The Cornucopian Text*; Halpern's argument linking copia to ideological control and its limits (*The Poetics of Primitive Accumulation*, 45–49); and Kerrigan's observations on copia and precedent ("The Articulation of the Ego," 272–73). Parker takes Erasmus's *De Copia* as the model for a twofold concern: "how to expand a discourse" and "how to control that expansion" (*Literary Fat Ladies*, 13–17, quotations at 13). K. Newman argues that a shift from copia to method increases emphasis on sexual hierarchy and taxonomy (*Fashioning Femininity*, 20–25). Hutson connects exemplarity to rhetorics of husbandry and domestic hierarchy (*The Usurer's Daughter*, esp. 30–41). See also Ferguson's powerful argument concerning "partial literacy" and its implications for the project of educating feminine subjects (*Dido's Daughters*, esp. 31–170).

15. Laqueur, *Making Sex*, 35. For summaries of the effects of maternal imagination, see Culpeper, *A Directory for Midwives*, esp. 140; and *The Problemes of Aristotle*, esp. sig. F1–F1v.

16. *The Problemes of Aristotle*, sig. E7v.

17. See Dolan's argument that heterosocial contracts can produce subjective elimination: "The notion of marriage as an economy of scarcity facilitates the development of a particular kind of subject, but only one. The other spouse serves as the object to that subject" (*Marriage and Violence*, 4).

18. Austin, *Haec Homo*, 67, emphasis in original. Rambuss cautions against regarding clichés as empty of meaning: "Too often interpretation desists at the point of such a determination, as if the status of being conventional would make a discursive construct or a sentiment any less thick with significance" (*Closet Devotions*, 1–2).

19. Rich, *The Excellency of good women*, 7–8. Rich adds that an unchaste woman is like a ship with too many merchants (12).

20. Jardin, *A Discourse of the Married and Single Life*, 110.

21. Rich, *The Excellency of good women*, 8.

22. Wall, *Staging Domesticity*, 1, 15. Other scholars also emphasize the uncanniness of domesticity. In her analysis of domestic crime, Dolan writes, "the threat usually lies in the familiar rather than the strange, in the intimate rather than the invader" (*Dangerous Familiars*, 4; on the dangers of an estranged familiarity, see esp. chap. 1). Korda focuses on alienated property; she describes the husband as haunted by the wife's role in household economies, by "the specter of her unsupervised spending and disposing of property" (*Shakespeare's Domestic Economies*, 31). Wall's association of domesticity with nationalism expands the implications of estrangement: "tension between the familiar and unfamiliar provides the material and conditions of a domestic, and sometimes national, fantasy" (28). In connection with this point, see Gowing's complication and critique of a family/state analogy secured by "the idea of natural hierarchy illustrated by patriarchy" (*Domestic Dangers*, esp. 22–29, quotation at 26).

23. Tilney, *A briefe and pleasant discourse of duties in Mariage*, sig. B6. Cleaver writes, "The husband ought not to bee satisfied that he hath robd his wife of her virginitie, but in that he hath possession and use of her will." He, too, describes the dangers of failure: "it is easie to beleeve that she desireth not long life unto her husband, with whom she passeth a time so tedious and irksome" (*A Godlie Forme of Householde Government*, 168–69).

24. Dolan observes, "the reassertion of male dominance operates as a cover story for more complex distributions of power within marriage" (*Marriage and Violence*, 28). See also Ezell, *The Patriarch's Wife*, 162.

25. Traub, *The Renaissance of Lesbianism*, 181

26. Bright, *A Treatise of Melancholy*, 70.

27. In a discussion of the "Shakespearean figure of the *second*," Parker cites "the larger problem of the fidelity of the agent or representative," and complicates assumptions about precedence: "Shakespearean evocations of seconds, including the representation of an authorizing authority, author, or 'will,' while they iterate the language of the secondary prevalent in the culture contemporary with the plays, also undermine the very hierarchy of first and second, model and copy, original and translative decline" (*Shakespeare from the Margins*, 9).

28. Wojciehowski, *Old Masters, New Subjects*, 10.

29. Rackin describes the dangers of feminine knowledge and intention in her powerful account of women in Shakespeare's history plays: "As bearers of the life that names, titles, and historical records could never fully represent, the women were keepers of the unspoken and unspeakable reality that always threatened to belie the words that pretended to describe it" ("Anti-Historians," 343). Schalkwyk identifies that threat as central to one of Shakespeare's late romances: "patriarchy in *The Winter's Tale* is predicated upon a

paradox: its greatest need is at the same time the source of its deepest fears and insecurity. Nothing but a woman's word can justify the legitimacy of its bloodline" ("A Lady's 'Verily,'" 269).

30. This is Cixous's phrase for the body that has been "more than confiscated" from women, "the ailing or dead figure, which so often turns out to be the nasty companion, the cause and location of inhibitions" ("The Laugh of the Medusa," esp. 250).

31. Butler, *Gender Trouble*, 137–49; Irigaray, *This Sex Which Is Not One*, esp. 76; Žižek, *"Da Capo senza Fine,"* 220; and Bersani, "Is the Rectum a Grave," 209.

32. Halberstam, *Female Masculinity*, 9.

33. See, for example, Adelman, *Suffocating Mothers*; Amussen, *An Ordered Society*; Belsey, *Shakespeare and the Loss of Eden* and *The Subject of Tragedy*; Berry, *Of Chastity and Power*; Dolan, *Dangerous Familiars* and *Marriage and Violence*; Ezell, *The Patriarch's Wife*; Ferguson, *Dido's Daughters*; Gowing, *Domestic Dangers*; Howard and Rackin, *Engendering a Nation*; Hutson, *The Usurer's Daughter*; Jankowski, *Pure Resistance*; Jardine, *Still Harping on Daughters*; Jordan, *Renaissance Feminism*; Kahn, *Man's Estate*; Kelly and Leslie, eds., *Menacing Virgins*; Korda, *Shakespeare's Domestic Economies*; Miller and Yavneh, eds., *Maternal Measures*; Neely, *Broken Nuptials*; K. Newman, *Fashioning Femininity*; Paster, *The Body Embarrassed* and *Humoring the Body*; Rose, *The Expense of Spirit*; Shannon, *Sovereign Amity*; Traub, *The Renaissance of Lesbianism*; Wall, *Staging Domesticity*; Willis, *Malevolent Nurture*. This list is necessarily suggestive rather than exhaustive.

34. K. Newman, *Fashioning Femininity*, 30. Newman refers here to the emergence of women writers, but her study gives broad scope to tactical mimesis; see her discussion of ideology as "an Imaginary, unfixed, phantasmagoric, at once enabling and at the same time oppressive" (12). See also Belsey: "an affirmation and its opposite, power and resistance, may share the same inscription" (*Shakespeare and the Loss of Eden*, 15).

35. Bartels illustrates this duality in her analysis of strategic submission, which, she argues, "allows women to be actors: to speak out through, rather than against, established postures and make room for self-expression within self-suppressing roles. Under the cover of male authority, women could modify its terms and sanction their moves without direct resistance. They could be good wives *and* desiring subjects, obedient *and* self-assertive, silent *and* outspoken" ("Strategies of Submission," 419). Crocker makes a related argument about *The Taming of the Shrew*: "By accepting the model of femininity foisted on her, Katharine gains a degree of autonomy. By speaking the category of feminine virtue that masculine discourse would define, she steps outside the boundaries of subjectivity imagined by Petruchio" ("Affective Resistance," 155–56).

36. Althusser's theory of internal distance resonates here; he suggests that works of art might "make us 'perceive' (but not know) in some sense *from the inside*, by an *internal distance*, the very ideology in which they are held." However, he argues that this reinforces ideology as determinative: "The fact that the content of the work of Balzac and Tolstoy is 'detached' from their political ideology and in some way makes us 'see' it from the *outside*, makes us 'perceive' it by a distantiation inside that ideology, *presupposes that ideology itself*" ("A Letter on Art," 222–25, quotations at 223, 225, emphasis in original).

37. Jordan, *Renaissance Feminism*, 160.

38. Case, "Toward a Butch-Femme Aesthetic," 305.

39. Kelso, *Doctrine for the Lady of the Renaissance*, 24.

40. Butler, *Excitable Speech*, 38.

41. Rich, *The Excellency of good women*, 5.

42. Baldwin, *A treatyce of Moral philosophy*, fol. 134; fol. 132v. As Belsey concludes in her account of Eve's ambiguity, "No wonder women cannot be read: the good and bad wife are one and the same person" (*Shakespeare and the Loss of Eden*, 77).

43. This is hardly an abstract proposition, as Dolan has shown: "By asserting her entitlement to grievance and self-will and endeavoring to reshape her circumstances by means of violence, the murderous wife calls into question the legal conception of a wife as subsumed by her husband and largely incapable of legal or moral agency. She also violates the vigorous and persistent, if not necessarily descriptive, cultural constructions of women as incapable of initiative or autonomous action" (*Dangerous Familiars*, 26).

44. Gosynhyll, *The prayse of all women*, sig. E1v.

45. Belsey's reading of *Lucrece* argues that self-sacrifice can challenge social formations: "[Lucrece] reaffirms her own sovereignty in an action that is deliberately and independently chosen. The effect is a change of regime to one based on consent: *propriety* will no longer be synonymous with *property*" ("Tarquin Dispossessed," 333, emphasis in original). In debates over feminine sexual agency, the rape of Lucrece is a crux; see for example Bromley, "Lucrece's Re-Creation"; Fineman, "Shakespeare's *Will*"; Greenstadt, " 'Read it in me' "; Kahn, "The Rape in Shakespeare's *Lucrece*"; Little, *Shakespeare Jungle Fever*, esp. 25–48; Maus, "Taking Tropes Seriously"; and J. Newman, " 'And Let Mild Women.' "

46. Vives, *Instruction of a Christen woman*, 36–36v.

47. Brathwait, *The English Gentlewoman*, 126.

48. Heywood, *Gynaikeion*, 280.

49. [Edgar], *The Lawes Resolutions*, 377–78.

50. If such figures seem odd models for socialized femininity, they are nonetheless highly conventional: see for example Agrippa, *Female Pre-eminence*, esp. 64–67; Bercher, *The Nobility of Women*, esp. 136; Heale, *An Apologie for Women*, esp. 15; Heywood, *The Exemplary Lives*, passim; and Rich, *The Excellency of good women*, esp. 2–3. J. Newman notes that feminine self-sacrifice is only part of the story; see her extensive account of "a complex tradition of women participating in sacrificial rites of revenge and expiation [that] existed in antiquity and continued to be transmitted in the Renaissance" (" 'And Let Mild Women,' " quotation at 325).

51. de Certeau, *The Practice of Everyday Life*, 38, 36–37.

52. de Certeau, *The Practice of Everyday Life*, 36, 37–38.

53. Shannon, *Sovereign Amity*, 68.

54. Shannon, *Sovereign Amity*, 39–40.

55. Schalkwyk addresses the intricacies of reciprocity, affect, and obligation when he argues that "literal service, sexual desire, and loving devotion intersect in complex ways" in Shakespeare's *Sonnets* and *Twelfth Night*: "The submission required by service infringes on the possibility, quality, and reciprocity of love and desire. Yet service also makes love possible. The ideal of reciprocity that informs the concept of service also holds out the

promise of reciprocity in sexual love" ("Love and Service," 95). He develops the theory of willing subordination in *Shakespeare, Love and Service*, locating a nuanced discussion of constraint and choice within a nexus of affective, economic, political, and ideological discourses; see esp. 16–56. See also Greenstadt: "One implication of my analysis, then, is that the apparently polarized positions of autonomous individual and subjected other that have constrained recent attempts to theorize intentionality are in fact interdependent: that they arose in the early modern period as *versions* of each other" (*Rape and the Rise of the Author*, 5).

56. Althusser, "Ideology and Ideological State Apparatuses," 162, emphasis in original.

57. Traub, *The Renaissance of Lesbianism*, 21. See also Dolan, *Dangerous Familiars*, 3.

58. Callaghan, *Shakespeare Without Women*, 13–14. See also Belsey: "we *make* a relation, in both senses of that term, out of *our* reading practices and *their* documents. We produce, that is to say, a past which is both the consequence of our analysis and its motive. I take it for granted that the real existed then as now; but I take it equally for granted that the real was no more knowable then than it is now" (*Shakespeare and the Loss of Eden*, 12, emphasis in original).

59. Jardin, *A Discourse of the Married and Single Life*, 17–18.

60. Hutson, *The Invention of Suspicion*, 114.

61. Willbern, *Poetic Will*, 3.

62. R. Wilson, *Will Power*, 21. Wilson links Shakespeare's authorial will to historical changes in testamentary practice; he connects the testator's expanded rights to the emerging idea of the proprietary author, and concludes of the will as legal instrument, "Authority and authorship coincide in this document as they had not done before Shakespeare's lifetime, and would never do so possessively again" (184–237, quotation at 232). His introduction ends with a challenge to Shakespeare's will, both as intention and as legacy; see esp. 21. See also Fineman's comment on reading as resistance to legacy ("Shakespeare's *Will*," 215).

63. Freinkel, *Reading Shakespeare's Will*, 232.

64. Fineman, "Shakespeare's *Will*," 165–221, quotation at 187. Fineman writes, "the impression of psychologistic person in Shakespeare's texts characteristically effects and is effected by the mark of Shakespeare's person" (169). Greenblatt usefully summarizes the case for Shakespeare's implication; see "Introduction: Joel Fineman's 'Will,'" esp. xvi.

65. Whigham, *Seizures of the Will*, 5.

66. Williams, *A Glossary of Shakespeare's Sexual Language*, 337–38; see also his *Dictionary*.

67. Greenstadt, *Rape and the Rise of the Author*, 17–18. The point draws on Turner's argument in *One Flesh*; see Turner, esp. 43–44. Greenstadt goes on to argue that the invisibility of female pleasure in Augustine's account preserves the possibility of chaste feminine will; see 18.

68. For two evocative examples, see Partridge, *Shakespeare's Bawdy*, 218–19; and Onions, *A Shakespeare Glossary*, 318. Partridge writes, "In *Sonnets* 135 and 136, *will* does, as I have said, mean 'sexual desire; lust', but it also means, now the male, now the female,

sexual organ, as a number of scholars have, ever since the book first appeared in 1947, hastened to tell me" (218). Onions lists nine meanings of "will"—five as a noun, four as a verb—and cites the *Sonnets* at the last nominal definition: "5 (euphemistically, usu. with quibble on other senses) Male or female sexual organ SON 135.5" (318).

69. See Chapter 5 for development of this point, its critical context, and its implications for intersubjectivity in the *Sonnets*.

70. Chambers speculates that *Lear* brought Shakespeare close to a breakdown, which manifests its effects in *Timon of Athens*; see *William Shakespeare*, 1: 86.

71. I do not suggest that feminine will becomes an issue only in Shakespeare's later works. The recuperative machinations of Portia and Rosalind, for example, anticipate Helena and Isabella. Earlier still, in *The Taming of the Shrew*, Katharine's synopsis of patriarchal ideology poses a famously stubborn crux. See K. Newman on Katharine's final lines: "Such a representation of gender, what might be termed the 'female dramatizable,' is always at once patriarchally suspect and sexually ambivalent" (*Fashioning Femininity*, 48). Crocker draws on Žižek's theory of over-identification to develop "the agency involved in passivity": "by *taking on* the ideology of femininity that Petruchio promotes, [Katharine] *takes from* Petruchio the feminine submission he purports to desire" (Crocker, "Affective Resistance," 156, emphasis in original).

72. Charnes, *Notorious Identity*, 107. See her discussion of belatedness and notoriety, esp. 7–11.

73. Freinkel, *Reading Shakespeare's Will*, 166.

74. L. Wilson, *Theaters of Intention*, 5. Hutson writes, "[The] judicial pedagogy of narrative fostered an awareness of the 'facts' as having been generated by the order and coherence of their telling," and argues that forensic transactions, informed by the reciprocal motives of persuasion and verification, construct the illusion of character (*The Invention of Suspicion*, esp. 7). See also Willbern's discussion of character as "an active *figure of speech*" (*Poetic Will*, 11, emphasis in original).

75. Althusser, "Ideology and Ideological State Apparatuses," 161.

76. Ferguson points out that silence is not the default position of constrained subjects: "The image of the skeptical or resistant female occurs often enough in late medieval and early modern texts to complicate any notion that women as a group were substantially silenced either by their illiteracy or by normative ideologies of femininity" (*Dido's Daughters*, 96).

77. Althusser, "Ideology and Ideological State Apparatuses," 169, emphasis in original.

Chapter 1. Willing Women

1. Augustine would recur to the contradiction between individual choice and divine purpose; see "On Nature and Grace," 521–79; and "On Grace and Free Will," 733–74. See also "Appendix: St. Augustine's Review (AD 427) of *The Problem of Free Choice* (*Retractions* bk. 1 ch. 9)," in *The Problem of Free Choice*, 221–28.

2. L. Wilson, *Theaters of Intention*, 29. Wilson derives this concept from structuralist and poststructuralist analytic modes; he describes "the exclusion of the predicative relationship from accounts of practice even where the language of practical reason is introduced to describe the production and reproduction of social structures," and concludes, "The result is what may be called a hysteresis effect: the language of action persists despite the cessation or disappearance of the intending subject that constitutes its logical and grammatical cause if not necessarily its historical derivation" (27).

3. Althusser, "Ideology and Ideological State Apparatuses," 169, emphasis in original.

4. For a summary of the classical tradition which addresses relationships between ethics and desire, and which underlies Augustine's theories of will and choice, see Freinkel, *Reading Shakespeare's Will*, esp. 50. See also Eden's discussion of Aristotelian, Augustinian, and Stoic concepts of will in *Poetic and Legal Fiction*, esp. 76–81, 128–32, 97–105; and Tilmouth's accounts of Aristotle, Aquinas, and Augustine in *Passion's Triumph*, esp. 20–30, 157–68.

5. Althusser, "Ideology and Ideological State Apparatuses," 161, emphasis in original.

6. For a discussion of the conversion of will which, for Augustine, resolves the conflict between spirit and flesh, see Freinkel, esp. 244. For Althusser's theory of internal distantiation, see "A Letter on Art in Reply to André Daspre," esp. 222–25; for his comments on science, see "Ideology and Ideological State Apparatuses," esp. 162.

7. L. Wilson, *Theaters of Intention*, 14.

8. K. Kelly describes virginity as "an abstract idea residing in an anatomical metonym"; see her detailed analysis of unknowable bodily states (*Performing Virginity*, esp. 1–39, quotation at 7).

9. Korda compellingly analyzes the constrained yet self-determined roles women played in domestic property relations; see her discussion of "the subtle, coercive forms of power and resistance, discipline and self-discipline, that shaped female subjectivity during the period" (*Shakespeare's Domestic Economies*, esp. 1–51, quotation at 12).

10. Freinkel, *Reading Shakespeare's Will*, 134. See also her analysis of letter and spirit, esp. 255.

11. Whigham, *Seizures of the Will*, 1.

12. Paster, *Humoring the Body*, 8. See also her causal connection between the volatile humoral body and the emphasis on individual self-control and social codes of regulation, esp. 18–20. Rowe makes a related argument about the tension between humoral inconstancy and social contract; see "Inconstancy."

13. Erasmus, *A Diatribe or Sermon Concerning Free Will*, 20; Luther, *The Bondage of the Will*, 113. On this debate, see Freinkel, *Reading Shakespeare's Will*, esp. 245–47; and Wojciehowski, *Old Masters, New Subjects*, esp. 94–97.

14. Erasmus, *A Diatribe or Sermon Concerning Free Will*, "Summary and Conclusion," 85–86.

15. Luther, *The Bondage of the Will*, "Refutation of Erasmus' Preface," 113.

16. Wojciehowski, *Old Masters, New Subjects*, 185.

17. See for example Bates, *Masculinity, Gender and Identity*; Breitenberg, *Anxious Masculinity*; Finucci, *The Manly Masquerade*; and Vaught, *Masculinity and Emotion*.

18. Charron, *Of Wisdome*, 69.

19. Charron, *Of Wisdome*, 70.

20. Wright, *The Passions of the minde*, 58; 57. See also Elyot, *Of the Knowledeg [sic] whiche maketh a wise man*, 52–53; and Hooker, *Of the Lawes of Ecclesiasticall Politie*, 60.

21. Wright, *The Passions of the minde*, 10.

22. Dolan, *Marriage and Violence*, 23. For Dolan's detailed analysis of conflicts between marital models in both early modern and twentieth-century contexts, see esp. 26–66. For a reading of such conflicts across dramatic genres, see Rose, *The Expense of Spirit*. See also Ezell's discussion of "the Good Wife" (*The Patriarch's Wife*, esp. 37–42); and Gowing's analysis of impracticable prescriptions and marital equilibrium (*Domestic Dangers*, esp. 185–88).

23. Strier, "The Refusal to be Judged," 76.

24. Phillips, *English Fictions of Communal Identity*, 5; 12.

25. Jardine, "Cultural Confusion," 3, emphasis in original. After this synopsis, Jardine outlines earlier feminist methodologies—including her own—and interrogates "the pressure on the textual critic to embrace the fiction that there exists a reliable body of social and cultural historical 'fact,' to be 'tested' somehow against the 'fiction' of the literary representation" (3–4). For an elaboration of the social paradigm she summarizes in the essay, see Jardine, *Still Harping on Daughters*, esp. chap. 2. See also Jordan's analysis of tensions among responsibility, autonomy, and subjection (*Renaissance Feminism*, esp. 22–29).

26. Butler, *Gender Trouble*, 45. Butler defines this dynamic in her reading of Jacques Lacan: "[The] process of meaning-constitution requires that women reflect that masculine power and everywhere reassure that power of the reality of its illusory autonomy. This task is confounded, to say the least, when the demand that women reflect the autonomous power of masculine subject / signifier becomes essential to the construction of that autonomy and, thus, becomes the basis of a radical dependency that effectively undercuts the function it serves" (*Gender Trouble*, 45). See Lacan, "The Signification of the Phallus," esp. 289.

27. Butler, *Gender Trouble*, 45. Montrose discusses the negative aspects of this "pre-individuated" fantasy in early modern thought; see his account of "a collective anxiety about the power of the female not only to dominate or reject the male but to create and destroy him" ("'Shaping Fantasies,'" quotation at 36).

28. Butler, "Restaging the Universal," 22.

29. Scarry, "Consent and the Body," 881.

30. Freud, "Femininity," 131.

31. Scarry, "Consent and the Body," 883.

32. Davies, *Mirum in modum*, sig. D4. See also Burton's comment on reason, will, and "the *Sensitive* and *Moving Appetite*": "there was an excellent consent and harmony betwixt them, but that is now dissolved, they often jar" (*The Anatomy*, 1.1.2.11, p. 30).

33. Fletcher, *The Purple Island*, 81 (Canto 6, Stanza 66), 79 (Canto 6, Stanzas 57, 60).

34. Dolan, *Marriage and Violence*, 51.

35. Ezell, *The Patriarch's Wife*, 162. See also Dolan's comment on the tension between hierarchy and equality: "Since equality is understood as encouraging battles of the will, only a hierarchy, according to which one submits to the other, can resolve conflicts so that the occasional or apparent achievement of union becomes possible" (*Marriage and Violence*, 26). Rowe's reading of *The Duchess of Malfi* shows that conflicting logics of contract—status and affective allegiance, self-subjection and self-interest, consent and social obligation—are highlighted by the role of will within marriage (*Dead Hands*, esp. 90–97). Paster challenges the idea that marriage must eliminate female agency, noting that, according to humoral theory, the transition to sexual maturity increases that agency (*Humoring the Body*, 77–134; see esp. 86–89). More generally, feminist scholarship has revealed a range of complex relationships between marriage and volition; see for example Amussen, *An Ordered Society*; Belsey, *Shakespeare and the Loss of Eden*; Dolan, *Dangerous Familiars*; Fletcher, *Gender, Sex, and Subordination*; Gohlke, "'I wooed thee with my sword'"; Gowing, *Domestic Dangers* and *Common Bodies*; Neely, *Broken Nuptials*; K. Newman, *Fashioning Femininity*; Rose, *The Expense of Spirit*; Traub, *The Renaissance of Lesbianism*; and Wall, *Staging Domesticity*.

36. Bullinger, *The Christen state*, fols. 15v–16. For the rules, rituals, and spaces of self-definition that attend the process of contracting marriage, see Gowing's account of courtship, esp. 139–84. Gowing writes, "If young women evading commitment turned to the idea of dependence, women who gave themselves freely—or who were argued at court to have done so—expressed in the language of marital choice an assertion of autonomy" (*Domestic Dangers*, 157).

37. Bullinger, *The Christen state*, fol. 16.

38. Perhaps for this reason, critics often invoke will in their analyses of moments at which socialized desire might fail. In a reading of *All's Well That Ends Well*, Sullivan cites Baker's synopsis of faculty theory, and writes, "In this account of Bertram's case, the will has broken free of reason's control—the maintenance of which depends in part on memory—and has been misdirected by lust" ("'Be This Sweet Helen's Knell,'" 64). In her analysis of *The Rape of Lucrece*, Belsey also describes an unruly, erratic force: "In Shakespeare's poem Tarquin's irresistible 'will,' which both repudiates reason and distorts rational argument, is invested in the poem with all the ambiguity of the term in the period" ("Tarquin Dispossessed," 325). Freinkel suggests that a constrained will may threaten comic ideals as much as a will that is uncontrolled, reading the marital dilemma of *The Merchant of Venice* through a Lutheran model of bondage: "Portia's will, curbed as it is by the law of the father, is a will that has no choice in its willing, that is unfree insofar as it is bound to choose" (*Reading Shakespeare's Will*, 249).

39. Gataker, "A Wife in Deed," 54, emphasis in original.

40. Rowe, *Dead Hands*, 95, emphasis in original.

41. Gataker, "A Wife in Deed," 60, emphasis in original.

42. Belsey, "Alice Arden's Crime," 147. In Belsey's succinct and striking formulation, "The chain of bondage had given way to a net of power" (146). See also Jordan, *Renaissance Feminism*, esp. 286–95; and K. Newman, *Fashioning Femininity*, esp. 23.

43. La Primaudaye, *The Second Part of the French Academie*, 205–6. La Primaudaye emphasizes that will makes its own choices, which may refuse to engage with or reflect the counsels of reason: "the whole consultation lieth in the liberty and choyce of Will" (212). Davies makes a similar point in *Microcosmos*: "And though shee waites on *Reason* to, and fro, / Yet shee makes *Reason* waite her will to kno" (46).

44. Rowe, *Dead Hands*, 18.

45. Willbern describes the intention / desire simultaneity as a contradiction within a term: "Paradoxically, in Shakespeare's time the same word meant 'primitive, involuntary desire' and 'conscious volition'" (Willbern, xiv; see also xiv–xvii). Jordan writes of will, "It is best expressed in oxymoron, as the controlled (or disciplined) emotion or the emotional (or compassionate) control that determines moral choice" (*Renaissance Feminism*, 257). Freinkel gives a theological account of the relationship between intention and desire, contrasting the figural tradition, which reconciles spirit and flesh, with the Lutheran insistence on their dualism; see *Reading Shakespeare's Will*, esp. 118–19.

46. Davies, *Microcosmos*, 39.

47. Wright, *The Passions of the minde*, 58. See also Davies, *Mirum in modum*, sig. A4.

48. Elyot, *Of the Knowledeg [sic] whiche maketh a wise man*, 52. See also Nemesius on "the *selfe-will* of that *Soul*": "if shee had not voluntarily yeelded her selfe to those distemperatures, she might have overcome them, and beene in good case" (*The Nature of Man*, 560).

49. La Primaudaye, *The Second Part of the French Academie*, 208.

50. Hooker, *Of the Lawes of Ecclesiasticall Politie*, 66; Elyot, *Of the Knowledeg [sic] whiche maketh a wise man*, 57–57v. On the analogy between unruly will and adultery, see also Nemesius, *The Nature of Man*, 556–57; and Burton's comment on Phaedra in *The Anatomy of Melancholy* (1.1.2.11, p. 30). For a more positive account of feminine eroticism, see Bacon; in his discussion of how best to move the will, he cites Plato's scheme of seductive alliance between virtue and imagination (*The Twoo Bookes*, The Second Booke, 67).

51. Barckley, *A Discourse of the Felicitie of Man*, 574, 576.

52. Davies, *Mirum in modum*, sig. B3v–B4. See also Burton, 1.2.3.2, p. 94.

53. Maus, *Inwardness and Theater*, 196.

54. La Primaudaye, *The Second Part of the French Academie*, 213. Davies equates free will with subjection: "This liberty of *Monarchizing* thus / Shee deemeth good, what ill so ere ensues; / Which *libertie*, is *bondage* base to us, / And *free* we were, if our *will* could not chuse / But use His *will*, that gave us *wils* to use" (*Microcosmos*, 47).

55. Davies, *Microcosmos*, 45. This is the first use of "caeserizes" recorded by the *Oxford English Dictionary*.

56. La Primaudaye, *The Second Part of the French Academie*, 206; Davies, *Microcosmos*, 47, emphasis in original.

57. Elyot, *Of the Knowledeg [sic] whiche maketh a wise man*, 52. See also Wright: "as an uncarefull Magistrate neglecteth the good of the Common-weale, to avoyde some particular mens displeasure; so the Will, being afrayde to displease sense, neglecteth the care she ought to have over it" (*The Passions of the minde*, 58).

58. *Microcosmos* describes "the *will* witt-abus'd" in post-lapsarian terms: "drown'd in that damned *juyce*, / (*Synnes* Syder) from *Eaves* fatall *Apple* bruiz'd, / (Be'ing deadly drunck) makes stil the worser choise, / Wherein (like *Sow* in mire) it doth rejoyce" (40).

59. Elyot, *Of the Knowledeg [sic] whiche maketh a wise man*, 52; Davies, *Microcosmos*, 39; Nemesius, *The Nature of Man*, 560.

60. La Primaudaye, *The Second Part of the French Academie*, 206, 213.

61. Davies, *Microcosmos*, 47, emphasis in original.

62. Gataker, "A Good Wife Gods Gift," 2, emphasis in original.

63. Sir John Davies, *Nosce teipsum*, 52.

64. Sir John Davies, *Nosce teipsum*, 51.

65. La Primaudaye, *The Second Part of the French Academie*, 204–5.

66. Davies, *Microcosmos*, 43.

67. Baker, *The Image of Man*, 290–91. See also Dowden, "Elizabethan Psychology," 331.

68. "As a mediate faculty lying between sense and reason, the will was particularly vulnerable; it could, and often did, let the objects of sense rather than the objects of reason determine its conduct, and when it did, the result was disastrous" (Baker, *The Image of Man*, 292).

69. Baker, *The Image of Man*, 292.

70. Anderson, *Elizabethan Psychology*, 138.

71. Wright, *The Passions of the minde*, 58

72. Batman, *Batman uppon Bartholome*, fol. 16.

73. Even Ralegh, who celebrates will without ambivalence, registers the possibility of deception: "we desire that good which the understanding comprehendeth to be such indeed or in appearance" ("A Treatise of the Soul," 586).

74. La Primaudaye, *The Second Part of the French Academie*, 204.

75. La Primaudaye, *The Second Part of the French Academie*, 206.

76. Hooker, *Of the Lawes of Ecclesiasticall Politie*, 61.

77. Dowden, "Elizabethan Psychology," 332.

78. See Nemesius, *The Nature of Man*, esp. 549–58; and Charron, *Of Wisdome*, 55.

79. Davies, *Mirum in modum*, sig. C2.

80. Charron still more explicitly locates ethical responsibility in will rather than in knowledge: "As of all the goods that are in man, vertue or honestie is the first and principall, and which doth farre excell knowledge, dexteritie; so wee can not but confesse, that the will where vertue and goodnesse lodgeth, is of all others the most excellent: and to say

the trueth, a man is neither good nor wicked, honest nor dishonest, because he understandeth and knoweth those things that are good, and faire, and honest, or wicked and dishonest; but because he loveth them, and hath desire and will towards them" (*Of Wisdome*, 69). See also Burton, *The Anatomy of Melancholy*, 1.1.2.11, pp. 29–30; and Elyot's distinction between intentions that follow understanding and those that succumb to the senses (*Of the Knowledeg [sic] whiche maketh a wise man*, 50v).

81. Charron, *Of Wisdome*, 69.

82. Knowledge of that prerogative is suggestively deferred: Charron ends his discussion of will with the promise, "How we are to direct and rule our willes, shall be sayd heereafter" (*Of Wisdome*, 70), but follows this with sixteen chapters on passions and affections, after which he begins an entirely new section titled "The second Consideration of Man, by *comparing him with all other creatures*" (101, emphasis in original).

83. Ralegh, "A Treatise of the Soul," 586–87.

84. Bacon, *The Twoo Bookes*, The Second Booke, 66v. Bacon expresses confidence in rhetoric, but stresses the stakes of the battle: "if the affections in themselves were plyant and obedient to Reason, it were true, there shoulde bee no great use of perswasions and insinuations to the Will . . . [but] Reason would become Captive and servile, if *Eloquence of Perswasions*, did not practise and winne the *Imagination*, from the *affections* part" (67–67v).

85. Paster, *Humoring the Body*, 11.

86. Hooker, *Of the Lawes of Ecclesiasticall Politie*, 60.

87. Coeffeteau, *A Table of Humane Passions*, 55, 71. Coeffeteau argues that well-governed passions are both necessary and useful: "they are the instruments and objects of vertue, and as it were lively sparkes which inflame desires in our soules; and as *Aristotle* speakes, they are the armes of reason" (69).

88. Davies, *Mirum in modum*, sig. C2v.

89. Bright gives form to this strenuous artifice when he addresses the question, "How the soule by one simple faculty performeth so many and divers actions": "So many actions diverse in kinde rise from one simple first motion, by reason of variety of joynts in one engine. . . . And this appeareth in such sort as carie their motion within them selves. In water works I have seene a mill driven with the winde, which hath both served for grist, and avoiding of rivers of water out of drowned fens and marishes, which to an American ignorant of the devise, would seme to be wrought by a lively action of every part, and not by such a generall mover as the wind is" (*A Treatise of Melancholy*, 65, 66–67). Bright's analogy describes an organic process, but identifies the reader with that ignorant American who sees only disparate and inexplicable results.

90. Vives, *An Introduction to wysedome*, sig. B3v.

91. Elyot, *Of the Knowledeg [sic] whiche maketh a wise man*, 51.

92. Forset, *A Comparative Discourse*, 18.

93. Davies, *Microcosmos*, 107.

94. Sidney, *An Apologie*, sig. C2–C2v. Sidney argues that poetry can surpass the

highest works of nature, but that both creation and reception must contend with post-lapsarian distortion.

95. Vives, *An Introduction to wysedome*, sig. F2.

96. Barckley, *A Discourse of the Felicitie of Man*, 565.

97. Wright, *The Passions of the minde*, 58–59. Elyot argues that only proper hierarchy averts such transformations: "but that the soule have understanding alway at her elbowe, whiche shall bydde raison correcte Wylle, if he be conversaunt with these affectes. And than shall man stylle remayne without any of the sayde transformations that we before spake of" (*Of the Knowledeg [sic] whiche maketh a wise man*, 57v–58). Burton cites Agrippa in attributing metamorphoses to uncontrolled desire, also termed imagination or fantasy: "that some are turned to Wolves, from Men to Women, and Women again to Men (which is constantly believed) . . . or from Men to Asses, Dogs, or any other shapes" (*The Anatomy of Melancholy*, 1.2.3.2, p. 95). Davies, too, warns that ungoverned will invites the ascend-ance of "*Fantacie*"; see *Mirum in modum*, sig. C2v.

98. Burton, *The Anatomy of Melancholy*, 1.1.2.11, pp. 29–30.

99. Charron, *Of Wisdome*, 69.

100. James, *Passion and Action*, 2. See also Paster, Rowe, and Floyd-Wilson, eds., *Reading the Early Modern Passions*; and Tilmouth's account of "the decline (from an initial position of dominance) of an austerely rationalist model of self-governance, one centred on ideas of psychomachia and a hostility to the passions" (*Passion's Triumph*, esp. 1–36, quotation at 1).

101. Burton, *The Anatomy of Melancholy*, 1.2.3.2, p. 96, emphasis in original.

102. Burton, *The Anatomy of Melancholy*, 1.2.3.2, p. 96.

103. Scarry, "Consent and the Body," 882.

104. Scarry, "Consent and the Body," 883.

Chapter 2. Willful Speech: Metonymy and Mastery

1. Parker, *Literary Fat Ladies*, 2. Parker connects this explicitly to anxieties about domestic hierarchy: "It is not necessary to read far in the handbooks of rhetoric or discus-sions of language in the English Renaissance . . . to perceive an intimate and ideologically motivated link between the need to control the movement of tropes and contemporary exigencies of social control, including, though not limited to, the governance of the house-hold" (98).

2. Fenner, *The Artes of Logike and Rethorike*, sig. D2. Barton comments emphatically on the mystifying effect of doubleness: "whereas I have made Metonymie twofold, Perfect and Elliptick, I say boldly, that nothing in all Rhetorick doth more puzzle scholars, then not being made acquainted with this difference of Metonymicall examples" (*The Art of Rhetorick*, sig. A4).

3. Jakobson, "Two Aspects of Language," 132. See also de Man, who, in his scrutiny of the apparent preeminence of metaphor, refers to "the contingency of a metonymy

based only on the casual encounter of two entities that could very well exist in each other's absence" (*Allegories of Reading*, 63).

4. Parker, *Literary Fat Ladies*, 111. See also the more general point made by the editors of *Renaissance Figures of Speech*: "The figures, then, refuse to be contained within textbooks and school exercises, but permeate Renaissance literature and culture as dynamic and evolving nuclei of thought and expression" (Adamson, Alexander, and Ettenhuber, "Introduction," 11).

5. Bacon, *The Twoo Bookes of Francis Bacon*, The Second Booke, 60.

6. Bacon, *The Twoo Bookes of Francis Bacon*, The Second Booke, 57.

7. Parker observes that "women, excluded from the study of rhetoric, figure curiously and prominently in Renaissance English discussions of rhetoric, and particularly in relation to questions of decorum and control" (*Literary Fat Ladies*, 107).

8. Cummings, "Metalepsis," 229.

9. Puttenham, *The Arte of English Poesie*, 114.

10. Sherry, *A treatise of Schemes and Tropes*, sig. C4v. See Poole's study of stylistic taxonomy, in which he traces the logic that links rhetorical deviation to error or fault: "For if the vices of style represent deviations from licit rhetoric, might this return us to the prior problem that rhetoric is itself a deviation from common speech?" (Poole, "The Vices of Style," 237).

11. Menon, *Wanton Words*, 4.

12. Peacham, *The Garden of Eloquence* (1577), sig. C4. See also his comments on Metaphora, Metonimia, Onomatopeia, and Acyrologia (sig. B2–D1).

13. Day, *The English Secretary*, Book 2, 77.

14. Puttenham, *The Arte of English Poesie*, 152.

15. Peacham, *The Garden of Eloquence* (1577), sig. B1v. See also T. Wilson, *The Arte of Rhetorique*, fol. 91v.

16. Gataker, "A Wife in Deed," 1, 4, emphasis in original.

17. Dollimore, *Sexual Dissidence*, 33.

18. Gataker, "A Wife in Deed," 6. In "A Good Wife Gods Gift," Gataker notes that peril increases with nearness, and wives are nearest of all: "It is no small vexation for a man to find untoward and unfaithful cariage toward him *in those that eat his bread*, that feed at his boord; much more to sustaine it at the hands *of her*, that taketh up the same bed with him, *that lieth in his bosome*. No evill to a bad bed-fellow, to a bosome-evill, to that evill that lieth next the heart, either within or about the breast" (3, emphasis in original).

19. Sherry, *A Treatise of the Figures of Grammer and Rhetorike*, fol. 24.

20. Kristeva writes, "As we know, Freud specifies two fundamental 'processes' in the work of the unconscious: *displacement* and *condensation*. Kruszewski and Jakobson introduced them, in a different way, during the early stages of structural linguistics, through the concepts of *metonymy* and *metaphor*, which have since been interpreted in light of psychoanalysis" (*Revolution in Poetic Language*, 59).

21. Cummings, "Metalepsis," 230.

22. Ainsworth, *The Art of Logick*, 3.

23. Cuddon, *A Dictionary of Literary Terms*, 394.

24. Burke, "Four Master Tropes," 506.

25. "Metonyms," conceived in this way, recall the synecdochic processes that take part for whole. For influential accounts of the relationship between synecdoche and metonymy, see Burke, "Four Master Tropes," esp. 507–11; and Jakobson, "Two Aspects of Language," esp. 130–31. In his analysis of homosexuality and inscription, Edelman notes a similar impulse to restrict and reify metonymic volatility: "Metaphor, that is, binds the arbitrary slippages characteristic of metonymy into units of 'meaning' that register as identities or representational presences" (*Homographesis*, 9). Such "units" facilitate motivated objectification, as when one modern dictionary gives this example of metonymy: "ogling the heavily mascaraed *skirt* at the next table" (*Webster's Third New International Dictionary, Unabridged*, emphasis in original).

26. Newman, *Fashioning Femininity*, 4–5.

27. Sherry, *A treatise of Schemes and Tropes*, sig. C5v.

28. Brathwait, *The English Gentlewoman*, 40. If Brathwait seems to have a somewhat tenuous grasp on what we might call reproductive realities, his point is reinforced by the now familiar fact that female sexual anatomy was often imagined as an inverted and imperfect version of idealized maleness. For explication of the Galenic "one-sex model," see Laqueur, *Making Sex*, and Greenblatt, *Shakespearean Negotiations*, esp. chap. 3. For challenges to the idea of this model's dominance in the early modern period, see Adelman, "Making Defect Perfection," and Schleiner, "Early Modern Controversies about the One-Sex Model."

29. Laqueur, *Making Sex*, 35. Montrose elucidates the defensive social fantasy behind this reproductive conceit, writing that *A Midsummer Night's Dream* "formulate[s] in poetic discourse, a proposition about the genesis of gender and power: men make women, and make themselves through the medium of women" ("'Shaping Fantasies,'" 42).

30. Jonson, *The Masque of Beauty*, l. 310.

31. Parker, *Literary Fat Ladies*, 14.

32. Sherry, *A treatise of Schemes and Tropes*, sig. C5v. Sherry's "Metonomya, Transnominacion," becomes, for T. Wilson, "Transmutacion," "the whiche is when a woorde hath a proper signification of the owne, and beyng referred to an other thyng, hath an other meanyng, the Grecians cal it Metonymia the whiche is diverse waies used" (*The Arte of Rhetorique*, fol. 93).

33. Lacan, "The Agency of the Letter in the Unconscious," 167, emphasis in original.

34. Fraunce, *The Arcadian Rhetorike*, sig. A5.

35. With similar logic, Fenner conflates "the subject" with "that whiche hath anie thing adjoyned" (*The Artes of Logike and Rethorike*, sig. D2). Menon writes, "What ties metonymy to itself is a vaguely-defined affinity, rather than a physically determinable resemblance. . . . There is, therefore, a certain level of arbitrariness where metonymy is concerned" (*Wanton Words*, 42).

36. Puttenham, *The Arte of English Poesie*, 150, 148.

37. Puttenham, *The Arte of English Poesie*, 151.

38. Menon, *Wanton Words*, 42.

39. In this context, metonymic transpositions of cause and effect reflect a central paradox of feminine will: virtuous sexual choice may be an effect of social stability, in the sense that it answers a purpose other than its own; but it is also and inescapably the cause. For present-day definitions of metonymy as the figure of causal substitution or reversal, see Alexander, "Prosopopoeia," 99; and Cummings, "Metalepsis," 222.

40. Ferguson, *Dido's Daughters*, 127. This formulation emerges from Ferguson's reading of Dante's *De vulgari eloquentia*, which offers "illustrated prescriptions for an illustrious language" that she describes as "flagrantly, even deliriously, ideological" (127).

41. Sherry, *A Treatise of the Figures of Grammer and Rhetorike*, fol. 23v.

42. Peacham, *The Garden of Eloquence* (1577), sig. C2.

43. Fraunce, *The Arcadian Rhetorike*, sig. A6.

44. Puttenham, *The Arte of English Poesie*, 150.

45. *The Oxford English Dictionary*, s.v. "hypallage." The OED notes that in Quintilian "the word (written as Greek) has the sense of metonymy," and adds, "English authors have sometimes applied it loosely or incorrectly to other variations from natural forms of expression, esp. to the transference of attributes from their proper subjects to others." See Day's definitions of metonymy and hypallage in *The English Secretary*, Book 2, 78, 83. For a direct equation of the terms, see Peacham, *The Garden of Eloquence* (1593), 19.

46. Puttenham, *The Arte of English Poesie*, 143–44.

47. Drayton, *Englands Heroicall Epistles*, 4v.

48. Day, *The English Secretary*, Book 1, 135. For additional examples, see 134–38.

49. Bunny, *Of Divorce for Adulterie*, 115.

50. Bulwer, *Chirologia*, 172.

51. Speght, *A mouzell for Melastomus*, 9, emphasis in original.

52. Žižek, "*Da Capo senza Fine*," 217–20, quotations at 217.

53. Reynolds conveys the errant power of figuration in his critique of "*Anaphoras, Epistrophes, Metaphors, Metonymyes, Synecdoches* and those their other potent Tropes and Figures"; his distinction between "Accidents or appendixes" and "the Essentiall Forme, of true Poësy" stresses that figures pose the dual threat of deliberate and accidental misuse, a threat turned both toward a credulous audience and back on an injudicious expositor (*Mythomystes*, sig. A3–A3v).

54. Middleton and Rowley, *A Courtly Masque*, sig. C2.

55. Derrida, ". . . That Dangerous Supplement . . . ," 154. On the topic of presence and escape, it seems wonderfully suggestive that *Renaissance Figures of Speech*, which I cite several times, includes no essay on metonymy, although several of the contributors invoke metonymic figuration at densely complex analytic moments. This is of course an artifact of anthology-making; as the editors note, "comprehensive coverage has not been our aim" (Adamson, Alexander, and Ettenhuber, "Introduction," 14). But for me the omission recalls Hillman and Mazzio's introduction to *The Body in Parts*, in which they write (in

parentheses), "We should perhaps point out that the most notably absent sexual organ in this volume is the penis. An argument could be made, however, that the male member functions almost literally as a floating signifier, surfacing throughout this volume in perhaps the most unexpected of places" (xx). While I would emphatically *not* equate metonymy with the penis, I might argue that making the "male member" a floating signifier is a metonymic effect.

56. Merbecke, *A Booke of Notes and Common places*, 266. He writes, "For first the vessell is taken for that which is conteined in the vessell, as the Cup for the wine which is within the Cup. Then the wine is called the Covenant or Testament, whereas in deede, it is but the signe of the Testament, or rather of the bloud of Christ, whereby the Testament was made" (266). For a catalogue of religious uses of metonymy, see T. Wilson, *A Christian Dictionarie*; Wilson's examples include the city, the cross, the crown, the tongue, unclean spirits, weak flesh, and the fruits of an unregenerate will. For a critique of figurative attenuation, see Fisher's comments on the distortion of scripture by "those *Metonymical and improper names*" (*Rusticus Ad Academicos*, "The Third Apologetical, and Expostulatory Exercitation," 153).

57. Ramus, *A Compendium of the Art of Logick and Rhetorick*, 288. See also Fenner, *The Artes of Logike and Rethorike*, sig. D2; and Fraunce, *The Arcadian Rhetorike*, sig. A3.

58. Ramus, *A Compendium of the Art of Logick and Rhetorick*, 292.

59. Derrida, ". . . That Dangerous Supplement. . . ," 147.

60. Gallop, "Reading the Mother Tongue," 320. For theoretical accounts of women as previous to, excluded by, or otherwise alienated from a dominant, ideologically invested language, see for example Irigaray, *This Sex Which Is Not One*, and Cixous, "The Laugh of the Medusa."

61. For analyses of early modern efforts to impose silence on women, see for example Boose, "Scolding Brides and Bridling Scolds"; Jardine, *Still Harping on Daughters*, esp. 103–40; Parker, *Literary Fat Ladies*, esp. 8–35; and Stallybrass, "Patriarchal Territories."

62. Ferguson, *Dido's Daughters*, 124. See also Enterline, *The Rhetoric of the Body*, esp. 35. For discussion of the gender ambiguity of the tongue, and of language itself, see Mazzio, "Sins of the Tongue," esp. 60; and Stallybrass, "Reading the Body," esp. 215.

63. Attersoll, *The Badges of Christianity*, 232. See Mazzio's nuanced discussion of Reformation attacks on "mindless iteration or ignorant mimesis" (*The Inarticulate Renaissance*, 19–55, quotation at 21); she writes, "Reformation polemic doubled as a form of self-defense about the vulnerable status of the English tongue" (23).

64. Freccero, *Queer/Early/Modern*, 18. See also Kristeva's definition of the semiotic as "a 'second' return of instinctual functioning within the symbolic, as a negativity introduced into the symbolic order, and as the transgression of that order" (*Revolution in Poetic Language*, 69).

65. Scholarship on early modern maternity has greatly expanded our understanding of its complexity, and of the ambivalence it might provoke. See for example Adelman, *Suffocating Mothers*; Eccles, *Obstetrics and Gynaecology*; Kahn, *Man's Estate*; Miller and Yavneh, eds., *Maternal Measures*; Paster, *The Body Embarrassed*, esp. 163–280; Rose, "Where are the Mothers in Shakespeare?"; H. Smith, "Gynecology and Ideology in

Seventeenth–Century England"; Willis, *Malevolent Nurture*; and R. Wilson, "Observations on English Bodies."

66. T. Wilson, *The Arte of Rhetorique*, fol. 86. See, too, Lever's distinction between the preservation and the corruption of linguistic genealogy: "We therfore, that devise understandable termes, compounded of true and auncient english woords, do rather maintain and continue the antiquitie of our mother tongue: then they, that with inckhorne termes doe chaunge and corrupt the same, making a mingle mangle of their native speache, and not observing the propertie thereof" (*The Arte of Reason*, sig. *6v [pages inserted before sig. A1]).

67. Austin, *Haec Homo*, 133.

68. Sutcliffe, *A True Relation of Englands Happinesse*, 2. Wiburn makes a similar point; see *A Checke or reproofe*, fol. 124v–125.

69. Annand, *Fides Catholica*, 64.

70. Mazzio, "Sins of the Tongue," 54. Mazzio develops this relation through emblems of the detached but animate tongue, writing, "The spectacle of the independent organ of speech, mobile even while dislodged from its bodily surround, in many ways perfectly embodies anxieties about reference itself, not only about the movement of speech *away* from the individual body but also about the movement of signs away from any singularly discernable, naturalized context" (54).

71. Marston, *What You Will*, Act 2, Scene 1, sig. C4v.

72. Wall, "'Household Stuff,'" 15.

73. Dekker and Webster, *West-Ward Hoe*, Actus Primus, Scaena Prima, sig. B2.

74. Michaelis, *The Admirable Historie*, sig. A6. See also Scot, *Scot's Discovery of Witchcraft*, 308. This link between witchcraft and the mother tongue is also cited to comment on the language in which knowledge of witches is conveyed; see for example Heywood, *Gynaikeion*, 406; and Torquemada, *The Spanish Mandevile of Miracles*, fol. 81.

75. Abbot, *The Reasons Which Doctour Hill Hath Brought, for the upholding of Papistry*, 37–38. Leigh—another woman who made a book—addresses her reader "to entreate and desire you, and in some sort to commaund you, that all your children, be they Males or Females, may in their youth learne to read the Bible in their owne mother tongue; for I know, it is a great helpe to true godlinesse" (*The Mothers Blessing*, 24).

76. Enterline, *The Rhetoric of the Body*, 37.

77. Seneca, *Hippolitus Translated out of Seneca by Edmund Prestwich*, 74. This poem gestures toward the effect Mazzio describes in *The Inarticulate Renaissance*: "disruptions in conversational encounters might produce not only shame, awkwardness, alienation, or a sense of participatory insufficiency but also a heightened awareness of the (suddenly disrupted) protocols governing selves and others" (9).

78. Ferguson, *Dido's Daughters*, 125. Ferguson analyzes our inheritance of "that notion of the Renaissance as a rebirth, a notion that carries with it a powerful masculinist ideology": "This includes, as one of its many strands, the idea that *biological* mothers, and the mother tongues of the vernacular, are less culturally valuable than intellectual fathers and the ancient languages of Hebrew, Greek, and Latin, languages often figured as paternal, as more unified and enduring than the vernaculars, and, in some cases, as

directly descended from the Word of God the Father" (133). See also Ong: "The cleavage between the vernacular world and the Latin world did not coincide with the division between literacy and illiteracy, but it did coincide with the division between family life and a certain type of extra-familial life and with a division between a world in which women had some say and an almost exclusively male world" ("Latin Language Study," 107–8).

79. Ainsworth, *The Art of Logick*, 216.

80. Sidney, *An Apologie for Poetrie*, sig. B2–B2v. Kerrigan describes the formation of the "linguistic ego" in related terms, arguing that students of Latin could return to English as masters: "these men internalized a masculine language and then, mature in words, fathered a great literature in its image" ("The Articulation of the Ego," 287). Intriguingly, however, Kerrigan complicates that model by asserting that maternal influence made the return to English possible. "The turn from Latin to English that gave us the English literature of the Renaissance was more than a gesture of linguistic nationalism or a flight from paternal priority: it was also a trust in the mother as the true progenitrix of time, the mistress of futurity" (288).

81. Harington, "An Advertisement to the Reader," sig. A1.

82. The translator's dedication that prefaces Erasmus's *Paraphrase* describes the vulnerability of a generally available text to indiscriminate or ill-willed reading. "Out of one and the same floure the Bee gathereth honey, and the spider sucketh venome: so great diversitie of operacion there is in good and civill natures. And the common faulte that malignaunt persones doe allege against the publishing of Goddes worde in the mother tongue, and against the setting foorth of holesome and godly exposicions upon the same, is, that suche bookes cause sedicion against the doctrine" (Erasmus, *The first tome or volume of the Paraphrase of Erasmus*, Fol. xvi^v).

83. Parker, "Virile Style," 201, 206, 216.

84. Guazzo, *The Civile Conversation*, Book 2, fol. 18v.

85. Younge, *The Drunkard's Character*, 104.

86. Barckley, *A Discourse of the Felicitie of Man*, 307. Dallington, too, conflates linguistic and sexual improprieties in order to displace them, attributing both to "this French tongue being no Mother tongue of it self"; see *The View of Fraunce*, sig. V3.

87. Wall, "'Household Stuff,'" 29.

88. Prynne, *Histrio-mastix*, 611–12. The sidenote suggests that theatricality is both contagious and chronic: "Therefore they may not act academicall Enterludes in Colledges" (612).

89. Stephens, *Essayes and Characters, Ironicall, and Instructive*, 410–11, 414.

90. Alexander, "Prosopopoeia," 102.

91. Goodman, *The Fall of Man*, 302–3. See also Perkins's account of the fall into language: "If thou have many tongues and knowest not howe to use them well: hee which hath but his mother tongue, ordering it aright, is a better linguist then thou" (*A Direction for the Government of the Tongue*, 58–59, quotation at 59). Brathwait draws a rather different picture of excess and lack in his character "A Zealous Brother": "Hee holds his Mother tongue to be the Originall tongue; and in that only he is constant, for he hath none to

change it withall. Hee wonders how *Babel* should have such a confused variety of *tongues*, and hee understand but one" (*Whimzies*, 198).

92. Purchas, too, links loss of name to linguistic surfeit: "Hee that seeth how *John* or *James* are transported in such unlike sounds from the Originall, in *Greeke, Latine, French, Dutch, Spanish, Italian, English*, and other languages, in all so unlike and diversified, would scarcely acknowledge them brothers, or to have any kindred either to the mother tongue, or in those many sister languages: and so is it commonly with other names" (*Purchas His Pilgrimes*, Book 1, 22).

93. Bacon, *The Twoo Bookes of Francis Bacon*, The Second Booke, 60; Bacon, *The Two Bookes of Sr. Francis Bacon* (1629), 111; Bacon, *The Two Bookes of Sr. Francis Bacon* (1633), 211. (In the 1629 edition, the pages between 199 [misnumbered 169] and 233 are numbered 100–132.)

94. Mazzio, *The Inarticulate Renaissance*, 12.

95. Winter, "To his Translation," sig. A1v.

96. Breton, *Characters upon Essaies Morall, and Divine*, sig. A6.

97. Spenser, *The Shepheardes Calender*, sig. ¶2v (pages inserted before sig. A1).

98. Enterline writes, "Alienation from one's own tongue is both a physical predicament in Ovidian narrative and, at the same time, the condition of being able to speak at all" (*The Rhetoric of the Body*, 31).

99. Butler, *Excitable Speech*, 26.

100. Butler, *Excitable Speech*, 25.

101. T. Wilson, *The Arte of Rhetorique*, fol. 93; Sherry, *A treatise of Schemes and Tropes*, sig. C5v; Sherry, *A Treatise of the Figures of Grammer and Rhetorike*, fol. 24.

102. Sherry, *A Treatise of the Figures of Grammer and Rhetorike*, fols. 23v–24.

103. Foucault, *The Order of Things*, xv.

104. Foucault, *The Order of Things*, xvi.

105. T. Wilson, *The Arte of Rhetorique*, "The Table," sig. Hh4v.

106. Foucault, *The Order of Things*, ix.

107. Lodge, *Catharos*, 25v.

108. Lodge, *Catharos*, 26.

109. Mazzio, *The Inarticulate Renaissance*, 189. For a related point, see Mazzio's reading of misogyny and self-estrangement in *The Purple Island* ("Sins of the Tongue," 58).

Chapter 3. Acts of Will: Misogyny and Masquerade

1. Johnson, "The Alchemy of Style and Law," 173–74, emphasis in original.

2. Bourdieu, "On Symbolic Power," 166.

3. Bourdieu, "On Symbolic Power," 164.

4. Scarry, "Consent and the Body," 882; 877, emphasis in original. Bourdieu himself opens up a space of contest within the field of complicity: "What creates the power of words and slogans, a power capable of maintaining or subverting the social order, is the belief in the legitimacy of words and of those who utter them" (170). That split capacity,

to maintain or subvert, suggests the multiple positions from which an ordering discourse necessarily speaks.

5. Bacon, *The Twoo Bookes of Francis Bacon*, The Second Booke, 63–63v.

6. Bacon, *The Twoo Bookes of Francis Bacon*, The Second Booke, 62.

7. Wayne, "Historical Differences," 165.

8. Swetnam, *The Araignment*, 59.

9. Butler, *Excitable Speech*, 20.

10. Butler, *Excitable Speech*, 19.

11. "Historicism and Its Discontents," Rutgers University, October 12, 2007. I take the heading of this section from symposium promotion materials.

12. qutd. in Orlin, "A Case for Anecdotalism," 75.

13. Orlin, "A Case for Anecdotalism," 74.

14. Rackin, *Shakespeare and Women*, 8.

15. Orlin, "A Case for Anecdotalism," 75.

16. Wayne, "Historical Differences," 174.

17. Rackin, *Shakespeare and Women*, 15.

18. Wayne, "Historical Differences," 174.

19. Orlin, "A Case for Anecdotalism," 77.

20. See for example Ezell, *The Patriarch's Wife*, esp. 6–8, 16–20; Gowing, *Domestic Dangers*, esp. 4–9; Korda, *Shakespeare's Domestic Economies*, esp. 39–47; Orlin, "A Case for Anecdotalism," esp. 74; and Rackin, *Shakespeare and Women*, esp. 19–25. In a different mode, but to similar effect, Papp and Kirkland vividly imagine the response to misogynist texts: "No doubt the Elizabethan women who could read them didn't know whether to laugh or cry at all the stereotypes, simplifications, and gross exaggerations contained in these booklets" (*Shakespeare Alive!* 77). Belsey offers a nuanced account of the relationship between cultural vocabularies and material practices: "Culture is lived as *a relation to* practice, as commitment or resistance, or as an uneasy alliance between the two, an anxious, undecided ambivalence" (*Shakespeare and the Loss of Eden*, esp. 4–8, quotation at 8, emphasis in original).

21. Gowing, *Domestic Dangers*, 4. Gowing argues against the idea of a coherent, univocal system of sexual morals: "Moral principles, and the understandings of honour that were consequent on them, were not a monolithic system, but arose as a series of perceptions, from different sources and with different purposes and effects" (4).

22. Wayne, "Historical Differences," 158. See also Traub's account of misogyny in medical discourse: "The exculpatory strategies of medical texts demonstrate that misogyny, whatever form its mobilization takes, is radically unstable" (*The Renaissance of Lesbianism*, 122).

23. Wayne, "Historical Differences"; see her reading of *Othello*, esp. 167–70.

24. Traub, *The Renaissance of Lesbianism*, 122.

25. Mullaney, "Mourning and Misogyny," 157.

26. Agrippa, *Female Pre-Eminence*, 77–78, emphasis in original.

27. Allott, *Wits Theater*, 101v–102.

28. Pontaymeri, *A Womans Woorth*, 30–30v.

29. Swetnam, *The Araignment*, 15.

30. Rich, *The Excellency of good women*, 5.

31. Ezell, *The Patriarch's Wife*, 51–52; for her survey of the pattern of attack and defense, see 46–54. See also her discussion of the tradition of the "Good Wife," esp. 37–42.

32. Belsey, *Shakespeare and the Loss of Eden*, 15.

33. Baldwin, *A treatyce of Moral philosophy*, fols. 131–33.

34. Swetnam, *The Araignment*, sig. A2v; 28.

35. Rose, *The Expense of Spirit*, 4. Rose contrasts a fallen view of marriage to "the Protestant (largely Puritan) idealization of 'holy matrimony'" (4), and contends that idealization construes marriage in heroic terms; she writes of Jacobean tragedy, "Furthermore, the heroism being constructed is one of patient suffering, rather than willful action; as such, I argue, it is a heroism particularly suited to women" (9). See her readings of *Othello* and *The Duchess of Malfi*, esp. 131–77. See also Jordan: "Misogyny was the inevitable by-product of the concept of Christian marriage as the union of rational man with passionate woman" (*Renaissance Feminism*, 54).

36. Swetnam, *The Araignment*, 36. Burton gives a detailed catalogue of mismatches, which also obviates useful distinctions; see *The Anatomy of Melancholy*, 3.2.6.3, pp. 568–69.

37. Gowing, *Domestic Dangers*, 276.

38. Dekker, trans., *The Batchelars Banquet*, epigraph.

39. Swetnam, *The Araignment*, 5.

40. Jardin, *A Discourse of the Married and Single Life*, 107.

41. Copland, *The seven sorowes*, sig. C1v–C2.

42. Dolan, *Dangerous Familiars*, 57–58.

43. Cited by Jardin in *A Discourse of the Married and Single Life*, 108–9. For a full history of this myth, see Bowen, ed., *One Hundred Renaissance Jokes*, 17.

44. Swetnam, *The Araignment*, 6.

45. Jardin, *A Discourse of the Married and Single Life*, 105–6.

46. Allott, *Wits Theater*, 102–4.

47. Agrippa, *Female Pre-Eminence*, 3, emphasis in original; Pontaymeri, *A Womans Woorth*, sig. A10. Pontaymeri is identified as the author of the main text, but the translator's and editor's identities are unclear; the epistle I cite is signed "Yours in all duety. *Anonimus*" (sig. A10v).

48. Ezell, *The Patriarch's Wife*, 55. For her detailed discussion of the debate over marital hierarchy, see 54–64. See also Jordan's comment on the Latin Fathers of the early church: "Such theological opinions demonstrate how teleological doctrine—that by Eve's creation and sin the pattern for all subsequent relations between men and women is established—could be interpreted to express a fear of woman and of sexuality in general" (*Renaissance Feminism*, 26).

49. Bullinger, *The Christen state*, fol. 2v.

50. Gataker, "A Wife in Deed," 9, emphasis in original.

51. Gataker, "A Wife in Deed," 37, emphasis in original.

52. Bullinger, *The Christen state*, fol. 15v.

53. Allott, *Wits Theater*, 102. See also More, *A lytle and bryefe treatyse*, sig. A4v; and Bulwer, *Chirologia*, 71–2.

54. Swetnam, *The Araignment*, 1 (sig. B1).

55. More, *A Lytle and bryefe treatyse*, sig. A4v; Huarte, *The Examination of mens Wits*, sig. A7.

56. Gosynhyll, *The Schole house of women*, sig. B4v–C1.

57. Austin, *Haec Homo*, 50, emphasis in original. Other authors make the same point; see anon., *An other defence of womens vertues*, 63; and Speght, *A Mouzell for Melastomus*, 10.

58. Austin, *Haec Homo*, 47–48, emphasis in original.

59. Agrippa, *Female Pre-Eminence*, 10, emphasis in original.

60. Ezell concludes, "Obviously, the manner of Eve's creation did not show *anything* sufficiently clearly to settle the controversy over the extent of patriarchal authority in the seventeenth century" (*The Patriarch's Wife*, 60, emphasis in original). See also Belsey, *Shakespeare and the Loss of Eden*, esp. 76–77.

61. Bloch attributes this coherent purpose to misogynist discourse: "to remove individual women from the realm of events" (*Medieval Misogyny*, 5). Jordan points out that praise often serves the ends of segregation and subjection (*Renaissance Feminism*, esp. 8, 18–19).

62. Averell, *A Dyall for dainty Darlings*, sig. F4.

63. Speght, *A Mouzell for Melastomus*, 10, emphasis in original.

64. Austin, *Haec Homo*, 3–4. See Jordan's observation: "concepts crucial to the idea of a society organized according to principles inimical to patriarchy—heterogeneity in nature and its creatures, androgyny as the bigendering of each sex, and the equality of men and women in human society—were enunciated in feminist discourse of the sixteenth century" (*Renaissance Feminism*, 28–29).

65. Speght, *A Mouzell for Melastomus*, 10. The critique of physical abuse is common; for analyses of its implications, see Jordan, *Renaissance Feminism*, esp. 97; and Dolan, *Dangerous Familiars*, esp. 31–38.

66. Belsey, *Shakespeare and the Loss of Eden*, 77.

67. Gataker, "A Good Wife Gods Gift," 20, emphasis in original.

68. Allott, *Wits Theater*, 102.

69. Newman, *Fashioning Femininity*, 10.

70. Vickers, "Diana Described," 109.

71. Newman, *Fashioning Femininity*, 12.

72. Parker, *Literary Fat Ladies*, 127.

73. B. Smith, *Homosexual Desire*, 260. See also Parker, *Literary Fat Ladies*, esp. 126–54; Parker describes "an imagery of opening and controlling something gendered as female before spectators and possessors gendered as male, in a process in which ostentatious display, *copia*, or 'increase' is constrained within an economy of mastery and ownership" (154).

74. Sawday, *The Body Emblazoned*, 212.

75. Sawday, *The Body Emblazoned*, 9.

76. Freud, "Medusa's Head," 274.

77. Enterline, *The Rhetoric of the Body*, 29. On the complexities of cross-gendered authorial voice, see also Harvey, *Ventriloquized Voices*; Wall, *The Imprint of Gender*; and Greenstadt, *Rape and the Rise of the Author*.

78. For readings of subjectivity and voice that complicate Vickers's model, see for example Enterline, *The Rhetoric of the Body*, 36–38; Dubrow, *Echoes of Desire*, 36–48; and Bates, *Masculinity, Gender and Identity*. Many scholars have noted that sonnet sequences unsettle autonomous mastery; on Shakespeare's *Sonnets* and this critical tradition, see Chapter 5.

79. Traub argues that anatomies undercut naturalized oppositions in a way that implicates both anatomist and corpse; see "Gendering Mortality," esp. 50.

80. There is also the possibility that pieces might operate on their own terms. In the introduction to *The Body in Parts*, Hillman and Mazzio point out that fragments often possess independent capacities: "the part, in the "Historicall" and "Scientificall" texts of the period, is a subject, both in the sense that it is increasingly marked and elaborated upon in a range of visual and textual spaces, and in the sense that it is frequently imagined to take on attributes of agency and subjectivity" (xii). This sparks a vision of blazons run amok, in which a part may gesture neither toward the next part nor toward the desired whole, but toward its own willful act.

81. Banister, *The Historie of Man*, 88v. See Traub's cogent comment on authorial self-protection: "the female body performed a crucial service to scientific production: absorbing within her flesh the danger and ambivalence involved in unveiling and publicizing nature's secrets" (*The Renaissance of Lesbianism*, 79).

82. Maus, *Inwardness and Theater*, 196.

83. Burton, *The Anatomy of Melancholy*, 3.2.2.2, p. 465.

84. Hutson, *The Usurer's Daughter*, 7. Hutson writes, "humanism relocates the instrumentality of male friendship, translating it from alliance and gift-exchange to persuasive communication," and argues that this cultural shift, with its emphasis on rhetorics of husbandry and wife-training, limits the representational scope for feminine agency (11). See also 17–51.

85. *A Brief Anatomie of Women*, 2–3. For a blazon that identifies women's bodies with their adornments, conflating sexual and financial costs to men, see Jardin, *A Discourse of the Married and Single Life*, 61–64. Jardin also imagines that sexual desire might insert men into the structure of the blazon, with monstrous results: "O wretched man that intendest to marry a woman! thou must goe unto the eyes of *Argus*, to keep her; the eares of *Faues*, to hearken after her; the nosethrils of a Wolfe, that thou maist smel out her defects: The tongue of a Fish, that thou be silent at her brawlings: The stomake of an Estridge, to disgest her reproches: The necke of a Bull, to support the heavy yoke: the Crowne of *Pan* woven with thornes, to cover thy horne: The feete of a Hart to runne from her snares" (66–67).

86. *Haec Vir* links the female sexual body to literal weapons, describing "a shorne, powdered, borrowed Hayre, a naked, lascivious, bawdy Bosome, a *Leaden-Haft* Dagger, a High-way Pistoll, and a mind and behaviour sutable or exceeding every repeated deformi-tie" (sig. A4).

87. Rich, *The Excellency of good women*, 13.

88. *Hic Mulier*, sig. B4.

89. Vickers, "Members Only," 17.

90. Swetnam, *The Araignment*, 16. See also Bullinger's apocalyptic vision: "The lyp-pes of an harlot are as a swete droppynge honye combe, and her throte is softer then oyle: but her ende is bitterer then death, and as sharpe as a two edged sweard. Her feete lead unto death, and her pathe drawethe unto hell" (*The Christen state*, fol. 26).

91. Kristeva, *Revolution in Poetic Language*, 50.

92. Burton, *The Anatomy of Melancholy*, 3.2.6.3, p. 561.

93. Jordan, *Renaissance Feminism*, 53.

94. Burton, *The Anatomy of Melancholy*, 3.2.6.3, p. 569, emphasis in original.

95. Jardin, *A Discourse of the Married and Single Life*, 17–18.

96. Jardin, *A Discourse of the Married and Single Life*, 102.

97. *Good Vibrations* catalogue, 38–39.

98. Riviere, "Womanliness as a Masquerade," 101.

99. Tuke, *A Discourse Against Painting*, 10. For a reading of this passage in terms of "a double-bind of either being pure but not seeming so or seeming so but not according to male conventions," see Eaton, "Beatrice-Joanna and the Rhetoric of Love," esp. 275.

100. Brathwait, *The English Gentlewoman*, sig. Gg2v, emphasis in original.

101. Gowing writes, "the potential consequences of a woman's unchastity under-mine the very basis of a society structured—practically and conceptually—in familial terms"; as her detailed analysis of court cases demonstrates, the unstable connection be-tween language and practice forms a site of fierce contest (*Domestic Dangers*, 4). See also L. Wilson's account of the interplay between pretense and intention: "because pretense tends toward action—because it is an outward and visible (and false) declaration of in-tent—the prefix pre- takes both temporal and spatial senses of 'before,' with the result that intent acquires ethical and social meaning in the form of a promise that is a *pretense* both because it comes before and is an earnest of action, and because it is a setting before, a (duplicitous) *presentation*" (*Theaters of Intention*, 11, emphasis in original).

102. Jardin, *A Discourse of the Married and Single Life*, 44.

103. Crocker, "Affective Resistance," 156.

104. Riviere, "Womanliness as a Masquerade," 94.

105. Shakespeare, *Timon of Athens*, 3.6.78–79.

106. Case, "Toward a Butch-Femme Aesthetic," 304.

107. Duggan and McHugh, "A Fem(me)inist Manifesto," 165, emphasis in original.

108. Halberstam, *Female Masculinity*, 237–38. Bersani argues that gay male camp can usefully defamiliarize conventional feminine roles, even if it expresses antagonism toward women: "The gay male parody of a certain femininity, which, as others have argued, may itself be an elaborate social construct, is both a way of giving vent to the hostility toward

women that probably afflicts every male (and which male heterosexuals have of course expressed in infinitely nastier and more effective ways) *and* could also paradoxically be thought of as helping to deconstruct that image for women themselves" ("Is the Rectum a Grave," 208, emphasis in original).

109. Traub, "The Perversion of 'Lesbian' Desire," 40. Traub traces a historical shift in perceptions of feminine homoeroticism, concluding, "by the end of the seventeenth century, chaste femme love became the object of cultural anxiety" (25).

110. Case, "Toward a Butch-Femme Aesthetic," 305.

111. Duggan and McHugh, "A Fem(me)inist Manifesto," 166.

112. Freccero, *Queer/Early/Modern*, 80.

Chapter 4. "My Intents Are Fix'd": Constant Will in *All's Well That Ends Well*

1. Barnet, "Introduction: *All's Well That Ends Well*," 1050.

2. Patterson, "Intention," 145.

3. Baldwin, *A treatyce of Moral philosophy*, fols. 130v–131. See also Markham, *The English House-wife*, 4.

4. Althusser, "Ideology and Ideological State Apparatuses," 169.

5. Žižek, *The Sublime Object of Ideology*, 21, emphasis in original.

6. Žižek, *The Sublime Object of Ideology*, 112.

7. Žižek, *The Sublime Object of Ideology*, 112.

8. Shakespeare, *All's Well That Ends Well*, in *The Riverside Shakespeare*. Subsequent citations follow this edition; bracketed passages in this edition are silently retained.

9. Brathwait, *Ar't asleepe Husband?* 4, emphasis in original. Brathwait makes this claim in response to a charge of innate female autocracy: "Shee was made of a *Crookt* Subject, a *Rib*: and out of her crooked disposition (will some say, who stand ill-affected to the *Salique* state) shee will not stick to tyrannize over a sheepish husband, and give him *rib-roast*" (3–4).

10. Buoni, *Problemes of Beautie*, 47.

11. Baldwin, *A treatyce of Moral philosophy*, 132v–133. Caninius, in Elyot's *The Defence of Good Women*, follows this argument as well: "But their moste unperfection is their inconstancye, whiche procedeth of their said naturall debilitie. For where as the affection of muche dread or muche love aboundeth, stabilitie lacketh, and witte littell prevaileth" (sig. B7v).

12. La Perrière, *The Theater of Fine Devices*, 88, emblem LXXXVIII.

13. Alberti, *Hecatonphila. The Arte of Love*, 34v.

14. Rowe, "Inconstancy," 91. Rowe concludes, "the stereotype of female inconstancy marks conceptual conflicts in English Renaissance writing, between the demands of contractual subjectivity and the constraints of humoral psychology" (100). For an extended discussion of inconstancy framed in terms of nationalism, ethnicity, and geohumoralism, see Floyd-Wilson, *English Ethnicity and Race*, esp. 48–66.

15. McCandless discusses the tensions surrounding Helena's occupation of "the masculine position of desiring subject"; see "Helena's Bed-trick," esp. 450. A number of readers have traced the play's complication of patriarchy to the value it places on bonds among women. See for example Asp, "Subjectivity, Desire and Female Friendship," esp. 59; Adelman, *Suffocating Mothers*, esp. 79–80; and Neely, *Broken Nuptials*, esp. 74–78. In a compelling challenge to the priority of dyadic, heterosexual marriage plots, J. Crawford argues for a "*systemic* and *contingent* (as opposed to teleological) notion of marriage" in *All's Well*, and emphasizes "the multiply influenced and systemic nature of the familial, socioeconomic, and affective same-sex bonds so central to marriage in Shakespeare's play" ("*All's Well*," 39, 45, emphasis in original).

16. Brathwait, *The English Gentlewoman*, 126.

17. See for example Snyder, "'*All's Well*,'" esp. 74; Asp, "Subjectivity, Desire, and Female Friendship," 56; and Jardine, "Cultural Confusion," esp. 11. Earlier criticism often describes Helena's transformation in moral terms; for two opposed views, see Calderwood, "Styles of Knowing," 282; and Chambers, *Shakespeare: A Survey*, 205.

18. Adelman, *Suffocating Mothers*, 85. See also Snyder, "'*All's Well*,'" 66; and Neely, *Broken Nuptials*, 67. Bevington describes Helena in terms of "unified feminine duality" ("All's Well That Plays Well," 170). See also Kay's account of Helena's multiple roles in "Reforming the Prodigal," esp. 119.

19. Quiller-Couch, "Introduction," xxxi; and Kastan, "Limits of Comedy," 579.

20. For example, see Chambers, *Shakespeare: A Survey*, 200–207; Quiller-Couch, "Introduction," xxxi; and Leech, "The Theme of Ambition," 17–29. For more recent examples, see Levin, "'*All's Well*,'" 131–44; and Berkeley and Keesee, "Bertram's Blood-Consciousness," 247–58. For a survey of the practice of judging Helena, see McCandless, "Helena's Bed-trick," 454n13.

21. Bevington, "All's Well That Plays Well," 170.

22. Lewis and Short, *A Latin Dictionary*, s.v. "intentio," I, II, IIA–IIC.

23. *The Oxford English Dictionary*, s.v. "intention" (n.), 4, 5, 7.

24. L. Wilson, *Theaters of Intention*, 7. For an overview of the modern genesis of "an action-oriented account of intention," and the questions it raises about the relationship between intention and act, see Patterson, "Intention," esp. 137–40, quotation at 137.

25. Lewis and Short, *A Latin Dictionary*, s.v. "intentio," IIE

26. Charron, *Of Wisdome*, 69–70. A later translation by Stanhope accentuates the effect of personification: "Here the Soul goes as it were out of it self, it stretches and moves forward toward the Object; it seeks and runs after it with open Arms, and is eager to take up its Residence, and dwell with the Thing desired and beloved" (*Of Wisdom*, 165).

27. Hooker, *Of the Lawes of Ecclesiasticall Politie*, 59.

28. La Primaudaye, *The Second Part of the French Academie*, 207.

29. *A Midsummer Night's Dream*, in *The Riverside Shakespeare*, 3.2.463; 3.2.461.

30. Hodgdon, "The Making of Virgins and Mothers," 59, emphasis in original.

31. Jardine, "Cultural Confusion," 12.

32. [Chamberlayne], *The Compleat Midwife's Practice Enlarged*, 308.

33. Crooke, *Mikrokosmographia*, 197. See also Banister's refusal to discuss the female generative organs in the vernacular, in *The Historie of Man*, 85. For other early modern discussions of this problem of knowledge and the forms of its articulation, see for example Gale, *Certaine Workes of Chirurgerie*, sig. *4; and Culpeper, *A Directory for Midwives*, 4. For critical analyses of these concerns, see for example Eccles, *Obstetrics and Gynaecology*; McLaren, *Reproductive Rituals*; H. Smith, "Gynecology and Ideology"; Traub, *The Renaissance of Lesbianism*, esp. 107–24; and R. Wilson, "Observations on English Bodies."

34. Raynalde argues that feminine understanding may be a practical impossibility: "the aunswere of the Phisition and reasonable allegation of causes to the same infirmitie, is manye tymes obscure, darke, and straunge, to be comprehended by the woman, for lacke of due knowledge" (*The Birth of Mankynde*, sig. B2v). Culpeper, too, takes on that problem; see *A Directory for Midwives*, 4. As discourses on generation address themselves to both masculine and feminine readers, this limitation appears increasingly artificial.

35. Traub, *The Renaissance of Lesbianism*, 122. Traub notes that strategies which pursue and convey corporeal knowledge "reveal a complex and contradictory cultural calculus": anxieties about the illicit are mediated through and mitigated by female bodies, but those bodies also figure the precarious qualities of the new epistemological regime. See esp. 122–24.

36. *The Oxford English Dictionary*, s.v. "empiric" (n.), 2.

37. Oberndorff, *The Anatomyes of the True Physition*, 3–4. The audience's credulity is critiqued as well: "For they delighting altogether in Noveltie, and loathing their old accustomed Physitions, though never so learned, if there come any straunge Beast, or Monster, out of Barbary, or Jacke an Apes from Cataia, they doo gaze upon him with Admiration, flocke after him by whole Troupes, and set him out, in highest Degrees of Commendations" (13).

38. Oberndorff, *The Anatomyes of the True Physition*, 29.

39. Forset, *A Comparative Discourse*, 93.

40. Gataker, "A Wife in Deed," 33.

41. Rowe, *Dead Hands*, 27. See also L. Wilson, who describes the anatomy theater as a space of mutual constitution and constant exchange ("William Harvey's *Prelectiones*," esp. 72).

42. Traub, "Gendering Mortality," 55, 45. For further discussion of the complex and often precarious positions of anatomist and corpse, see Rowe, *Dead Hands*, 24–51; Sawday, "The Fate of Marsyas" and *The Body Emblazoned*; and L. Wilson, "William Harvey's *Prelectiones*." See also Park, "The Criminal and the Saintly Body" and "The Life of the Corpse."

43. Shakespeare makes this explicit in *King John*, when Lady Faulconbridge names her son a bastard. His resemblance to Cordelion has been recognized, but he remains the son and heir of Faulconbridge until his mother declares him otherwise. His response— "Ay, my mother, / With all my heart I thank thee for my father!" (1.1.269–70)— acknowledges that her affirmation redefines his identity; without those socially transformative words, the relations among bodies remain mute.

44. Jardine, "Cultural Confusion," 7.

45. McCandless, "Helena's Bed-trick," 454.

46. Lacan, "The Mirror Stage," 4.

47. Neely describes the narrow scope of Bertram's choice: "Unlike both the heroes of the comedies, who are usually parentless, and those of tragedy, who often struggle with fathers or father figures, Bertram either submits or flees" (*Broken Nuptials*, 66). Even when Bertram runs, he runs in place, claiming a new identity by taking service in another's name. For a theoretical analysis of reproductive futurism and the regressive priorities of repetition and sameness, see Edelman, *No Future*, esp. 59–66.

48. In a critique of feminist readings, Cook writes, "[Shakespeare's] focus excludes a textual basis for exaggerated feminist concern with patriarchy, since the King, Lafew, the French Lords, and Bertram hardly constitute oppressive male authority" ("Helena: The Will and the Way," 14). If the proliferation of authorized men fails to impress, this perhaps registers a deficit of persuasive autonomy.

49. Bevington, "All's Well That Plays Well," 168.

50. Sullivan, "'Be this sweet Helen's knell,'" 60. For Sullivan's cogent account of the interplay of memory and forgetting in Helena's social reinvention, see 59–61.

51. Adelman, *Suffocating Mothers*, 82.

52. For speculations concerning this contradiction, see for example *All's Well That Ends Well*, New Folger Library Shakespeare, 72n94–96; *The Norton Shakespeare*, 2203n5; and *All's Well That Ends Well*, Arden, 3rd rev. ed., 55n86–88.

53. Asp, "Subjectivity, Desire and Female Friendship," 54. See also Hodgdon, "The Making of Virgins and Mothers," 66; Adelman, *Suffocating Mothers*, 82–83; and Bevington, "All's Well That Plays Well," 176.

54. Žižek, *The Sublime Object of Ideology*, 75. I am indebted to Jonathan Gil Harris for the suggestion that the play's resolution has this sinthomatic quality.

55. Žižek, *The Sublime Object of Ideology*, 75.

56. Kastan, "Limits of Comedy," 580. See also Gross, "The Conclusion to *All's Well That Ends Well*," esp. 272; Donaldson, "Shakespeare's Play of Endings," esp. 52; and Briggs, "Shakespeare's Bed-Tricks," esp. 312. Even Asp's account of effective feminine subjectivity concludes without full closure ("Subjectivity, Desire and Female Friendship," 61). See also Hodgdon's comments on compromise ("The Making of Virgins and Mothers," 68) and Snyder's speculation that the uneasiness of the ending may originate with the author ("'All's Well,'" 75).

57. For a Lacanian reading of the play, see Snyder, "'The King's not here.'"

58. Kastan perceives a conflict between means and ends and between comic convention and ethical behavior; see "Limits of Comedy," esp. 585. Godshalk examines the strain the play places on the configurations of the morality tale; see "*All's Well* and the Morality Play." Wheeler describes an incoherence between psychological realism and structural artifice ("The King and the Physician's Daughter" and *Shakespeare's Development*, esp. 34–91); Warren, between structural constraint and autobiographical impulse ("Why Does It End Well?"); Adelman, "between male autonomy and female desire" (*Suffocating Mothers*, 83); Briggs, "between artistic resolution and uncontainable desire" ("Shakespeare's

Bed-Tricks,'" 305); and Friedman, "between male bonding and marriage" ("Male Bonds and Marriage," 232).

59. Cartelli, "Shakespeare's 'Rough Magic,'" 123.

60. Žižek, *The Sublime Object of Ideology*, 84, emphasis in original.

61. Harris, "All Swell That End Swell," 180.

62. Neely, *Broken Nuptials*, 65. J. Crawford notes an impulse to stabilize that marriage at the expense of more intricate, nuanced relational systems: "The marriage that ends the play is not the single-minded triumph of heterosexuality critics so often strain to see it as" ("*All's Well*," 45).

63. Snyder, "'*All's Well*,'" 77.

64. van Veen, "Love in enduring death," *Amorum Emblemata*, 185.

Chapter 5. "Will in Overplus": Recasting Misogyny in the *Sonnets*

Epigraph: Shakespeare, sonnet 136, in *Shakespeare's Sonnets*, ed. Duncan-Jones. Hereafter cited parenthetically by sonnet and line number.

1. Fineman, *Shakespeare's Perjured Eye*, 27.

2. See Williams, *A Glossary*, 337–38.

3. Sedgwick, *Between Men*, 38.

4. Freinkel, *Reading Shakespeare's Will*, 225. For a particularly well annotated example, see Booth, ed., *Shakespeare's Sonnets*, 466–67. See also Willbern's more general comments on will: "The term occupies a densely overdetermined semantic nexus within which notions of erotic *appetite* or *desire*, sexual and procreative *organs*, *aggression* (the will to power), *wish, whim, inclination, volition, conscious intention, purpose*, and *bequest* or *testament* co-exist at varying levels of potentiality" (*Poetic Will*, xiv, emphasis in original).

5. Freinkel, *Reading Shakespeare's Will*, 228. See also Sedgwick, who writes, "this double entendre means too many things. . . . Its gender bearings are, far from neutral, but wildly and, as it turns out, dangerously scattered" (*Between Men*, 38).

6. In considering the last 28 poems of the *Sonnets* as a sequence constructed in relation to a feminine addressee, I follow a convention that is assumed—see Booth, ed., *Shakespeare's Sonnets*, 434—but hardly uncontested. For a strong challenge to presumptions concerning the order of the sequence, see Dubrow, "'Incertainties now crown themselves assur'd.'" For an argument supporting the idea of a sequence ordered according to Shakespeare's intentions, see Duncan-Jones, "Was the 1609 *Shake-speares Sonnets* Really Unauthorized?" Kalas argues for a dialogic relationship between the two parts of the sequence; see "Fickle Glass," esp. 263. See also Fineman, *Shakespeare's Perjured Eye*, 172. Bell suggests that the last 28 sonnets divide their address between the dark lady and the young man; see "Rethinking Shakespeare's Dark Lady." Trevor argues that the sequence's investment in poetry itself subsumes the specificity of gendered identities and relations; see "Shakespeare's Love Objects."

7. See Traub, who writes, "despite some gender ambiguity in modes of linguistic

address, male and female *bodies* are cathected quite differently in these poems" ("Sex Without Issue," 442). A range of powerful readings have complicated the distinction between homosocial and heterosocial desire. See Bredbeck, *Sodomy and Interpretation*, esp. 172–80; de Grazia, "The Scandal of Shakespeare's Sonnets," esp. 41–44; and J. Goldberg, "Hal's Desire, Shakespeare's Idaho," esp. 41. See also Dubrow's discussion of the indeterminacy of the object in relation to the intersection of Petrarchan and anti-Petrarchan discourses in *Echoes of Desire*, esp. 122–25. For a reading of the relationship between heterosexuality and homosexuality in the context of editorial practice, see Stallybrass, "Editing as Cultural Formation"; Stallybrass writes, "The *Sonnets*, previously a marginal aspect of Shakespeare's corpus, became the ground on which 'sexual identity' was invented and contested" (103).

8. For a highly influential account of the link between Petrarchan sequences and the cultural imperatives that control and chastise women, see Vickers, "Diana Described." Vickers develops the social dimension of this strategy in her reading of anatomical blazons in "Members Only," esp. 13–14. See also B. Smith's account of the social, sexual, and rhetorical power relations of the Petrarchan sequence in *Homosexual Desire*, 259–60. For readings of feminine voice that complicate Vickers's model, see for example Enterline, *The Rhetoric of the Body*, 36–38; and Dubrow, *Echoes of Desire*, 36–48.

9. Bourdieu, *The Logic of Practice*, 55. B. Smith takes up Bourdieu's structure of conditioned and conditional freedom to argue for Shakespeare's redirection of heteronormative conceits toward homoerotic desire in the first 126 sonnets. See *Homosexual Desire*, 264–65.

10. Bourdieu, *The Logic of Practice*, 58. For characterizations of the "dark lady" sonnets as misogynist, see Duncan-Jones, introduction to *Shakespeare's Sonnets*, 47–49; Sedgwick, *Between Men*, 44; and Fineman, *Shakespeare's Perjured Eye*, esp. 17 and 288. In "Shakespeare's *Will*," Fineman makes misogyny a tenet of the "specific characterological profile" he draws of the *Sonnets*' speaker: "he—for this subject is conceived as male— experiences his own phenomenal substantiality as a materialized heterogeneity; he is subject of an unprecedentedly heterosexual, and therefore misogynist, desire for an object that is not admired" (171). The assumption recurs throughout Booth's commentary; see for example *Shakespeare's Sonnets*, 434, 476, 525. For overview and critique of such characterizations, see Dubrow, "'Incertainties now crown themselves assur'd,'" 128–30; and Bell, "Rethinking Shakespeare's Dark Lady," esp. 294 and 310. For a challenge to the "truth" of misogyny based on the speaker's unreliability, see Stapleton, "'My False Eyes.'" For discussion of these sonnets in relation to the negative cultural valuing of feminine sexuality, see Goldberg's seminal observation: "If anything like sodomy does appear in the sonnets, it is in relation to the so-called dark lady of the final poems, a woman with whom promiscuous, non-marital sex occurs; this is seen as debauched and transgressive sex, not least because it threatens to destroy the relation between the sonneteer and his beloved young man" ("Hal's Desire, Shakespeare's Idaho," 41). Both de Grazia and Traub draw on this point. De Grazia argues that the sonnets reflect a fear of ungoverned reproduction, and more specifically of miscegenation. See de Grazia, "The Scandal of Shakespeare's Sonnets," 41–49. Traub instead describes misogyny as a response

to nonreproductive sex and contested generation: "Misogyny here is an *ideological effect* generated from a conflict over who is going to control (discourses of) reproduction" ("Sex Without Issue," 445). See also Halpern's comments on sodomy and sterility in *Shakespeare's Perfume*, 27–28.

11. Charron, *Of Wisdome*, 69.

12. For accounts of the relationship between reason and will, see for example Charron, *Of Wisdome*, 55; Davies, *Mirum in modum*, sig. C2–C2v; Burton, *The Anatomy of Melancholy*, 1.1.2.11, pp. 26–30; Elyot, *Of the knowledeg whiche maketh a wise man*, 51–52v; Hooker, *Of the Lawes of Ecclesiasticall Politie*, 59–62; and La Primaudaye, *The Second Part of the French Academie*, 204–6.

13. Wright, *The Passions of the minde*, 58. See also Bacon, *The Twoo Bookes*, The Second Booke, 66v–67v; and Coeffeteau, *A Table of Humane Passions*, 54–55. For further discussions of will's consequential power of choice, see Burton, *The Anatomy of Melancholy*, 1.1.2.11, pp. 29–30; Hooker, *Of the Lawes of Ecclesiasticall Politie*, 59–60; and Sir John Davies, *Nosce teipsum*, 51–52.

14. Davies, *Microcosmos*, 45; see also La Primaudaye, *The Second Part of the French Academie*, 213; and Fletcher, *The Purple Island*, p. 79 (Canto 6, Stanza 57).

15. Fineman, *Shakespeare's Perjured Eye*, 27.

16. Freinkel, *Reading Shakespeare's Will*, 232.

17. de Grazia, "The Scandal of Shakespeare's Sonnets," 47. See also Sedgwick, *Between Men*, 45.

18. Traub develops the implications of this effect: "heteroeroticism in these poems ultimately involves not an immersion in (or celebration of) gender difference, but an anxious projection of similitude, an attempt to manage difference by reducing it to sameness" ("Sex Without Issue," 443–44). For a related point concerning "the pleasure of amalgamation, not in the first place with the receptive woman but with the other men received," see Sedgwick, *Between Men*, 38.

19. Sir John Davies, *Nosce teipsum*, 50. See Booth's comments on "sense" (*Shakespeare's Sonnets*, 486–87).

20. de Grazia, "Babbling Will," 128.

21. See Freinkel's important reading of this sonnet in the context of post-Reformation representation: "As that more-than-enough ornament, Shakespeare's *Will* seems, indeed, to take its cue from the *flesh* as Luther defines it: no mere figure, Luther's *Fleisch* is simultaneously too little and too much—both inadequate vessel and absolute fetish" (*Reading Shakespeare's Will*, 233). For a theological reading that connects the language of will to Babel, see de Grazia, "Babbling Will."

22. Schoenfeldt connects these images of appetite to an antagonistic relationship between unruly passion and privileged self-mastery; see "The Matter of Inwardnesss," esp. 307–11. Singh argues that Shakespeare's sonnets "differ from the moral philosophers in that they do not approach passions as a sensual threat to reason and morals—and as requiring ethical control and sublimation" ("'Th' expense of spirit,'" 288).

23. Phillips describes this as an effect of cultural longing: "The dream, so widespread in the Renaissance, of abolishing those two words, *thine* and *mine*, reveals a latent desire

to sublimate their lexical counterparts, *thou* and *I*, into a more perfect subject: *we*" (*English Fictions of Communal Identity*, 6).

24. Garber, *Vested Interests*, 11. See Fineman's comment on the intervention of a "third": "when the poet in this way becomes his 'Will' he becomes *to* himself an absent third person whose nowhere is what stands between, as missing connection, his otherwise identical first and second person" (*Shakespeare's Perjured Eye*, 27). Fineman further develops this idea; see 291–96.

25. de Man, "Autobiography as De-Facement," 75–76.

26. Enterline, *The Rhetoric of the Body*, 11. See also de Man's qualification: "despite the perfect closure of the system, the text contains elements that not only disrupt its balance but its principle of production" ("Autobiography as De-Facement," 76).

27. de Man, "Autobiography as De-Facement," 70.

28. Newman, "Directing Traffic," 50.

29. Strier, "The Refusal to be Judged," 84. Commenting on "the poem's insistence on intersubjectivity and (if there is a difference) either cooperation or collusion," Strier characterizes this as "a kind of grim utopianism" (83). For an unequivocally positive reading, see Snow, "Loves of Comfort and Despair"; Snow describes the relationship as "something workable, even strangely affirmative and idealistic" (462). In response, Feinberg describes a far more negative contract, framed in terms of enforced collusion, lies, and eventual silencing ("Erasing the Dark Lady"). See also Booth, *Shakespeare's Sonnets*, 476–81; his commentary begins by describing "logically improbable, unnatural, and uncomfortable unions" (477), and ends with a reference to "triumphantly mutual pronouns" (481). Schalkwyk refers to "a kind of mutual rather than unilateral transformation of a relationship through the acceptance of a lie," contrasting this performative effect to the "quasi-performative" mode deployed in the poems to the young man ("What May Words Do?" 268). Other readings also take up the idea of mutuality between speaker and feminine addressee in order to emphasize the complexity and opacity of the relationship to the young man. See for example B. Smith, *Homosexual Desire*, 257; and Gil, who writes of "a (perverse) mutuality between male lover and female beloved" in order to argue that "Shakespeare seeks to shield the Young Man (and the relationship Shakespeare has with him) from the entire homosocial/sodomitical dynamic" (*Before Intimacy*, 109, 111).

30. Bersani, "Sociality and Sexuality," 649; 651.

31. For an intriguing alternative to the focus on social interactions, see Gil, who argues for a discourse of sexuality through which the *Sonnets* "memorialize a weird, asocial experience whose felt reality is captured in depersonalized and depersonalizing emotions that connect bodies when a connection between socially legible persons has become impossible" (*Before Intimacy*, 135).

32. Kalas, "Fickle Glass," 270, emphasis in original. See also Snow, "Loves of Comfort and Despair," 471; Feinberg, "Erasing the Dark Lady," 104; and Fineman, *Shakespeare's Perjured Eye*, 166.

33. Fineman, *Shakespeare's Perjured Eye*, 22. For a critique of Fineman's exclusive

focus on the poet's subjectivity, see Kalas, who writes, "the sonnets appear to engage in a dialectic of subject and object that does not necessarily resolve itself in the absolute identity of the subject" ("Fickle Glass," 274).

34. Halpern, *Shakespeare's Perfume*, 30–31. Halpern cites the image of captivity as one of the "local parallels" between sonnet sequences and the Sadean novel: "In Sonnet 133, the Dark Lady becomes a Sadean torturer, locking both Shakespeare and the young man in her prison" (31).

35. I am indebted to Carolyn Dever for this formulation.

36. Bersani, "Is the Rectum a Grave?" 218.

37. Burton, *The Anatomy of Melancholy*, 3.2.2.2, p. 460. In her analysis of Vives, Weitz Miller writes, "A virgin whose appearance draws the male gaze is an agent of destruction to the soul of the man who sees her and is attracted to her: she is responsible for the gazer's response to her" ("Metaphor and the Mystification of Chastity," 139).

38. Buoni, *Problemes of Beautie*, 12.

39. Burton, *The Anatomy of Melancholy*, 3.2.2.2, p. 462. See also Swetnam, *The Araignment*, 14; Baldwin, *A treatyce of Moral philosophy*, 133; Jardin, *A Discourse of the Married and Single Life*, 97; and Buoni, *Problemes of Beautie*, 63–64.

40. Jardin, *A Discourse of the Married and Single Life*, 40.

41. Buoni, *Problemes of Beautie*, 18.

42. Wright, *The Passions of the minde*, 58. Buoni writes, "the *Beautie* of the minde is always joyned to the wit or understanding; and that of the body oftentimes violently enforced by the affections"; when will abdicates where it should mediate and govern—"the will placed upon fraile objects, and willing nothing but to satisfie the desires of the flesh"—it opens that gap between reason and passion (*Problemes of Beautie*, 46, 75).

43. Freinkel, *Reading Shakespeare's Will*, 210, emphasis in original.

44. Duncan-Jones, introduction to *Shakespeare's Sonnets*, 48. For a notably different understanding of tone, see Booth's claim that "the speaker's clown act in taking hyperbolic metaphors literally appears to have no target and no aim but to be funny" (*Shakespeare's Sonnets*, 454).

45. Sonnet 143 raises the stakes when the speaker represents himself as a child, and anchors his existence in a surrender to feminine will from which his own will—his identity, his self-possession—might take shape. "So will I pray that thou mayst have thy Will, / If thou turn back and my loud crying still" (143.13–14). For a reading of this sonnet's maternal imagery that explores "how conflicts between authority and sexuality frame the progress of desire," see Miller, "Playing 'the mother's part,'" esp. 350.

46. Gil, *Before Intimacy*, 108. See also Fineman's discussion of beauty and seeming in *Shakespeare's Perjured Eye*, esp. 172–76. For an account of the inscrutable relations between exterior and interior framed by early modern theories of color, see Harvey, "Flesh Colors." For the ways in which aesthetic and erotic response are inflected by perceptions of racial difference, see, for example, de Grazia, "The Scandal of Shakespeare's Sonnets"; Hall, *Things of Darkness* and "'These bastard signs of fair'"; Hunt, "Be Dark but Not Too Dark"; and Iyengar, *Shades of Difference*.

47. Epideixis and neoplatonism of course record their own contradictions and fail-
ures; on the complexities of the poetry of praise, see for example Fineman, *Shakespeare's
Perjured Eye*; Enterline, *The Rhetoric of the Body*; Dubrow, *Echoes of Desire*; and Kalas,
"Fickle Glass." On the intricacies of neoplatonism, see K. Crawford, "Marsilio Ficino,
Neoplatonism, and the Problem of Sex," and *The Sexual Culture of the French Renaissance*,
esp. chap. 3.

48. For an analysis that frames this problem in rhetorical terms, see Freinkel's account of the "abuse" of catachresis: "What is immortal, in the end, is not beauty, nor the
figure of beauty, but the abuse of beauty's figure: beauty's in-creasing catachresis. It is
beauty's carcass, its echoing and endlessly recycled voice, that death shall never claim"
(*Reading Shakespeare's Will*, 236).

49. Fineman, *Shakespeare's Perjured Eye*, 18, 22. For a compelling critique of Fineman that expands the issue of difference to include age, class, and race, see de Grazia,
"The Scandal of Shakespeare's Sonnets," 44–49.

50. Rich, *The Excellency of good women*, 21. See also Pontaymeri, *A Womans
Woorth*, 60v.

51. Jardin, *A Discourse of the Married and Single Life*, 16–17. See also Cecil, *Precepts*,
47; *A Brief Anatomie of Women*, 3; and Barbaro, *Directions for Love and Marriage*, 30–31.
This last text offers perhaps the most peculiar instance, basing the correlation between
beauty and unchastity on the beautiful woman's height.

52. *Hic Mulier*, sig. B3v.

53. Salter explicitly argues for a virtue based on semblance: "Also our good Matrone
shal give her to understande, how goodly a beautie and gallant ornament chastitie is in a
young Maiden, and if it apperes that she lenes her eare unto suche praies, and by semblance, desiereth not onely too seeme suche a one, but to bee suche a one, the signes wilbe
evident" (*A Mirrhor mete for all Mothers, Matrones, and Maidens*, sig. B2). Seeming paves
the way for being, and in the process overlays it with "signes" of feminine desire that
provide the only available evidence.

54. Buoni, *Problemes of Beautie*, 33.

55. Greene, *Unrequited Conquests*, 11–12.

56. Brathwait, *Ar't asleepe Husband?* 14.

57. Buoni, *Problemes of Beautie*, 12.

58. Dubrow, *Echoes of Desire*, 127.

59. Bredbeck, *Sodomy and Interpretation*, 178, 180.

60. Goldberg, "Hal's Desire, Shakespeare's Idaho," 41; Halpern, *Shakespeare's Perfume*, 31.

61. de Grazia, "The Scandal of Shakespeare's Sonnets," 41–49; B. Smith, "I, You,
He, She, and We," 427.

62. Freinkel, *Reading Shakespeare's Will*, 233–34.

63. Dubrow writes, "Just as sonnet 129 first deflects guilt about desire from the
subject to the abstract force of lust and subsequently to the woman, so in reading the
sequence as a whole, a number of Shakespeareans repeatedly identify a frailty whose name
is woman" ("'Incertainties now crown themselves assur'd,'" 130).

64. Dollimore, *Sexual Dissidence*, 33.

65. Greene, *Unrequited Conquests*, 3.

Chapter 6. "Twixt Will and Will Not": Chastity and Fracture in *Measure for Measure*

1. Shakespeare, *Measure for Measure*, in *The Riverside Shakespeare*. Subsequent citations follow this edition; bracketed passages in this edition are silently retained.

2. Shell discusses the problems of political and theological judgment caused by the conflation of sexual intentions and acts; see *The End of Kinship*, 79–93. See also Briggs, "Shakespeare's Bed-Tricks," esp. 307–11; she writes of Isabella's defense, "The suggestion of a pun on the word 'subject' exposes precisely that conflict between the freedom of the mind and the subjection of the body to the state and its rules that the bed-trick had temporarily reconciled" (311). Cunningham argues that the severance of intent from legal guilt silences "the secret erotic self" in the interests of the state; see "Opening Doubts," 325–36.

3. Adelman, *Suffocating Mothers*, 91. Marcus describes "a city which is paradoxically enslaved both by too much 'libertie' and by too much trust in the rigidities of law" (*Puzzling Shakespeare*, 171).

4. Watson analyzes the tension between "a dramatized treatise on the properties of government" and "an impassioned human story"; see "False Immortality" (quotations at 417).

5. Maus, *Inwardness and Theater*, 179. See also Magedanz, "Public Justice and Private Mercy," esp. 320–21; Watson, "False Immortality"; and Wheeler, *Shakespeare's Development*, 92–153. On the reconciliation of sexuality and stability, see Cunningham's argument concerning "the transience of the community and the effect of permanence that attends on social contracts, in this case, specifically marriage" ("Opening Doubts," 329); and Baines, who writes, "Enforcing chastity thus becomes not only a means of restoring societal health, but also the means of retrieving or buttressing patriarchal authority" ("Assaying the Power of Chastity," 285). A number of readers observe that the problem comedies challenge naturalized connections among comedy, marriage, and sexual hierarchy; see for example Neely, *Broken Nuptials*, 61–62; Adelman, *Suffocating Mothers*, 78; Riefer, "'Instruments,'" 169; and Jankowski, "Hymeneal Blood," esp. 101–2.

6. Dollimore, "Transgression and Surveillance," 83. See also Greenblatt's discussion of salutary anxiety (*Shakespearean Negotiations*, 133–42); and J. Goldberg, who writes, "the Duke even asserts control over what he cannot control" (*James I*, 235). For other discussions of the Duke's absolutism, see Tennenhouse, *Power on Display*, 154–59; Adelman, *Suffocating Mothers*, esp. 88; Marcus, *Puzzling Shakespeare*, esp. 178; Korda, *Shakespeare's Domestic Economies*, esp. 184–185; and Mullaney, *The Place of the Stage*, 88–115. Little contends that the Duke consolidates power through mockery; see "Absolute Bodies." For an incisive critique of the assumption that "the play is about the power of ruling ideologies to shape early modern subjects," see Crane, "Male Pregnancy," esp. 269–70, quotation at

269. For a reading that shifts the ground, "from the duplicities of political representation to those of ethical self-representation," see Berger, *Making Trifles*, 335–426, quotation at 365.

7. Adelman, *Suffocating Mothers*, 102. See also Riefer, "'Instruments'"; Baines, "Assaying the Power of Chastity," esp. 298; and Dollimore, "Transgression and Surveillance," esp. 83.

8. Arguments that invoke absolutism often also address the Duke's flawed mastery. See for example Greenblatt, *Shakespearean Negotiations*, 141; J. Goldberg, *James I*, 235; Cunningham, "Opening Doubts," 326; Korda, *Shakespeare's Domestic Economies*, 189–91; Lake, "Ministers, Magistrates," 180; Little, "Absolute Bodies," 125–26; and Shell, *The End of Kinship*, 89. Wheeler describes the Duke's "illusion of change and providential guidance" as theatrically effective, but at odds with the complexity of the play; see *Shakespeare's Development*, esp. 121–27, 149–53, quotation at 150. Cohen argues that the ideal of absolute monarchical power may be undermined by *Measure*'s divided generic conventions ("From Mistress to Master," esp. 456).

9. Korda, *Shakespeare's Domestic Economies*, 160.

10. 2.3.2; 3.1.152; 3.1.175.

11. In her meticulous "local reading" of jurisdictional tensions and anxieties about Catholic imperialism, Marcus concludes, "All it would take to activate the alternate 'paranoid' interpretation of *Measure for Measure* and its victory for unlocalized law would be sufficient fear of an as yet uncertain future for England under a monarch not yet well known" (*Puzzling Shakespeare*, 195).

12. Davies, *Microcosmos*, 48. See also Forset's analogy between self-government and the well-ordered state in *A Comparative Discourse*, esp. 17–18.

13. Bacon, *The Twoo Bookes of Francis Bacon*, The Second Booke, 46v. I have revised words that appear entirely in capital letters to lower-case form.

14. Crane comments on the Duke's "fantasy of solitary completeness and inviolability" and its vulnerability to contamination ("Male Pregnancy," 292). See also Adelman, *Suffocating Mothers*, 99, and Wheeler, *Shakespeare's Development*, esp. 133–39. Wehrs draws on Crane's reading of interpenetration to argue that vulnerability to others constitutes "redemptive potentialities inscribed by divine love into nature" ("Touching Words," 28).

15. J. Goldberg writes, "In the play, tautology is the Duke's truth, and with it all's good, all's one, reflecting him, serving his ends" (*James I*, 237).

16. J. Goldberg, *James I*, 239. See also Berger, *Making Trifles*, 390; McCandless, "'I'll Pray to Increase,'" 105; and Wheeler, *Shakespeare's Development*, 133–34.

17. Forset, *A Comparative Discourse*, 17.

18. Tennenhouse describes the brief popularity of "absent monarch plays" in the early seventeenth century; see *Power on Display*, esp. 154–59. See also Cohen's discussion of the relationship between romantic comedy and the "disguised monarch play" in *Measure* ("From Mistress to Master").

19. Berger, *Making Trifles*, 340; Berger argues that the Duke concerns himself instead with self-representation and exculpation. See also Shell, *The End of Kinship*, 90–91; Watson, "False Immortality," 420–21; and Wheeler, *Shakespeare's Development*, 132–33.

20. To see that gap clearly, we need only consider his attempt to persuade Barnardine to die. Barnardine refuses: "I will not consent to die this day, that's certain"; "I will not die today for any man's persuasion"; "for thence will I not today" (4.3.44; 47; 50). When the Duke encounters this effective will, he cannot impose his own.

21. Shakespeare, *A Midsummer Night's Dream*, 2.1.186; 5.1.114–15.

22. Goldberg reads doubling and division in terms of the relationship between sovereign and dramatic power; see *James I*, esp. 233.

23. See the note in the *Riverside Shakespeare*: "**generative**: male (?). Many editors adopt Theobald's *ungenerative* (= sexless); cf. *ungenitur'd* in line 174" (Shakespeare, *Measure for Measure*, note to line 112).

24. Huarte, *The Examination of mens Wits*, 150.

25. Coeffeteau writes, "the strivings of vertue consistes not wholy to roote all naturall *Passions* out of the soule, but to moderate and governe them by the rule of reason" (*A Table of Humane Passions*, 66).

26. Huarte, *The Examination of mens Wits*, 150–51.

27. Hayne argues that *Measure* highlights this disproportionate response to resist proposed laws that would in fact punish illicit sex with death ("Performing Social Practice," esp. 13–18).

28. Lake writes of Angelo, "Here he is speaking like the Calvinist God whose will was his law and whose law was his will" ("Ministers, Magistrates," 174). He describes Angelo's failure to distinguish human and divine law, and extends this critique to Isabella; see 176.

29. Crane, "Male Pregnancy," 285. See Crane's larger argument that no one in this play escapes interpenetration and contamination, and her comments on the relationship between linguistic and sexual permeability, esp. 280–91. On Angelo's attempts—and failures—to separate public authority from private desire, see Adelman, *Suffocating Mothers*, 90; Cunningham, "Opening Doubts," 325; Magedanz, "Public Justice and Private Mercy," 323; McCandless, "'I'll Pray to Increase,'" 90; Shell, *The End of Kinship*, 85–88; Wehrs, "Touching Words," 31; and Wheeler, *Shakespeare's Development*, 93–102.

30. Maus argues, "Angelo's yearning for a clandestine union is simply the flip side of his equally intense yearning for rigid containment" (*Inwardness and Theater*, 163). See Charron's equation of excess and lack: "Our will is sharpened by opposition, it opposeth it selfe against deniall. On the other side, our appetite contemneth and letteth passe that which it hath in possession, and runnes after that which it hath not. . . insomuch that the two extreames, the defect and the abundance, the desire and the fruition do put us to like paine" (*Of Wisdome*, 70).

31. Davies, *Microcosmos*, 47.

32. Coeffeteau, *A Table of Humane Passions*, 77.

33. Kamaralli writes, "*Measure* is unique in describing a class of people by their ability to seem" ("Writing About Motive," 55). Several readers discuss Angelo's hypocrisy in relation to Puritan stereotypes; see Lake, "Ministers, Magistrates," 168–169; and Hayne, "Performing Social Practice," 18–20.

34. See Berger's important discussion of the relationship between sin and crime in

this speech, and his reading of Isabella's plea as "a challenge flung at the Duke" (*Making Trifles*, 404). Shell connects Isabella's plea to the play's distinction between religious and political authority; see *The End of Kinship*, esp. 79.

35. Wehrs, "Touching Words," 1.

36. Heywood, *Gynaikeion*, 276.

37. Pontaymeri, *A Womans Woorth*, 44v.

38. [Edgar], *The Lawes Resolutions of Womens Rights*, 377.

39. Bullinger, *The Christen state*, fol. 15v.

40. Baines, "Assaying the Power of Chastity," 285. Baines contends that Isabella "is ignorant of how she, as subject, is constituted and subjected by her chastity" (288).

41. Korda reads Isabella's position outside marriage as a potent danger to that institution; see her account of the "threatening figure of the singlewoman whose refusal to assume the role of 'keeper' threatens to foreclose patrilineality entirely, from without" (*Shakespeare's Domestic Economies*, 175).

42. Watson writes of *Measure*, "From beginning to end, the dominant motive is the need to convert lustful fornication into fruitful married sexuality" ("False Immortality," 412). Many readers attribute this chastising function to the Duke, although often with some skepticism about his ethics or his efficacy. See Dollimore, "Transgression and Surveillance," 81–84; Adelman, *Suffocating Mothers*, 100; Tennenhouse, *Power on Display*, 158; Marcus, *Puzzling Shakespeare*, 178–79; Korda, *Shakespeare's Domestic Economies*, 188; and Lake, "Ministers, Magistrates," 178. Knoppers describes Isabella as the target of that chastisement: "Under the guise of comic correction and transformation, Isabella undergoes a punitive process of juridical shaming" ("(En)gendering Shame," 460). See also Riefer, "'Instruments,'" 159; Wheeler, *Shakespeare's Development*, 129–30; and Watson, "False Immortality," 424–27. By contrast, Kamaralli argues that Isabella makes autonomous decisions, and the Duke's control is an artifact of critical tradition; see "Writing About Motive," esp. 48. See also J. Rose's important questions about responsibility ("Sexuality," 106). For the intriguing suggestion that the Duke reprises the role of comic heroine, see Riefer, "'Instruments,'" 159; Tennenhouse, *Power on Display*, 155; Adelman, *Suffocating Mothers*, 101–2; and Cohen, "From Mistress to Master," 445.

43. Halberstam, *Female Masculinity*, 123.

44. Berger connects this slippage to the Duke's need to avoid detection; see *Making Trifles*, 373.

45. Lacan, "The Function and Field of Speech and Language," 66, 67.

46. Crane, "Male Pregnancy," 278–79.

47. For detailed analyses of early modern uncertainties concerning the virginal body, see Kelly, *Performing Virginity*, esp. 1–39, and Loughlin, *Hymeneutics*, esp. 13–52.

48. For a discussion of the relationship between identity and performance, see Kamaralli, who argues that Isabella shifts from a concern with appearance to an investment in truth ("Writing About Motive," esp. 53–55). By contrast, see Cunningham's analysis of *Measure* as "an instance of dramatic mooting," which privileges "the idea that identity is fundamentally improvisational and social" ("Opening Doubts," 318).

49. DiGangi, "Pleasure and Danger," 591. DiGangi describes "a fear of the dangers

thought to ensue from a woman's control over her own body" (590), and argues that marriage becomes a focal point for that fear; see esp. 604. See also Knoppers's argument that a structural analogy between "too little" and "too much" sexuality identifies Isabella with the play's prostitutes ("(En)gendering Shame," 464). Weitz cogently argues that the opposition of chastity to lust creates a conceptual link between them; see "Romantic Fiction," esp. 149–50.

50. Schwarz, "The Wrong Question" and "Chastity, Militant and Married."

51. Riefer, "'Instruments,'" 161.

52. Berger, *Making Trifles*, 406. See also McCandless, "'I'll Pray to Increase,'" 94–95; Knoppers, "(En)gendering Shame," esp. 462–63, 468; and J. Rose, "Sexuality," 117. Analyses of cultural prescription complicate earlier indictments of Isabella as deliberately seductive. A separate development of the question of sexual agency focuses on sadism and masochism. Brown connects this to monastic practices; see "Erotic Religious Flagellation." McCandless draws on Deleuze's theory of sadism to discuss "the sadopornographic nature of the punishments in *Measure for Measure*" ("I'll Pray to Increase," quotation at 90).

53. Jankowski, "Pure Resistance," 230. DiGangi describes "the resistances posed in the overlapping and contested spaces between virgin and wife, between wife and whore" ("Pleasure and Danger," 592). Slights and Holmes contend that Isabella's religious affiliation enables her to evade patriarchal assimilation ("Isabella's Order," esp. 289). Korda argues that Isabella threatens patrilineality through her link to the Order of Saint Clare (*Shakespeare's Domestic Economies*, esp. 189–91).

54. Slights and Holmes, 282. See also Jankowski's powerful reading of the relationship between "more" and "none" ("Pure Resistance," 229–31).

55. J. Rose, "Sexuality," 103. She adds, "In the critical debates about Isabella, it is as if we can see anxiety about aesthetic or representational cohesion turning into a sexual reproach" (105). See also Kamaralli, "Writing About Motive," 48; Riefer, "'Instruments,'" 157; and Watson, "False Immortality," 427.

56. Butler, *Bodies That Matter*, xi.

57. For readings of Isabella's own paternal inheritance, see Adelman, *Suffocating Mothers*, 97; and Wheeler, *Shakespeare's Development*, 114. By contrast, see McCandless's description of Angelo as "ruthless enforcer of the Law of the Father" ("'I'll Pray to Increase,'" 92).

58. Kamaralli, "Writing About Motive," 49.

59. Coeffeteau, *A Table of Humane Passions*, 76.

60. Some readers criticize Isabella for a narrowly physical understanding of virtue. See Shell's account of this tradition, and his response: "The position . . . not only fails to give physical chastity its political due; it also fails to take into account what chastity as 'a condition of the spirit' means within the logic of the plot of *Measure for Measure*" (*The End of Kinship*, 103).

61. Knoppers, "(En)gendering Shame," 463. Knoppers contends that this challenge, through which "civil authority is threatened by the very chastity it extols" (464), motivates the disciplinary project of shame. See also J. Rose, "Sexuality," 104; and Wheeler, *Shakespeare's Development*, 116.

62. Marcus writes, "In *Measure for Measure*, the rule of law is overthrown by something that may be divine transcendence, but can also look like royal whim, unruly 'license,' a mere recapitulation of the abuse it purports to rectify" (*Puzzling Shakespeare*, 182). See also Wheeler's point about generic dissonance: "*Measure for Measure* is guided to its comic conclusion by a character whose essence is the denial of family ties and sexuality, the denial, that is to say, of the essence of comedy" (*Shakespeare's Development*, 149).

63. For comments on the unpersuasive, disagreeable, untenable, or frankly punitive resolution imposed by marriage in *Measure*, see, for example, Adelman, *Suffocating Mothers*, 87; DiGangi, "Pleasure and Danger," 604; Maus, *Inwardness and Theater*, 179–80; J. Goldberg, *James I*, 235; Knoppers, "(En)gendering Shame," 471; Briggs, "Shakespeare's Bed-Tricks," 307–308; Marcus, *Puzzling Shakespeare*, 183; Neely, *Broken Nuptials*, 64, 102; Riefer, "'Instruments,'" 169; Wheeler, *Shakespeare's Development*, 7–8; Cohen, "From Mistress to Master," 453–55; Korda, *Shakespeare's Domestic Economies*, 188; and Lake, "Ministers, Magistrates," 179. Lake makes an interestingly qualified claim about Isabella: "Even if she may not (yet) quite want him, Isabella gets the prince" (180). As this suggests, punishment is by no means the only available reading. See Hayne on community expectations ("Performing Social Practice," 28); Magedanz on equity ("Public Justice and Private Mercy," 327); Friedman on reparation ("'O, let him marry her!'" esp. 454, 464); and Cunningham on "new public identities" ("Opening Doubts," 327). Complex discussions of the relationship between marriage and incest appear in Shell, *The End of Kinship*, 149–71, and Wheeler, *Shakespeare's Development*, esp. 104, 130. See also Watson's comments on the pragmatism of the state versus the desire of the individual ("False Immortality," esp. 417).

64. Neely summarizes this ambivalence: "Women are paradoxically loved and loathed for both their chastity and their sexuality" (*Broken Nuptials*, 100).

65. Neely, *Broken Nuptials*, 63.

66. Baines argues that Isabella sees no choice, but the bed trick nevertheless depends on feminine willingness to allow the exploitation of chastity ("Assaying the Power of Chastity," 295–96). Kamaralli claims that Isabella's new faith in "truth" justifies her participation ("Writing About Motive," 55). By contrast, Crane argues that the bed trick imposes penetration and shame on Isabella ("Male Pregnancy," 286; see also McCandless, "'I'll Pray to Increase,'" 105). Jankowski reads the bed trick as a critique of companionate marriage; see "Hymeneal Blood," esp. 97–98; 100–102. Other arguments describe it as the Duke's seduction by proxy, or as a device that inscribes Isabella into masculine exchange; for the first, see Shell, *The End of Kinship*, esp. 91–93, and Friedman, "'O, let him marry her!'" 461 n.31.; for the second, see Knoppers, "(En)gendering Shame," 451; Mullaney, *The Place of the Stage*, 109–10; and Adelman, *Suffocating Mothers*, 101–102.

67. Berry writes, "[Chastity] often seemed to connote, not the negation of woman's bodily difference, of her own sexual desires, but rather the survival of a quality of feminine autonomy and self-sufficiency which could not be appropriated in the self-serving interests of the masculine subject" (*Of Chastity and Power*, 18). For accounts of sexual self-possession as a challenge to heterosocial hierarchy—as an alternative, an escape, a weapon, a

mystification, or a screen—see Berry, 1–37 and passim; Shannon, *Sovereign Amity*, 54–89; Jordan, *Renaissance Feminism*, esp. 29–30, 82–83; Greenstadt, "'Read it in me'"; Rogers, "The Enclosure of Virginity"; Traub, "The Perversion of 'Lesbian' Desire"; Jankowski, *Pure Resistance*; Weitz Miller, "Metaphor and the Mystification of Chastity"; Kelly and Leslie, eds., *Menacing Virgins*; and Halpern, "Puritanism and Maenadism."

68. Greenstadt, *Rape and the Rise of the Author*, 27.

69. Friedman, "'O, let him marry her!'", 459–60. See also Knoppers, "(En)gendering Shame," 466, and Wheeler, *Shakespeare's Development*, 129.

70. Adelman, *Suffocating Mothers*, 76–77. See also Neely, *Broken Nuptials*, 93–95; and Briggs, "Shakespeare's Bed-Tricks," esp. 296–97, 311–12. Maus reads the bed trick through "a pervasive and complex pattern of substitutions, deputations, and interchanges"; see her nuanced discussion of vicarious identification and bodily reenactment (*Inwardness and Theater*, 171–77, quotation at 172). On the issue of substitution, see also Goldberg's reading of mystified analogies and "crucial though unfathomable" differences (*James I*, 232–34, quotation at 234); Wheeler's of deputation and scapegoating (*Shakespeare's Development*, 134–39); Watson's of the "indifference" of biological and political functions ("False Immortality," 429); and Shell's of "natural usury" and bodily exchange (*The End of Kinship*, 124–27).

71. Butler, *Gender Trouble*, 140, emphasis in original.

72. McCandless, "'I'll Pray to Increase,'" 108. He writes, "Her speechlessness becomes itself a mode of speech, a dialect that cannot be silenced, even if it cannot be fathomed" (108). See also Berger, *Making Trifles*, 426.

73. Spencer, "A Measure of Success"; Walker, "Death comes as a relief."

74. Billington, "Measure for Measure." See also Spencer's claim that "he always serves the text rather than his ego" ("A Measure of Success").

75. Bassett, "Antony and Cleopatra, Globe, London; Measure for Measure, Theatre Royal, Bath."

76. Billington, "Measure for Measure."

77. Brien, "Measure for Measure."

78. Nightingale, "Measure for Measure." See also Koenig's comment: "his sudden proposal does not seem the end of a quest for wisdom so much as another desperate, ill-judged effort at humanity" ("Measure for Measure, Theatre Royal, Bath").

79. Wood, "Measure for Measure."

80. Nightingale, "Measure for Measure." Nightingale writes of *Measure*, "If it is problematic, it's because it's hard to understand how Shakespeare could have written two-plus acts of such incisive intensity and then two-plus of such romantic idiocy."

81. Nightingale, "Measure for Measure"; Wood, "Measure for Measure." Wood asks, "What are we to make of the final scene and the various marriages—a deeply flawed tying up of loose ends by Shakespeare?" See also Walker: "Without any directorial flourishes, one is left only to dwell on the shortcomings of the plot and the cast" ("Death comes as a relief").

82. Marcus, *Puzzling Shakespeare*, 183. See Maus's account of "the problem of un-knowable inward truth" (*Inwardness and Theater*, 181). Maus and Marcus both comment on the importance of unresolved possibility (*Inwardness and Theater*, 180; *Puzzling Shake-speare*, 183), and Shell cautions against the distortion inherent in assuming an answer (*The End of Kinship*, 176). Berger reads silence as the "best escape" from the Duke's coercions (*Making Trifles*, 364); Korda connects uncertainty to "the divergent destinies of the inhabi-tants of dissolved nunneries in post-Reformation England" (*Shakespeare's Domestic Econo-mies*, 189); Hayne focuses on "the perilous ambiguity of betrothal" ("Performing Social Practice," 8); Wheeler writes of "a comic whole smaller than the sum of its parts" (*Shake-speare's Development*, 127); Knoppers concludes, "Isabella's silence blocks closure in the ending of *Measure for Measure* and exposes the play's complicity in the (en)genderings of shame it professes to interrogate" ("(En)gendering Shame," 471).

Chapter 7. "Fallen Out With My More Headier Will": Dislocation in *King Lear*

1. Strier, *Resistant Structures*, 178. On "will" as both the faculty of purpose and the instrument of legacy, see R. Wilson's discussion of *Lear* and historical changes in the rights of testators (*Will Power*, 184–237, esp. 220–29); and Willbern's comments on "legacy as an act of posthumous potency" (*Poetic Will*, xvii).

2. Strier does not assign responsibility to the women of the play; he attributes politi-cal crisis to Lear's subsequent errors, and writes, "The love-test is purely ceremonial, and the suggestion that it is part of the division merely a flourish" (180–81).

3. Shakespeare, *The History of King Lear*, ed. Orgel. I follow the 1608 quarto text; the 1623 folio text omits several key scenes that focus on women. The major differences are well known: the quarto contains Lear's mock trial of his daughters in 3.6; Albany's diatribe against Goneril and her response in 4.2; and the description of Cordelia in the scene that the Pelican Shakespeare edition has numbered 4.3a. I also address the quarto's use of "wit," rather than "will," at 4.5.263. In the discussion that follows, I cite the Pelican text edited by Orgel, which assigns act and scene numbers based on the folio, to enable cross-comparison with the folio and conflated texts. Unless otherwise indicated, all subse-quent quotations are cited parenthetically by act, scene, and line numbers taken from this edition.

4. Aylmer, *An Harborowe for Faithfull and Trewe Subjectes*, sig. G1.

5. Bourdieu, "On Symbolic Power," 170.

6. 3.6.71–72; 3.7.106; 4.2.50–51; 4.5.120–21.

7. Rudnytsky connects Cordelia to Regan and Goneril when he describes both ideal-ization and demonization as symptoms of "the play's underlying misogyny" ("'The Darke and Vicious Place,'" 301); see also Cox, "'An Excellent Thing,'" 143. Kelly complicates oppositions through analysis of a specific stage history; see "Performing Australian Iden-tity." Berger writes, "Thus, while the performativity of self-representation ensconces Cor-delia in the orthopsychic identity she desires and imagines for herself, the performativity

of her speech acts continuously structures the dramatic action to ensure both her complicity with her sisters and her ability to remain unaware of it" (*Making Trifles*, 305; see also 42–46, 300–305).

8. Berry, *Shakespeare's Feminine Endings*, 157. See also Kavanagh, "Shakespeare in Ideology," 157.

9. Several critics note that Lear misconstrues, collapses, or breaks links between the political or social and the personal. Brayton writes, "To Lear's outraged eyes, Cordelia displays a will beyond the bounds of official state sanction, outside of her father's control" ("Angling," 407; see his comments on misreading, esp. 410). Boose argues that Lear fundamentally misconceives the marriage ritual; see "The Father and the Bride," esp. 332–34. See also Holahan on "a divergence, within this patriarchal system, between royal commands and paternal appeals" ("'Look, Her Lips,'" 413); and Kavanagh on "an individualist ideology that lives the world as a field of calculation, self-gratification and perverse desire" ("Shakespeare in Ideology," 156). For metacritical approaches to tensions between personal and political concerns, see Halpern's hysterica/historica discussion in *The Poetics of Primitive Accumulation*, esp. 215–18; and Thompson's account of feminist and materialist readings in "Are There any Women?"

10. Boose, 333.

11. Agrippa, *The Commendation of Matrimony*, sig. B5. See also Tigurinus, *A most excellent Hystorie*, 192; and Bullinger, *The Christen state of Matrimony*, fols. 3v–4. Camden's *Remaines, Concerning Britaine* gives this argument to the daughter herself: "shee did thinke that one day it would come to passe, that shee should affect another more fervently, meaning her husband, when shee were married: Who being made one flesh with her, as God by commaundement had told, and nature had taught hir, shee was to cleave fast to, forsaking father and mother." The commentator concludes, "One referreth this to the daughters of King *Leir*" (248–49).

12. Hutson, *The Usurer's Daughter*, 8.

13. Boose writes, "Lear violates both his kingly role in the hierarchical universe and his domestic one in the family" ("The Father and the Bride," 332).

14. Bullinger, *The Christen state*, fol. 14. On the importance of parental consent, see Bullinger, esp. fols. 10v–14; and Stockwood, *A Bartholmew Fairing*, esp. 94–95.

15. Cecil, *Certaine Precepts*, 9.

16. Drayton, *The Tragicall Legend*, sig. H6. I am grateful to Donald Jellerson for drawing my attention to this passage.

17. Bryan, *The Vertuous Daughter*, 2.

18. Halpern, *The Poetics of Primitive Accumulation*, 249; Berger, *Making Trifles*, 303. See also Greenfield, "Excellent Things," esp. 47–49. Dollimore writes, "Cordelia's real transgression is not unkindness as such, but speaking in a way which threatens to show too clearly how the laws of human kindness operate in the service of property, contractual, and power relations" (*Radical Tragedy*, 198).

19. Scarry, "Consent and the Body," 877, emphasis in original.

20. For a discussion of Cordelia's "virago" role, see Cox, "'An Excellent Thing.'"

21. Scarry, "Consent and the Body," 875.

22. Holinshed, *The Historie of England*, 13. *The Mirour for Magistrates* gives Cordelia this line: "We came to *Britayne* with our royall campe to fight: / And manly fought so long our enmies vanquisht were" ([Higgins], fol. 50v). Both Cox and Whittier argue that Cordelia displays gender ambiguity in *Lear* ("'An Excellent Thing,'" esp. 153–57; "Cordelia as Prince," esp. 387–91).

23. Alfar, *Fantasies of Female Evil*, 97, 19. Hoover also characterizes Goneril and Regan as masculine ("Goneril and Regan," 49–65).

24. See Callaghan's cogent observation: "The problem with the category of woman is in keeping it *in* its place and *out* of the ideal order. This process is, however, always and necessarily incomplete" (*Woman and Gender*, 109).

25. Davies, *Microcosmos*, 47.

26. *Haec Vir*, sig. B4v. Alfar writes, "Goneril both asserts her position as the law and scorns the power structure for which her husband stands" (*Fantasies of Female Evil*, 102).

27. Bloch, *Medieval Misogyny*, 5.

28. Žižek, "*Da Capo senza Fine*," 220, emphasis in original.

29. Rowe, "Inconstancy," 91. See also Charnes: "'pathology' in individual subjects is always organized around (and even authorized by) misrecognition, displacement, and denial in the social" (*Notorious Identity*, 14). Amussen historicizes the displacement of disorder onto women; see *An Ordered Society*, Chapter 4, esp. 122–23; and Chapter 6, esp. 181–83. Brayton traces this pattern in *Lear*: "the demonic kingdom of female faults and unlicensed wills becomes the site of deception that Lear consistently blames for his own dissolving powers" (410).

30. Berger, *Making Trifles*, 66.

31. The play's seamless misogyny has long been open to question. In 1959, Block described Goneril and Regan as "reasonable" in their early opposition to Lear, arguing that sympathy shifts only when they banish him into the storm ("*King Lear*," 504–8). S. L. Goldberg offers an attentive reading of Goneril (*An Essay on "King Lear"*, esp. 113). Berger describes a mimetic relationship between Lear's behavior and that of his daughters (*Making Trifles*, 32–35). See also Reid's psychoanalytic account ("In Defense of Goneril and Regan"). Hoover refers misogyny to Lear's own conflicts about sexuality and responsibility ("Women, Centaurs, and Devils"). Brayton writes, "[Lear's] uncontrolled fomenting at his daughters provokes them to institute the calculus of the zero in their relations with their father" ("Angling," 410).

32. Alfar, *Fantasies of Female Evil*, 81.

33. Sir John Davies, *Nosce teipsum*, 51.

34. Sir John Davies, *Nosce teipsum*, 52.

35. For "wit" as "cunning," see Shakespeare, *The History of King Lear*, Pelican ed., n. to 4.5.263, and Norton ed., n. to 20.259. For "will" as "lust," see Shakespeare, *The Tragedy of King Lear*, Riverside ed., n. to 4.6.271, and Signet ed., n. to 4.5.273; for "desire," see Shakespeare, *The Tragedy of King Lear*, New Folger Library ed., n. to 4.6.300; for "appetite," see Shakespeare, *King Lear*, Bantam ed., n. to 4.6.275. The Norton edition glosses "will" as "wilfullness," and adds, "'will' might also refer to a woman's genitals" (*The Tragedy of King Lear*, n. to 4.5.263).

36. See Brayton's account of how "the female will is equated with alterity, what cannot be mapped," and his link between misogynist conventions and the rhetoric of demonic possession ("Angling," 411–21, quotation at 413).

37. Important scholarship has illuminated the motivated but often invisible effects of editing, and has analyzed the layers of mediation that produce "authoritative" texts. See Marcus, *Unediting the Renaissance*; de Grazia, *Shakespeare Verbatim*; Maguire, *Shakespearean Suspect Texts*; Orgel, "What Is a Text?" and "The Authentic Shakespeare"; Masten, "More or Less"; and Stallybrass, "Editing as Cultural Formation." See also Hutson's discussion of "unediting" and dramatic mimesis (*The Invention of Suspicion*, 108–11).

38. Jardin, *A Discourse of the Married and Single Life*, sig. A7–A7v.

39. Tennenhouse describes the brief popularity of "absent monarch plays" in the early seventeenth century; see *Power on Display*, 154–59.

40. Brayton, "Angling," 421. For assessments of Lear's sovereignty, see Halpern's discussion of political authority and property relations (*The Poetics of Primitive Accumulation*, 215–69); Kahn's reading of a repressed desire for the maternal ("The Absent Mother"); Dodd's contention regarding the play's "aspirations for a consensual, disarmed image of political authority" ("Impossible Worlds," 501); Kavanagh's point that Lear "substitut[es] stubborn vanity for the authority of his position" ("Shakespeare in Ideology," 156); Boose's comments on the disrupted marriage ritual ("The Father and the Bride," 332–35); Brayton's analysis of sovereignty, territory, and provisional illusion ("Angling"); Rudnytsky's reading of patriarchy, female sexuality, and incest fantasies ("'The Darke and Vicious Place'"); R. Wilson's claim that a conflict between patriarchy and paternalism appears in Lear's autocratic use of testamentary powers (*Will Power*, 220–29, esp. 226–28); Shannon's contrast between animal sovereignty and the "privative sense of man" ("Poor, Bare, Forked," quotation at 196); and Strier's argument concerning virtuous disobedience (*Resistant Structures*, 177–99). This list cannot be exhaustive, but it suggests the range of methodologies that identify sovereignty as contingent, deficient, alienated, or demystified.

41. Kahn, "The Absent Mother," 36; Halpern, *The Poetics of Primitive Accumulation*, 220.

42. The back cover of Harold Bloom's *Shakespeare's King Lear* displays this quotation, attributed to Bloom: "[Lear] is the most awesome of all the poet's originals. No one else in Shakespeare is so legitimate a representation of supreme authority."

43. Tennenhouse, *Power on Display*, 142.

44. Tennenhouse, *Power on Display*, 142, emphasis in original.

45. Halpern, *The Poetics of Primitive Accumulation*, 215. Charnes offers a provocative proposal for a "new hystericism" (*Notorious Identity*, 18–19).

46. McLuskie, "The Patriarchal Bard," 102. Thompson's survey of criticism leads her to pose a question about polarization: "So must we accept that feminist readings and materialist readings are indeed incompatible in the case of *King Lear*, that we can attend either to the personal level of the play (which is at least partially female) or to the political level (which is pretty solidly male), but not to both?" ("Are There Any Women," 125).

47. Dollimore, *Radical Tragedy*, 203. Kavanagh notes that the visibility of *Lear's*

contradictions "makes it a text that fixes an ideological position only tenuously" ("Shakespeare in Ideology," 160).

48. Averell, *A Dyall for dainty Darlings,* sig. E3v. See also the reunion of Apollonius and his daughter Tharsia, described in Twyne, *The Patterne of painefull Adventures,* sig. I3.

49. Kahn, "The Absent Mother," 49. See also Adelman, *Suffocating Mothers,* 128–29. Cavell implicates the audience, too, in a response that appropriates Cordelia through identification with her; see *Disowning Knowledge,* 73. Holahan echoes Lear's fantasy: "A strange dialogue across existential spaces and times joins two different characters, preserving a difference in speech yet folding the two voices into the one body of the king" ("'Look, Her Lips,'" 424).

50. Cavell, *Disowning Knowledge,* 69.

51. Scarry, "Consent and the Body," 873, emphasis in original.

52. Becon, *A new Catechisme,* fol. 532 (misnumbered 536). Kelso summarizes this doctrine: "But the art of speech for the girl, and the woman as well, was reduced for the most part to one simple rule: Silence" (*Doctrine for the Lady of the Renaissance,* 50).

53. Jardin, *A Discourse of the Married and Single Life,* sig. A6v.

54. Callaghan, *Woman and Gender,* 87.

55. Filmer, *Patriarcha,* 20–21.

56. Alfar writes, "It is not possible, historically or textually, to read Goneril's and Regan's defenses of their nation as either a mistake or as a monstrous arrogation of power" (*Fantasies of Female Evil,* 107).

57. Bushnell, "Tyranny and Effeminacy," 342.

58. Spenser, *The Faerie Queene,* Book 2, Canto 10, Stanza 32, ll. 1–5.

59. Geoffrey of Monmouth, *The British History,* 59.

60. Holinshed, *The Historie of England,* 13.

61. [Higgins], *The Mirour for Magistrates,* fol. 51.

62. *The True Chronicle History of King Leir,* sig. I4v.

63. Geoffrey of Monmouth, *The British History,* 60; Spenser, *The Faerie Queene,* Book 2, Canto 10, Stanza 33, l. 9.

64. Tennenhouse writes, "To ask why Cordelia, in my reading of the situation, has to die, is virtually to provide the answer: because the patriarchal principle itself rather than the identity of the monarch's natural body is in question" (*Power on Display,* 141). See Adelman and Kahn, who interrogate the reduction of Cordelia to an instrument (Adelman, *Suffocating Mothers,* 125–29; and Kahn, "The Absent Mother," 46–49). See also Boose: "Initially barren of mothers, the play concludes with the death of all the fathers and all the daughters; the only figures who survive to emphasize the sterility of the final tableau are Albany, a widower, and Edgar, an unmarried son" ("The Father and the Bride," 335).

65. Tate, *The History of King Lear,* 67.

66. Shakespeare, *The Plays of William Shakespeare,* ed. Samuel Johnson, 6: 159.

67. Tate, "Epilogue," *The History of King Lear.*

Epilogue. Or: The Roman Matron

1. Agrippa, *Female Pre-eminence*, 65–66, emphasis in original.

2. Harding, "Woman's Fantasy of Manhood," 245.

3. Sheridan, *Coriolanus: or, The Roman Matron*.

4. Žižek, "*Da Capo senza Fine*," 220.

5. Shakespeare, *Coriolanus*, in *The Riverside Shakespeare*, 2.1.198–200. Subsequent citations follow this edition; bracketed passages in this edition are silently retained.

6. *The Oxford English Dictionary*, s.v. "repeal": v.[1], 1a, 1b, 2, 3b, 3e, 4; v.[2]

Bibliography

Abbot, George. *The Reasons Which Doctour Hill Hath Brought, for the upholding of Papistry, which is falselie termed the Catholike Religion: Unmasked, and shewed to be very weake*. Oxford: Joseph Barnes for Simon Waterson, 1604.

Adamson, Sylvia, Gavin Alexander, and Katrin Ettenhuber. "Introduction." In *Renaissance Figures of Speech*, ed. Sylvia Adamson, Gavin Alexander, and Katrin Ettenhuber, 1–14. Cambridge: Cambridge University Press, 2007.

Adelman, Janet. "'Anger's My Meat': Feeding, Dependency, and Aggression in *Coriolanus*." In *Representing Shakespeare: New Psychoanalytic Essays*, ed. Murray M. Schwartz and Coppélia Kahn, 129–49. Baltimore: Johns Hopkins University Press, 1980.

———. "Making Defect Perfection: Shakespeare and the One-Sex Model." In *Enacting Gender on the English Renaissance Stage*, ed. Viviana Comensoli and Anne Russell, 23–52. Urbana: University of Illinois Press, 1999.

———. *Suffocating Mothers: Fantasies of Maternal Origin in Shakespeare's Plays*, Hamlet *to* The Tempest. New York: Routledge, 1992.

Agrippa von Nettesheim, Heinrich Cornelius. *The Commendation of Matrimony*. Trans. David Clapam. London: in aedibus Thomae Bertheleti, 1540.

———. *Female Pre-eminence: or the Dignity and Excellency of that sex, above the Male*. Trans. Henry Care. London: T. R. and M. D. for Henry Million, 1670.

Ainsworth, Henry. *The Art of Logick; or, The Entire Body of Logick in English . . . The Second Edition, corrected and amended*. London: Printed for John Streater, 1657.

Alberti, Leon Battista. *Hecatonphila. The Arte of Love. Or, Love discovered in an hundred severall kindes*. London: P.S. for William Leake, 1598.

Alexander, Gavin. "Prosopopoeia: The Speaking Figure." In *Renaissance Figures of Speech*, ed. Sylvia Adamson, Gavin Alexander, and Katrin Ettenhuber, 97–112. Cambridge: Cambridge University Press, 2007.

Alfar, Cristina León. *Fantasies of Female Evil: The Dynamics of Gender and Power in Shakespearean Tragedy*. Newark: University of Delaware Press, 2003.

Allott, Robert. *Wits Theater of the little World*. London: J[ames] R[oberts] for N[icholas] L[ing], 1599.

Althusser, Louis. "Ideology and Ideological State Apparatuses: Notes Towards an Investigation." In *Lenin and Philosophy and Other Essays*, trans. Ben Brewster, 121–73. London: New Left Books, 1971.

———. "A Letter on Art in Reply to André Daspre." In *Lenin and Philosophy and Other Essays*, trans. Ben Brewster, 221–27. New York: Monthly Review Press, 1971.

Amussen, Susan Dwyer. *An Ordered Society: Gender and Class in Early Modern England*. Oxford: Blackwell, 1988.

Anderson, Ruth Leila. *Elizabethan Psychology and Shakespeare's Plays*. Ed. Franklin H. Potter. University of Iowa Humanistic Studies 3, 4. Iowa City: University of Iowa, 1927.

Annand, William. *Fides Catholica. Or, The Doctrine of the Catholick Church: In Eighteen Grand Ordinances*. London: T. R. for Edward Brewster, 1661.

Anon. *An other defence of womens vertues*. Bound with Alexandre de Pontaymeri, *A Womans Woorth*. London: John Wolfe, 1599.

Asp, Carolyn. "Subjectivity, Desire and Female Friendship in *All's Well That Ends Well*." *Literature and Psychology* 32, 4 (1986): 48–63.

Attersoll, William. *The Badges of Christianity*. London: W. Jaggard, 1606.

Augustine of Hippo. "On Grace and Free Will," trans. P. Holmes. In *Basic Writings of Saint Augustine*. Ed. Whitney J. Oates. 2 vols. 1: 733–74. New York: Random House, 1948.

———. "On Nature and Grace," trans. P. Holmes. In *Basic Writings of Saint Augustine*, 1: 521–79.

———. *The Problem of Free Choice* (De Libero Arbitrio). Ed. and trans. Dom Mark Pontifex. London: Longmans, Green, 1955.

Austin, William. *Haec Homo Wherein the Excellency of the Creation of Woman is described*. London: Richard Olton for Ralph Mabb, 1637.

Averell, William. *A Dyall for dainty Darlings, rockt in the cradle of Securitie*. London: Printed for Thomas Hackette, 1584.

Aylmer, John. *An Harborowe for Faithfull and Trewe Subjectes, agaynst the late blowne Blaste, concerning the Government of Wemen*. London: John Daye, 1559.

Bacon, Francis. *The Twoo Bookes of Francis Bacon. Of the proficience and advancement of Learning, divine and humane*. London: Printed for Henrie Tomes, 1605.

———. *The Two Bookes of Sr. Francis Bacon. Of The Proficience and Advancement of Learning, Divine and Humane*. London: Printed for William Washington, 1629.

———. *The Two Bookes of Sr. Francis Bacon Of The Proficience and Advancement of Learning, Divine and Humane*. Oxford: Printed by I. L. for Thomas Huggins, 1633.

Baines, Barbara. "Assaying the Power of Chastity in *Measure for Measure*." *SEL: Studies in English Literature, 1500–1900* 30, 2 (1990): 283–301.

Baker, Herschel. *The Image of Man: A Study of the Idea of Human Dignity in Classical Antiquity, the Middle Ages, and the Renaissance*. New York: Harper and Row, 1947, 1961.

Baldwin, William. *A treatyce of Moral philosophy containing the sayinges of the wise*. London: Rycharde Tottill, 1564.

Banister, John. *The Historie of Man, sucked from the sappe of the most approved Anathomistes*. London: John Daye, 1578.

Barbaro, Francesco. *Directions for Love and Marriage*. London: John Leigh and Tho. Burrell, 1677.

Barckley, Richard. *A Discourse of the Felicitie of Man: Or His Summum bonum*. London: Printed for William Ponsonby, 1598.

Barnet, Sylvan. "Introduction: *All's Well That Ends Well*." In *The Complete Signet Classic Shakespeare*, ed. Sylvan Barnet, 1050–56. New York: Harcourt Brace Jovanovich, 1972.

Bartels, Emily. "Strategies of Submission: Desdemona, the Duchess, and the Assertion of Desire." *SEL: Studies in English Literature, 1500–1900* 36, 2 (1996): 417–33.

Barton, John. *The Art of Rhetorick Concisely and Compleatly Handled, Exemplified out of holy Writ*. London: Printed for Nicolas Alsop, 1634.

Bassett, Kate. "Antony and Cleopatra, Globe, London; Measure for Measure, Theatre Royal, Bath; The Rocky Horror Show, Playhouse, London." *The Independent*, 16 July 2006. http://www.independent.co.uk/arts-entertainment/theatre-dance/reviews/antony-and-cleopatra-globe-londonbr-measure-for-measure-theatre-royal-bathbr-the-rocky-horror-show-playhouse-london-407945.html.

Bates, Catherine. *Masculinity, Gender and Identity in the English Renaissance Lyric*. Cambridge: Cambridge University Press, 2007.

Batman, Stephen. *Batman uppon Bartholome, his Booke De Proprietatibus Rerum, Newly corrected, enlarged and amended*. London: Thomas East, 1582.

Becon, Thomas. *A new Catechisme*. In *The worckes of Thomas Becon*. London: John Day, 1564.

Bell, Ilona. "Rethinking Shakespeare's Dark Lady." In *A Companion to Shakespeare's Sonnets*, ed. Michael Schoenfeldt, 293–313. Oxford: Blackwell, 2007.

Belsey, Catherine. "Alice Arden's Crime: *Arden of Faversham* (c. 1590)." In *Staging the Renaissance: Reinterpretations of Elizabethan and Jacobean Drama*, ed. David Scott Kastan and Peter Stallybrass, 133–50. New York: Routledge, 1991.

———. *Shakespeare and the Loss of Eden: The Construction of Family Values in Early Modern Culture*. Basingstoke: Macmillan, 1999.

———. *The Subject of Tragedy: Identity and Difference in Renaissance Drama*. London: Methuen, 1985.

———. "Tarquin Dispossessed: Expropriation and Consent in *The Rape of Lucrece*." *Shakespeare Quarterly* 52, 3 (2001): 315–35.

Bercher, William. *The Nobility of Women* (1559). Ed. R. Warwick Bond. London: privately printed for presentation to the members of the Roxburghe Club, 1904.

Berger, Harry, Jr. *Making Trifles of Terrors: Redistributing Complicities in Shakespeare*. Ed. Peter Erickson. Stanford, Calif: Stanford University Press, 1997.

Berkeley, David S. and Donald Keesee. "Bertram's Blood-Consciousness in *All's Well That Ends Well*." *SEL: Studies in English Literature, 1500–1900* 31, 2 (1991): 247–58.

Berry, Philippa. *Of Chastity and Power: Elizabethan Literature and the Unmarried Queen*. London: Routledge, 1989, 1994.

———. *Shakespeare's Feminine Endings: Disfiguring Death in the Tragedies*. London: Routledge, 1999.

Bersani, Leo. "Is the Rectum a Grave?" *October 43, AIDS: Cultural Analysis/Cultural Activism* (Winter 1987): 197–222.

———. "Sociality and Sexuality." *Critical Inquiry* 26, 4 (Summer 2000): 641–56.

Bevington, David. "All's Well That Plays Well." In *Subjects on the World's Stage: Essays on British Literature of the Middle Ages and the Renaissance*, ed. David G. Allen and Robert A. White, 162–80. Newark: University of Delaware Press, 1995.

Billington, Michael. "Measure for Measure." Guardian.co.uk, 14 July 2006. http://www .guardian.co.uk/stage/2006/jul/14/theatre

Bloch, R. Howard. *Medieval Misogyny and the Invention of Western Romantic Love*. Chicago: University of Chicago Press, 1991.

Block, Edward A. "*King Lear*: A Study in Balanced and Shifting Sympathies." *Shakespeare Quarterly* 10, 4 (1959): 499–512.

Bloom, Harold. *Shakespeare's King Lear*. New York: Riverhead Books, 2005.

Boose, Lynda E. "The Father and the Bride in Shakespeare." *PMLA* 97, 3 (1982): 325–47.

———. "Scolding Brides and Bridling Scolds: Taming the Woman's Unruly Member." In *Materialist Shakespeare: A History*, ed. Ivo Kamps, 239–79. London: Verso, 1995.

Booth, Stephen, ed. *Shakespeare's Sonnets*. New Haven, Conn: Yale University Press, 1977.

Bourdieu, Pierre. *The Logic of Practice*. Trans. Richard Nice. Stanford, Calif.: Stanford University Press, 1990.

———. "On Symbolic Power." In *Language and Symbolic Power*, ed. John B. Thompson, trans. Gino Raymond and Matthew Adamson, 163–70. Cambridge, Mass.: Harvard University Press, 1991.

Bowen, Barbara C., ed. *One Hundred Renaissance Jokes*. Birmingham, Ala.: Summa Publications, 1988.

Brathwait, Richard. *Ar't asleepe Husband? A Boulster Lecture*. London: R. Bishop for Richard Best, 1640.

———. *The English Gentlewoman, drawne out to the full Body*. London: B. Alsop and T. Fawcet for Michaell Sparke, 1631.

———. *Whimzies: Or, A New Cast of Characters*. London: F. K. for Ambrose Rithirdon, 1631.

Brayton, Dan. "Angling in the Lake of Darkness: Possession, Dispossession, and the Politics of Discovery in *King Lear*." *ELH* 70, 2 (2003): 399–426.

Bredbeck, Gregory. *Sodomy and Interpretation: Marlowe to Milton*. Ithaca, N.Y.: Cornell University Press, 1991.

Breitenberg, Mark. *Anxious Masculinity in Early Modern England*. Cambridge: Cambridge University Press, 1996.

Breton, Nicholas. *Characters upon Essaies Morall, and Divine*. London: Edw. Griffin for John Gwillim, 1615.

———. *A Poste with a Packet of madde letters. The second part*. London: R. B. for John Browne and John Smethicke, 1606.

A Brief Anatomie of Women: Being an Invective against, and Apologie for, The Bad and Good Of that Sexe. London: E. Alsop, 1653.

Brien, Jeremy. "Measure for Measure." *The Stage*, 13 July 2006. http://www.thestage.co .uk/reviews/review.php/13217

Briggs, Julia. "Shakespeare's Bed-Tricks." *Essays in Criticism* 44, 4 (1994): 293–314.

Bright, Timothy. *A Treatise of Melancholy. Contayning the causes thereof, and reasons of the straunge effects it worketh in our minds and bodies*. London: John Windet, 1586.

Bromley, Laura G. "Lucrece's Re-Creation." *Shakespeare Quarterly* 34, 2 (1983): 200–211.

Brown, Carolyn. "Erotic Religious Flagellation and Shakespeare's *Measure for Measure*." *English Literary Renaissance* 16, 1 (1986): 139–65.

Browne, Sir Thomas. *Religio Medici*. London: Printed for Andrew Crooke, 1642.

Brownmiller, Susan. *Femininity*. New York: Fawcett Columbine, 1984.

Bryan, John. *The Vertuous Daughter*. London: Thomas Harper for Lawrence Chapman, 1636.

Bullinger, Heinrich. *The Christen state of matrimony*. Trans. Miles Coverdale. London: John Mayler for John Gough, 1546.

Bulwer, John. *Chirologia: Or The Naturall Language of the Hand . . . Whereunto is added Chironomia: Or, the Art of Manuall Rhetoricke*. London: Thomas Harper for R. Whitaker, 1644.

Bunny, Edmund. *Of Divorce for Adulterie, and Marrying againe: that there is no sufficient warrant so to do*. Oxford: Joseph Barnes, 1610.

Buoni, Thommaso. *Problemes of Beautie and all humane affections*. Trans. S. L. London: G. Eld for Edward Blount and William Aspley, 1606.

Burke, Kenneth. "Four Master Tropes," in *A Grammar of Motives*, 503–17. Berkeley: University of California Press, 1945; 1969.

Burks, Deborah G. " 'I'll Want My Will Else': *The Changeling* and Women's Complicity with Their Rapists." *ELH* 62, 4 (1995): 759–90.

Burton, Robert. *The Anatomy of Melancholy. What it is, With all the kinds, causes, symptomes, prognostickes, and severall cures of it*. The Sixt. Edition, corrected and augmented by the Author. Oxford: Printed for Henry Cripps, 1651.

Bushnell, Rebecca. "Tyranny and Effeminacy in Early Modern England." In *Reconsidering the Renaissance*, ed. Mario A. Di Cesare, 339–54. Binghamton, N.Y.: Medieval and Renaissance Texts and Studies, 1992.

Butler, Judith. *Bodies That Matter: On the Discursive Limits of "Sex"*. New York: Routledge, 1993.

———. *Excitable Speech: A Politics of the Performative*. New York: Routledge, 1997.

———. *Gender Trouble: Feminism and the Subversion of Identity*. New York: Routledge, 1990.

———. *The Psychic Life of Power: Theories in Subjection*. Stanford, Calif.: Stanford University Press, 1997.

———. "Restaging the Universal: Hegemony and the Limits of Formalism." In Judith

Butler, Ernesto Laclau, and Slavoj Žižek, *Contingency, Hegemony, Universality: Contemporary Dialogues on the Left*, 11–43. London: Verso, 2000.

Calderwood, James L. "Styles of Knowing in *All's Well*." *Modern Language Quarterly* 25 (1964): 272–94.

Callaghan, Dympna. *Shakespeare Without Women: Representing Gender and Race on the Renaissance Stage*. London: Routledge, 2000.

———. *Woman and Gender in Renaissance Tragedy: A Study of* King Lear, Othello, The Duchess of Malfi, *and* The White Devil. Atlantic Highlands, N.J.: Humanities Press International, 1989.

Camden, Carroll. *The Elizabethan Woman*. Houston: Elsevier Press, 1952.

Camden, William. *Remaines, Concerning Britaine: But especially England, and the Inhabitants thereof*. London: John Legatt for Simon Waterson, 1614.

Carroll, Lewis. *Through the Looking-Glass*. In *Alice's Adventures in Wonderland & Through the Looking-Glass*, ed. Martin Gardner. New York: Signet Classic, 2000.

Cartelli, Thomas. "Shakespeare's 'Rough Magic': Ending as Artifice in *All's Well That Ends Well*." *Centennial Review* 27, 2 (1983): 117–34.

Case, Sue-Ellen. "Toward a Butch-Femme Aesthetic." In *The Lesbian and Gay Studies Reader*, ed. Henry Abelove, Michèle Aina Barale, and David M. Halperin, 294–306. New York: Routledge, 1993.

Cave, Terence. *The Cornucopian Text: Problems of Writing in the French Renaissance*. Oxford: Clarendon Press, 1979.

Cavell, Stanley. *Disowning Knowledge in Six Plays of Shakespeare*. Cambridge: Cambridge University Press, 1987.

Cecil, William, Baron Burghley. *Certaine Precepts or Directions, for the well ordering and carriage of a mans life*. London: T. C. and B. A. for Ri. Meighen and Thom. Jones, 1617.

[Chamberlayne, Thomas]. *The Compleat Midwife's Practice Enlarged. In the most weighty and high Concernments of the Birth of Man . . . The second Edition corrected*. London: Printed for Nath. Brook, 1659.

Chambers, E. K. *Shakespeare: A Survey*. London: Sidgwick & Jackson, 1925.

———. *William Shakespeare: A Study of Facts and Problems*. 2 vols. Oxford: Clarendon, 1930.

Charnes, Linda. *Notorious Identity: Materializing the Subject in Shakespeare*. Cambridge, Mass.: Harvard University Press, 1993.

Charron, Pierre. *Of Wisdom Three Books*. Trans. George Stanhope. London: M. Gillyflower and others, 1697.

———. *Of Wisdome Three Bookes, Written in French by Peter Charron*. Trans. Samson Lennard. London: Printed for Edward Blount and Will: Aspley, 1608.

Cixous, Hélène. "The Laugh of the Medusa." Trans. Keith Cohen and Paula Cohen. In *New French Feminisms: An Anthology*, ed. Elaine Marks and Isabelle de Courtivron, 245–64. Amherst: University of Massachussetts Press, 1980.

Cleaver, Robert. *A Godlie Forme of Householde Government: For the Ordering of Private Families, according to the direction of Gods word*. London: Felix Kingston for Thomas Man, 1598.

Coeffeteau, Nicolas. *A Table of Humane Passions. With their Causes and Effects*. Translated into English by Edw. Grimeston. London: Nicholas Okes, 1621.

Cohen, Stephen. "From Mistress to Master: Political Transition and Formal Conflict in *Measure for Measure*." *Criticism* 41, 4 (1999): 431–64.

Cook, Dorothy. "Helena: The Will and the Way." *The Vpstart Crow* 10 (1990): 14–31.

Copland, Robert. *The seven sorowes that women have when theyr husbandes be deade*. London: Wyllyam Copland, ca. 1565.

Cox, Catherine S. "'An Excellent Thing in Woman': Virgo and Viragos in *King Lear*." *Modern Philology* 96, 2 (1998): 143–57.

Crane, Mary Thomas. "Male Pregnancy and Cognitive Permeability in *Measure for Measure*." *Shakespeare Quarterly* 49, 3 (1998): 269–92.

Crawford, Julie. "*All's Well That Ends Well*: Or, Is Marriage Always Already Heterosexual?" In *Shakesqueer: A Queer Companion to the Complete Works of Shakespeare*, ed. Madhavi Menon, 39–47. Durham, N.C.: Duke University Press, 2011.

Crawford, Katherine. "Marsilio Ficino, Neoplatonism, and the Problem of Sex." *Renaissance and Reformation/Renaissance et Réforme* 28, 2 (2004): 3–35.

———. *The Sexual Culture of the French Renaissance*. Cambridge: Cambridge University Press, 2010.

Crocker, Holly A. "Affective Resistance: Performing Passivity and Playing A-Part in *The Taming of the Shrew*." *Shakespeare Quarterly* 54, 2 (Summer 2003): 142–59.

Crooke, Helkiah. *Mikrokosmographia: A Description of the Body of Man*. London: William Jaggard, 1615.

Cuddon, J. A. *A Dictionary of Literary Terms*. Rev. ed. New York: Penguin, 1979.

Culpeper, Nicholas. *A Directory for Midwives: Or, A Guide for Women*. London: Peter Cole, 1651.

Cummings, Brian. "Metalepsis: The Boundaries of Metaphor." In *Renaissance Figures of Speech*, ed. Sylvia Adamson, Gavin Alexander, and Katrin Ettenhuber, 217–33. Cambridge: Cambridge University Press, 2007.

Cunningham, Karen. "Opening Doubts Upon the Law: *Measure for Measure*." In *A Companion to Shakespeare's Works*, vol. 4, ed. Richard Dutton and Jean E. Howard, 316–32. London: Blackwell, 2003.

Dallington, Robert. *The View of Fraunce*. London: Symon Stafford, 1604.

Davies, John. *Microcosmos. The Discovery of the Little World, with the government thereof*. Oxford: Joseph Barnes for John Barnes, 1603.

———. *Mirum in modum. A Glimpse of Gods Glorie and The Soules Shape*. London: Printed for William Aspley, 1602.

Davies, Sir John. *Nosce teipsum*. London: Richard Field for John Standish, 1599.

Day, Angel. *The English Secretary . . . Devided into two bookes*. London: P. S. for C. Burbie, 1599.

de Grazia, Margreta. "Babbling Will in *Shake-speares Sonnets* 127 to 154." *Spenser Studies* 1 (1980): 121–34.

———. "The Scandal of Shakespeare's Sonnets." *Shakespeare Survey* 46 (1994): 35–49.

———. *Shakespeare Verbatim: The Reproduction of Authenticity and the 1790 Apparatus.* Oxford: Clarendon Press, 1991.

de Man, Paul. "Autobiography as De-Facement." In *The Rhetoric of Romanticism*, 67–81. New York: Columbia University Press, 1984.

———. *Allegories of Reading: Figural Language in Rousseau, Nietzsche, Rilke and Proust.* New Haven, Conn.: Yale University Press, 1979.

Dekker, Thomas, trans. *The Batchelars Banquet.* London: T. C. for T. P., 1603.

Dekker, Thomas and John Webster. *West-Ward Hoe. As it hath beene divers times Acted by the Children of Paules.* London: William Jaggard for John Hodgets, 1607.

Derrida, Jacques. ". . . That Dangerous Supplement . . ." In *Of Grammatology*, trans. Gayatri Chakravorty Spivak, 141–64. Baltimore: Johns Hopkins University Press, 1974.

DiGangi, Mario. "Pleasure and Danger: Measuring Female Sexuality in *Measure for Measure.*" *ELH* 60, 3 (1993): 589–609.

Dodd, William. "Impossible Worlds: What Happens in *King Lear*, Act 1, Scene 1." *Shakespeare Quarterly* 50, 4 (1999): 477–507.

Dolan, Frances E. *Dangerous Familiars: Representations of Domestic Crime in England, 1550–1700.* Ithaca, N.Y.: Cornell University Press, 1994.

———. *Marriage and Violence: The Early Modern Legacy.* Philadelphia: University of Pennsylvania Press, 2008.

Dollimore, Jonathan. *Radical Tragedy: Religion, Ideology and Power in the Drama of Shakespeare and His Contemporaries.* New York: Harvester Wheatsheaf, 1984, 1989.

———. *Sexual Dissidence: Augustine to Wilde, Freud to Foucault.* Oxford: Clarendon Press, 1991.

———. "Transgression and Surveillance in *Measure for Measure.*" In *Political Shakespeare: New Essays in Cultural Materialism*, ed. Jonathan Dollimore and Alan Sinfield, 72–87. Ithaca, N.Y.: Cornell University Press, 1985.

Donaldson, Ian. "*All's Well That Ends Well*: Shakespeare's Play of Endings." *Essays in Criticism* 27 (1977): 34–55.

Dowden, Edward. "Elizabethan Psychology." In *Essays Modern and Elizabethan*. London: J. M. Dent and Sons, 1910.

Drayton, Michael. *Englands Heroicall Epistles.* London: J[ames] R[oberts] for N. Ling, 1597.

———. *The Tragicall Legend of Robert, Duke of Normandy . . . With the Legend of Matilda the chast.* London: Ia. Roberts for N. L., 1596.

Dubrow, Heather. "'Incertainties now crown themselves assur'd': The Politics of Plotting Shakespeare's Sonnets." In *Shakespeare's Sonnets: Critical Essays*, ed. James Schiffer, 113–33. New York: Garland, 1999.

———. *Echoes of Desire: English Petrarchism and its Counterdiscourses.* Ithaca, N.Y.: Cornell University Press, 1995.

Duggan, Lisa and Kathleen McHugh. "A Fem(me)inist Manifesto." In *Brazen Femme: Queering Femininity*, ed. Chloë Brushwood Rose and Anna Camilleri, 165–70. Vancouver: Arsenal Pulp Press, 2002.

Duncan-Jones, Katherine. "Was the 1609 *Shake-speares Sonnets* Really Unauthorized?" *Review of English Studies* 34, 134 (1983): 151–71.

Eaton, Sara. "Beatrice-Joanna and the Rhetoric of Love: *The Changeling* (1622)." In *Staging the Renaissance: Reinterpretations of Elizabethan and Jacobean Drama*, ed. David Scott Kastan and Peter Stallybrass, 275–89. New York: Routledge, 1991.

Eccles, Audrey. *Obstetrics and Gynaecology in Tudor and Stuart England*. Kent, Oh.: Kent State University Press, 1982.

Edelman, Lee. *No Future: Queer Theory and the Death Drive*. Durham, N.C.: Duke University Press, 2004.

———. *Homographesis: Essays in Gay Literary and Cultural Theory*. New York: Routledge, 1994.

Eden, Kathy. *Poetic and Legal Fiction in the Aristotelian Tradition*. Princeton, N.J.: Princeton University Press, 1986.

[Edgar, Thomas]. *The Lawes Resolutions of Womens Rights: Or, The Lawes Provision for Woemen*. London: Printed by the assignes of John More for John Grove, 1632.

Elyot, Sir Thomas. *The Defence of Good Women*. London: in aedibus Thomae Bertheleti, 1545.

———. *Of the Knowledeg [sic] whiche maketh a wise man*. London: In aedibus Thomae Bertheleti, 1533.

Enterline, Lynn. *The Rhetoric of the Body from Ovid to Shakespeare*. Cambridge: Cambridge University Press, 2000.

Erasmus, Desiderius. *A Diatribe or Sermon Concerning Free Will*. In *Discourse on Free Will*, ed. trans. Ernst F. Winter. New York: Frederick Ungar, 1961.

———. *The first tome or volume of the Paraphrase of Erasmus upon the newe testamente*. London: Edwarde Whitchurche, 1548.

Ezell, Margaret J. M. *The Patriarch's Wife: Literary Evidence and the History of the Family*. Chapel Hill: University of North Carolina Press, 1987.

Feinberg, Nona. "Erasing the Dark Lady: Sonnet 138 in the Sequence." *Assays* 4 (1987): 97–108.

Fenner, Dudley. *The Artes of Logike and Rethorike, plainelie set foorth in the Englishe tounge*. Middelburg: R. Schilders, 1584.

Ferguson, Margaret W. *Dido's Daughters: Literacy, Gender, and Empire in Early Modern England and France*. Chicago: University of Chicago Press, 2003.

Filmer, Sir Robert. *Patriarcha: Or the Natural Power of Kings*. London: Walter Davis, 1680.

Fineman, Joel. *Shakespeare's Perjured Eye: The Invention of Poetic Subjectivity in the Sonnets*. Berkeley: University of California Press, 1986.

———. "Shakespeare's *Will*: The Temporality of Rape." In *The Subjectivity Effect in Western Literary Tradition: Essays Toward the Release of Shakespeare's Will*, 165–221. Cambridge, Mass.: MIT Press, 1991.

Finucci, Valeria. *The Manly Masquerade: Masculinity, Paternity, and Castration in the Italian Renaissance.* Durham, N.C.: Duke University Press, 2003.

Fisher, Samuel. *Rusticus Ad Academicos . . . The Rustick's Alarm to the Rabbies: or, The Country Correcting the University, and Clergy.* London: Printed for Robert Wilson, 1660.

Fletcher, Anthony. *Gender, Sex, and Subordination in England, 1500–1800.* New Haven, Conn.: Yale University Press, 1995.

Fletcher, Phineas. *The Purple Island, or The Isle of Man: Together with Piscatorie Eclogs and Other Poeticall Miscellanies.* Cambridge: Printed by the Printers to the Universitie of Cambridge, 1633.

Floyd-Wilson, Mary. *English Ethnicity and Race in Early Modern Drama.* Cambridge: Cambridge University Press, 2003.

Forset, Edward. *A Comparative Discourse of the Bodies Natural and Politique.* London: Printed for John Bill, 1606.

Foucault, Michel. *Discipline and Punish: The Birth of the Prison.* Trans. Alan Sheridan. New York: Vintage, 1979.

———. "Governmentality." In *The Foucault Effect: Studies in Governmentality*, ed. Graham Burchell, Colin Gordon, and Peter Miller, 87–104. London: Harvester Wheatsheaf, 1991.

———. *The Order of Things: An Archaeology of the Human Sciences.* New York: Vintage, 1973.

Fraunce, Abraham. *The Arcadian Rhetorike.* London: Thomas Orwin, 1588.

———. *The lawiers logike.* London: William How for Thomas Gubbin and T. Newman, 1588.

Freccero, Carla. *Queer/Early/Modern.* Durham, N.C.: Duke University Press, 2006.

Freinkel, Lisa. *Reading Shakespeare's Will: The Theology of Figure from Augustine to the Sonnets.* New York: Columbia University Press, 2002.

Freud, Sigmund. "Femininity." In *New Introductory Lectures on Psycho-Analysis.* In *The Standard Edition of the Complete Psychological Works of Sigmund Freud*, 22: 112–35. Trans. and ed. James Strachey. 24 vols. London: Hogarth Press, 1974.

———. "Medusa's Head." In *The Standard Edition*, 18: 273–74.

Friedman, Michael D. "'O, let him marry her!': Matrimony and Recompense in *Measure for Measure.*" *Shakespeare Quarterly* 46, 4 (1995): 454–64.

———. "Male Bonds and Marriage in *All's Well* and *Much Ado.*" *SEL: Studies in English Literature, 1500–1900* 35, 2 (1995): 231–49.

Gale, Thomas. *Certaine Workes of Chirurgerie, newly compiled.* London: Rouland Hall, 1563.

Gallop, Jane. "Reading the Mother Tongue: Psychoanalytic Feminist Criticism." *Critical Inquiry* 13, 2 (1987): 314–29.

Garber, Marjorie. *Vested Interests: Cross-Dressing and Cultural Anxiety.* New York: Harper-Perennial, 1993.

Gataker, Thomas. "A Good Wife Gods Gift." In *A Good Wife Gods Gift: And, A Wife Indeed. Two Mariage Sermons.* London: John Haviland for Fulke Clifton, 1623.

———. "A Wife in Deed." In *A Good Wife Gods Gift: And, A Wife Indeed.*

Geisel, Theodor Seuss (Dr. Seuss). *Horton Hatches the Egg.* New York: Random House, 2004.

Geoffrey of Monmouth. *The British History.* Trans. Aaron Thompson. London: Printed for J. Bowyer et al, 1718.

Gil, Daniel Juan. *Before Intimacy: Asocial Sexuality in Early Modern England.* Minneapolis: University of Minnesota Press, 2006.

Godshalk, W. L. "*All's Well* and the Morality Play." *Shakespeare Quarterly* 25 (1974): 61–70.

Gohlke, Madelon. "'I wooed thee with my sword': Shakespeare's Tragic Paradigms." In *Representing Shakespeare: New Psychoanalytic Essays,* ed. Murray M. Schwartz and Coppélia Kahn, 170–87. Baltimore: Johns Hopkins University Press, 1980.

Goldberg, Jonathan. "Hal's Desire, Shakespeare's Idaho." In *Henry IV, Parts One and Two,* ed. Nigel Wood, 35–64. Buckingham: Open University Press, 1995.

———. *James I and the Politics of Literature: Jonson, Shakespeare, Donne, and their Contemporaries.* Baltimore: Johns Hopkins University Press, 1983.

Goldberg, S. L. *An Essay on "King Lear."* Cambridge: Cambridge University Press, 1974.

Good Vibrations catalogue: "SupraVibra and the Quest for Pleasure." Fall 2004.

Goodman, Godfrey. *The Fall of Man, or the Corruption of Nature, Proved by the light of our naturall Reason.* London: Felix Kyngston for Richard Lee, 1616.

Gosynhyll, Edward (attributed author). *Here begynneth a lytle boke named the Schole house of women.* London: Thomas Petyt, 1541.

Gosynhyll, Edward. *The prayse of all women, called Mulierum Pean.* London: Wyllyam Myddylton, ca. 1542.

Gowing, Laura. *Common Bodies: Women, Touch, and Power in Seventeenth-Century England.* New Haven, Conn.: Yale University Press, 2003.

———. *Domestic Dangers: Women, Words, and Sex in Early Modern London.* Oxford: Clarendon Press, 1996.

Greenblatt, Stephen. "Introduction: Joel Fineman's 'Will.'" In Joel Fineman, *The Subjectivity Effect in Western Literary Tradition: Essays Toward the Release of Shakespeare's Will,* ix–xix. Cambridge, Mass.: MIT Press, 1991.

———. *Shakespearean Negotiations: The Circulation of Social Energy in Renaissance England.* Oxford: Clarendon, 1988.

Greene, Roland. *Unrequited Conquests: Love and Empire in the Colonial Americas.* Chicago: University of Chicago Press, 1999.

Greenfield, Thomas A. "Excellent Things in Women: The Emergence of Cordelia." *South Atlantic Bulletin* 42, 1 (1977): 44–52.

Greenstadt, Amy. *Rape and the Rise of the Author: Gendering Intention in Early Modern England.* Surrey: Ashgate, 2009.

———. "'Read it in me': The Author's Will in *Lucrece.*" *Shakespeare Quarterly* 57, 1 (2006): 45–70.

Gross, Gerard J. "The Conclusion to *All's Well That Ends Well.*" *SEL: Studies in English Literature, 1500–1900* 23, 2 (1983): 257–76.

Guazzo, Stefano. *The Civile Conversation of M. Steeven Guazzo.* Trans. George Pettie. London: Richard Watkins, 1581.

Haec-Vir: Or The Womanish-Man: Being an Answere to a late Booke intituled Hic-Mulier. London: Printed for J. T., 1620.

Halberstam, Judith. *Female Masculinity.* Durham, N.C.: Duke University Press, 1998.

Hall, Kim F. "'These bastard signs of fair': Literary Whiteness in Shakespeare's Sonnets." In *Post-Colonial Shakespeares,* ed. Ania Loomba and Martin Orkin, 64–83. London: Routledge, 1998.

———. *Things of Darkness: Economies of Race and Gender in Early Modern England.* Ithaca, N.Y.: Cornell University Press, 1995.

Halpern, Richard. *The Poetics of Primitive Accumulation: English Renaissance Culture and the Genealogy of Capital.* Ithaca, N.Y.: Cornell University Press, 1991.

———. "Puritanism and Maenadism in *A Mask.*" In *Rewriting the Renaissance,* ed. Margaret W. Ferguson, Maureen Quilligan, and Nancy J. Vickers, 88–105. Chicago: University of Chicago Press, 1986.

———. *Shakespeare's Perfume: Sodomy and Sublimity in the Sonnets, Wilde, Freud, and Lacan.* Philadelphia: University of Pennsylvania Press, 2002.

Harding, D. W. "Women's Fantasy of Manhood: A Shakespearian Theme." *Shakespeare Quarterly* 20, 3 (1969): 245–53.

Harington, Sir John. "An Advertisement to the Reader." In Lodovico Ariosto, *Orlando Furioso in English Heroical Verse, by John Harington.* London: Richard Field, 1591.

Harris, Jonathan Gil. "All Swell That End Swell: Dropsy, Phantom Pregnancy, and the Sound of Deconception in *All's Well That Ends Well.*" *Renaissance Drama* 35 (2006): 169–89.

Harvey, Elizabeth D. "Flesh Colors and Shakespeare's Sonnets." In *A Companion to Shakespeare's Sonnets,* ed. Michael Schoenfeldt, 314–28. Oxford: Blackwell, 2007.

———. *Ventriloquized Voices: Feminist Theory and English Renaissance Texts.* London and New York: Routledge, 1992.

Hayne, Victoria. "Performing Social Practice: The Example of *Measure for Measure.*" *Shakespeare Quarterly* 44, 1 (1993): 1–29.

Heale, William. *An Apologie for Women.* Oxford: Joseph Barnes, 1609.

Heywood, Thomas. *The Exemplary Lives And Memorable Acts of Nine The Most Worthy Women Of The World.* London: Tho. Cotes for Richard Royston, 1640.

———. *Gynaikeion: or, Nine Bookes of Various History. Concerninge Women.* London: Adam Islip, 1624.

Hic Mulier: Or, The Man-Woman: Being a Medicine to cure the Coltish Disease of the Staggers in the Masculine-Feminines of our Times. London: Printed for J. T., 1620.

[Higgins, John]. *The First parte of the Mirour for Magistrates, containing the falles of the first infortunate Princes of this lande.* London: Thomas Marshe, 1574.

Hillman, David, and Carla Mazzio. "Introduction: Individual Parts." In *The Body in Parts: Fantasies of Corporeality in Early Modern Europe,* ed. David Hillman and Carla Mazzio, xi–xxix. New York and London: Routledge, 1997.

Hodgdon, Barbara. "The Making of Virgins and Mothers: Sexual Signs, Substitute Scenes and Doubled Presences in *All's Well That Ends Well*." *Philological Quarterly* 66, 1 (1987): 47–71.

Holahan, Michael. "'Look, Her Lips': Softness of Voice, Construction of Character in *King Lear*." *Shakespeare Quarterly* 48, 4 (1997): 406–31.

Holinshed, Raphael. *The Historie of England, from the time that it was first inhabited, untill the time that it was last conquered*. Separately paginated in *The First and second volumes of Chronicles . . . now newlie augmented and continued*. London: Henry Denham, 1587.

Hooker, Richard. *Of the Lawes of Ecclesiasticall Politie. Eyght Bookes*. London: John Windet, 1593.

Hoover, Claudette. "Goneril and Regan: 'So Horrid as in Woman.'" *San Jose Studies* 10, 3 (1984): 49–65.

———. "Women, Centaurs, and Devils in *King Lear*." *Women's Studies* 16, 3–4 (1989): 349–59.

Howard, Jean E. and Phyllis Rackin. *Engendering a Nation: A Feminist Account of Shakespeare's English Histories*. London: Routledge, 1997.

Huarte, Juan. *The Examination of mens Wits . . . Translated out of the Spanish tongue by M. Camillo Camilli. Englished out of his Italian, by R. C. Esquire*. London: Adam Islip, 1596.

Hunt, Marvin. "Be Dark But Not Too Dark: Shakespeare's Dark Lady as a Sign of Color." In *Shakespeare's Sonnets: Critical Essays*, ed. James Schiffer, 368–89. New York: Garland, 1999.

Hutson, Lorna. *The Invention of Suspicion: Law and Mimesis in Shakespeare and Renaissance Drama*. Oxford: Oxford University Press, 2007.

———. *The Usurer's Daughter: Male Friendship and Fictions of Women in Sixteenth-Century England*. London: Routledge, 1994.

Irigaray, Luce. *This Sex Which Is Not One*. Trans. Catherine Porter with Carolyn Burke. Ithaca, N.Y.: Cornell University Press, 1977, 1985.

Iyengar, Sujata. *Shades of Difference: Mythologies of Skin Color in Early Modern England*. Philadelphia: University of Pennsylvania Press, 2005.

Jakobson, Roman. "Two Aspects of Language and Two Types of Aphasic Disturbances." In *On Language*, ed. Linda R. Waugh and Monique Monville-Burston, 115–33. Cambridge, Mass.: Harvard University Press, 1990.

James, Susan. *Passion and Action: The Emotions in Seventeenth-Century Philosophy*. Oxford: Clarendon Press, 1997.

Jankowski, Theodora A. "Hymeneal Blood, Interchangeable Women, and the Early Modern Marriage Economy in *Measure for Measure* and *All's Well That Ends Well*." In *A Companion to Shakespeare's Works*, vol. 4, ed. Richard Dutton and Jean E. Howard, 89–105. London: Blackwell, 2003.

———. "Pure Resistance: Queer(y)ing Virginity in William Shakespeare's *Measure for*

Measure and Margaret Cavendish's *The Convent of Pleasure.*" *Shakespeare Studies* 26 (1998): 218–55.

———. *Pure Resistance: Queer Virginity in Early Modern English Drama.* Philadelphia: University of Pennsylvania Press, 2000.

Jardin, Roland du. *A Discourse of the Married and Single Life. Wherein, by Discovering the Misery of the one, is plainely declared the felicity of the other.* London: Printed for Jonas Man, 1621.

Jardine, Lisa. "Cultural Confusion and Shakespeare's Learned Heroines: 'These are old paradoxes.'" *Shakespeare Quarterly* 38, 1 (1987): 1–18.

———. *Still Harping on Daughters: Women and Drama in the Age of Shakespeare.* Sussex: Harvester Press, 1983.

Johnson, Barbara. "The Alchemy of Style and Law." In *The Feminist Difference: Literature, Psychoanalysis, Race, and Gender,* 165–82. Cambridge, Mass.: Harvard University Press, 1998.

Jonson, Ben. *The Masque of Beauty* (1608). In *The Complete Masques,* ed. Stephen Orgel. New Haven, Conn.: Yale University Press, 1969.

Jordan, Constance. *Renaissance Feminism: Literary Texts and Political Models.* Ithaca, N.Y.: Cornell University Press, 1990.

Kahn, Coppélia. "The Absent Mother in *King Lear.*" In *Rewriting the Renaissance: The Discourses of Sexual Difference in Early Modern Europe,* ed. Margaret W. Ferguson, Maureen Quilligan, and Nancy J. Vickers, 33–49. Chicago: University of Chicago Press, 1987.

———. *Man's Estate: Masculine Identity in Shakespeare.* Berkeley: University of California Press, 1981.

———. "The Rape in Shakespeare's *Lucrece.*" *Shakespeare Studies* 9 (1976): 45–72.

Kahn, Victoria. "Margaret Cavendish and the Romance of Contract." *Renaissance Quarterly* 50, 2 (1997): 526–66.

Kalas, Rayna. "Fickle Glass." In *A Companion to Shakespeare's Sonnets,* ed. Michael Schoenfeldt, 261–76. Oxford: Blackwell, 2007.

Kamaralli, Anna. "Writing About Motive: Isabella, the Duke and Moral Authority." *Shakespeare Survey* 58 (2005): 48–59.

Kastan, David Scott. "*All's Well That Ends Well* and the Limits of Comedy." *ELH* 52, 3 (1985): 575–89.

Kavanagh, James H. "Shakespeare in Ideology." In *Alternative Shakespeares,* ed. John Drakakis, 144–65. London: Methuen, 1985.

Kay, W. David. "Reforming the Prodigal: Dramatic Paradigms, Male Sexuality, and the Power of Shame in *All's Well That Ends Well.*" In *Re-Visions of Shakespeare: Essays in Honor of Robert Ornstein,* ed. Evelyn Gajowski, 108–27. Newark: University of Delaware Press, 2004.

Kelly, Kathleen Coyne. *Performing Virginity and Testing Chastity in the Middle Ages.* London: Routledge, 2000.

Kelly, Kathleen Coyne and Marina Leslie, eds. *Menacing Virgins: Representing Virginity in the Middle Ages and Renaissance*. Newark: University of Delaware Press, 1999.

Kelly, Philippa. "Performing Australian Identity: Gendering *King Lear*." *Theatre Journal* 57, 2 (2005): 205–27.

Kelso, Ruth. *Doctrine for the Lady of the Renaissance*. Urbana: University of Illinois Press, 1956.

Kerrigan, William. "The Articulation of the Ego in the English Renaissance." In *The Literary Freud: Mechanisms of Defense and the Poetic Will*, ed. Joseph H. Smith, M.D., 261–308. New Haven, Conn.: Yale University Press, 1980.

King, Margaret L. *Women of the Renaissance*. Chicago: University of Chicago Press, 1991.

Knoppers, Laura Lunger. "(En)gendering Shame: *Measure for Measure* and the Spectacles of Power." *English Literary Renaissance* 23, 3 (1993): 450–71.

Koenig, Rhoda. "Measure for Measure, Theatre Royal, Bath." *The Independent*, 14 July 2006. http://www.independent.co.uk/arts-entertainment/theatre-dance/reviews/measure-for-measure-theatre-royal-bath-none-onestar-twostar-fourstar-fivestar-407917.html

Korda, Natasha. *Shakespeare's Domestic Economies: Gender and Property in Early Modern England*. Philadelphia: University of Pennsylvania Press, 2002.

Kristeva, Julia. *Revolution in Poetic Language*. Trans. Margaret Waller. New York: Columbia University Press, 1984.

La Perrière, Guillaume de. *The Theater of Fine Devices, containing an hundred morall Emblemes*. Trans. Thomas Combe. London: Richard Field, 1614.

La Primaudaye, Pierre de. *The Second Part of the French Academie*. London: G. B[ishop], R[alph] N[ewbery], and R. B[arker], 1594.

Lacan, Jacques. "The Agency of the Letter in the Unconscious." In *Écrits: A Selection*, trans. Alan Sheridan, 146–78. New York: Norton, 1977.

———. "The Function and Field of Speech and Language in Psychoanalysis." In *Écrits: A Selection*, 30–113.

———. "The Mirror Stage." In *Écrits: A Selection*, 1–7.

———. "The Signification of the Phallus." In *Écrits: A Selection*, 281–91.

Lake, Peter. "Ministers, Magistrates, and the Production of 'Order' in *Measure for Measure*." *Shakespeare Survey* 54 (2001): 165–81.

Laqueur, Thomas. *Making Sex: Body and Gender from the Greeks to Freud*. Cambridge, Mass.: Harvard University Press, 1990.

Leech, Clifford. "The Theme of Ambition in 'All's Well That Ends Well.'" *ELH* 12 (1954): 17–29.

Leigh, Dorothy. *The Mothers Blessing*. London: Printed for John Budge, 1616.

Lever, Ralph. *The Arte of Reason, rightly termed, Witcraft*. London: H. Bynneman, 1573.

Levin, Richard A. "*All's Well That Ends Well*, and 'All Seems Well.'" *Shakespeare Studies* 13 (1980): 131–44.

Lewis, Charlton T. and Charles Short. *A Latin Dictionary*, rev. ed. (1879). Repr. Oxford: Clarendon Press, 1966.

Little, Arthur L., Jr. "Absolute Bodies, Absolute Laws: Staging Punishment in *Measure for Measure.*" In *Shakespearean Power and Punishment*, ed. Gillian Murray Kendall, 113–29. London: Associated University Presses, 1998.

———. *Shakespeare Jungle Fever: National-Imperial Re-Visions of Race, Rape, and Sacrifice.* Stanford, Calif.: Stanford University Press, 2000.

Lodge, Thomas. *Catharos. Diogenes in his Singularitie.* London: William Hoskins and John Danter for John Busbie, 1591.

Loughlin, Marie H. *Hymeneutics: Interpreting Virginity on the Early Modern Stage.* Lewisburg, Pa.: Bucknell University Press, 1997.

Luther, Martin. *The Bondage of the Will.* In *Discourse on Free Will*, ed. trans. Ernst F. Winter. New York: Frederick Ungar, 1961.

Maclean, Ian. *The Renaissance Notion of Woman: A Study in the Fortunes of Scholasticism and Medical Science in European Intellectual Life.* Cambridge: Cambridge University Press, 1980.

Magedanz, Stacy. "Public Justice and Private Mercy in *Measure for Measure.*" *SEL* 44, 2 (2004): 317–32.

Maguire, Laurie E. *Shakespearean Suspect Texts: The "Bad" Quartos and Their Contexts.* Cambridge: Cambridge University Press, 1996.

Marcus, Leah S. *Puzzling Shakespeare: Local Reading and Its Discontents.* Berkeley: University of California Press, 1988.

———. *Unediting the Renaissance: Shakespeare, Marlowe, Milton.* New York: Routledge, 1996.

Markham, Gervase. *The English House-wife. Containing The inward and outward Vertues which ought to be in a complete Woman.* London: Nicholas Okes for John Harison, 1631.

Marston, John. *What You Will.* London: G. Eld for Thomas Thorppe, 1607.

Masten, Jeffrey. "More or Less: Editing the Collaborative." *Shakespeare Studies* 29 (2001): 109–31.

Maus, Katharine Eisaman. *Inwardness and Theater in the English Renaissance.* Chicago: University of Chicago Press, 1995.

———. "Taking Tropes Seriously: Language and Violence in Shakespeare's *Rape of Lucrece.*" *Shakespeare Quarterly* 37, 1 (1986): 66–82.

Mazzio, Carla. *The Inarticulate Renaissance: Language Trouble in an Age of Eloquence.* Philadelphia: University of Pennsylvania Press, 2009.

———. "Sins of the Tongue." In *The Body in Parts: Fantasies of Corporeality in Early Modern Europe*, ed. David Hillman and Carla Mazzio, 53–79. New York: Routledge, 1997.

McCandless, David. "'I'll Pray to Increase Your Bondage': Power and Punishment in *Measure for Measure.*" In *Shakespearean Power and Punishment*, ed. Gillian Murray Kendall, 89–112. London: Associated University Presses, 1998.

———. "Helena's Bed-trick: Gender and Performance in *All's Well That Ends Well.*" *Shakespeare Quarterly* 45, 4 (1994): 449–68.

McLaren, Angus. *Reproductive Rituals: The Perception of Fertility in England from the Six-teenth Century to the Nineteenth Century.* London: Methuen, 1984.

McLuskie, Kathleen. "The Patriarchal Bard: Feminist Criticism and Shakespeare: *King Lear* and *Measure for Measure.*" In *Political Shakespeare: New Essays in Cultural Mate-rialism,* ed. Jonathan Dollimore and Alan Sinfield, 88–108. Ithaca, N.Y.: Cornell University Press, 1985.

Menon, Madhavi. *Wanton Words: Rhetoric and Sexuality in English Renaissance Drama.* Toronto: University of Toronto Press, 2004.

Merbecke, John. *A Booke of Notes and Common places, with their expositions.* London: Thomas East, 1581.

Michaelis, Sébastien. *The Admirable Historie of the Possession and Conversion of a Penitent woman. Seduced by a Magician That Made her to become a Witch.* Trans. W. B. London: Felix Kingston for William Aspley, 1613.

Middleton, Thomas and William Rowley. *A Courtly Masque: The Device Called The World tost at Tennis.* London: George Purslowe for Edward Wright, 1620.

Miller, Naomi J. "Playing 'the mother's part': Shakespeare's Sonnets and Early Modern Codes of Maternity." In *Shakespeare's Sonnets: Critical Essays,* ed. James Schiffer, 347–67. New York: Garland, 1999.

Miller, Naomi and Naomi Yavneh, eds. *Maternal Measures: Figuring Caregiving in the Early Modern Period.* Aldershot: Ashgate, 2000.

Montrose, Louis. "'Shaping Fantasies': Figurations of Gender and Power in Elizabethan Culture." In *Representing the English Renaissance,* ed. Stephen Greenblatt, 31–64. Berkeley: University of California Press, 1988.

More, Edward. *A Lytle and bryefe treatyse, called the defence of women, and especially of Englyshe women, made agaynst the Schole house of women.* London: John Kynge, 1560.

Muld Sacke: Or The Apologie of Hic Mulier. London: [William Stansby] for Richard Meighen, 1620.

Mullaney, Steven. "Mourning and Misogyny: *Hamlet, The Revenger's Tragedy,* and the Final Progress of Elizabeth I, 1600–1607." *Shakespeare Quarterly* 45, 2 (1994): 139–162.

———. *The Place of the Stage: License, Play, and Power in Renaissance England.* Chicago: University of Chicago Press, 1988.

Neely, Carol Thomas. *Broken Nuptials in Shakespeare's Plays.* New Haven, Conn.: Yale University Press, 1985.

Nemesius. *The Nature of Man. A learned and usefull Tract, written in Greek by Nemesius, surnamed the Philosopher.* Trans. George Wither. London: M. F. for Henry Taunton, 1636.

Newman, Jane O. "'And Let Mild Women to Him Lose Their Mildness': Philomela, Female Violence, and Shakespeare's *The Rape of Lucrece.*" *Shakespeare Quarterly* 45, 3 (1994): 304–26.

Newman, Karen. "Directing Traffic: Subjects, Objects, and the Politics of Exchange." *differences* 2, 2 (1990): 41–54.

————. *Fashioning Femininity and English Renaissance Drama*. Chicago: University of Chicago Press, 1991.

Nightingale, Benedict. "Measure for Measure." *The Times*, 14 July 2006. http://entertain ment.timesonline.co.uk/tol/arts_and_entertainment/article6 87307.ece

Oberndorff, John. *The Anatomyes of the True Physition, and Counterfeit Mounte-banke*. Trans. F[rancis] H[erring]. London: Printed for Arthur Johnson, 1602.

Ong, Walter J. "Latin Language Study as a Renaissance Puberty Rite." *Studies in Philology* 56, 2 (April 1959): 103–24.

————. "Tudor Writings on Rhetoric, Poetic, and Literary Theory." In *Rhetoric, Romance, and Technology: Studies in the Interaction of Expression and Culture*, 48–103. Ithaca, N.Y.: Cornell University Press, 1971.

Onions, C. T. *A Shakespeare Glossary*, enlarged and revised throughout by Robert D. Eagleson. Oxford: Clarendon Press, 1986.

Orgel, Stephen. "The Authentic Shakespeare." *Representations* 21 (Winter 1988), 1–25.

————. "What Is a Text?" In *Staging the Renaissance: Reinterpretations of Elizabethan and Jacobean Drama*, ed. David Scott Kastan and Peter Stallybrass, 83–87. New York: Routledge, 1991.

Orlin, Lena Cowen. "A Case for Anecdotalism in Women's History: The Witness Who Spoke When the Cock Crowed." *English Literary Renaissance* 31, 1 (2001): 52–77.

Papp, Joseph and Elizabeth Kirkland. *Shakespeare Alive!* Toronto: Bantam Books, 1988.

Park, Katharine. "The Criminal and the Saintly Body: Autopsy and Dissection in Renaissance Italy." *Renaissance Quarterly* 47, 1 (1994): 1–33.

————. "The Life of the Corpse: Division and Dissection in Late Medieval Europe." *Journal of the History of Medicine and Allied Sciences* 50, 1 (1995): 111–32.

Parker, Patricia. *Literary Fat Ladies: Rhetoric, Gender, Property*. London: Methuen, 1987.

————. *Shakespeare from the Margins: Language, Culture, Context*. Chicago and London: University of Chicago Press, 1996.

————. "Virile Style." In *Premodern Sexualities*, ed. Louise Fradenburg and Carla Freccero, 201–22. New York: Routledge, 1996.

Partridge, Eric. *Shakespeare's Bawdy: A Literary & Psychological Essay and a Comprehensive Glossary*, rev. and enlarged. London: Routledge & Kegan Paul, 1968.

Paster, Gail Kern. *The Body Embarrassed: Drama and the Disciplines of Shame in Early Modern England*. Ithaca, N.Y.: Cornell University Press, 1993.

————. *Humoring the Body: Emotions and the Shakespearean Stage*. Chicago: University of Chicago Press, 2004.

Paster, Gail Kern, Katherine Rowe, and Mary Floyd-Wilson, eds. *Reading the Early Modern Passions: Essays in the Cultural History of Emotion*. Philadelphia: University of Pennsylvania Press, 2004.

Patterson, Annabel. "Intention." In *Critical Terms for Literary Study*, ed. Frank Lentricchia and Thomas McLaughlin, 135–46. Chicago: University of Chicago Press, 1990.

Peacham, Henry. *The Garden of Eloquence Conteyning the Figures of Grammer and Rhetorick*. London: H. Jackson, 1577.

————. *The Garden of Eloquence Conteining the Most Excellent Ornaments, Exornations,*

Lightes, flowers, and formes of speech . . . Corrected and augmented by the first Author. London: R. F. for H. Jackson, 1593.

Perkins, William. *A Direction for the Government of the Tongue according to Gods word.* Cambridge: Printed by John Legate Printer to the University of Cambridge, 1593.

Phillips, Joshua. *English Fictions of Communal Identity, 1485–1603.* Farnham: Ashgate, 2010.

Pontaymeri, Alexandre de. *A Womans Woorth, defended against all the men in the world.* Ed. Anthony Gibson. London: John Wolfe, 1599.

Poole, William. "The Vices of Style." In *Renaissance Figures of Speech*, ed. Sylvia Adamson, Gavin Alexander, and Katrin Ettenhuber, 237–51. Cambridge: Cambridge University Press, 2007.

The Problemes of Aristotle, with other Philosophers and Phisitions. Wherein are contayned divers questions, with their answers, touching the estate of mans bodie. At Edenborough: Robert Waldgrave, 1595.

Prynne, William. *Histrio-mastix. The Players Scourge or, Actors Tragaedie.* London: Printed by E. A. and W. J. for Michael Sparke, 1633.

Purchas, Samuel. *Purchas his Pilgrimes. In Five Bookes.* The First Part. London: William Stansby for Henrie Fetherstone, 1625.

Puttenham, George. *The Arte of English Poesie.* London: Richard Field, 1589.

Quiller-Couch, Sir Arthur. "Introduction." *All's Well That Ends Well.* Cambridge: Cambridge University Press, 1929.

Rackin, Phyllis. "Anti-Historians: Women's Roles in Shakespeare's Histories." *Theatre Journal* 37, 3 (1985): 329–44.

———. *Shakespeare and Women.* Oxford: Oxford University Press, 2005.

Ralegh, Sir Walter. "A Treatise of the Soul." In *The Works of Sir Walter Ralegh, Kt., Now First Collected: To Which are Prefixed, the Lives of the Author, by Oldys and Birch*, 8: 571–91. 8 vols. Oxford: At the University Press, 1829.

Rambuss, Richard. *Closet Devotions.* Durham, N.C.: Duke University Press, 1998.

Ramus, Petrus (Pierre de la Ramée). *A Compendium of the Art of Logick and Rhetorick in the English Tongue. Containing All that Peter Ramus, Aristotle, and Others have writ thereon.* London: Thomas Maxey, 1651.

Raynalde, Thomas. *The Birth of Mankynde, otherwyse named the womans booke.* London: Richard Jugge, 1565.

Reid, Stephen. "In Defense of Goneril and Regan." *American Imago* 27 (1970): 226–44.

Reynolds, Henry. *Mythomystes Wherein a Short Survay Is Taken of the Nature and Value of True Poesy.* London: George Purslowe for Henry Seyle, 1632.

Rich, Barnabe. *The Excellency of good women. The honour and estimation that belongeth unto them. The infallible markes whereby to know them.* London: Thomas Dawson, 1613.

Riefer, Marcia. "'Instruments of Some More Mightier Member': The Constriction of Female Power in *Measure for Measure*." *Shakespeare Quarterly* 35, 2 (1984): 157–69.

Riviere, Joan. "Womanliness as a Masquerade" (1929). In *The Inner World and Joan Riviere: Collected Papers: 1920–1958*, ed. Athol Hughes, 89–101. London: Karnac for the Melanie Klein Trust, 1991.

Rogers, John. "The Enclosure of Virginity: The Poetics of Sexual Abstinence in the English Revolution." In *Enclosure Acts: Sexuality, Property, and Culture in Early Modern England*, ed. Richard Burt and John Michael Archer, 229–50. Ithaca, N.Y.: Cornell University Press, 1994.

Rose, Jacqueline. "Sexuality in the Reading of Shakespeare: *Hamlet* and *Measure for Measure*." In *Alternative Shakespeares*, ed. John Drakakis, 95–118. London: Methuen, 1985.

Rose, Mary Beth. *The Expense of Spirit: Love and Sexuality in English Renaissance Drama*. Ithaca, N.Y.: Cornell University Press, 1988.

———. "Where Are the Mothers in Shakespeare? Options for Gender Representation in the English Renaissance." *Shakespeare Quarterly* 42, 3 (Fall 1991): 291–314.

Rowe, Katherine. *Dead Hands: Fictions of Agency, Renaissance to Modern*. Stanford, Calif.: Stanford University Press, 1999.

———. "Inconstancy: Changeable Affections in Stuart Dramas of Contract." In *Environment and Embodiment in Early Modern England*, ed. Mary Floyd-Wilson and Garrett A. Sullivan, Jr., 90–102. New York: Palgrave Macmillan, 2007.

Rudolph, Julia. "Rape and Resistance: Women and Consent in Seventeenth-Century English Legal and Political Thought." *Journal of British Studies* 39, 2 (2000): 157–84.

Rudnytsky, Peter. "'The Darke and Vicious Place': The Dread of the Vagina in *King Lear*." *Modern Philology* 96, 3 (1999): 291–311.

Salter, Thomas. *A Mirrhor mete for all Mothers, Matrones, and Maidens, intituled the Mirrhor of Modestie*. London: Edward White, 1579.

Sawday, Jonathan. *The Body Emblazoned: Dissection and the Human Body in Renaissance Culture*. London: Routledge, 1995.

———. "The Fate of Marsyas: Dissecting the Renaissance Body." In *Renaissance Bodies: The Human Figure in English Culture c. 1540–1660*, ed. Lucy Gent and Nigel Llewellyn, 111–35. London: Reaktion Books, 1990.

Scarry, Elaine. "Consent and the Body: Injury, Departure, and Desire." *New Literary History* 21, 4, Papers from the Commonwealth Center for Literary and Cultural Change (1990): 867–96.

Schalkwyk, David. "'A Lady's 'Verily' is as Potent as a Lord's': Women, Word and Witchcraft in *The Winter's Tale*." *English Literary Renaissance* 22, 2 (1992): 242–72.

———. "Love and Service in *Twelfth Night* and the Sonnets." *Shakespeare Quarterly* 56, 1 (2005): 76–100.

———. *Shakespeare, Love and Service*. Cambridge: Cambridge University Press, 2008.

———. "What May Words Do? The Performative of Praise in Shakespeare's Sonnets." *Shakespeare Quarterly* 49, 3 (1998): 251–68.

Schleiner, Winfried. "Early Modern Controversies About the One-Sex Model." *Renaissance Quarterly* 53, 1 (2000): 180–91.

Schoenfeldt, Michael. "The Matter of Inwardness: Shakespeare's Sonnets." In *Shakespeare's Sonnets: Critical Essays*, ed. James Schiffer, 305–24. New York: Garland, 1999.

Schwarz, Kathryn. "Chastity, Militant and Married: Cavendish's Romance, Milton's Masque." *PMLA* 118, 2 (2003): 270–85.

————. "The Wrong Question: Thinking Through Virginity." *differences* 13, 2 (2002): 1–34.

Scot, Reginald. *Scot's Discovery of Witchcraft*. London: Printed by R. C. for Giles Calvert, 1651.

Scott, Joan W. "The Evidence of Experience." *Critical Inquiry* 17, 4 (1991): 773–97.

Sedgwick, Eve Kosofsky. *Between Men: English Literature and Male Homosocial Desire*. New York: Columbia University Press, 1985.

Seneca, Lucius Annaeus. *Hippolitus Translated out of Seneca by Edmund Prestwich. Together with divers other Poems of the same Authors*. London: G. D. for George Boddington, 1651.

Shakespeare, William. *All's Well That Ends Well*, ed. Barbara A. Mowat and Paul Werstine. New Folger Edition. New York: Washington Square Press, 2006.

————. *All's Well That Ends Well*, ed. G. K. Hunter. Arden: 3rd rev. ed. London: Methuen, 1959.

————. *All's Well That Ends Well*. In *The Riverside Shakespeare*, 2nd ed., general ed. G. Blakemore Evans. Boston: Houghton Mifflin, 1997.

————. *King Lear*, ed. David Bevington. Bantam ed. New York: Bantam Books, 1988.

————. *The History of King Lear*. In *King Lear: The 1608 Quarto and 1623 Folio Texts*, ed. Stephen Orgel. The Pelican Shakespeare. New York: Penguin Books, 2000.

————. *The History of King Lear*. In *The Norton Shakespeare*, gen. ed. Stephen Greenblatt. New York and London: Norton, 1997.

————. *Measure for Measure*. In *The Riverside Shakespeare*, 2nd ed., general editor G. Blakemore Evans. Boston: Houghton Mifflin, 1997.

————. *A Midsummer Night's Dream*. In *The Riverside Shakespeare*, 2nd ed., general editor G. Blakemore Evans. Boston: Houghton Mifflin, 1997.

————. *The Plays of William Shakespeare*, ed. Samuel Johnson. 8 vols. London: Printed for J. and R. Tonson et al, 1765.

————. *Shakespeare's Sonnets*, ed. Katherine Duncan-Jones. Arden: 3rd Series. London: Thomas Nelson, 1997.

————. *Timon of Athens*. In *The Riverside Shakespeare*, 2nd ed., general editor G. Blakemore Evans. Boston: Houghton Mifflin, 1997.

————. *The Tragedy of King Lear*, ed. Barbara A. Mowat and Paul Werstine. New Folger Edition. New York: Washington Square Press, 1993.

————. *The Tragedy of King Lear*. In *The Complete Signet Classic Shakespeare*, gen. ed. Sylvan Barnet. New York: Harcourt Brace Jovanovich, 1972.

————. *The Tragedy of King Lear*. In *The Norton Shakespeare*, gen. ed. Stephen Greenblatt. New York and London: Norton, 1997.

————. *The Tragedy of King Lear*. In *The Riverside Shakespeare*, gen. ed. G. Blakemore Evans. Boston: Houghton Mifflin, 1974.

Shannon, Laurie. "Poor, Bare, Forked: Animal Sovereignty, Human Negative Exceptionalism, and the Natural History of *King Lear*." *Shakespeare Quarterly* 60, 2 (2009): 168–96.

———. *Sovereign Amity: Figures of Friendship in Shakespearean Contexts*. Chicago: University of Chicago Press, 2002.

Shaw, George Bernard. *The Philanderer*. In *Plays Pleasant and Unpleasant*, 75–161. New York: Brentano's, 1906.

Shell, Marc. *The End of Kinship:* Measure for Measure, *Incest, and the Ideal of Universal Siblinghood*. Stanford, Calif.: Stanford University Press, 1988.

Sheridan, Thomas. *Coriolanus: or, The Roman Matron. A Tragedy. Taken from Shakespear and Thomson*. London: printed for A. Millar, 1755.

Sherry, Richard. *A treatise of Schemes and Tropes very profytable for the better understanding of good authors, gathered out of the best Grammarians & Oratours*. London: John Day, 1550.

———. *A Treatise of the Figures of Grammer and Rhetorike, profitable for al that be studious of Eloquence*. London: in aedibus Ricardi Totteli, 1555.

Sidney, Sir Philip. *An Apologie for Poetrie*. London: Printed for Henry Olney, 1595.

Singh, Jyotsna G. "'Th' expense of spirit in a waste of shame': Mapping the 'Emotional Regime' of Shakespeare's Sonnets." In *A Companion to Shakespeare's Sonnets*, ed. Michael Schoenfeldt, 277–89. Oxford: Blackwell, 2007.

Slights, Jessica and Michael Morgan Holmes. "Isabella's Order: Religious Acts and Personal Desires in *Measure for Measure*." *Studies in Philology* 95, 3 (1998): 263–92.

Smith, Bruce R. *Homosexual Desire in Shakespeare's England: A Cultural Poetics*. Chicago: University of Chicago Press, 1991, 1994.

———. "I, You, He, She, and We: On the Sexual Politics of Shakespeare's Sonnets." In *Shakespeare's Sonnets: Critical Essays*, ed. James Schiffer, 411–29. New York: Garland, 1999.

Smith, Hilda. "Gynecology and Ideology in Seventeenth-Century England." In *Liberating Women's History: Theoretical and Critical Essays*, ed. Berenice A. Carroll, 97–114. Urbana: University of Illinois Press, 1976.

Snow, Edward A. "Loves of Comfort and Despair: A Reading of Shakespeare's Sonnet 138." *ELH* 47, 3 (1980): 462–83.

Snyder, Susan. "*All's Well That Ends Well* and Shakespeare's Helens: Text and Subtext, Subject and Object." *English Literary Renaissance* 18, 1 (1988): 66–77.

———. "'The King's Not Here': Displacement and Deferral in *All's Well That Ends Well*." *Shakespeare Quarterly* 43, 1 (1992): 20–32.

Speght, Rachel. *A Mouzell for Melastomus*. London: Nicholas Okes for Thomas Archer, 1617.

Spencer, Charles. "A Measure of Success." Telegraph.co.uk, 14 July 2006. http://www.tele graph.co.uk/culture/theatre/drama/3653794/A-measure-of-success.html

Spenser, Edmund. *The Faerie Queene*. Ed. Thomas P. Roche, Jr. New York: Viking Penguin, 1978, 1987.

———. *The Shepheardes Calender*. London: Hugh Singleton, 1579.

Stallybrass, Peter. "Editing as Cultural Formation: The Sexing of Shakespeare's Sonnets." *Modern Language Quarterly* 54, 1 (1993): 91–103.

———. "Patriarchal Territories: The Body Enclosed." In *Rewriting the Renaissance: The*

Discourses of Sexual Difference in Early Modern Europe, ed. Margaret W. Ferguson, Maureen Quilligan, and Nancy J. Vickers, 123–42. Chicago: University of Chicago Press, 1986.

———. "Reading the Body and the Jacobean Theater of Consumption." In *Staging the Renaissance: Reinterpretations of Elizabethan and Jacobean Drama*, ed. David Scott Kastan and Peter Stallybrass, 210–20. New York: Routledge, 1991.

Stapleton, M. L. "'My False Eyes': The Dark Lady and Self-Knowledge." *Studies in Philology* 90, 2 (1993): 213–30.

Stephens, John. *Essayes and Characters, Ironicall, and Instructive. The second impression.* London: E. Allde for Phillip Knight, 1615.

Stockwood, John. *A Bartholmew Fairing for Parentes, to bestow upon their sonnes and daughters.* London: John Wolfe for John Harrison the younger, 1589.

Strier, Richard. "The Refusal to Be Judged in Petrarch and Shakespeare." In *A Companion to Shakespeare's Sonnets*, ed. Michael Schoenfeldt, 73–89. Oxford: Blackwell, 2007.

———. *Resistant Structures: Particularity, Radicalism, and Renaissance Texts.* Berkeley: University of California Press, 1995.

Sullivan, Garrett A., Jr. "'Be this sweet Helen's knell, and now forget her': Forgetting, Memory, and Identity in *All's Well That Ends Well.*" *Shakespeare Quarterly* 50, 1 (1999): 51–69.

Sutcliffe, Matthew. *A True Relation of Englands Happinesse, Under the Raigne of Queene Elizabeth.* London, 1629.

Suzuki, Mihoko. *Subordinate Subjects: Gender, the Political Nation, and Literary Form in England, 1588–1688.* Aldershot: Ashgate, 2003.

Swetnam, Joseph. *The Araignment of Lewd, Idle, Froward, and unconstant women.* London: George Purslowe for Thomas Archer, 1615.

Tate, Nahum. *The History of King Lear. Acted at the Duke's Theatre. Reviv'd with Alterations. By N. Tate.* London: Printed for E. Flesher, 1681.

Tennenhouse, Leonard. *Power on Display: The Politics of Shakespeare's Genres.* New York: Methuen, 1986.

Thompson, Ann. "Are There any Women in *King Lear?*" In *The Matter of Difference: Materialist Feminist Criticism of Shakespeare*, ed. Valerie Wayne, 117–28. Ithaca, N.Y.: Cornell University Press, 1991.

Tigurinus, Chelidonius. *A most excellent Hystorie, Of the Institution and firste beginning of Christian Princes.* Trans. James Chillester. London: H. Bynneman, 1571.

Tilmouth, Christopher. *Passion's Triumph over Reason: A History of the Moral Imagination from Spenser to Rochester.* Oxford: Oxford University Press, 2007.

Tilney, Edmund. *A briefe and pleasant discourse of duties in Mariage, called the Flower of Friendshippe.* London: Henrie Denham, 1571.

Torquemada, Antonio de. *The Spanish Mandevile of Miracles. Or The Garden of curious Flowers.* London: J[ames] R[oberts] for Edmund Matts, 1600.

Traub, Valerie. "Gendering Mortality in Early Modern Anatomies." In *Feminist Readings of Early Modern Culture: Emerging Subjects*, ed. Valerie Traub, M. Lindsay Kaplan, and Dympna Callaghan, 44–92. Cambridge: Cambridge University Press, 1996.

———. "The Perversion of 'Lesbian' Desire." *History Workshop Journal* 41 (1996): 23–49.

———. *The Renaissance of Lesbianism in Early Modern England*. Cambridge: Cambridge University Press, 2002.

—. "Sex Without Issue: Sodomy, Reproduction, and Signification in Shakespeare's Sonnets." In *Shakespeare's Sonnets: Critical Essays*, ed. James Schiffer, 431–52. New York: Garland, 1999.

Trevor, Douglas. "Shakespeare's Love Objects." In *A Companion to Shakespeare's Sonnets*, ed. Michael Schoenfeldt, 225–41. Oxford: Blackwell, 2007.

The True Chronicle History of King Leir, and his three daughters, Gonorill, Ragan, and Cordella. London: Simon Stafford for John Wright, 1605.

Tuke, Thomas. *A Discourse Against Painting and Tincturing of Women*. London: Printed for Edward Marchant, 1616.

Turner, James Grantham. *One Flesh: Paradisal Marriage and Sexual Relations in the Age of Milton*. Oxford: Clarendon Press, 1987.

Twyne, Laurence. *The Patterne of painefull Adventures*. London: Valentine Simmes for the Widow Newman, 1594.

van Veen, Otto. *Amorum Emblemata*. Antwerp, 1608.

Vaught, Jennifer. *Masculinity and Emotion in Early Modern English Literature*. Aldershot: Ashgate, 2008.

Vickers, Nancy. "Diana Described: Scattered Woman and Scattered Rhyme." In *Writing and Sexual Difference*, ed. Elizabeth Abel, 95–109. Chicago: University of Chicago Press, 1982.

———. "Members Only." In *The Body in Parts: Fantasies of Corporeality in Early Modern Europe*, ed. David Hillman and Carla Mazzio, 3–21. New York: Routledge, 1997.

Vives, Juan Luis. *An Introduction to wysedome . . . translated into Englyshe by Rycharde Morysine*. London: in aedibus Thom[ae] Bertheleti, 1540.

———. *A Very Fruteful and Pleasant boke callyd the Instruction of a Christen woman . . . tourned oute of latyne into Englysshe by Richard Hyrde*. London: in [a]edibus Thom[a]e Berth[eleti], 1541.

Walker, Tim. "Death comes as a relief." Telegraph.co.uk, 16 July 2006. http://www.telegraph.co.uk/culture/3653881/Death-comes-as-a-relief.html

Wall, Wendy. "'Household Stuff': The Sexual Politics of Domesticity and the Advent of English Comedy." *ELH* 65, 1 (1998): 1–45.

———. *The Imprint of Gender: Authorship and Publication in the English Renaissance*. Ithaca, N.Y.: Cornell University Press, 1993.

———. *Staging Domesticity: Household Work and English Identity in Early Modern Drama*. Cambridge: Cambridge University Press, 2002.

Warren, Roger. "Why Does It End Well? Helena, Bertram, and the Sonnets." *Shakespeare Survey* 22 (1969): 79–92.

Watson, Robert N. "False Immortality in *Measure for Measure*: Comic Means, Tragic Ends." *Shakespeare Quarterly* 41, 4 (1990): 411–32.

Wayne, Valerie. "Historical Differences: Misogyny and *Othello*." In *The Matter of Difference: Materialist Feminist Criticism of Shakespeare*, ed. Valerie Wayne, 153–79. Ithaca, N.Y.: Cornell University Press, 1991.

Wehrs, Donald R. "Touching Words: Embodying Ethics in Erasmus, Shakespearean Comedy, and Contemporary Theory." *Modern Philology* 104, 1 (2006): 1–33.

Weitz Miller, Nancy. "Metaphor and the Mystification of Chastity in Vives's *Instruction of a Christen Woman*." In *Menacing Virgins: Representing Virginity in the Middle Ages and Renaissance*, ed. Kathleen Coyne Kelly and Marina Leslie, 132–45. Newark: University of Delaware Press, 1999.

Weitz, Nancy. "Romantic Fiction, Moral Anxiety, and Social Capital in Cavendish's 'Assaulted and Pursued Chastity." In *Authorial Conquests: Essays on Genre in the Writings of Margaret Cavendish*, ed. Line Cottegnies and Nancy Weitz, 145–60. Madison, N.J.: Fairleigh Dickinson University Press, 2003.

Wheeler, Richard P. "The King and the Physician's Daughter: *All's Well That Ends Well* and the Late Romances." *Comparative Drama* 8, 4 (1974–75): 311–24.

———. *Shakespeare's Development and the Problem Comedies: Turn and Counter-Turn*. Berkeley: University of California Press, 1981.

Whigham, Frank. *Seizures of the Will in Early Modern English Drama*. Cambridge: Cambridge University Press, 1996.

Whittier, Gayle. "Cordelia as Prince: Gender and Language in *King Lear*." *Exemplaria* 1, 2 (1989): 367–99.

Wiburn, Perceval. *A Checke or reproofe of M. Howlets untimely shreeching in her Majesties eares*. London: Thomas Dawson for Toby Smyth, 1581.

Willbern, David. *Poetic Will: Shakespeare and the Play of Language*. Philadelphia: University of Pennsylvania Press, 1997.

Williams, Gordon. *A Dictionary of Sexual Language and Imagery in Shakespearean and Stuart Literature*. 3 vols. London: Athlone, 1994.

———. *A Glossary of Shakespeare's Sexual Language*. London: Athlone, 1997.

Willis, Deborah. *Malevolent Nurture: Witch-Hunting and Maternal Power in Early Modern England*. Ithaca, N.Y.: Cornell University Press, 1995.

Wilson, Luke. *Theaters of Intention: Drama and the Law in Early Modern England*. Stanford, Calif.: Stanford University Press, 2000.

———. "William Harvey's *Prelectiones*: The Performance of the Body in the Renaissance Theater of Anatomy." *Representations* 17 (Winter 1987): 62–95.

Wilson, Richard. "Observations on English Bodies: Licensing Maternity in Shakespeare's Late Plays." In *Enclosure Acts: Sexuality, Property, and Culture in Early Modern England*, ed. Richard Burt and John Michael Archer, 121–50. Ithaca, N.Y.: Cornell University Press, 1994.

———. *Will Power: Essays on Shakespearean Authority*. Detroit: Wayne State University Press, 1993.

Wilson, Thomas. *The Arte of Rhetorique, for the use of all suche as are Studious of Eloquence*. London: Richardus Graftonus, 1553.

Wilson, Thomas. *A Christian Dictionarie*. London: Printed by William Jaggard, 1612.

Winter, Thomas. "To his Translation." In Guillaume de Salluste Du Bartas, *The Second Day of the First Weeke of the most excellent, learned, and divine Poet, William, Lord Bartas*. Trans. Thomas Winter. London: Printed for James Shaw, 1603.

Wojciehowski, Dolora A. *Old Masters, New Subjects: Early Modern and Poststructuralist Theories of Will*. Stanford, Calif.: Stanford University Press, 1995

Wollstonecraft, Mary. *A Vindication of the Rights of Woman*. In *A Vindication of the Rights of Men; A Vindication of the Rights of Woman; An Historical and Moral View of the French Revolution*, ed. Janet Todd, 63–284. New York: Oxford University Press, 2008.

Wood, Pete. "Measure for Measure." *The British Theatre Guide*, 2006. http://www.british theatreguide.info/reviews/TRBmeasure-rev.htm.

Woodbridge, Linda. *Women and the English Renaissance: Literature and the Nature of Womankind, 1540 to 1620*. Urbana: University of Illinois Press, 1984.

Wright, Thomas. *The Passions of the minde in generall. Corrected, enlarged, and with sundry new discourses augmented*. London: Valentine Simmes for Walter Burre, 1604.

Younge, Richard. *The Drunkard's Character*. London: R. Badger for George Latham, 1638.

Žižek, Slavoj. "*Da Capo senza Fine*." In Judith Butler, Ernesto Laclau, and Slavoj Žižek, *Contingency, Hegemony, Universality: Contemporary Dialogues on the Left*, 213–62. London: Verso, 2000.

———. *The Sublime Object of Ideology*. London: Verso, 1989.

Index

Abbot, George, 68

abdication, 17, 21, 122, 157, 159–61, 182–84, 190–92, 249n42

abjection, 33, 67–68, 116

absent monarch plays, 160, 197, 252n18

Adamson, Sylvia, 229n4, 231n55

Adelman, Janet, 83, 110, 121, 157, 158, 176, 200, 218n33, 230n28, 232n65, 244n58, 254n42, 262n64

adultery, 10, 39, 63, 70, 100–101, 165, 225n50. *See also* inconstancy

agency: and authority, 34; constraints on, 6, 24, 29, 60, 72, 109–10, 128, 156–63, 200–3, 239n84; duality of, 2–3, 33–34, 38, 47, 113, 177; and language, 53, 56–57, 60–62, 67–68; and mediation, 5–6, 8, 11, 30, 32–34, 44–45, 113–14, 217n27; and personification, 28, 34–35, 38, 41, 56–57, 239n80; and social subjectivity, 3–11, 14–16, 26–30, 32–36, 40–42, 60–62, 84–90, 99–103, 112–14, 118–23, 131–32, 135–42, 166–74, 175–77, 200–203, 215n2, 221n71; of will, 2–3, 16, 28, 30, 38, 40–42, 44–47, 132–33; of women, 2–4, 6–11, 13–16, 21, 26–27, 30, 32–36, 40–42, 60–62, 67–68, 84–90, 95–103, 112–14, 118–25, 128, 135–42, 166–74, 175–77, 182–83, 187–89, 190–94, 197–98, 210–14, 219nn43, 45, 221n71, 224n35, 249n37. *See also* choice; cultural literacy; discipline

Agrippa von Nettesheim, Heinrich Cornelius, 83–84, 88, 91, 186–87, 210–11, 219n50, 228n97

Ainsworth, Henry, *The Art of Logick*, 59, 63, 69

Alberti, Leon Battistai, *The Arte of Love*, 110

Alexander, Gavin, 70–71, 229n4, 231nn39, 55

Alfar, Cristina León, 191, 195–96, 198, 260n26, 262n56

alienation: of critical methods, 198–99; in language, 52–53, 57–58, 65–72, 103, 232n60, 233n77, 235n98; within systems of order, 6, 9, 14, 16, 19–21, 32–33, 35, 74, 78–79, 95–96, 98–99, 103, 119, 140–41, 167–68, 199–203; of will, 32–33, 35, 44–45, 157–65, 182–89, 199–203. *See also* alterity

All's Well That Ends Well (Shakespeare), 12, 17, 19, 21, 105–128, 176, 224n38

allegory, 35, 117, 167–68, 188–89

Allott, Robert, *Wits Theater of the little World*, 84, 87–88, 90, 93

alterity, 10, 21, 65–66, 95–96, 185, 195–96, 198, 261n36. *See also* alienation

Althusser, Louis, 15, 21, 24–26, 107, 218n36, 222n6

Amussen, Susan Dwyer, 218n33, 224n35, 260n29

analogic relations, 2–3, 16, 28, 30–32, 35–36, 40–41, 45–48, 53–54, 55, 61, 92, 113–14, 122–23, 159, 164, 188–89, 196, 216n9, 217n22, 225n50, 227n89, 252n12

anatomies: of the body, 38, 93–95, 118, 239n79, 243n41, 42, 246n8; of the psyche, 28, 46; of social relations, 132, 173, 184, 198

Anderson, Ruth Leila, 43

Annand, William, 67

Asp, Carolyn, 122

Attersoll, William, 66

Augustine, 19, 24–26, 28, 147, 156, 163, 220n67, 221n1, 222nn4, 6

Austin, William, *Haec Homo*, 7, 67, 91, 92

autonomy, 2–4, 9, 11, 15, 18, 21, 27, 30, 33, 38, 40, 42, 62, 72, 87, 89–90, 101, 113, 118, 131,

Acknowledgments

This book has benefited from many acts of generosity. Research grants from the American Council of Learned Societies, the Folger Shakespeare Library, the Huntington Library, and the Newberry Library gave me access to invaluable resources, as did support from the Research Scholars Grant Program and the Robert Penn Warren Center for the Humanities, both at Vanderbilt University.

It is difficult to offer adequate thanks to all the people who read essays and chapters, invited me to present work, talked through ideas, and in so many ways supported, encouraged, and inspired me. I am grateful to Thomas Anderson, Rebecca Chapman, Jonathan Crewe, Holly Crocker, Lisa Duggan, Carla Freccero, Julia Garrett, Jonathan Goldberg, Roland Greene, Jonathan Gil Harris, Donald Jellerson, Leah Marcus, Jeffrey Masten, Carla Mazzio, Miranda Nesler, Gail Kern Paster, Richard Rambuss, Katherine Rowe, David Schalkwyk, Elizabeth Spiller, Henry Turner, and Wendy Wall for their thoughtful contributions at various stages. I owe particular thanks to Emily Bartels, Julie Crawford, Carolyn Dever, Lynn Enterline, Madhavi Menon, Ifeoma Nwankwo, and Laurie Shannon; their fierce intelligence has stimulated me even as their friendship has sustained me.

Jerry Singerman took on the project, made suggestions that strengthened it, and provided calm good sense at every turn. He has been an editor in the most capacious sense of the word. Alison Anderson saw the book through production; I have benefited both from her advice and from her patience. Frances E. Dolan and Karen Newman read the manuscript for the press, and I could not have asked for better interlocutors. Their generous engagements and acute insights have shaped the book from title to epilogue.

This book is in some sense the result of an interrupted life. Deb Bartle, Katherine Crawford, Lynn Dobrunz, Lisa Duggan, Julia Garrett, Barbara Landy, Dianne McCarthy, Bill Schwarz, and Susan Schwarz were with me when a future seemed less than likely; I am indebted beyond measure to their love and strength. Emma, Zoey, Biscuit, and particularly Sammy have illustrated the power of intention and desire in inimitable (and formidable) ways. The illustration in Chapter 1 is a small tribute to their spirit. Finally, it seems only fitting that I dedicate a book on will to Katherine Crawford; her constant will has been my touchstone.

Earlier versions of Chapter 4 and Chapter 5 appeared in *Shakespeare Quarterly* 58, 2 (2007): 200–227 and *ELH* 75, 3 (2008): 737–66 respectively. Both are reprinted by permission of the Johns Hopkins University Press.